THE COMPLETE WORKS OF ROBERT BROWNING

The Complete works of Robert Browning

With Variant Readings & Annotations

OHIO UNIVERSITY PRESS

ATHENS, OHIO 1969

Library of Congress Catalog Number 68-18389

Manufactured in the United States of America by
Wm. J. Keller Inc., Buffalo, New York

Contents

PREFACE

I CONTENTS

This edition of the works of Robert Browning is intended to be complete. It is expected to run to thirteen volumes and will contain:

1. The full contents of the first editions of Browning's work, arranged in chronological order. The poems included in *Dramatic Lyrics, Dramatic Romances and Lyrics,* and *Men and Women* appear in the order of their first publication rather than the order in which Browning rearranged them for later publication.

2. All prefaces, dedications, and advertisements which Browning wrote for his own works or for those of Elizabeth Barrett Browning and others.

3. The two known prose essays which Browning published: the review of a book on Tasso, generally referred to as "The Essay on Chatterton," and the preface for a collection of letters supposed to have been written by Percy Bysshe Shelley, generally referred to as "The Essay on Shelley."

4. The front matter and the table of contents of each of the collected editions (1849, 1863, 1868, 1888–89a, and 1889) which Browning himself saw through the press. The table of contents will include both the pagination of the original volume and of this edition.

5. Poems by Browning published during his lifetime but not collected by him.

6. Unpublished poems by Browning which have come to light since his death.

7. John Forster's *Thomas Wentworth, Earl of Strafford* to which Browning contributed significantly, though to what precise extent cannot be determined.

II GENERAL TEXTUAL PRINCIPLES

The assumptions on which we have prepared the text are, we think, reasonably straightforward, if not entirely conventional. Our principal departure from current textual theory is that we question the conventional meanings of *text* and *author*. For a work which varies in a series of documents and editions, there is no such empirical entity as the *text*. Consequently, the problem of *the transmission of the text* is not a real one; rather, the real problem is to understand the character of the decisions which were responsible for the successive and varying states of the work. Conventionally, it is assumed that only those texts should be used for which evidence of authorial control can be demonstrated, but, as with *text,* the *author* is a constructed entity; not only is it the fact that the *author* (conceived as a static entity) no longer exists; it is equally the case that the *author* (so conceived) never did exist. Our focus, therefore, shifts from *text* and *author* conceived as static metaphysical entities to the dynamic process of creating and editing involved in the compilation of a series of documents.

Any writer's work consists of two processes: he generates an utterance and he corrects that utterance by balancing his current conception of the coherence of what he has so far written, and his grasp of the conventions applicable to the kind of discourse he is composing as they then obtain and as he understands them. Thus, instead of making a distinction between *author* and *editor,* we make a distinction between *authorial function* and *editorial function*. It appears to us that in exercising his editorial functions the author's basis for his activity is continually changing, and may continue to change throughout his life. His grasp of both the coherence of his work and of the conventions may improve or deteriorate; he may come to feel that the conventions are either more or less binding on him. *Author* refers, then, not to a stable entity but to an unstable and continuously innovating continuum.

Furthermore, a writer's attitude towards the exercise of the editorial function may vary from an insistence that he alone has the right to exercise it to an acceptance of virtually any editorial decision made by another. The explanation for this phenomenon is that the author, as every practicing author knows, is not necessarily the one best equipped to balance the two demands at work in the editorial decision-making process. If he is unusually intelligent and richly cultivated at the high cultural level, however, the probability that he is best equipped increases, especially if his cultural situation is relatively limited and stable and imposes upon him a demanding notion of the editorial function. Consequently, there is no logical difference between an author's exercise of the editorial function and an editor's, who is also an unstable and continuously innovating continuum, but whose editorial function is precisely the same as the author's.

Other individuals also exercise the editorial function: the compositor, the printer, and the copyreader. In the history of printing, each of these has been responsible for variants, and insofar as such variants reflect a grasp of the coherence of the work and of current conventions, they cannot be classified as errors. An error is a variant which self-evidently damages the coherence of the text and departs from the conventions as the textual critic himself understands both factors as they were at work in the historical situation from which the work emerged. The history of printing has moved in the direction of trying to limit the printer to errors, to train the compositor to set only what is before him, and to restrict the copyreader to the detection of errors by requiring him to refer questionable variants to the editor and author. Actual practice varies from house to house, within the history of each house, and according to the kind of discourse.

We also depart from one line of current textual theory by assuming that punctuation is not to be categorized as an accidental. An accidental, we maintain, is a variant that cannot alter the semantic function of the semiotic data. Spelling, for example, can delay the recognition of a semantic function, but if the current standard spelling can be unequivocally substituted, then it is truly an accidental, and so with word divisions and the like. But whatever the semantic function of punctuation may be—and it is a matter which is little understood—everyone feels it, though some feel it more than others, and this instability of semiotic response is also true of authors. Punctuation, under which we include paragraphing, does not merely *affect* the semantic continuum; it is part of that continuum. Thus, the study of a series of editorial decisions in a passage involving only punctuational variants can, and usually does, have both an interesting and an important effect upon the interpretation of a passage. It seems to us, therefore, that particularly in a nineteenth or twentieth century work, punctuational variants must be considered as substantive changes and so recorded.

The problem, then, is this. Given a work which varies in a series of documents and editions, which document exhibits evidence of the most adequate exercise of the editorial function, and on what grounds is this decision to be made? Or, given a work which so varies but apparently has never had adequate editing, to what degree should the textual editor carry out the task? The textual editor must recognize that he is not restoring or establishing a text, but is continuing the editorial function initiated by the author. When it comes to what variants to record and what emendations to make, the textual critic cannot console himself by falling back on a nonexistent metaphysical entity, the *author*.

III SPECIFIC PROBLEMS IN EDITING BROWNING'S WORKS

The works of Browning offer few problems (though some are of genuine interest) and provide a great redundance of data. Aside from a handful of uncollected poems, all short, everything but *Asolando* went through two or more editions during Browning's lifetime. Except for *Pauline, Strafford,* and *Sordello,* everything published before 1849 was republished in newly edited form in the 1849 collection. *Strafford* and *Sordello* were newly edited for the collection of 1863, as were all other works in that edition. The 1868 collection added a newly edited *Pauline* and *Dramatis Personae* to the other works, which were themselves re-edited. The 1888–89a collection in sixteen volumes included everything so far published in volumes (certain poems published only in periodicals were not included; *Asolando* was added as Volume XVII after Browning's death). The printing of this edition was completed in July, 1889, and the exhaustion of some of the early volumes led Browning to correct the first ten volumes before he left for Italy in late August. The second edition of this sixteen volume collection is dated 1889 on the titlepages; the first eight volumes of the first edition are dated 1888, the rest, 1889. We have designated Volumes IX to XVI of the first edition 1889*a*.

We have designated the existing manuscripts and editions either as primary or secondary materials. The primary materials include:

1. The manuscript of each volume (when such exists; see table at the end of preface);

2. The proof sheet (when such exists);

3. The original edition of each volume (and subsequent separate editions where such exist);

4. The collected editions over which Browning exercised editorial control:

1849–*Poems by Robert Browning*. Two Volumes. London: Chapman and Hall.

1863–*The Poetical Works*. Three Volumes. London: Chapman and Hall.

1868–*The Poetical Works*. Six Volumes. London: Smith, Elder and Company.

1888–*The Poetical Works*. Volumes 1–8. London: Smith, Elder and Company.

1889a–*The Poetical Works*. Volumes 9–16. London: Smith, Elder and Company.

1889–*The Poetical Works*. Volumes 1–16. London: Smith, Elder and Company. (Vols. 1–10, a revision of 1888–1889a; Vols. 11–16, a reprint of 1889a).

All other relevant materials now known to exist or which may be discovered while this edition is being prepared will be called secondary. Examples of such materials are: the copy of the first edition of *Pauline* which contains annotations by Browning and John Stuart Mill; the copy of the first edition of *Paracelsus* which contains corrections in Browning's hand; Elizabeth Barrett's suggestions for the revision of *A Soul's Tragedy* and certain of the short poems which composed *Dramatic Romances and Lyrics* (1845); and the edition of *Strafford* by Miss Emily Hickey for which Browning made suggestions.

Given all these diverse materials, our first problem is to determine the nature of the decisions for the variants. We are concerned, of course, with all kinds of substantive variants, not only of word and line but also of punctuation. That Browning was responsible for changes of words and lines seems obvious. As far as our records indicate, no one other than Elizabeth Barrett recommended specific changes in the actual wording of Browning's poems. Of the numerous suggestions which she made for changes in the poems which composed *Dramatic Romances and Lyrics* (1845), he accepted some and rejected others. In the case of *Paracelsus,* for example, there are no differences in wording or lines between Browning's corrected manuscript and the printed first edition which suggest that an editor other than Browning was responsible for word changes in the text. Here, then, we need ask only if he were also responsible for changes in punctuation, or if these were imposed upon his poems by the publisher.

To begin with available evidence, the practice of Tennyson and of Swinburne, for example, suggests there was a strong tendency in the nineteenth century to allow a poet general control over the punctuation of his own work. Byron (not very typically) sought editorial help in punctuating; but, as a rule, English poets seem to have been able to insist that even their eccentricities in pointing be followed by compositors—both before the 1840's, when punctuation practice tended to be more anarchic, as well as after the publication of John Wilson's comprehensive, systematic, and highly influential *A Treatise on Grammatical Punctuation* (Manchester, 1844). Thus, the general practice today of publishers deferring to the editorial function of the author according to his literary status seems already to have been in existence, and the similar practice of ascribing high status to a poet, or at least higher than that granted to a novelist, seems to have been obtained.

We do know that for the final 1889 edition Browning had full control over all variants, including punctuation. Indeed, the probabilities indicate that by at least 1863 Browning had principal control over the editorial function. Moreover, in writing to Chapman in the 1850's he shows concern for punctuation. ("I attach importance to the mere stops . . . ." *New Letters of Robert Browning,* eds. William Clyde DeVane and Kenneth Knickerbocker, New Haven, 1950, p. 83.)

Still earlier, the history of the *Paracelsus* texts is of the highest interest and importance. The manuscript of that poem exhibits either an ignorance of punctuation conventions or a refusal to consider them very seriously. For whatever reason, Browning exhibits in this manuscript a wide latitude of innovation even from a variety of conflicting current punctuational conventions. The manuscript shows, however, housestyling, or the exercise of the editorial function by someone other than Browning for one leaf in Act I and all but the first and last pages of Act III. Several other pages show editorial changes in punctuation which may be Browning's. What precisely happened to the styling of some of the manuscript before it was finally printed is uncertain. Either a new manuscript was prepared, or proof was set up from the manuscript as it stood after partial editing and was then thoroughly revised. The manuscript shows signs of heavy use, indications for the signatures (corrected for one signature), and what are evidently compositors' names. The second possibility, then, seems the more likely. The results are significant. First, although the printed punctuation of the edited portions of the manuscript does not correspond with that editing, it is in the same style as that editing. Second, the printed punctuation of the unedited portions is in the same style as the printed versions of the edited portions, and thus of the editing in the manuscript. Third, subsequent published works for which no manuscript exists are in the same style as the printed 1835 *Paracelsus.* Finally, the next available manuscript of major significance, that for *Christmas Eve and Easter Day,* prepared for the printer by Elizabeth and Robert, shows virtually no variation from the first edition of 1850. Everything leads to the probability that Browning exercised final control of the punctuation from the printed 1835 *Paracelsus* through the rest of his career. Indeed, we are aware of Mrs. Sutherland Orr's statement (*Life and Letters of Robert Browning,* London, 1891) that Browning invariably sent proof sheets of his work to his French friend Joseph Milsand for corrections. There is no indication, however, that, in seeking such help, Browning relinquished his own final editorial function.

All evidence, then, indicates that from 1835 onward Browning was responsible for all substantive variants to be found in the several editions of his works over which he had nominal supervision.

(There were indeed during his lifetime a number of editions and selections over which he exercised no control and which, as a result, we have eliminated from consideration here.)

IV CHOICE OF TEXT

By 1889, Browning was the most experienced editor of his own poetic discourse. It seems to us, therefore, that the 1889 edition of his works provides the most satisfactory basic text, not just because it is chronologically the last one he worked on. Rather, the probability is that in 1888 and 1889 he had a better grasp of the coherence of individual works and of this particular style of the conventions, including the conventions of punctuation, than anyone else. The text we have presented is the 1889 text for the contents of the first ten volumes, emended only to correct a few obvious compositor's or printer's errors; the 1888 text for the contents of the last six volumes, emended in the same way; and the 1889 first edition of *Asolando,* similarly emended for the contents of that volume. The text for the uncollected material is based on the original publication. Compared with the textual critic of an Elizabethan play, the textual critic of Browning has on the whole an easy decision to make about what edition to select as the basis for his own text and what further editorial functions are to be exercised.

V PRESENTATION OF VARIANTS

The presentation of the variants is not conventional. Indeed, there is no standard way to offer variants. Initially, we attempted to follow a system sometimes adhered to but, because of the nature of the materials, found it inadequate. We were forced therefore to improvise. We believe that the style we have adopted, which is explained in detail below, has the advantage of presenting the history of the variants in the order in which they appeared, from the first form through the final one, and in a way in which the full text of each line of each edition is most accurately and readily reconstructed.

In presenting the variants from the 1889 text we print at the bottom of the page variants found in the manuscripts, when available, and in the first and subsequent editions—that is, variants found in the primary materials. It seems to us that we can give a clearer, more concise notion of Browning's editorial function if we separate primary materials from secondary materials. Moreover, we must assume that additional manuscripts may become available between now and the time the last volume of this edition is published, making a supplemental volume of variants necessary. We have decided, therefore, that it would be logical to place all variants derived from secondary materials together in a final volume. This final volume will also include *Thomas Wentworth, Earl of Strafford* by John Forster, to which Browning's contribution was considerable but indeterminable.

TABLE OF SIGNS

All signs used by Browning himself have been avoided. The symbols essential to an understanding of the variant notes are set out in the following table of signs:

§ . . . §	Editor's note
<>	Words omitted
/	Line break
//,///, . . .	Line break plus one or more lines without internal variants

All variants are placed at the bottom of the page of text to which they refer. A variant is generally preceded and followed by a pickup and a drop word *(a)*. No note terminates with a punctuation mark unless the punctuation mark comes at the end of a line. If a variant drops or adds a punctuation mark, the next word is added *(b)*. If the normal pickup word has appeared previously in the same line, the note begins with the word preceding it. If the normal drop word appears subsequently in the line, the next word is added *(c)*. A single capitalized pickup word indicates the beginning of a line of poetry. When a capitalized pickup word occurs within the line, it is accompanied by the preceding word *(d)*.

No pickup word, however, is used for any variant consisting of an internal change, for example, a hyphen in a compounded word, an apostrophe, a tense change, or a spelling change. Nor is a drop word used when the variant comes at the end of a line *(e)*. Illustrations from *Pauline:*

a **47**| *1833:* thee, and *1868:* thee and

b **130**| *1833:* hope, or part, or care, in *1868:* hope or part or care in

131| *1833:* cares, and strife, and toil, *1868:* cares and strife and toil *1888:* care

c **654**| *1833:* selfishness, this still decaying *1888:* selfishness, the still-decaying

24| *1833:* altars, and stand *1868:* altars and stand

d [166]| *1833:* And creatures of my own were mixed with them, *1888:* And with them creatures of my own were mixed,

[34]| *1833:* on Fancy's wings, and *1868:* on fancy's wings and

e [215]| *1833:* tho' *1868:* though

Each recorded variant will be assumed to be incorporated in the next edition if there is no indication otherwise.

Punctuational variants (the use of parentheses rather than square brackets, and of abbreviation rather than full spelling and other such genuine accidentals) which occur in the presentation of casts of characters, place locations, stage directions, and character designations are not listed.

Two kinds of variants which we regard as genuine accidentals have been emended and not recorded. For a time during Browning's career it was the practice, as every student of Victorian literature is aware, to precede every line of a quotation with a quotation mark. We have eliminated all but the first and last quotation mark, in accordance with modern practice and with the practice of some of the original Browning editions. Secondly, during most of his career, a space was left in contractions of two words; thus "it's" was printed "it 's." These we have closed up, in accordance with modern practice.

VI COLLATION

Finally, there remains the question of collation within an edition. In the first place all printings of the 1868 edition except the first have been eliminated. Those volumes were evidently sold separately, for some of them were reprinted, according to the dates on the title pages, a number of times. There is also evidence that, though the edition may have been stereotyped, there was some resetting. Since there is no indication that Browning had anything to do with the resetting and since, for the reasons given above, we have decided that his editorial decisions are to be preferred when known, we have disregarded these versions. In any case, it would be impossible to be sure that all of them had been discovered, even a representative sampling. As for the other editions, Browning was not a popular author and the editions were small. A sampling of various exemplars of several editions has not revealed a significant yield among them. However, in case of doubt about incomplete inking and dropped endline punctuation and letters, a sample collation with other exemplars of the same edition has been undertaken.

VII ANNOTATIONS

Browning scholarship is not yet fully mature. The notes we have presented, therefore, are not intended to be exhaustive or final. The format of the edition has been planned to allow for revision of the notes without disturbing the text. If the text prove satisfactory, it can be reprinted indefinitely with new sets of notes.

As a general principle, we have annotated proper names, phrases that function as proper names, and words or groups of words the full meaning of which require factual, historical, or literary background. Thus, we have attempted to hold interpretation to a minimum, although we realize that the act of selection itself is to some extent interpretative.

Specifically, we have annotated the following: (1) proper names; (2) geographical locations; (3) allusions to Biblical and other literature; (4) words not included in *Webster's Collegiate Dictionary,* Seventh Edition (since some limits must be imposed upon our work and because this dictionary is generally accepted and readily available; we annotate words either not in or used by Browning in a sense other than that given in the desk dictionary; for a more accurate understanding of the meaning which Browning gives to words we have relied heavily upon Samuel Johnson's dictionary); other items requiring factual information which is not of current common knowledge or easily available. All passages in a language other than English are translated into English. Occasional quotations from Browning's sources are included when such source quotations seem especially pertinent and are of difficult access.

For notes, particularly on historical figures and events, we have tended to prefer fullness and even to risk the tangential and unessential. As a result, some of the information provided may be perhaps unnecessary for the mature scholar. On the other hand, it is impossible to assume that all who use this edition—the ordinary reader and the undergraduate and graduate students, for example—will be fully equipped to assimilate unaided all of Browning's copious literary, historical, and mythological allusions. Thus we have directed our efforts toward an audience conceived as a continuum from the relatively uninformed to the trained.

TABLE OF ABBREVIATIONS USED IN ANNOTATIONS

B	Browning
Orr *Hbk*	*Handbook to The Works of Robert Browning.* Mrs. Sutherland Orr, London, 1885.
P-C	*The Complete Works of Robert Browning.* Eds. Charlotte Porter and Helen A. Clarke. 12 Volumes. New York, 1900.

VIII TABLE OF MANUSCRIPTS

The following manuscripts are known to exist in the locations indicated:

Paracelsus
Forster and Dyce Collection,
Victoria and Albert Museum, Kensington

Christmas Eve and Easter Day
Forster and Dyce Collection,
Victoria and Albert Museum, Kensington

Dramatis Personae
Pierpont Morgan Library, New York

The Ring and the Book
British Museum

Balaustion's Adventure
Balliol College Library, Oxford

Prince Hohenstiel-Schwangau
Balliol College Library, Oxford

Fifine at the Fair
Balliol College Library, Oxford

Red Cotton Night-Cap Country
Balliol College Library, Oxford

Aristophanes' Apology
Balliol College Library, Oxford

The Inn Album
Balliol College Library, Oxford

Of Pacchiarotto and How He Worked in Distemper
Balliol College Library, Oxford

The Agamemnon of Aeschylus
Balliol College Library, Oxford

La Saisaiz and The Two Poets of Croisic
Balliol College Library, Oxford

Dramatic Idyls First Series
Balliol College Library, Oxford

Dramatic Idyls Second Series
Balliol College Library, Oxford
Jocoseria
Balliol College Library, Oxford
Ferishtah's Fancies
Balliol College Library, Oxford
Parleyings With Certain People of Importance in Their Day
Balliol College Library, Oxford
Asolando
Pierpont Morgan Library, New York

Each manuscript is fully described in this edition in the section given to annotations on the corresponding text.

The following manuscripts are not known to be extant:

Pauline
Strafford
Sordello
Pippa Passes
King Victor and King Charles
"The Essay on Chatterton"
Dramatic Lyrics
The Return of the Druses
A Blot in the 'Scutcheon
Colombe's Birthday
Dramatic Romances and Lyrics
Luria
A Soul's Tragedy
"The Essay on Shelley"
Men and Women

We should like to request that anyone with information about any of the manuscripts which are presently unknown to the scholarly world communicate with the Director of the Ohio University Press, Athens, Ohio.

IX REQUEST FOR CORRECTIONS

We have tried to make this edition free from error, but we know that the history of printing proves that such an ambition is impossible of fulfillment. We urgently request that whoever discovers errors will report them to the Ohio University Press, Athens, Ohio, where a file of such errors will be kept so that any future printings can take advantage of such reports.

X ACKNOWLEDGMENTS

We express our appreciation especially to the following: the Ohio University Press, the Ohio University Library, and the Ohio University English Department for providing money and services which have made it possible for us to assemble the vast materials required for preparation of this edition; The Armstrong Browning Library, Baylor University, Waco, Texas, and its director Professor Jack Herring for various favors including permission to use and to reproduce the 1835 silver-copper daguerreotype of Robert Browning, the original of which is in the Baylor collection (see *Robert Browning's Portraits, Photographs and Other Likenesses* by Grace Elizabeth Wilson, Baylor University Interests, Series Fourteen, 1943); The Victoria and Albert Museum, Kensington, England, for permission to reproduce and use the manuscript of *Paracelsus*. We have also received valuable assistance in securing and preparing materials to appear in later volumes from the British Museum; Balliol College Library, Oxford; Mr. Philip Kelley, New York; and Mr. John Murray, London. We also gratefully acknowledge the assistance of Mr. Marshall Lee, New York, for helping to design the format of the edition.

The Editors
Athens, Ohio
1969

TABLE OF EDITIONS REFERRED TO IN VOLUME I

1833 *Pauline: A Fragment of a Confession.*
London: Saunders and Otley.

1835 *Paracelsus.*
London: Effingham Wilson.

1849 *Poems.* Two Volumes.
London: Chapman and Hall.

1863 *The Poetical Works.*
Three Volumes. London: Chapman and Hall.

1868 *The Poetical Works.*
Six Volumes. London: Smith, Elder, and Company.

1888 *The Poetical Works.*
Volumes 1–8. London: Smith, Elder, and Company.

1889a *The Poetical Works.*
Volumes 1–16. London: Smith Elder, and Company.

1889 *The Poetical Works.*
Sixteen Volumes. London: Smith Elder, and Company.

A full description of each of these may be found in Section A, pp. 1–60 of *Robert Browning: A Bibliography,* 1830–1950. Compiled by Leslie Nathan Broughton, Clark Sutherland Northup, and Robert Pearsall: Cornell University Press, 1953.

PAULINE

Edited by John Berkey

"Eyes calm beside thee"

PARACELSUS

Edited by Morse Peckham

PAULINE

Edited by John Berkey

PAULINE;

A FRAGMENT OF A CONFESSION.

Plus ne suis ce que j'ai été,
Et ne le sçaurois jamais être.—Marot.

Non dubito, quin titulus libri nostri raritate sua quamplurimos alliciat ad legendum: inter quos nonnulli obliquæ opinionis, mente languidi, multi etiam maligni, et in ingenium nostrum ingrati accedent, qui temeraria sua ignorantia, vix conspecto titulo clamabunt. Nos vetita docere, hæresium semina jacere: piis auribus offendiculo, præclaris ingeniis scandalo esse: . . . . adeo conscientiæ suæ consulentes, ut nec Apollo, nec Musæ omnes, neque Angelus de cœlo me ab illorum execratione vindicare queant: quibus et ego nunc consulo, ne scripta nostra legant, nec intelligant, nec meminerint: nam noxia sunt, venenosa sunt: Acherontis ostium est in hoc libro, lapides loquitur, caveant, ne cerebrum illis excutiat. Vos autem, qui æqua mente ad legendum venitis, si tantam prudentiæ discretionem adhibueritis, quantam in melle legendo apes, jam securi legite. Puto namque vos et utilitatis haud parum et voluptatis plurimum accepturos. Quod si qua repereritis, quæ vobis non placeant, mittite illa, nec utimini. NAM ET EGO VOBIS ILLA NON PROBO, SED NARRO. Cætera tamen propterea non respuite. . . . . Ideo, si quid liberius dictum sit, ignoscite adolescentiæ nostræ, qui minor quam adolescens hoc opus composui.—*Hen. Corn. Agrippa, De Occult. Philosoph. in Præfat.*

London: January 1833.
V. A. XX. Vixi Annos Viginti I was 20 years old.

[This introduction would appear less absurdly pretentious did it apply, as was intended, to a completed structure of which the poem was meant for only a beginning and remains a fragment.]

1| *1833:* suâ *1868:* sua 4| *1833:* temerarià suâ ignorantiâ vix <> clamabunt: Nos *1868:* temeraria sua ignorantia, *1888:* clamabunt Nos *1889:* clamabunt. Nos 6| *1833:* adeò *1868:* adeo 8| *1833:* execrationè *1868:* execratione 11| *1833:* æquâ *1868:* æqua 14| *1833:* parùm <> plurimùm *1868:* parum <> plurimum. 17| *1833:* uite . . . . Ideo *1868:* uite . . . . . . Ideo *1888:* uite . . . . . Ideo, 18| *1833: H. Cor.* *1868: Hon. Corn.* 19| *1833: Phil.* *1868: Philosoph. in Prefat.* *1888: Philosoph. in Præfat.* 20| *1833: London, January, 1833.* *1888:* LONDON: *January 1833.*
§ Bracketed passage omitted in 1833, 1868. §

PAULINE

1833

Pauline, mine own, bend o'er me—thy soft breast
Shall pant to mine—bend o'er me—thy sweet eyes,
And loosened hair and breathing lips, and arms
Drawing me to thee—these build up a screen
To shut me in with thee, and from all fear;
So that I might unlock the sleepless brood
Of fancies from my soul, their lurking-place,
Nor doubt that each would pass, ne'er to return
To one so watched, so loved and so secured.
But what can guard thee but thy naked love?
Ah dearest, whoso sucks a poisoned wound
Envenoms his own veins! Thou art so good,
So calm—if thou shouldst wear a brow less light
For some wild thought which, but for me, were kept
From out thy soul as from a sacred star!
Yet till I have unlocked them it were vain
To hope to sing; some woe would light on me;
Nature would point at one whose quivering lip
Was bathed in her enchantments, whose brow burned
Beneath the crown to which her secrets knelt,
Who learned the spell which can call up the dead,
And then departed smiling like a fiend
Who has deceived God,—if such one should seek

---

§ Ed. 1833, 1868, 1888, 1889. § 3| *1833:* hair, and breathing *1868:* hair and breathing 5| *1833:* fear, *1868:* fear; 7| *1833:* lurking place, *1868:* lurking-place 9| *1833:* loved, and *1868:* loved and 11| *1833:* dearest! whoso *1868:* dearest, whoso 12| *1833:* veins,—thou *1868:* veins! Thou 13| *1833:* should'st *1888:* shouldst 15| *1833:* soul, as <> star. *1868:* soul as <> star! 17| *1833:* me, *1868:* me; 18| *1833:* one, whose *1868:* one whose 19| *1833:* enchantments—whose *1868:* enchantments, whose 20| *1833:* crown, to <> knelt; *1868:* crown to <> knelt, 22| *1833:* departed, smiling *1868:* departed smiling 23| *1833:* deceived God. If *1868:* deceived God,—if

Again her altars and stand robed and crowned
Amid the faithful! Sad confession first,
Remorse and pardon and old claims renewed,
Ere I can be—as I shall be no more.

I had been spared this shame if I had sat
By thee for ever from the first, in place
Of my wild dreams of beauty and of good,
Or with them, as an earnest of their truth:
No thought nor hope having been shut from thee,
No vague wish unexplained, no wandering aim
Sent back to bind on fancy's wings and seek
Some strange fair world where it might be a law;
But, doubting nothing, had been led by thee,
Thro' youth, and saved, as one at length awaked
Who has slept through a peril. Ah vain, vain!

Thou lovest me; the past is in its grave
Tho' its ghost haunts us; still this much is ours,
To cast away restraint, lest a worse thing
Wait for us in the dark. Thou lovest me;
And thou art to receive not love but faith,
For which thou wilt be mine, and smile and take
All shapes and shames, and veil without a fear
That form which music follows like a slave:
And I look to thee and I trust in thee,
As in a Northern night one looks alway
Unto the East for morn and spring and joy.

---

[24]| *1833:* altars, and stand *1868:* altars and stand [25]| *1833:* faithful: sad *1888:* faithful! Sad [26]| *1833:* pardon, and *1868:* pardon and [28]| *1833:* shame, if <> sate *1868:* shame if <> sat [29]| *1833:* ever, from *1868:* ever from [31]| *1833:* truth. *1868:* truth: [32]| *1833:* hope, having *1868:* hope having [33]| *1833:* unexplained—no *1868:* unexplained, no [34]| *1833:* Fancy's wings, and *1868:* fancy's wings and [35]| *1833:* world, where *1868:* world where [36]| *1833:* But doubting *1888:* But, doubting [37]| *1833:* awaked, *1868:* awaked [38]| *1833:* thro' <> Ah! vain *1868:* through <> Ah vain [39]| *1833:* me—the <> grave, *1868:* me; the <> grave [40]| *1833:* us—still *1868:* us; still [42]| *1833:* darkness <> me, *1868:* me; *1888:* dark [43]| *1833:* love, but *1868:* love but [44]| *1833:* smile, and *1868:* smile and [45]| *1833:* shapes, and *1868:* shapes and [46]| *1833:* slave; *1868:* slave: [47]| *1833:* thee, and *1868:* thee and [49]| *1833:* morn, and spring *1868:* morn and spring

Thou seest then my aimless, hopeless state,
And, resting on some few old feelings won
Back by thy beauty, wouldst that I essay
The task which was to me what now thou art:
And why should I conceal one weakness more?

Thou wilt remember one warm morn when winter
Crept aged from the earth, and spring's first breath
Blew soft from the moist hills; the black-thorn boughs,
So dark in the bare wood, when glistening
In the sunshine were white with coming buds,
Like the bright side of a sorrow, and the banks
Had violets opening from sleep like eyes.
I walked with thee who knew'st not a deep shame
Lurked beneath smiles and careless words which sought
To hide it till they wandered and were mute,
As we stood listening on a sunny mound
To the wind murmuring in the damp copse,
Like heavy breathings of some hidden thing
Betrayed by sleep; until the feeling rushed
That I was low indeed, yet not so low
As to endure the calmness of thine eyes.
And so I told thee all, while the cool breast
I leaned on altered not its quiet beating:
And long ere words like a hurt bird's complaint
Bade me look up and be what I had been,
I felt despair could never live by thee:
Thou wilt remember. Thou art not more dear
Than song was once to me; and I ne'er sung

51| *1833:* And resting <> feelings, won *1868:* And, resting <> feelings won **52**| *1833:* would'st *1868:* wouldst **53**| *1833:* task, which *1868:* task which **55**| *1833:* morn, when Winter *1868:* morn when winter **56**| *1833:* Spring's *1868:* spring's **57**| *1833:* hills—the *1868:* hills; the **58**| *1833:* wood; when *1868:* wood, when **60**| *1833:* sorrow—and *1868:* sorrow, and **61**| *1833:* eyes— *1868:* eyes. **62**| *1833:* thee, who knew *1868:* thee who *1888:* knew'st **63**| *1833:* words, which *1868:* words which **64**| *1833:* it—till <> mute; *1868:* it till <> mute, **68**| *1833:* sleep—until *1868:* sleep; until **70**| *1833:* eyes; *1888:* eyes. **72**| *1833:* beating; *1868:* beating, *1888:* beating: **73**| *1833:* words, like <> complaint, *1868:* words like <> complaint **75**| *1833:* thee. *1868:* thee: **76**| *1833:* remember:—thou *1868:* remember. Thou

But as one entering bright halls where all
Will rise and shout for him: sure I must own
That I am fallen, having chosen gifts
Distinct from theirs—that I am sad and fain
Would give up all to be but where I was,
Not high as I had been if faithful found,
But low and weak yet full of hope, and sure
Of goodness as of life—that I would lose
All this gay mastery of mind, to sit
Once more with them, trusting in truth and love
And with an aim—not being what I am.

Oh Pauline, I am ruined who believed
That though my soul had floated from its sphere
Of wild dominion into the dim orb
Of self—that it was strong and free as ever!
It has conformed itself to that dim orb,
Reflecting all its shades and shapes, and now
Must stay where it alone can be adored.
I have felt this in dreams—in dreams in which
I seemed the fate from which I fled; I felt
A strange delight in causing my decay.
I was a fiend in darkness chained for ever
Within some ocean-cave; and ages rolled,
Till through the cleft rock, like a moonbeam, came
A white swan to remain with me; and ages
Rolled, yet I tired not of my first free joy
In gazing on the peace of its pure wings:
And then I said "It is most fair to me,
Yet its soft wings must sure have suffered change

78| *1833:* halls, where *1868:* halls where 79| *1833:* him. Sure *1868:* him: sure 80| *1833:* fallen—having *1868:* fallen, having 81| *1833:* sad—and *1868:* sad and 82| *1833:* was; *1868:* was, 83| *1833:* been, if <> found— *1868:* been if <> found, 84| *1833:* weak; yet *1868:* weak yet 87| *1833:* love, *1888:* love 88–89| § no space in 1833, 1868. § 89| *1833:* Oh, Pauline! I am ruined! who *1868:* Oh Pauline, I am ruined who 90| *1833:* tho' *1868:* though 91| *1833:* Of wide dominion *1868:* Of wild dominion 92| *1833:* ever:— *1868:* ever! 98| *1833:* decay; *1888:* decay. 99| *1833:* fiend, in *1868:* fiend in 101| *1833:* thro' *1868:* through 103| *1833:* first joy *1888:* first free joy 104| *1833:* wings. *1868:* wings: 105| *1833:* said, "It *1868:* said "It

From the thick darkness, sure its eyes are dim,
Its silver pinions must be cramped and numbed
With sleeping ages here; it cannot leave me,
For it would seem, in light beside its kind,
Withered, tho' here to me most beautiful."
And then I was a young witch whose blue eyes,
As she stood naked by the river springs,
Drew down a god: I watched his radiant form
Growing less radiant, and it gladdened me;
Till one morn, as he sat in the sunshine
Upon my knees, singing to me of heaven,
He turned to look at me, ere I could lose
The grin with which I viewed his perishing:
And he shrieked and departed and sat long
By his deserted throne, but sunk at last
Murmuring, as I kissed his lips and curled
Around him, "I am still a god—to thee."

Still I can lay my soul bare in its fall,
Since all the wandering and all the weakness
Will be a saddest comment on the song:
And if, that done, I can be young again,
I will give up all gained, as willingly
As one gives up a charm which shuts him out
From hope or part or care in human kind.
As life wanes, all its care and strife and toil
Seem strangely valueless, while the old trees
Which grew by our youth's home, the waving mass
Of climbing plants heavy with bloom and dew,

107| *1833:* darkness—sure <> dim— *1868:* darkness, sure <> dim, 110| *1833:* light, beside *1868:* light beside 111| *1833:* Withered—tho' *1868:* Withered, tho' 112| *1833:* witch, whose *1868:* witch whose 114| *1833:* god—I *1868:* god; I *1888:* god: I 115| *1833:* radiant—and *1868:* radiant and *1888:* radiant, and 119| *1833:* perishing. *1868:* perishing: 120| *1833:* departed, and *1868:* departed and 121| *1833:* throne—but <> last, *1868:* throne, but <> last 123–124| § No space in 1833, 1868. § 125| *1833:* For all *1888:* Since all 126| *1833:* song. *1868:* song: 128| *1833:* gained as *1868:* gained, as 130| *1833:* hope, or part, or care, in *1868:* hope or part or care in 131| *1833:* cares, and strife, and toil, *1868:* cares and strife and toil *1888:* care 133| *1833:* home—the *1868:* home, the 134| *1833:* plants, heavy <> dew— *1868:* plants heavy <> dew,

The morning swallows with their songs like words,
All these seem clear and only worth our thoughts:
So, aught connected with my early life,
My rude songs or my wild imaginings,
How I look on them—most distinct amid
The fever and the stir of after years!

I ne'er had ventured e'en to hope for this,
Had not the glow I felt at His award,
Assured me all was not extinct within:
His whom all honour, whose renown springs up
Like sunlight which will visit all the world,
So that e'en they who sneered at him at first,
Come out to it, as some dark spider crawls
From his foul nets which some lit torch invades,
Yet spinning still new films for his retreat.
Thou didst smile, poet, but can we forgive?

Sun-treader, life and light be thine for ever!
Thou art gone from us; years go by and spring
Gladdens and the young earth is beautiful,
Yet thy songs come not, other bards arise,
But none like thee: they stand, thy majesties,
Like mighty works which tell some spirit there
Hath sat regardless of neglect and scorn,
Till, its long task completed, it hath risen
And left us, never to return, and all
Rush in to peer and praise when all in vain.

135| *1833:* words,— *1868:* words, 136| *1833:* thoughts. *1868:* thoughts: 137| *1833:* So aught <> life —— § Long dash after life § *1868:* So, aught <> life, 141| *1868:* ventured e'er to <> this; *1888:* ventured e'en to <> this, 143| *1833:* within. *1868:* within: 144| *1833:* HIM <> honor—whose *1868:* HIS <> honor, whose *1888:* honour 145| *1833:* world; *1868:* world, 148| *1833:* nets, which *1868:* nets which 149| *1833:* retreat.— *1868:* retreat. 150| *1833:* poet,—but, can *we* *1868:* poet, but can we 150–151| § No space in 1868 § 151| *1833:* Sun-treader—life <> ever; *1868:* Sun-treader, life <> ever! 152| *1833:* us—years go by—and *1868:* us; years go by and 153| *1833:* Gladdens, and <> beautiful, *1868:* not, other 155| *1833:* thee—they stand—thy *1868:* thee: they stand, thy 156| *1833:* Spirit *1868:* spirit 159| *1833:* return: and *1868:* return, and

The air seems bright with thy past presence yet,
But thou art still for me as thou hast been
When I have stood with thee as on a throne
With all thy dim creations gathered round
Like mountains, and I felt of mould like them,
And with them creatures of my own were mixed,
Like things half-lived, catching and giving life.
But thou art still for me who have adored
Tho' single, panting but to hear thy name
Which I believed a spell to me alone,
Scarce deeming thou wast as a star to men!
As one should worship long a sacred spring
Scarce worth a moth's flitting, which long grasses cross,
And one small tree embowers droopingly—
Joying to see some wandering insect won
To live in its few rushes, or some locust
To pasture on its boughs, or some wild bird
Stoop for its freshness from the trackless air:
And then should find it but the fountain-head,
Long lost, of some great river washing towns
And towers, and seeing old woods which will live
But by its banks untrod of human foot,
Which, when the great sun sinks, lie quivering
In light as some thing lieth half of life
Before God's foot, waiting a wondrous change;
Then girt with rocks which seek to turn or stay
Its course in vain, for it does ever spread
Like a sea's arm as it goes rolling on,
Being the pulse of some great country—so
Wast thou to me, and art thou to the world!

162| *1833:* me, as *1868:* me as 163| *1833:* thee, as *1868:* thee as 156| *1833:* mountains,—and *1868:* mountains, and 166| *1833:* And creatures of my own were mixed with them, *1888:* And with them creatures of my own were mixed, 168| *1833:* me, who have adored, *1868:* adored *1888:* me who 169| *1833:* name, *1868:* name 171| *1833:* wert <> men— *1868:* wast <> men! 174| *1833:* droopingly, *1888:* droopingly— 175| *1833:* won, *1868:* won 176| *1833:* rushes—or *1868:* rushes, or 177| *1833:* boughs—or *1868:* boughs, or 178| *1833:* air, *1868:* air: 180| *1833:* river—washing *1868:* river washing 182| *1833:* banks, untrod *1868:* banks untrod 185| *1833:* foot—waiting <> change *1868:* foot, waiting <> change; 186| *1833:*—Then *1868:* Then 190| *1833:* Wert <> me—and <> world. *1868:* Wast <> me, and <> world!

And I, perchance, half feel a strange regret
That I am not what I have been to thee:
Like a girl one has silently loved long
In her first loneliness in some retreat,
When, late emerged, all gaze and glow to view
Her fresh eyes and soft hair and lips which bloom
Like a mountain berry: doubtless it is sweet
To see her thus adored, but there have been
Moments when all the world was in our praise,
Sweeter than any pride of after hours.
Yet, sun-treader, all hail! From my heart's heart
I bid thee hail! E'en in my wildest dreams,
I proudly feel I would have thrown to dust
The wreaths of fame which seemed o'erhanging me,
To see thee for a moment as thou art.

And if thou livest, if thou lovest, spirit!
Remember me who set this final seal
To wandering thought—that one so pure as thou
Could never die. Remember me who flung
All honour from my soul, yet paused and said
"There is one spark of love remaining yet,
For I have nought in common with him, shapes
Which followed him avoid me, and foul forms
Seek me, which ne'er could fasten on his mind;

191| *1833:* regret, *1888:* regret **193**| *1833:* has loved long silently, *1868:* silently *1888:* has silently loved long **194**| *1833:* first loveliness, in *1868:* loveliness in *1888:* first loneliness in **195**| *1833:* When first emerged *1868:* When, first *1888:* When, late emerged **196**| *1833:* eyes, and soft hair, and lips which bleed *1868:* eyes and soft hair and *1888:* which bloom **197**| *1833:* berry. Doubtless *1868:* berry: doubtless **198**| *1833:* adored—but *1868:* adored, but **199**| *1833:* Moments, when < > in his praise, *1868:* Moments when *1888:* in our praise, **201**| *1833:* Sun-treader, all hail!—from *1868:* sun-treader, all hail! From **202**| *1833:* hail!—e'en *1868:* hail! E'en **203**| *1833:* I am proud to feel < > thrown up all *1888:* I proudly feel < > thrown to dust **204**| *1833:* wreathes *1868:* wreaths **205**| *1833:* To have seen thee, for a moment, as *1868:* thee for a moment as *1888:* To see thee **205–206**| § No space in 1868 § **206**| *1833:* livest—if *1868:* livest, if **207**| *1833:* me, who *1868:* me who **209**| *1833:* me, who *1868:* me who **210**| *1833:* honor < > soul—yet < > said, *1868:* soul, yet *1888:* honour < > said **212**| *1833:* him—shapes *1868:* him, shapes

And though I feel how low I am to him,
Yet I aim not even to catch a tone
Of harmonies he called profusely up;
So, one gleam still remains, although the last."
Remember me who praise thee e'en with tears,
For never more shall I walk calm with thee;
Thy sweet imaginings are as an air,
A melody some wondrous singer sings,
Which, though it haunt men oft in the still eve,
They dream not to essay; yet it no less
But more is honoured. I was thine in shame,
And now when all thy proud renown is out,
I am a watcher whose eyes have grown dim
With looking for some star which breaks on him
Altered and worn and weak and full of tears.

Autumn has come like spring returned to us,
Won from her girlishness; like one returned
A friend that was a lover, nor forgets
The first warm love, but full of sober thoughts
Of fading years; whose soft mouth quivers yet
With the old smile, but yet so changed and still!
And here am I the scoffer, who have probed
Life's vanity, won by a word again
Into my own life—by one little word
Of this sweet friend who lives in loving me,
Lives strangely on my thoughts and looks and words,
As fathoms down some nameless ocean thing

215| *1833:* tho' *1868:* though **217**| *1833:* Of all the harmonies which he called up, *1868:* called up; *1888:* Of harmonies he called profusely up; **218**| *1833:* So one <> altho' *1868:* So, one <> although **219**| *1833:* me—who *1868:* me who **222**| *1833:* melody, some wond'rous *1868:* melody some wondrous **224**| *1833:* less, *1868:* less **225**| *1833:* honored *1888:* honoured **227**| *1833:* watcher, whose *1868:* watcher whose **228**| *1833:* star—which <> him, *1868:* star which <> him **229**| *1833:* Altered, and worn, and weak, and *1868:* Altered and worn and weak and **230**| *1833:* come—like Spring *1868:* come like spring **231**| *1833:* girlishness—like *1868:* girlishness; like **232**| *1833:* lover—nor *1868:* *1888:* lover, nor **235**| *1833:* smile—but *1868:* smile but *1888:* smile, but **238**| *1833:* life—for one *1888:* life—by one **239**| *1833:* friend, who *1868:* friend who **240**| *1833:* thoughts, and looks, and *1868:* thoughts and looks and

Its silent course of quietness and joy.
O dearest, if indeed I tell the past,
May'st thou forget it as a sad sick dream!
Or if it linger—my lost soul too soon
Sinks to itself and whispers we shall be
But closer linked, two creatures whom the earth
Bears singly, with strange feelings unrevealed
Save to each other; or two lonely things
Created by some power whose reign is done,
Having no part in God or his bright world.
I am to sing whilst ebbing day dies soft,
As a lean scholar dies worn o'er his book,
And in the heaven stars steal out one by one
As hunted men steal to their mountain watch.
I must not think, lest this new impulse die
In which I trust! I have no confidence:
So, I will sing on fast as fancies come;
Rudely, the verse being as the mood it paints.

I strip my mind bare, whose first elements
I shall unveil—not as they struggled forth
In infancy, nor as they now exist,
When I am grown above them and can rule
But in that middle stage when they were full
Yet ere I had disposed them to my will;
And then I shall show how these elements
Produced my present state, and what it is.

243| *1833:* if, indeed, I *1868:* if indeed I **244**| *1833:* dream; *1868:* Mayst <> dream! *1888:* May'st **246**| *1833:* itself, and whispers, we *1868:* itself and *1888:* whispers we **247**| *1833:* linked—two *1868:* linked, two **248**| *1833:* singly—with <> feelings, unrevealed *1868:* singly, with <> feelings unrevealed **249**| *1833:* But to *1888:* Save to **250**| *1833:* some Power, whose *1868:* power whose **251**| *1833:* in God, or <> world, *1868:* in God or <> world. **252**| *1833:* sing; whilst *1868:* sing whilst **253**| *1833:* dies, worn *1868:* dies worn **254**| *1833:* by one, *1868:* by one **256**| *1833:* think—lest *1868:* think, lest **257**| *1833:* trust. I <> confidence, *1868:* trust; I <> confidence: **258**| *1833:* So I <> on—fast <> come *1868:* So, I <> on fast <> come; **259**| *1833:* Rudely—the *1868:* Rudely, the § period omitted by error in 1888, 1889 § **260**| *1833:* bare—whose *1868:* bare, whose **263**| *1833:* That I <> them, and can rule them, *1868:* them and can rule— *1888:* When I <> rule **264**| *1833:* stage, when <> full, *1868:* stage when <> full **267–268**| § Space §

I am made up an intensest life,
Of a most clear idea of consciousness
Of self, distinct from all its qualities,
From all affections, passions, feelings, powers;
And thus far it exists, if tracked, in all:
But linked, in me, to self-supremacy,
Existing as a centre to all things,
Most potent to create and rule and call
Upon all things to minister to it;
And to a principle of restlessness
Which would be all, have, see, know, taste, feel, all—
This is myself; and I should thus have been
Though gifted lower than the meanest soul.

And of my powers, one springs up to save
From utter death a soul with such desire
Confined to clay—of powers the only one
Which marks me—an imagination which
Has been a very angel, coming not
In fitful visions but beside me ever
And never failing me; so, though my mind
Forgets not, not a shred of life forgets,
Yet I can take a secret pride in calling
The dark past up to quell it regally.

A mind like this must dissipate itself.
But I have always had one lode-star; now,
As I look back, I see that I have halted
Or hastened as I looked towards that star—
A need, a trust, a yearning after God:

270| *1833:* self—distinct *1868:* self, distinct 272| *1833:* tracked in all, *1868:* all: *1888:* tracked, in 273| *1833:* linked in *1868:* linked, in 275| *1833:* create, and rule, and *1868:* create and rule and 279| *1833:* been, *1868:* been 282| *1833:* desires *1868:* desire 283| *1833:* clay—which is the *1888:* clay—of powers the 285| *1833:* been an angel to me—coming *1868:* me, coming *1888:* been a very angel, coming 286| *1833:* visions, but < > ever, *1868:* visions but < > ever 287| *1833:* so tho' *1868:* so, though 288| *1833:* not—not < > forgets— *1868:* not, not < > forgets, 290| *1833:* up—to *1868:* up to 291| *1833:* itself, 293| *1833:* have wasted, *1868:* wasted *1888:* have halted 294| *1833:* Or progressed as < > toward *1868:* towards *1888:* Or hastened as 295| *1833:* after God, *1868:* after God:

A feeling I have analysed but late,
But it existed, and was reconciled
With a neglect of all I deemed his laws,
Which yet, when seen in others, I abhorred.
I felt as one beloved, and so shut in
From fear: and thence I date my trust in signs
And omens, for I saw God everywhere;
And I can only lay it to the fruit
Of a sad after-time that I could doubt
Even his being—e'en the while I felt
His presence, never acted from myself,
Still trusted in a hand to lead me through
All danger; and this feeling ever fought
Against my weakest reason and resolve.

And I can love nothing—and this dull truth
Has come the last: but sense supplies a love
Encircling me and mingling with my life.

These make myself: I have long sought in vain
To trace how they were formed by circumstance,
Yet ever found them mould my wildest youth
Where they alone displayed themselves, converted
All objects to their use: now see their course!

They came to me in my first dawn of life
Which passed alone with wisest ancient books
All halo-girt with fancies of my own;

301| *1833:* fear—and *1868:* fear: and **302**| *1833:* omens—for <> every where; *1868:* omens, for <> everywhere; **305**| *1833:* being—having always felt *1888:* being—e'en the while I felt **306**| *1833:* presence—never acting *1868:* presence, never *1888:* acted **307**| *1833:* trusting <> hand that leads *1888:* trusted <> hand to lead **308**| *1833:* feeling still has fought *1888:* feeling ever fought **309**| *1833:* resolves. *1868:* resolve.
311| *1833:* last—but *1868:* last: but **313**| *1833:* myself—for I have sought *1868:* myself: for *1888:* myself: I have long sought **315**| *1833:* For I still find them—turning my wild youth *1868:* them turning *1888:* Yet ever found them mould my wildest youth **316**| *1833:* converting *1888:* converted
317| *1833:* use—now *1868:* use: now <> course. *1888:* course!
318| *1833:* life, *1868:* life **319**| *1833:* books, *1868:* books
320| *1833:* own, *1868:* own;

And I myself went with the tale—a god
Wandering after beauty, or a giant
Standing vast in the sunset—an old hunter
Talking with gods, or a high-crested chief
Sailing with troops of friend to Tenedos.
I tell you, nought has ever been so clear
As the place, the time, the fashion of those lives:
I had not seen a work of lofty art,
Nor woman's beauty nor sweet nature's face,
Yet, I say, never morn broke clear as those
On the dim clustered isles in the blue sea,
The deep groves and white temples and wet caves:
And nothing ever will surprise me now—
Who stood beside the naked Swift-footed,
Who bound my forehead with Proserpine's hair.

And strange it is that I who could so dream
Should e'er have stooped to aim at aught beneath—
Aught low or painful; but I never doubted:
So, as I grew, I rudely shaped my life
To my immediate wants; yet strong beneath
Was a vague sense of power though folded up—
A sense that, though those shades and times were past,
Their spirit dwelt in me, with them should rule.

Then came a pause, and long restraint chained down
My soul till it was changed. I lost myself,

321| *1833:* god, *1868:* god **322**| *1833:* beauty—or a giant, *1868:* beauty, or a giant **323**| *1833:* hunter, *1868:* hunter **324**| *1833:* gods—or <> chief, *1868:* gods, or *1888:* chief **325**| *1833:* friends to Tenedos;— *1868:* Tenedos. **327**| *1833:* lives. *1868:* lives: **329**| *1833:* beauty, nor *1868:* beauty nor **331**| *1833:* sea: *1868:* sea, **332**| *1833:* groves, and white temples, and wet caves— *1868:* groves and white temples and wet caves: *1888:* caves **336**| *1833:* An' <> is, that <> dream, *1868:* And <> is that <> dream **338**| *1833:* low, or painful, but <> doubted; *1868:* painful; but <> doubted, *1888:* low or <> doubted: **339**| *1833:* So as *1868:* So, as **340**| *1833:* wants, yet *1868:* wants; yet **341**| *1833:* powers folded *1888:* power though folded **342**| *1833:* that tho' those shadowy times *1868:* though <> past *1888:* that, though those shades and times were past, **343**| *1833:* me, and I should *1888:* me, with them should **345**| *1833:* soul, till *1868:* soul till

And were it not that I so loathe that loss,
I could recall how first I learned to turn
My mind against itself; and the effects
In deeds for which remorse were vain as for
The wanderings of delirious dream; yet thence
Came cunning, envy, falsehood, all world's wrong
That spotted me: at length I cleansed my soul.
Yet long world's influence remained; and nought
But the still life I led, apart once more,
Which left me free to seek soul's old delights,
Could e'er have brought me thus far back to peace.

As peace returned, I sought out some pursuit;
And song rose, no new impulse but the one
With which all others best could be combined.
My life has not been that of those whose heaven
Was lampless save where poesy shone out;
But as a clime where glittering mountain-tops
And glancing sea and forests steeped in light
Give back reflected the far-flashing sun;
For music (which is earnest of a heaven,
Seeing we know emotions strange by it,
Not else to be revealed,) is like a voice,
A low voice calling fancy, as a friend,
To the green woods in the gay summer time:
And she fills all the way with dancing shapes
Which have made painters pale, and they go on

346| *1833:* loathe that time, *1888:* loathe that loss, 348| *1833:* effects, *1868:* effects 349| *1833:* vain, as *1868:* vain as 351| *1833:* falsehood, which so long *1888:* falsehood, all world's wrong 352| *1833:* Have spotted me—at <> I was restored, *1868:* me: at <> restored. *1888:* That spotted <> I cleansed my soul. 353| *1833:* long the influence *1888:* long world's influence 354| *1833:* apart from all, *1888:* apart once more, 355| *1833:* left my soul to seek its old *1888:* left me free to seek soul's old 356–357| § No space in 1833, 1868 § 357| *1833:* pursuit: *1868:* pursuit; 358| *1833:* rose—no new impulse—but *1868:* rose, no new impulse but 361| *1833:* lampless, save *1868:* lampless save 362| *1833:* clime, where <> mountain-tops, *1868:* clime where <> mountain-tops 363| *1833:* sea, and <> light, *1868:* sea and <> light 365| *1833:* music, (which *1868:* music (which 367| *1833:* is as a *1888:* is like a 368| *1833:* Fancy *1868:* fancy 369| *1833:* time. *1868:* time: 370| *1833:* shapes, *1868:* shapes 371| *1833:* pale; and *1868:* pale, and

Till stars look at them and winds call to them
As they leave life's path for the twilight world
Where the dead gather. This was not at first,
For I scarce knew what I would do. I had
An impulse but no yearning—only sang.

And first I sang as I in dream have seen
Music wait on a lyrist for some thought,
Yet singing to herself until it came.
I turned to those old times and scenes where all
That's beautiful had birth for me, and made
Rude verses on them all; and then I paused—
I had done nothing, so I sought to know
What other minds achieved. No fear outbroke
As on the works of mighty bards I gazed,
In the first joy at finding my own thoughts
Recorded, my own fancies justified,
And their aspirings but my very own.
With them I first explored passion and mind,—
All to begin afresh! I rather sought
To rival what I wondered at than form
Creations of my own; if much was light
Lent by the others, much was yet my own.

I paused again: a change was coming—came:

372| *1833:* While stars < > them, and < > to them, *1868:* them and < > to them *1888:* Till stars 373| *1833:* world, *1868:* world 376| *1833:* No wish to paint, no yearning—but I sang. *1868:* yearning; but *1888:* An impulse but no yearning—only sang. 377| *1833:* sang, as < > seen, *1868:* sang as < > seen 380| *1833:* scenes, where *1868:* scenes where 384| *1833:* What mind had yet achieved. No fear was mine *1888:* What other minds achieved. No fear outbroke 385| *1833:* As I gazed on < > bards, *1888:* As on < > bards I gazed, 387| *1833:* Recorded, and my powers exemplified, *1868:* Recorded and *1888:* Recorded, my own fancies justified, 388| *1833:* And feeling their aspirings were my own. *1888:* And their aspirings but my very own. 389| *1833:* And then I < > mind; *1888:* With them I < > mind,— 390| *1833:* And I began afresh; I *1888:* All to begin afresh! I 391| *1833:* at, than *1888:* at than 392| *1833:* own; so much *1868:* so, much *1888:* own; if much 393| *1833:* Lent back by others, yet much was my *1888:* Lent by the others, much was yet my 394| *1833:* ¶ I < > again—a < > coming on, *1868:* I < > again, a *1888:* again: a < > coming—came:

I was no more a boy, the past was breaking
Before the future and like fever worked.
I thought on my new self, and all my powers
Burst out. I dreamed not of restraint, but gazed
On all things: schemes and systems went and came,
And I was proud (being vainest of the weak)
In wandering o'er thought's world to seek some one
To be my prize, as if you wandered o'er
The White Way for a star.

And my choice fell
Not so much on a system as a man—
On one, whom praise of mine shall not offend,
Who was as calm as beauty, being such
Unto mankind as thou to me, Pauline,—
Believing in them and devoting all
His soul's strength to their winning back to peace;
Who sent forth hopes and longings for their sake,
Clothed in all passion's melodies: such first
Caught me and set me, slave of a sweet task,
To disentangle, gather sense from song:
Since, song-inwoven, lurked there words which seemed
A key to a new world, the muttering
Of angels, something yet unguessed by man.

395| *1833:* boy—the *1868:* boy, the 396| *1833:* the coming, and *1868:* coming and *1888:* the future and 397| *1833:* I first thought on myself—and here my *1868:* myself, and *1888:* I thought on my new self, and all my
398| *1868:* out: I <> restraint but *1888:* out. I <> restraint, but
400| *1833:* weak), *1868:* weak) 401| *1833:* o'er them, to seek out some *1868:* them to *1888:* o'er thought's world to seek some 402| *1833:* my own; as one should wander o'er *1868:* own, as *1888:* my prize, as if you wandered o'er 403| *1833:* white way *1888:* White Way 403–405| *1833:* star. / ° ° ° ° / On *1868:* star. § space § ¶ And my choice fell / Not so much on a system as a man— / On 406| *1833:* beauty—being *1868:* beauty, being
407| *1833:* Pauline, *1868:* Pauline,— 408| *1833:* them, and *1868:* them and 411| *1833:* melodies, which first *1888:* melodies: such first
412| *1833:* me, and set me, as to a *1868:* me and *1888:* me, slave of a
413| *1833:* To gather every breathing of his songs. *1868:* songs: *1888:* To disentangle, gather sense from song: 414| *1833:* And woven with them there were words, which *1868:* words which *1888:* Since, song-inwoven, lurked there words 415| *1833:* world; the *1868:* world, the 416| *1833:* angels, of some thing unguessed *1868:* angels of *1888:* angels, something yet unguessed

How my heart leapt as still I sought and found
Much there, I felt my own soul had conceived,
But there living and burning! Soon the orb
Of his conceptions dawned on me; its praise
Lives in the tongues of men, men's brows are high
When his name means a triumph and a pride,
So, my weak voice may well forbear to shame
What seemed decreed my fate: I threw myself
To meet it, I was vowed to liberty,
Men were to be as gods and earth as heaven,
And I—ah, what a life was mine to prove!
My whole soul rose to meet it. Now, Pauline,
I shall go mad, if I recall that time!

    Oh let me look back ere I leave for ever
The time which was an hour one fondly waits
For a fair girl that comes a withered hag!
And I was lonely, far from woods and fields,
And amid dullest sights, who should be loose
As a stag; yet I was full of bliss, who lived
With Plato and who had the key to life;
And I had dimly shaped my first attempt,
And many a thought did I build up on thought,

417| *1833:* heart beat, as I went on, and *1868:* beat as <> on and *1888:* heart lept as still I sought and 418| *1833:* there! I <> own mind had *1868:* there, I *1888:* own soul had 419| *1833:* burning; soon the whole *1868:* burning! Soon *1888:* the orb 420| *1833:* me; their praise *1888:* me; its praise 421| *1833:* Is in <> men; men's *1868:* men, men's *1888:* Lives in 422| *1833:* pride; *1868:* pride, 423| *1833:* So my weak hands may <> to dim *1868:* So, my *1888:* weak voice may <> to shame
424| *1833:* What then seemed my bright fate *1888:* What seemed decreed my fate 425| *1833:* it. I *1868:* it, I 426| *1833:* gods, and <> heaven. *1868:* gods and <> heaven, 427| *1833:* ah! what <> to be, *1868:* ah, what <> be! *1888:* to prove! 429| *1833:* time. *1868:* time!
429–430| § 1833: space with ° ° ° ° Later editions: space § 430| *1833:* O <> back, e'er *1868:* Oh <> back e'er *1888:* ere 431| *1833:* time, which <> hour, that one waits *1868:* time which <> hour that one waits *1888:* hour one fondly waits 432| *1833:* girl, that <> hag. *1868:* girl that <> hag!
433| *1833:* lonely,—far *1868:* lonely, far 435| *1833:* stag—yet <> of joy—who *1868:* stag; yet <> joy, who *1888:* of bliss, who 436| *1833:* With Plato—and <> life. *1868:* With Plato and <> life;

As the wild bee hangs cell to cell; in vain,
For I must still advance, no rest for mind.

'Twas in my plan to look on real life,
The life all new to me; my theories
Were firm, so them I left, to look and learn
Mankind, its cares, hopes, fears, its woes and joys;
And, as I pondered on their ways, I sought
How best life's end might be attained—an end
Comprising every joy. I deeply mused.

And suddenly without heart-wreck I awoke
As from a dream: I said " 'Twas beautiful,
Yet but a dream, and so adieu to it!"
As some world-wanderer sees in a far meadow
Strange towers and high-walled gardens thick with trees,
Where song takes shelter and delicious mirth
From laughing fairy creatures peeping over,
And on the morrow when he comes to lie
For ever 'neath those garden-trees fruit-flushed
Sung round by fairies, all his search is vain.
First went my hopes for perfecting mankind,

439| *1833:* cell—in vain; *1868:* cell; in vain, **440**| *1833:* still go on: my mind rests not. *1868:* on, my. *1888:* still advance, no rest for mind. **441**| *1868:* life *1888:* life, **442**| *1833:* Which was all *1888:* The life all **443**| *1833:* so I left them, to look upon *1888:* so them I left, to look and learn **444**| *1833:* Men, and their cares, and hopes, and fears, and *1868:* Men and their cares and hopes and fears and *1888:* Mankind, its <> its woes and **445**| *1833:* on them all, I *1868:* And as <> all I *1888:* And, as <> on their ways, I **448**| *1833:* suddenly, without heart-wreck, I *1868:* suddenly without heart-wreck I **449**| *1833:* dream—I said, 'twas *1868:* dream: I said " 'Twas beautiful *1888:* beautiful, **450**| *1833:* dream; and <> it. *1868:* dream, and <> it!" **452**| *1833:* towers, and walled gardens, thick *1868:* towers and <> gardens thick *1888:* and high-walled gardens **453**| *1833:* Where singing goes on, and <> mirth, *1868:* on and *1888:* Where song takes shelter and <> mirth **454**| *1833:* And laughing *1888:* From laughing **455**| *1833:* morrow, when <> to live *1868:* morrow when *1888:* to lie **456**| *1833:* ever by those springs, and trees, fruit-flushed *1868:* springs and trees fruit-flushed *1888:* ever 'neath those garden-trees fruit-flushed **457**| *1833:* And fairy bowers—all *1868:* bowers, all *1888:* Sung round by fairies, all
457–458| *1833:* vain. / Well I remember ° ° ° ° / First

Next—faith in them, and then in freedom's self
And virtue's self, then my own motives, ends
And aims and loves, and human love went last.
I felt this no decay, because new powers
Rose as old feelings left—wit, mockery,
Light-heartedness; for I had oft been sad,
Mistrusting my resolves, but now I cast
Hope joyously away: I laughed and said
"No more of this!" I must not think: at length
I looked again to see if all went well.

My powers were greater: as some temple seemed
My soul, where nought is changed and incense rolls
Around the altar, only God is gone
And some dark spirit sitteth in his seat.
So, I passed through the temple and to me
Knelt troops of shadows, and they cried "Hail, king!
We serve thee now and thou shalt serve no more!
Call on us, prove us, let us worship thee!"
And I said "Are ye strong? Let fancy bear me
Far from the past!" And I was borne away,
As Arab birds float sleeping in the wind,
O'er deserts, towers and forests, I being calm.
And I said "I have nursed up energies,
They will prey on me." And a band knelt low

459| *1833:* And faith in them—then freedom in itself, *1868:* them, then <> itself *1888:* Next—faith in them, and then in freedom's self 460| *1833:* And virtue in itself—and then my motives' end, *1868:* itself, and <> motives, ends *1888:* And virtue's self, then my own motives 461| *1833:* And powers and loves; and *1868:* loves, and *1888:* And aims and loves 463| *1868:* mockery *1888:* mockery, 464| *1833:* And happiness; for *1888:* Lightheartedness; for 465| *1833:* resolves: but *1868:* resolves, but 466| *1833:* away—I <> said, *1868:* away: I <> said 467| *1833:* this"—I <> think; at *1868:* this!" I <> think: at 468| *1833:* look'd <> see how all went on. *1868:* looked *1888:* see if all went well. 470| *1833:* changed, and *1868:* changed and 471| *1833:* altar—only <> gone, *1868:* altar, only <> gone 472| *1833:* seat! *1868:* seat. 473| *1833:* So I <> temple; and *1868:* So, I <> temple and 474| *1833:* shadows; and they cried, "Hail, *1868:* shadows, and they cried "Hail, 475| *1833:* now, and *1868:* now and 477| *1833:* said, "Are ye strong—let *1868:* said "Are ye strong? Let 478| *1833:* past."—And <> away *1868:* past!" And <> away, 480| *1833:* towers, and <> calm; *1868:* towers and *1888:* calm. 481| *1833:* said, "I *1868:* said "I 482| *1833:* low, *1868:* low

And cried "Lord, we are here and we will make
Safe way for thee in thine appointed life!
But look on us!" And I said "Ye will worship
Me; should my heart not worship too?" They shouted
"Thyself, thou art our king!" So, I stood there
Smiling—oh, vanity of vanities!
For buoyant and rejoicing was the spirit
With which I looked out how to end my course;
I felt once more myself, my powers—all mine;
I knew while youth and health so lifted me
That, spite of all life's nothingness, no grief
Came nigh me, I must ever be light-hearted;
And that this knowledge was the only veil
Betwixt joy and despair: so, if age came,
I should be left—a wreck linked to a soul
Yet fluttering, or mind-broken and aware
Of my decay. So a long summer morn
Found me; and ere noon came, I had resolved
No age should come on me ere youth was spent,
For I would wear myself out, like that morn
Which wasted not a sunbeam; every hour

483| *1833:* cried, "Lord, <> here, and *1868:* cried "Lord, <> here and 484| *1833:* A way for thee—in <> life *1868:* thee in <> life! *1888:* Safe way 485| *1833:* O look <> said, "Ye *1868:* said "Ye *1888:* But look 486| *1833:* Me; but my heart must worship too." They shouted, *1868:* shouted *1888:* Me; should my heart not worship too?" They 487| *1833:* "Thyself—thou <> So I *1868:* "Thyself, thou <> So, I 488| *1833:* Smiling ° ° ° ° ° § only word in line. Space between lines § *1868:* Smiling . . . . . . § only word in line. No space between lines § *1888:* Smiling—oh, vanity of vanities! § no space § 489| *1833:* And buoyant *1888:* For buoyant 490| *1833:* my days; *1888:* my course; 491| *1833:* myself—my powers were mine; *1868:* myself, my *1888:* powers—all mine; 492| *1833:* I found that youth or health <> me, *1868:* me *1888:* I knew while youth and health 493| *1833:* life's vanity, no *1888:* life's nothingness, no 494| *1833:* me—I *1868:* me, I 495| *1833:* this feeling was *1888:* this knowledge was 496| *1833:* Betwixt me and <> so if *1868:* so, if *1888:* Betwixt joy and 497| *1833:* be as a *1888:* be left—a 498| *1833:* mind-broken, and *1868:* mind-broken and 500| *1833:* e'er *1888:* ere 501| *1833:* me, ere youth's hopes went, *1868:* me ere *1888:* ere youth was spent, 502| *1833:* out—like *1868:* out, like 503| *1833:* sunbeam—every joy *1868:* sunbeam; every

I would make mine, and die.

And thus I sought
To chain my spirit down which erst I freed
For flights to fame: I said "The troubled life
Of genius, seen so gay when working forth
Some trusted end, grows sad when all proves vain—
How sad when men have parted with truth's peace
For falsest fancy's sake, which waited first
As an obedient spirit when delight
Came without fancy's call: but alters soon,
Comes darkened, seldom, hastens to depart,
Leaving a heavy darkness and warm tears.
Bùt I shall never lose her; she will live
Dearer for such seclusion. I but catch
A hue, a glance of what I sing: so, pain
Is linked with pleasure, for I ne'er may tell
Half the bright sights which dazzle me; but now
Mine shall be all the radiance: let them fade
Untold—others shall rise as fair, as fast!
And when all's done, the few dim gleams transferred,"—
(For a new thought sprang up how well it were,

504| *1833:* die; and *1868:* die. And § no space or half-line division in 1833, 1868 § 505| *1833:* down, which I had fed *1868:* down which *1888:* which erst I freed 506| *1833:* With thoughts of fame. I said, the *1868:* fame: I said "The *1888:* For flights to fame 507| *1833:* genius seen so bright when *1868:* genius, seen *1888:* genius seen so gay when 508| *1833:* end, seems sad, when all in vain— *1868:* sad when *1888:* end, grows sad when all proves vain— 509| *1833:* Most sad, when <> with all joy *1868:* sad when *1888:* How sad <> with truth's peace 510| *1833:* For their wild fancy's <> first, *1868:* first *1888:* For falsest fancy's 511| *1833:* spirit, when *1868:* spirit when 512| *1833:* Came not with her alone, but *1868:* alone; but *1888:* Came without fancy's call: but 513| *1833:* Coming <> hasting *1868:* Comes <> hastening *1888:* hastens 514–515| § space in 1833 § 516| *1833:* Brighter for <> seclusion—I *1868:* seclusion. I *1888:* Dearer for 517| *1833:* sing, so pain *1868:* so, pain *1888:* sing: so 519| *1833:* The radiant sights *1888:* Half the bright sights 520| *1833:* They shall be all my own, and let *1868:* own; and *1888:* Mine shall be all the radiance: let 521| *1833:* fast. *1868:* fast! 522| *1833:* transferred,— *1868:* transferred,"— 523| *1833:* sprung up—that it were well *1868:* up that *1888:* sprang up how well it were,

Discarding shadowy hope, to weave such lays
As straight encircle men with praise and love,
So, I should not die utterly,—should bring
One branch from the gold forest, like the knight
Of old tales, witnessing I had been there)—
"And when all's done, how vain seems e'en success—
The vaunted influence poets have o'er men!
'Tis a fine thing that one weak as myself
Should sit in his lone room, knowing the words
He utters in his solitude shall move
Men like a swift wind—that tho' dead and gone,
New eyes shall glisten when his beauteous dreams
Of love come true in happier frames than his.
Ay, the still night brings thoughts like these, but morn
Comes and the mockery again laughs out
At hollow praises, smiles allied to sneers;
And my soul's idol ever whispers me
To dwell with him and his unhonoured song:
And I foreknow my spirit, that would press
First in the struggle, fail again to make
All bow enslaved, and I again should sink.

"And then know that this curse will come on us,
To see our idols perish; we may wither,

524| *1833:* To leave all shadowy hopes, and weave *1868:* hope *1888:* Discarding shadowy hope, to weave 525| *1833:* As would encircle me with <> love; *1868:* love, *1888:* As straight encircle men with 526| *1833:* So I <> utterly—I should *1868:* So. I <> utterly, I *1888:* utterly,—should
528| *1833:* there,)— *1868:* there)— 529| *1833:* And <> success, *1868:* "And <> success *1888:* success— 530| *1833:* And all the influence *1888:* The vaunted influence 531| *1833:* one, weak as myself, *1868:* one weak as myself 534| *1833:* tho' he be forgotten, *1888:* tho' dead and gone,
535| *1833:* Fair eyes *1888:* New eyes 537| *1833:* brought *1888:* brings 538| *1833:* Came, and <> laughed *1888:* Comes and <> laughs 539| *1833:* praises, and smiles, almost sneers; *1868:* smiles almost *1888:* praises, smiles allied to sneers; 540| *1833:* idol seemed to whisper *1888:* idol ever whispers 541| *1833:* unhonoured name— *1868:* name: *1888:* unhonoured song: 542| *1833:* I well knew my <> would be *1888:* I foreknow my <> would press 543| *1833:* struggle, and again would make *1888:* struggle, fail again to make 544| *1833:* bow to it; and I would sink again. *1868:* it, and I should sink *1888:* bow enslaved, and I again should sink. 544–545| *1833:* § space with ° ° ° ° ° Later editions: space §
546| *1833:* perish—we *1868:* perish; we

No marvel, we are clay, but our low fate
Should not extend to those whom trustingly
We sent before into time's yawning gulf
To face what dread may lurk in darkness there.
To find the painter's glory pass, and feel
Music can move us not as once, or, worst,
To weep decaying wits ere the frail body
Decays! Nought makes me trust some love is true,
But the delight of the contented lowness
With which I gaze on him I keep for ever
Above me; I to rise and rival him?
Feed his fame rather from my heart's best blood,
Wither unseen that he may flourish still."

Pauline, my soul's friend, thou dost pity yet
How this mood swayed me when that soul found thine,
When I had set myself to live this life,
Defying all past glory. Ere thou camest
I seemed defiant, sweet, for old delights
Had flocked like birds again; music, my life,
Nourished me more than ever; then the lore

547| *1833:* Nor marvel—we are clay; but *1868:* marvel, we are clay, but *1888:* No marvel 548| *1833:* extend them, whom *1868:* extend to them *1888:* to those whom 549| *1833:* Time's <> gulf, *1868:* time's <> gulf 550| *1833:* what e'er may <> there— *1868:* whate'er might <> there. *1888:* what dread may lurk 551| *1833:* To see the painters' *1888:* To find the painter's 552| *1833:* Sweet music move <> or worst, *1868:* or, worst, *1888:* Music can move 553| *1833:* To see decaying *1888:* To weep decaying 554| *1833:* Decays. Nought <> trust in love so really, *1868:* Decays! Nought *1888:* trust some love is true, 555| *1833:* As the delight *1888:* But the delight 556| *1833:* on souls I'd keep *1888:* on him I keep 557| *1833:* In beauty—I'd be sad to equal them; *1868:* beauty; I'd *1888:* Above me; I to rise and rival him? 558| *1833:* I'd feed their fame e'en from *1888:* Feed his fame rather from 559| *1833:* Withering unseen, that they might flourish still. *1868:* unseen that <> still." *1888:* Wither unseen that he may flourish 559–560| § 1833: space with ° ° ° ° Later editions: space § 560| *1833:* my sweet friend thou dost not forget *1888:* my soul's friend thou dost pity yet 561| *1833:* me, when thou first wert mine, *1868:* me when <> wast *1888:* when that soul found thine, 563| *1833:* all opinion. Ere *1888:* all past glory. Ere 564| *1833:* I was most happy, sweet, *1888:* I seemed defiant, sweet, 565| *1833:* Had come like *1888:* Had flocked like 566| *1833:* I nourished more than ever, and old lore *1888:* Nourished me more than ever; then the lore

Loved for itself and all it shows—that king
Treading the purple calmly to his death,
While round him, like the clouds of eve, all dusk,
The giant shades of fate, silently flitting,
Pile the dim outline of the coming doom;
And him sitting alone in blood while friends
Are hunting far in the sunshine; and the boy
With his white breast and brow and clustering curls
Streaked with his mother's blood, but striving hard
To tell his story ere his reason goes.
And when I loved thee as love seemed so oft,
Thou lovedst me indeed: I wondering searched
My heart to find some feeling like such love,
Believing I was still much I had been.
To soon I found all faith had gone from me,
And the late glow of life, like change on clouds,
Proved not the morn-blush widening into day,
But eve faint-coloured by the dying sun
While darkness hastens quickly. I will tell
My state as though 'twere none of mine—despair
Cannot come near us—this it is, my state.

Souls alter not, and mine must still advance;
Strange that I knew not, when I flung away
My youth's chief aims, their loss might lead to loss

567| *1833:* itself, and <> shows—the king *1868:* itself and *1888:* shows—that king 569| *1833:*—While *1868:* While 571| *1833:* doom, *1868:* doom; 572| *1833:*—And <> blood, while *1868:* And <> blood while 573| *1833:* boy, *1868:* boy 577| *1833:* thee, as I've loved so *1868:* thee as *1888:* as love seemed so 578| *1833:* me, and I wondered, and looked in *1868:* wondered and *1888:* me indeed: I wondering searched 580| *1833:* still what I had been; *1888:* still much I had been. 581| *1833:* And soon *1888:* Too soon 582| *1833:* life—changing like clouds, *1868:* life, changing *1888:* life, like change on clouds, 583| *1833:* 'Twas not *1888:* Proved not 584| *1833:* But evening, coloured *1868:* evening coloured *1888:* But eve faint-coloured 585| *1833:* darkness is quick hastening:—I *1868:* hastening. I *1888:* darkness hastens quickly. I 587| *1833:* near me—thus it is with me. *1888:* near us—this it is, my state. 587–588| § no space in 1833, 1868 § 588| *1833:* must progress still; *1888:* must still advance; 589| *1833:* And this I knew not when *1888:* Strange that I knew not, when 590| *1833:* aims. I ne'er supposed the loss *1888:* aims, their loss might lead to loss

Of what few I retained, and no resource
Be left me: for behold how changed is all!
I cannot chain my soul: it will not rest
In its clay prison, this most narrow sphere:
It has strange impulse, tendency, desire,
Which nowise I account for nor explain,
But cannot stifle, being bound to trust
All feelings equally, to hear all sides:
How can my life indulge them? yet they live,
Referring to some state of life unknown.

My selfishness is satiated not,
It wears me like a flame; my hunger for
All pleasure, howsoe'er minute, grows pain;
I envy—how I envy him whose soul
Turns its whole energies to some one end,
To elevate an aim, pursue success
However mean! So, my still baffled hope
Seeks out abstractions; I would have one joy,
But one in life, so it were wholly mine,
One rapture all my soul could fill: and this
Wild feeling places me in dream afar
In some vast country where the eye can see

591| *1833:* retained; for no *1868:* retained, for *1888:* retained, and no **592**| *1833:* Awaits me—now behold the change of all. *1868:* me: now *1888:* Be left me: for behold how changed is all! **593**| *1833:* soul, it *1888:* soul: it **594**| *1833:* prison; this <> sphere— *1868:* prison, this <> sphere: **595**| *1833:* strange powers, and feelings, and desires, *1868:* powers and feelings and *1888:* strange impulse, tendency, desire, **596**| *1833:* Which I cannot account for, nor *1868:* for nor *1888:* Which nowise I account **597**| *1833:* But which I stifle not, being *1888:* But cannot stifle, being **598**| *1833:* equally—to *1868:* equally, to **599**| *1833:* Yet I cannot indulge them, and they *1888:* How can my life indulge them? yet they **600**| *1833:* state or life unknown . . . . . *1868:* unknown. *1888:* state of life **603**| *1833:* is pain; *1888:* grows pain; **604**| *1833:* whose mind *1888:* whose soul **605**| *1833:* Turns with its energies <> end! *1868:* end, *1888:* Turns its whole energies **606**| *1833:* elevate a sect, or a pursuit, *1868:* sect or a pursuit *1888:* elevate an aim, pursue success **607**| *1833:* mean—so my <> hopes *1868:* mean! So, my *1888:* hope **608**| *1833:* Seek <> have but one *1888:* Seeks <> have one **609**| *1833:* Delight on earth, so <> mine; *1868:* mine, *1888:* But one in life, so **610**| *1833:* fill—and *1868:* fill: and **611**| *1833:* afar, *1868:* afar **612**| *1833:* some wide country, where *1868:* some wild country where *1888:* some vast country

No end to the far hills and dales bestrewn
With shining towers and towns, till I grow mad
Well-nigh, to know not one abode but holds
Some pleasure, while my soul could grasp the world,
But must remain this vile form's slave. I look
With hope to age at last, which quenching much,
May let me concentrate what sparks it spares.

This restlessness of passion meets in me
A craving after knowledge: the sole proof
Of yet commanding will is in that power
Repressed; for I beheld it in its dawn,
The sleepless harpy with just-budding wings,
And I considered whether to forego
All happy ignorant hopes and fears, to live,
Finding a recompense in its wild eyes.
And when I found that I should perish so,
I bade its wild eyes close from me for ever,
And I am left alone with old delights;
See! it lies in me a chained thing, still prompt
To serve me if I loose its slightest bond:
I cannot but be proud of my bright slave.

How should this earth's life prove my only sphere?
Can I so narrow sense but that in life

614| *1833:* and dwellings. I *1868:* dwellings: I *1888:* and towns, til I **616**| *1833:* pleasure—for my <> grasp them all, *1868:* pleasure, for <> all *1888:* pleasure, while my <> grasp the world, **617**| *1833:* remain with this vile form. I *1888:* remain this vile form's slave. I **619**| *1833:* concentrate the sparks *1888:* concentrate what sparks **622**| *1833:* Of a *1888:* Of yet **624**| *1833:* That sleepless harpy, with its budding wings *1868:* harpy with *1888:* The sleepless harpy with just-budding wings **625**| *1833:* whether I should yield *1888:* whether to forego **626**| *1833:* All hopes <> live alone with it, *1888:* All happy ignorant hopes <> live, **627**| *1833:* eyes; *1888:* eyes. **629**| *1833:* ever;— *1868:* ever, **630**| *1833:* with my delights,— *1868:* delights; *1888:* with old delights; **631**| *1833:* So it <> thing—still ready *1868:* So, it <> thing, still *1888:* See! it <> still prompt **632**| *1833:* me, if <> bond— *1868:* me if <> bond: **634**| *1833:* And thus I know this earth is not my sphere, *1888:* How should this earth's life prove my only sphere? **635**| *1833:* For I cannot so narrow me, but *1868:* me but *1888:* Can I so narrow sense but

Soul still exceeds it? In their elements
My love outsoars my reason; but since love
Perforce receives its object from this earth
While reason wanders chainless, the few truths
Caught from its wanderings have sufficed to quell
Love chained below; then what were love, set free,
Which, with the object it demands, would pass
Reason companioning the seraphim?
No, what I feel may pass all human love
Yet fall far short of what my love should be.
And yet I seem more warped in this than aught,
Myself stands out more hideously: of old
I could forget myself in friendship, fame,
Liberty, nay, in love of mightier souls;
But I begin to know what thing hate is—
To sicken and to quiver and grow white—
And I myself have furnished its first prey.
Hate of the weak and ever-wavering will,
The selfishness, the still-decaying frame . . .
But I must never grieve whom wing can waft
Far from such thoughts—as now. Andromeda!
And she is with me: years roll, I shall change,
But change can touch her not—so beautiful

636| *1833:* I still exceed it; in *1868:* it: in *1888:* Soul still exceeds it? In
637| *1833:* love would pass my reason—but since here *1868:* reason; but *1888:* love outsoars my <> since love **638**| *1833:* Love must receive its objects <> earth, *1868:* earth *1888:* Perforce receives its object
639| *1833:* reason will be chainless, *1888:* reason wanders chainless,
641| *1833:* All love below;—then what must be that love *1868:* below; then *1888:* Love chained below; then what were love, set free, **642**| *1833:* would quell *1888:* would pass **643**| *1833:* Reason, tho' it soared with the *1868:* Reason tho' *1888:* Reason companioning the **644**| *1833:* No—what <> love, *1868:* No, what <> love **645**| *1833:* be: *1868:* be.
647| *1833:* For here myself stands <> hideously. *1868:* hideously: *1888:* Myself <> hideously: of old **648**| *1833:* I can forget *1888:* I could forget
649| *1833:* Or liberty, or love of mighty souls. § space with ° ° ° § *1868:* souls; *1888:* Liberty, nay in love of mightier souls; **651**| *1833:* sicken, and to quiver, and grow white, *1868:* sicken and to quiver and grow white— **653**| *1833:* All my sad weaknesses, this wavering will, *1888:* Hate of the weak and ever-wavering will, **654**| *1833:* selfishness, this still decaying *1888:* selfishness, the still-decaying **655**| *1833:* grieve while I can pass *1888:* grieve whom wing can waft **656**| *1833:* now—Andromeda! *1868:* now, Andromeda! *1888:* now, Andromeda! **657**| *1833:* me—years *1868:* me: years

With her fixed eyes, earnest and still, and hair
Lifted and spread by the salt-sweeping breeze,
And one red beam, all the storm leaves in heaven,
Resting upon her eyes and hair, such hair,
As she awaits the snake on the wet beach
By the dark rock and the white wave just breaking
At her feet; quite naked and alone; a thing
I doubt not, nor fear for, secure some god
To save will come in thunder from the stars.
Let it pass! Soul requires another change.
I will be gifted with a wondrous mind,
Yet sunk by error to men's sympathy,
And in the wane of life, yet only so
As to call up their fears; and there shall come
A time requiring youth's best energies;
And lo, I fling age, sorrow, sickness off,
And rise triumphant, triumph through decay.

And thus it is that I supply the chasm
'Twixt what I am and all I fain would be:
But then to know nothing, to hope for nothing,
To seize on life's dull joys from a strange fear
Lest, losing them, all's lost and nought remains!

There's some vile juggle with my reason here;

659| *1833:* her dark eyes, *1888:* her fixed eyes, 660| *1833:* breeze; *1868:* breeze, 661| *1833:* red-beam, *1868:* red beam, 662| *1833:* eyes and face and hair, *1868:* hair *1888:* and hair, such hair, 663| *1833:* beach, *1868:* beach 664| *1833:* rock, and *1868:* rock and 665| *1833:* alone,—a *1868:* alone; a 666| *1833:* You doubt <> secure that God *1888:* I doubt <> secure some god 667| *1833:* Will come in thunder from the stars to save her. *1888:* To save will come in thunder from the stars. 668| *1833:* pass—I will call another *1868:* pass! I *1888:* pass! Soul requires another
669| *1833:* wond'rous soul, *1868:* wondrous *1888:* wondrous mind,
671| *1833:* life; yet *1868:* life, yet 672| *1833:* fears, and *1868:* fears; and 674| *1833:* And strait I *1888:* And lo, I 675| *1833:* And I rise triumphing over my decay. *1888:* And rise triumphant, triumphant through decay. 675–676| § space with ° ° ° ° in 1833 § 677| *1833:* all that I would be. *1868:* be: *1888:* all I fain would 678| *1833:* nothing—to hope for nothing— *1868:* nothing, to hope for nothing, 679| *1833:* fear, *1868:* fear 680| *1833:* lost, and nought remains. *1868:* lost and nought remains! 680–681| § space with ° ° ° ° in 1833 § 681| *1833: here— 1868: here;*

I feel I but explain to my own loss
These impulses: they live no less the same.
Liberty! what though I despair? my blood
Rose never at a slave's name proud as now.
Oh sympathies, obscured by sophistries!—
Why else have I sought refuge in myself,
But from the woes I saw and could not stay?
Love! is not this to love thee, my Pauline?
I cherish prejudice, lest I be left
Utterly loveless? witness my belief
In poets, though sad change has come there too;
No more I leave myself to follow them—
Unconsciously I measure me by them—
Let me forget it: and I cherish most
My love of England—how her name, a word
Of hers in a strange tongue makes my heart beat!

Pauline, could I but break the spell! Not now—
All's fever—but when calm shall come again,
I am prepared: I have made life my own.
I would not be content with all the change
One frame should feel, but I have gone in thought
Thro' all conjuncture, I have lived all life
When it is most alive, where strangest fate

683| *1833:* impulses—they *1868:* impulses; they *1888:* impulses; they
684| *1833:* despair—my *1868:* despair? my 685| *1833:* Rose not at <> proudlier than now, *1888:* Rose never at <> proud as now. 686| *1833:* And sympathy <> sophistries. *1868:* sympathy, <> sophistries! *1888:* Oh sympathies, <> sophistries!— 687| *1833:* Why have not I *1888:* Why else have I 688| *1833:* But for the <> stay— *1868:* stay? *1888:* But from the 689| *1833:* And love!—do I not love *1868:* love! do *1888:* Love! is not this to love 689–690| § space with ° ° ° ° in 1833 § 691| *1833:* loveless—witness this belief *1888:* loveless? witness my belief 692| *1833:* tho' <> too *1868:* though <> too; 693| *1833:* them: *1868:* them—
694| *1833:* them. *1868:* them— 695| *1833:* it; and *1868:* it: and
696| *1833:* name—a *1868:* name, a 697| *1833:* her's <> beat! . . *1868:* beat! *1888:* hers 697–698| § space with ° ° ° ° in 1833 § 698| *1833:* Pauline, I could do any thing—not *1888:* Pauline, could I but break the spell! Not 699| *1833:* again— *1868:* again, 700| *1833:* prepared—I <> own— *1868:* prepared: I <> own. 702| *1833:* feel—but *1868:* feel, but 703| *1833:* conjuncture—I *1868:* conjuncture, I 704| *1833:* alive—where *1868:* alive, where

New-shapes it past surmise—the throes of men
Bit by some curse or in the grasps of doom
Half-visible and still-increasing round,
Or crowning their wide being's general aim.

These are wild fancies, but I feel, sweet friend,
As one breathing his weakness to the ear
Of pitying angel—dear as a winter flower,
A slight flower growing alone, and offering
Its frail cup of three leaves to the cold sun,
Yet joyous and confiding like the triumph
Of a child: and why am I not worthy thee?
I can live all the life of plants, and gaze
Drowsily on the bees that flit and play,
Or bare my breast for sunbeams which will kill,
Or open in the night of sounds, to look
For the dim stars; I can mount with the bird
Leaping airily his pyramid of leaves
And twisted boughs of some tall mountain tree,
Or rise cheerfully springing to the heavens;
Or like a fish breathe deep in the morning air
In the misty sun-warm water; or with flower
And tree can smile in light at the sinking sun
Just as the storm comes, as a girl would look
On a departing lover—most serene.

Pauline, come with me, see how I could build
A home for us, out of the world, in thought!

705| *1833:* New Shapes <> the tales of *1888:* New-shapes <> the throes of **706**| *1833:* curse—or *1868:* curse or **707**| *1833:* still increasing *1888:* still-increasing **708**| *1833:* aim . . . . *1868:* aim.
708–709| § space with ° ° ° ° in 1833 § **711**| *1833:* flower; *1868:* flower, **714**| *1833:* confiding, like *1868:* confiding like **715**| *1833:* child—and *1868:* child: and **715–716**| § space with ° ° ° ° in 1833 §
720| *1833:* bird, *1868:* bird **723**| *1833:* heavens— *1868:* heavens;
724| *1833:* breathe in the *1868:* breathe-in *1888:* breathe deep the
725| *1833:* water—or with flowers *1868:* water; or *1888:* flower
726| *1833:* And trees can <> sun, *1868:* sun *1888:* And tree can <> sun **727**| *1833:* comes—as *1868:* comes, as **729**| *1833:* me—see
730| *1833:* world; in thought— *1868:* world, in thought!

I am uplifted: fly with me, Pauline!

Night, and one single ridge of narrow path
Between the sullen river and the woods
Waving and muttering, for the moonless night
Has shaped them into images of life,
Like the uprising of the giant-ghosts,
Looking on earth to know how their sons fare:
Thou art so close by me, the roughest swell
Of wind in the tree-tops hides not the panting
Of thy soft breasts. No, we will pass to morning—
Morning, the rocks and valleys and old woods.
How the sun brightens in the mist, and here,
Half in the air, like creatures of the place,
Trusting the element, living on high boughs
That swing in the wind—look at the silver spray
Flung from the foam-sheet of the cataract
Amid the broken rocks! Shall we stay here
With the wild hawks? No, ere the hot noon come.
Dive we down—safe! See this our new retreat
Walled in with a sloped mound of matted shrubs,
Dark, tangled, old and green, still sloping down
To a small pool whose waters lie asleep
Amid the trailing boughs turned water-plants:
And tall trees overarch to keep us in,
Breaking the sunbeams into emerald shafts,
And in the dreamy water one small group
Of two or three strange trees are got together
Wondering at all around, as strange beasts herd

731| *1833:* am inspired—come with *1868:* inspired: come *1888:* am uplifted: fly with **734|** *1833:* muttering—for *1868:* muttering, for **737|** *1833:* fare. *1868:* fare: **740|** *1833:* breasts; no—we *1868:* breasts. No, we **741|** *1833:* Morning—the rocks, and vallies, and *1868:* Morning, the rocks and valleys and **742|** *1833:* here,— *1868:* here, **743|** *1833:* element—living *1868:* element, living **745|** *1833:* the golden spray. *1868:* spray *1888:* the silver spray **746|** *1833:* cataract, *1868:* cataract **747|** *1833:* rocks—shall *1868:* rocks! Shall **748|** *1833:* hawks?—no, ere < > come *1868:* hawks? No, ere < > come, **749|** *1833:* safe;—see *1868:* safe! See **751|** *1833:* green—still *1868:* green, still **753|** *1833:* water-plants *1868:* water-plants: **754|** *1833:* over-arch *1888:* overarch **757|** *1833:* together, *1868:* together **758|** *1833:* around—as *1868:* around, as

Together far from their own land: all wildness,
No turf nor moss, for boughs and plants pave all,
And tongues of bank go shelving in the lymph,
Where the pale-throated snake reclines his head,
And old grey stones lie making eddies there,
The wild-mice cross them dry-shod. Deeper in!
Shut thy soft eyes—now look—still deeper in!
This is the very heart of the woods all round
Mountain-like heaped above us; yet even here
One pond of water gleams; far off the river
Sweeps like a sea, barred out from land; but one—
One thin clear sheet has overleaped and wound
Into this silent depth, which gained, it lies
Still, as but let by sufferance; the trees bend
O'er it as wild men watch a sleeping girl,
And through their roots long creeping plants out-stretch
Their twined hair, steeped and sparkling; farther on,
Tall rushes and thick flag-knots have combined
To narrow it; so, at length, a silver thread,
It winds, all noiselessly through the deep wood
Till thro' a cleft-way, thro' the moss and stone,
It joins its parent-river with a shout.

Up for the glowing day, leave the old woods!
See, they part like a ruined arch: the sky!
Nothing but sky appears, so close the roots
And grass of the hill-top level with the air—
Blue sunny air, where a great cloud floats laden

759| *1833:* land—all wildness— *1868:* land: all wildness, **761**| *1833:* the waters, *1888:* the lymph, **763**| *1833:* there; *1868:* there, **764**| *1833:* wild mice <> dry-shod—deeper in— *1868:* dry-shod: deeper in! *1888:* wild-mice <> dry-shod. Deeper in! **765**| *1833:* in: *1868:* in! **766**| *1833:* woods—all round, *1868:* woods all round **767**| *1833:* Mountain-like, heaped *1868:* Mountain-like heaped **768**| *1833:* gleams—far *1868:* gleams; far **770**| *1833:* over-leaped *1888:* overleaped **774**| *1833:* thro' <> plants stretch out *1868:* through *1888:* through <> plants out-stretch **777**| *1833:* thread *1868:* thread, **778**| *1833:* noiselessly, thro' <> wood, *1868:* noiselessly through <> wood **779**| *1833:* cleft way, *1888:* cleft-way, **780–781**| § no space in 1833, 1868 § **781**| *1833:* day—leave <> woods: *1868:* day, leave <> woods! **782**| *1833:* part, like <> arch, the *1868:* arch: the **783**| *1833:* root *1868:* roots **785**| *1833:* floats, laden *1868:* floats laden

With light, like a dead whale that white birds pick,
Floating away in the sun in some north sea.
Air, air, fresh life-blood, thin and searching air,
The clear, dear breath of God that loveth us,
Where small birds reel and winds take their delight!
Water is beautiful, but not like air:
See, where the solid azure waters lie
Made as of thickened air, and down below,
The fern-ranks like a forest spread themselves
As though each pore could feel the element;
Where the quick glancing serpent winds his way,
Float with me there, Pauline!—but not like air.

Down the hill! Stop—a clump of trees, see, set
On a heap of rock, which look o'er the far plain:
So, envious climbing shrubs would mount to rest
And peer from their spread boughs; wide they wave, looking
At the muleteers who whistle on their way,
To the merry chime of morning bells, past all
The little smoking cots, mid fields and banks
And copses bright in the sun. My spirit wanders:
Hedgerows for me—those living hedgerows where
The bushes close and clasp above and keep

788| *1833:* Air, air—fresh life-blood—thin < > air— *1868:* Air, air, fresh life-blood, thin < > air, 789| *1833:* God, that loveth us: *1868:* God that loveth us, 790| *1833:* delight. *1868:* delight! 791| *1833:* air. *1868:* air: 792| *1833:* lie, *1868:* lie 794| *1833:* fern-ranks, like < > themselves, *1868:* fern-ranks like < > themselves 795| *1833:* tho' *1868:* though 796| *1833:* way— *1868:* way, 797| *1833:* Pauline, but *1868:* Pauline!—but 797–798| § no space in 1833, 1868 § 798| *1833:* hill—stop *1868:* hill! Stop 799| *1833:* rocks < > plains, *1888:* rock < > plain: 800| *1833:* And envious < > rest, *1868:* rest *1888:* So, envious 801| *1833:* boughs. There they *1868:* boughs; there *1888:* boughs; wide they 802| *1833:* muleteers, who whistle as they go *1868:* muleteers who *1888:* whistle on their way, 803| *1833:* of their morning bells, and all *1888:* of morning 804| *1833:* cots, and fields, and blanks, *1868:* cots and fields and banks *1888:* cots, mid fields 805| *1833:* copses, bright < > sun; my spirit wanders. *1868:* copses bright < > sun. My spirit wanders: 806| *1833:* Hedge-rows for me—still, living, hedge-rows, where *1868:* living hedge-rows where *1888:* Hedgerows for me—those living hedgerows 807| *1833:* close, and clasp above, and *1868:* close and clasp above and

Thought in—I am concentrated—I feel;
But my soul saddens when it looks beyond:
I cannot be immortal, taste all joy.

O God, where do they tend—these struggling aims?*

*Je crains bien que mon pauvre ami ne soit pas toujours parfaitement compris dans ce qui reste à lire de cet étrange fragment, mais il est moins propre que tout autre à éclaircir ce qui de sa nature ne peut jamais être que songe et confusion. D'ailleurs je ne sais trop si en cherchant à mieux coordonner certaines parties l'on ne courrait pas le risque de nuire au seul mérite auquel une production si singulière peut prétendre, celui de donner une idée assez précise du genre qu'elle n'a fait qu'ébaucher. Ce début sans prétention, ce remuement des passions qui va d'abord en accroissant et puis s'apaise par degrés, ces élans de l'âme, ce retour soudain sur soimême, et par-dessus tout, la tournure d'esprit tout particulière de mon ami, rendent les changemens presque impossibles. Les raisons qu'il fait valoir ailleurs, et d'autres encore plus puissantes, ont fait trouver grâce à mes yeux pour cet écrit qu'autrement je lui eusse conseillé de jeter au feu. Je n'en crois pas moins au grand principe de toute composition—à ce principe de Shakespeare, de Rafaelle, de Beethoven, d'où il suit que la concentration des idées est due bien plus à leur conception qu'à leur mise en exécution: j'ai tout lieu de craindre que la première de ces qualités ne soit encore étrangère à mon ami, et je doute fort qu'un redoublement de travail lui fasse acquérir la seconde. Le mieux serait de brûler ceci; mais que faire?

Je crois que dans ce qui suit il fait allusion à un certain examen qu'il fit autrefois de l'âme, ou plutôt de son âme, pour découvrir la suite des objets auxquels il lui serait possible d'atteindre, et dont chacun une fois obtenu devait former une espèce de plateau d'où l'on pouvait apercevoir d'autres buts, d'autres projets, d'autres jouissances qui, à leur tour, devaient être surmontés. Il en

2| *1833:* fragment—mais *1868:* fragment, mais 6| *1833:* singuliere *1868:* singuliére 6| *1833:* prétendre—celui *1868:* prétendre, celui 7| *1833:* que' ébaucher.—Ce *1868:* qu'ébaucher. Ce 8| *1833:* puis s'appaise par *1888:* puis s'apaise par 9| *1833:* soi-même.—Et par dessus < > ami rendent *1868:* soi-même, et par-dessus < > ami, rendent 12| *1833:* feu—Je *1868:* feu. Je 13| *1833:* Shakspeare, de Raffaelle, < > d'où *1868:* Shakespeare, de Rafaelle, < > 'ou *1888:* Shakespeare, de Rafaelle, < > d'où 15| *1833:* est dûe bien < > conception, qu'à *1868:* conception qu'à *1888:* est due bien < > conception qu'à 15–16| *1833:* execution . . . j'ai *1868:* execution: j'ai 17| *1833:* ami—et *1868:* ami, et 17| *1833:* de bruler *1868:* de brûler 20| *1833:* l'âme ou plutot < > la suité *1868:* l'âme ou plutôt < > la suite *1888:* l'âme, ou plutot < > la suite 21| *1833:* d'attèndre, et *1888:* d'atteindre, et 22| *1833:* aperçevoir *1888:* apercevoir 808| *1833:* feel;— *1868:* feel; 809| *1833:* beyond; *1868:* beyond: 810| *1833:* immortal, nor taste all. *1868:* immortal nor *1888:* immortal, taste all joy. 810–811| § no space in 1833, 1868 § 811| *1833:* O God! where does this tend—< > aims!° *1868:* O God, where < > aims?° *1888:* O God, where do they—these résultait que l'oubli et le sommeil devaient tout terminer. Cette idée, que je ne saisis pas parfaitement, lui est peut-être aussi inintelligible qu'à moi.

PAULINE.

What would I have? What is this "sleep" which seems
To bound all? can there be a "waking" point
Of crowning life? The soul would never rule;
It would be first in all things, it would have
Its utmost pleasure filled, but, that complete,
Commanding, for commanding, sickens it.
The last point I can trace is—rest beneath
Some better essence than itself, in weakness;
This is "myself," not what I think should be:
And what is that I hunger for but God?

My God, my God, let me for once look on thee
As though nought else existed, we alone!
And as creation crumbles, my soul's spark
Expands till I can say,—Even from myself
I need thee and I feel thee and I love thee.
I do not plead my rapture in thy works
For love of thee, nor that I feel as one
Who cannot die: but there is that in me
Which turns to thee, which loves or which should love.

23| *1833:* idée que <> parfaitement lui *1868:* idée, que <> parfaitement, lui 24| *1833:* peutêtre aussi intelligible *1868:* peutêtre aussi inintelligible *1888:* peu-être aussi inintelligible 812| *1833:* have? what <> "sleep," which *1868:* have? What <> "sleep" which 814| *1833:* rule— *1868:* rule; 815| *1833:* things—it *1868:* things, it 816| *1833:* filled,—but the complete *1868:* filled, but, that complete, 817| *1833:* Commanding for commanding sickens *1868:* Commanding, for commanding, sickens
818| *1833:* point that I <> is, rest *1868:* point I <> is, rest, beneath *1888:* is—rest beneath 819| *1833:* itself—in *1868:* itself, in 820| *1833:* "myself"—not <> be, *1868:* "myself," not <> be: 821–822| § no space in 1833, 1868 § 822| *1833:* my God! let *1868:* my God, let 823| *1833:* tho' <> existed: we alone. *1868:* though <> existed, we alone!
825| *1833:* say, "Even *1868:* say,—Even 826| *1833:* thee, and I feel thee, and <> thee; *1868:* thee and <> thee and <> thee: *1888:* love thee.
828| *1833:* thee—or *1868:* thee, nor 829| *1833:* die—but *1868:* die: but 830| *1833:* loves, or <> love." *1868:* loves or <> love.
830–831| § space in 1833, 1888, 1889; no space in 1868 §

Why have I girt myself with this hell-dress?
Why have I laboured to put out my life?
Is it not in my nature to adore,
And e'en for all my reason do I not
Feel him, and thank him, and pray to him—now?
Can I forego the trust that he loves me?
Do I not feel a love which only ONE . . .
O thou pale form, so dimly seen, deep-eyed!
I have denied thee calmly—do I not
Pant when I read of thy consummate power,
And burn to see thy calm pure truths out-flash
The brightest gleams of earth's philosophy?
Do I not shake to hear aught question thee?
If I am erring save me, madden me,
Take from me powers and pleasures, let me die
Ages, so I see thee! I am knit round
As with a charm by sin and lust and pride,
Yet though my wandering dreams have seen all shapes
Of strange delight, oft have I stood by thee—
Have I been keeping lonely watch with thee
In the damp night by weeping Olivet,
Or leaning on thy bosom, proudly less,
Or dying with thee on the lonely cross,
Or witnessing thine outburst from the tomb.

A mortal, sin's familiar friend, doth here
Avow that he will give all earth's reward,
But to believe and humbly teach the faith,
In suffering and poverty and shame,

835| *1833:* to him?—*Now.* *1868:* to him—now? 837| *1833:* ONE . . . . . *1888:* ONE . . . 838| *1833:* deep-eyed, *1868:* deep-eyed! 840| *1833:* consummate deeds, *1888:* consummate power, 841| *1833:* calm, pure *1868:* calm pure 843| *1833:* thee? . . . . *1868:* thee? 843–844| § space in 1833 § 845| *1833:* powers, and pleasures—let *1868:* powers and pleasures, let 846| *1833:* thee: I *1868:* thee! I 847| *1833:* charm, by *1868:* charm by 848| *1833:* tho' *1868:* though 850| *1833:* thee, *1868:* thee 852| *1833:* less— *1868:* less, 853| *1833:* cross— *1868:* cross, 854| *1833:* witnessing thy bursting from the tomb! *1888:* witnessing thine outburst from the tomb. 855| *1833:* friend doth *1868:* friend, doth 858| *1888:* suffering, and poverty, and *1868:* suffering and poverty and

Only believing he is not unloved.

And now, my Pauline, I am thine for ever!
I feel the spirit which has buoyed me up
Desert me, and old shades are gathering fast;
Yet while the last light waits, I would say much,
This chiefly, it is gain that I have said
Somewhat of love I ever felt for thee
But seldom told; our hearts so beat together
That speech seemed mockery; but when dark hours come,
And joy departs, and thou, sweet, deem'st it strange
A sorrow moves me, thou canst not remove,
Look on this lay I dedicate to thee,
Which through thee I began, which thus I end,
Collecting the last gleams to strive to tell
How I am thine, and more than ever now
That I sink fast: yet though I deeplier sink,
No less song proves one word has brought me bliss,
Another still may win bliss surely back.
Thou knowest, dear, I could not think all calm,
For fancies followed thought and bore me off,
And left all indistinct; ere one was caught
Another glanced; so, dazzled by my wealth,

859| *1833:* unloved . . . . *1868:* unloved. **862**| *1833:* Deserting me: and old shades gathering on; *1868:* me, and *1888:* Desert <> shades are gathering fast; **863**| *1833:* while its last *1888:* while the last **864**| *1833:* And chiefly, I am glad that *1888:* This chiefly, it is gain that **865**| *1833:* That love which I have ever <> thee, *1868:* thee *1888:* Somewhat of love I ever **866**| *1833:* together, *1868:* together **867**| *1833:* speech is mockery, but <> come; *1868:* mockery; but <> come, *1888:* speech seemed mockery **868**| *1833:* And I feel sad; and <> strange; *1868:* sad, and <> strange *1888:* And joy departs, and **869**| *1833:* remove. *1868:* remove, **871**| *1833:* thro' <> began, and which I *1868:* through *1888:* which thus I **873**| *1833:* That I <> now— *1868:* now *1888:* How I **874**| *1833:* That I am sinking fast—yet tho' I sink, *1868:* fast: yet though *1888:* That I sink fast <> I deeplier sink, **875**| *1833:* less I feel that thou hast *1868:* bliss *1888:* less song proves one word has <> bliss, **876**| *1833:* And that I still may hope to win it back. *1888:* Another still may win bliss surely back. **877**| *1833:* know'st, dear friend, I *1868:* knowest *1888:* dear, I **878**| *1833:* For wild dreams followed me, and *1868:* me and *1888:* For fancies followed thought and **879**| *1833:* And all was indistinct. Ere *1868:* indistinct; ere *1888:* And left all indistinct **880**| *1833:* glanced: so dazzled *1868:* glanced; so, dazzled

I knew not which to leave nor which to choose,
For all so floated, nought was fixed and firm.
And then thou said'st a perfect bard was one
Who chronicled the stages of all life.
And so thou bad'st me shadow this first stage.
'Tis done, and even now I recognize
The shift, the change from last to past—discern
Faintly how life is truth and truth is good.
And why thou must be mine is, that e'en now
In the dim hush of night, that I have done,
Despite the sad forebodings, love looks through—
Whispers,—E'en at the last I have her still,
With her delicious eyes as clear as heaven
When rain in a quick shower has beat down mist,
And clouds float white above like broods of swans.
How the blood lies upon her cheek, outspread
As thinned by kisses! only in her lips
It wells and pulses like a living thing,
And her neck looks like marble misted o'er
With love-breath,—a Pauline from heights above,
Stooping beneath me, looking up—one look

881| *1833:* Knowing not *1888:* I knew not 882| *1833:* For all my thoughts so <> fixed— *1868:* fixed. *1888:* For all so <> fixed and firm. 884| *1833:* Who shadowed out the <> life, *1888:* Who chronicled the *1889:* life. 885| *1833:* badest me tell this my first stage;— *1868:* bad'st <> stage. *1888:* me shadow this first 886| *1833:* done: and <> I feel all dim the shift *1868:* done, and *1888:* I recognize 887| *1833:* Of thought. These are my last thoughts; I discern *1868:* thought; these *1888:* The shift, the change from last to past—discern 888| *1833:* Faintly immortal life, and truth, and good. *1868:* life and truth and *1888:* Faintly how life is truth and truth is good. 889| *1833:* now, *1868:* now 890| *1833:* night—that <> done— *1868:* night, that <> done, 891| *1833:* With fears and sad forebodings: I look thro' *1868:* forebodings, I look through *1888:* Despite the sad forebodings, love looks through— 892| *1833:* And say, "E'en *1868:* say,—E'en *1888:* Whispers,—E'en 893| *1833:* heaven, *1868:* heaven 895| *1833:* white in the sun like <> swans." *1868:* swans. *1888:* white above like. 896| *1833:* cheek, all spread *1888:* cheek, outspread 897| *1833:* kisses; only *1868:* kisses! only 899| *1833:* looks, like *1868:* looks like 900| *1833:* love-breath; a dear thing to kiss and love, *1868:* love-breath,—a *1888:* a Pauline from heights above, 901| *1833:* Standing beneath me—looking out to me, *1868:* me, looking *1888:* Stooping beneath me, looking up—one look

As I might kill her and be loved the more.

So, love me—me, Pauline, and nought but me,
Never leave loving! Words are wild and weak,
Believe them not, Pauline! I stained myself
But to behold thee purer by my side,
To show thou art my breath, my life, a last
Resource, an extreme want: never believe
Aught better could so look on thee; nor seek
Again the world of good thoughts left for mine!
There were bright troops of undiscovered suns,
Each equal in their radiant course; there were
Clusters of far fair isles which ocean kept
For his own joy, and his waves broke on them
Without a choice; and there was a dim crowd
Of visions, each a part of some grand whole:
And one star left his peers and came with peace
Upon a storm, and all eyes pined for him;
And one isle harboured a sea-beaten ship,
And the crew wandered in its bowers and plucked
Its fruits and gave up all their hopes of home;
And one dream came to a pale poet's sleep,
And he said, "I am singled out by God,
No sin must touch me." Words are wild and weak,
But what they would express is,—Leave me not,
Still sit by me with beating breast and hair

902| *1833:* loved for it. *1888:* loved the more. **903**| *1833:* Love me—love me, Pauline, love nought but me; *1868:* but me, *1888:* So, love me—me, **904**| *1833:* Leave me not. All these words are *1868:* not! All *1888:* Never leave loving! Words **905**| *1833:* Pauline. I stooped so low *1868:* Pauline! I *1888:* Pauline! I stained myself **907**| *1833:* breath—my life—a *1868:* breath, my life, a **908**| *1833:* Resource—an *1868:* Resource, an **909**| *1833:* look to thee, nor *1868:* look to thee; nor *1888:* look on thee **910**| *1833:* for me. *1868:* me! *1888:* for mine! **912**| *1833:* course. There *1868:* course; there **913**| *1833:* isles, which *1868:* isles which **915**| *1833:* choice. And *1868:* choice; and **916**| *1833:* of the dim whole. *1868:* whole: *1888:* of some grand whole: **917**| *1833:* And a star *1868:* And one star **918**| *1833:* him. *1868:* him; **920**| *1833:* bowers, and *1868:* bowers and **921**| *1833:* fruits, and <> hopes for home. *1868:* fruits and <> home; *1888:* hopes of home; **924**| *1833:* me." I am very weak, *1868:* weak *1888:* me." Words are wild and weak, **925**| *1833:* what I would *1888:* what they would **926**| *1833:* me—with beating breast, and *1868:* me with beating breast and

Loosened, be watching earnest by my side,
Turning my books or kissing me when I
Look up—like summer wind! Be still to me
A help to music's mystery which minds fails
To fathom, its solution, no mere clue!
O reason's pedantry, life's rule prescribed!
I hopeless, I the loveless, hope and love.
Wiser and better, know me now, not when
You loved me as I was. Smile not! I have
Much yet to dawn on you, to gladden you.

No more of the past! I'll look within no more.
I have too trusted my own lawless wants,
Too trusted my vain self, vague intuition—
Draining soul's wine alone in the still night,
And seeing how, as gathering films arose,
As by an inspiration life seemed bare
And grinning in its vanity, while ends
Foul to be dreamed of, smiled at me as fixed
And fair, while others changed from fair to foul
A young witch turns an old hag at night.

927| *1833:* Loosened—watching *1868:* Loosened, be watching **928**| *1833:* books, or *1868:* books or **929**| *1833:* wind. Be *1868:* wind! Be **930**| *1833:* A key to music's mystery, when mind fails, *1868:* mystery when *1888:* A help to music's mystery which mind fails **931**| *1833:* A reason, a solution and a clue. *1868:* clue! *1888:* To fathom, its solution, no mere clue! **932**| *1833:* You see I have thrown off my prescribed rules: *1888:* O reason's pedantry, life's rule prescribed! **933**| *1833:* I hope in myself—and hope, and pant, and love— *1868:* hope and pant and love. *1888:* I hopeless, I the loveless, hope and love. **934**| *1833:* You'll find me better—know me more than when *1868:* better, know *1888:* Wiser and better, know me now, not when **935**| *1833:* not; I *1868:* not! I **936**| *1833:* to gladden you—to dawn on you. *1868:* you, to *1888:* to dawn on you, to gladden you. **936–937**| § no space in 1868 § **937**| *1833:* past—I'll <> more— *1868:* past! I'll <> more. **938**| *1833:* trusted to my own wild wants— *1868:* wants, *1888:* trusted my own lawless wants, **939**| *1833:* trusted to myself—to intuition. *1868:* myself, to intuition— *1888:* trusted my vain self, vague intuition— **940**| *1833:* Draining the wine *1888:* Draining soul's wine **941**| *1833:* how—as *1868:* how, as **943**| *1833:* vanity, and ends *1888:* vanity, while ends **944**| *1833:* Hard to <> of, stared at <> fixed, *1888:* Foul to <> of, smiled at <> fixed **945**| *1833:* And others suddenly became all foul, *1868:* foul *1888:* And fair, while others changed from fair to foul **946**| *1833:* a fair witch turned an *1888:* As a young witch turns an

No more of this! We will go hand in hand,
I with thee, even as a child—love's slave,
Looking no farther than his liege commands.

And thou hast chosen where this life shall be:
The land which gave me thee shall be our home,
Where nature lies all wild amid her lakes
And snow-swathed mountains and vast pines begirt
With ropes of snow—where nature lies all bare.
Suffering none to view her but a race
Or stinted or deformed, like the mute dwarfs
Which wait upon a naked Indian queen.
And there (the time being when the heavens are thick
With storm) I'll sit with thee while thou dost sing
Thy native songs, gay as a desert bird
Which crieth as it flies for perfect joy,
Or telling me old stories of dead knights;
Or I will read great lays to thee—how she,
The fair pale sister, went to her chill grave
With power to love and to be loved and live:
Or we will go together, like twin gods
Of the infernal world, with scented lamp
Over the dead, to call and to awake,
Over the unshaped images which lie
Within my mind's cave: only leaving all,
That tells of the past doubt. So, when spring comes

947| *1833:* this—we *1868:* this! We 948| *1833:* I will go with <> child, love's *1888:* I with <> child—love's 949| *1833:* no further than thy sweet commands. *1868:* no farther than commands, *1888:* than his liege commands. 949–950| § no space in 1833, 1868 § 950| *1833:* be— *1868:* be: 953| *1833:* mountains, and vast pines all girt *1868:* mountains and *1888:* pines begirt 956| *1833:* Most stinted and deformed—like *1868:* deformed, like *1888:* Or stinted or deformed, like 959| *1833:* storms *1888:* storm 961| *1833:* Who crieth as he flies *1888:* Which crieth as it flies 962| *1833:* knights. *1868:* knights; 963| *1833:* read old lays *1888:* read great lays 965| *1833:* love, and <> loved, and live. *1868:* love and to be loved and live: 968| *1833:* dead—to call <> awake— *1868:* dead, to call <> awake, 970| *1833:* cave—only leaving all *1868:* cave: only leaving all, 971| *1833:* doubts. So when spring comes, *1868:* So, when *1888:* doubt <> comes

With sunshine back again like an old smile,
And the fresh waters and awakened birds
And budding woods await us, I shall be
Prepared, and we will question life once more,
Till its old sense shall come renewed by change,
Like some clear thought which harsh words veiled before;
Feeling God loves us, and that all which errs
Is but a dream which death will dissipate.
And then what need of longer exile? Seek
My England, and, again there, calm approach
All I once fled from, calmly look on those
The works of my past weakness, as one views
Some scene where danger met him long before.
Ah that such pleasant life should be but dreamed!

But whate'er come of it, and though it fade,
And though ere the cold morning all be gone,
As it may be;—tho' music wait to wile,
And strange eyes and bright wine lure, laugh like sin
Which steals back softly on a soul half saved,
And I the first deny, decry, despise,

972| *1833:* And sunshine comes again *1888:* With sunshine back again
973| *1833:* waters, and awakened birds, *1868:* waters and awakened birds
974| *1833:* us—I *1868:* us, I 975| *1833:* will go and think again, *1888:* will question life once more, 976| *1833:* And all old loves shall come to us—but changed *1868:* us, but *1888:* Till its old sense shall come renewed by change, 977| *1833:* As some sweet thought *1888:* Like some clear thought 978| *1833:* errs, *1868:* errs 979| *1833:* Is a strange dream <> dissipate; *1868:* dissipate. *1888:* Is but a dream 980| *1833:* then when I am firm we'll seek again *1868:* firm, we'll *1888:* then what need of longer exile? Seek 981| *1833:* My own land, and again I will approach *1888:* My England, and, again there, calm approach 982| *1833:* My old designs, and calmly look on all *1888:* All I once fled from, calmly look on those
985| *1833:* Ah! that *1868:* Ah that 986| *1833:* it—and tho' *1868:* it, and though 987| *1833:* tho' <> gone *1868:* though <> gone,
988| *1833:* wait for me, *1888:* wait to wile, 989| *1833:* And fair eyes <> wine, laughing like sin, *1868:* wine laughing like sin *1888:* And strange eyes <> wine lure, laugh like 990| *1833:* saved; *1868:* saved, 991| *1833:* And I be first to deny all, and despise *1888:* And I the first deny, decry, despise,

With this avowal, these intents so fair,—
Still be it all my own, this moment's pride!
No less I make an end in perfect joy.
E'en in my brightest time, a lurking fear
Possessed me: I well knew my weak resolves,
I felt the witchery that makes mind sleep
Over its treasure, as one half afraid
To make his riches definite: but now
These feelings shall not utterly be lost,
I shall not know again that nameless care
Lest, leaving all undone in youth, some new
And undreamed end reveal itself too late:
For this song shall remain to tell for ever
That when I lost all hope of such a change,
Suddenly beauty rose on me again.
No less I make an end in perfect joy,
For I, who thus again was visited.
Shall doubt not many another bliss awaits,
And, though this weak soul sink and darkness whelm,
Some little word shall light it, raise aloft,
To where I clearlier see and better love,
As I again go o'er the tracts of thought
Like one who has a right, and I shall live
With poets, calmer, purer still each time,
And beauteous shapes will come for me to seize,
And unknown secrets will be trusted me

992| *1833:* This verse, and these intents which seem so fair; *1868:* fair,— *1888:* With this avowal, these intents so fair,— 993| *1833:* Still this is all <> pride, *1888:* Still be it all <> pride! 996| *1833:* me. I *1868:* me: I 998| *1833:* treasures—as *1868:* treasure, as 999| *1833:* definite—but *1868:* definite: but 1001| *1833:* care, *1868:* care 1002| *1833:* Lest leaving *1868:* Lest, leaving 1004| *1833:* ever, *1868:* ever 1006| *1833:* Beauty *1868:* beauty 1008| *1833:* I, having thus again been visited, *1888:* I, who thus again was visited, 1010| *1833:* And tho' <> sink, and darkness come, *1868:* And, though <> sink and *1888:* darkness whelm, 1011| *1833:* it up again, *1888:* it, rise aloft, 1012| *1833:* And I shall see all clearer and love better; *1868:* better, *1888:* To where I clearlier see and better love, 1013| *1833:* I shall again <> thought, *1868:* thought *1888:* As I again 1014| *1833:* As one <> right; and *1868:* right, and *1888:* Like one 1015| *1833:* poets—calmer—purer *1868:* poets, calmer, purer 1016| *1833:* come to me again, *1888:* come for me to seize, 1017| *1833:* me, *1868:* me

Which were denied the waverer once; but now
I shall be priest and prophet as of old.

Sun-treader, I believe in God and truth
And love; and as one just escaped from death
Would bind himself in bands of friends to feel
He lives indeed, so, I would lean on thee!
Thou must be ever with me, most in gloom
If such must come, but chiefly when I die,
For I seem, dying, as one going in the dark
To fight a giant: but live thou for ever,
And be to all what thou hast been to me!
All in whom this wakes pleasant thoughts of me
Know my last state is happy, free from doubt
Or touch of fear. Love me and wish me well.

RICHMOND:
October 22, 1832.

1018| *1833:* were not mine when wavering—but *1868:* wavering; but *1888:* were denied the waverer once; but **1019**| *1833:* and lover, as *1868:* lover as *1888:* and prophet as **1020**| *1833:* in God, and truth, *1868:* in God and truth **1023**| *1833:* indeed—so <> thee; *1868:* indeed, so <> thee! **1024**| *1833:* me—most *1868:* me, most **1025**| *1833:* When such shall come—but *1868:* come, but *1888:* If such must come **1026**| *1833:* seem dying *1868:* seem, dying **1027**| *1833:* giant—and live *1868:* giant: and *1888:* giant: but live **1028**| *1833:* me— *1868:* me! **1029**| *1833:* me, *1888:* me **1030**| *1833:* happy—free from doubt, *1868:* happy, free from doubt **1031**| *1833:* well! *1888:* well.

"Eyes calm beside thee"

SONNET

"Eyes calm beside thee"

SONNET

EYES, calm beside thee, (Lady couldst thou know!)
  May turn away thick with fast-gathering tears:
I glance not where all gaze: thrilling and low
  Their passionate praises reach thee—my cheek wears
Alone no wonder when thou passest by;
Thy tremulous lids bent and suffused reply
To the irrepressible homage which doth glow
  On every lip but mine: if in thine ears
Their accents linger—and thou dost recall
  Me as I stood, still, guarded, very pale,
Beside each votarist whose lighted brow
Wore worship like an aureole, 'O'er them all
  My beauty,' thou wilt murmur, 'did prevail
Save that one only:'—Lady couldst thou know!
August 17, 1834

§ Monthly Repository, New Series, VIII, Oct., 1834, p. 712. §

PARACELSUS

Edited by Morse Peckham

PARACELSUS

INSCRIBED TO

AMÉDÉE DE RIPERT-MONCLAR

BY HIS AFFECTIONATE FRIEND

R. B.

LONDON: *March* 15, 1835

1835: INSCRIBED / TO / THE COMTE A. DE RIPART-MONCLAR, / BY HIS AFFECTIONATE FRIEND, / ROBERT BROWNING 1849: § omitted § *1863:* INSCRIBED TO / AMÉDÉE DE RIPERT-MONCLAR, / BY HIS AFFECTIONATE FRIEND, / R.B. *March* 15*th*, 1835. *1868:* RIPERT-MONCLAR / <> FRIEND R.B. / *London, March* 15, 1835.

I am anxious that the reader should not, at the very outset—mistaking my performance for one of a class with which it has nothing in common—judge it by principles on which it was never moulded, and subject it to a standard to which it was never meant to conform. I therefore anticipate his discovery, that it is an attempt, probably more novel than happy, to reverse the method usually adopted by writers whose aim it is to set forth any phenomenon of the mind or the passions, by the operation of persons and events; and that, instead of having recourse to an external machinery of incidents to create and evolve the crisis I desire to produce, I have ventured to display somewhat minutely the mood itself in its rise and progress, and have suffered the agency by which it is influenced and determined, to be generally discernible in its effects alone, and subordinate throughout, if not altogether excluded: and this for a reason. I have endeavoured to write a poem, not a drama; the canons of the drama are well known, and I cannot but think that, inasmuch as they have immediate regard to stage representation, the peculiar advantages they hold out are really such only so long as the purpose for which they were at first instituted is kept in view. I do not very well understand what is called a Dramatic Poem, wherein all those restrictions only submitted to on account of compensating good in the original scheme are scrupulously retained, as though for some special fitness in themselves—and all new facilities placed at an author's disposal by the vehicle he selects, as pertinaciously rejected. It is certain, however, that a work like mine depends more immediately on the intelligence and sympathy of the reader for its success—indeed were my scenes stars it must be his co-operating fancy which, supplying all chasms, shall connect the scattered lights into one constellation—a Lyre or a Crown. I trust for his indulgence towards a poem which had been imagined six months ago; and that even should he think slightingly of the present (an experiment I am in

---

§ Introduction in MS and 1835 only § § MS variants from 1835: §
1| Reader 11| Mood 14| throughout, if 15| Poem <> Drama;—the canons of the 16| Drama 17| stage-representation 22| scheme, are <> retained as tho' 23| themselves,—and 26| Reader 29| constellation -a Lyre

no case likely to repeat) he will not be prejudiced against other productions which may follow in a more popular, and perhaps less difficult form.

15th March, 1835.

PERSONS.

AUREOLUS PARACELSUS, *a student.*

FESTUS *and* MICHAL, *his friends.*

APRILE, *an Italian poet.*

1835: AUREOLOUS PARACELSUS. / FESTUS & MICHAL, his friends. / APRILE. / N.B.—*For the localities and dates, see the note at the end.* *1849:* APRILE, an Italian Poet. § *N.B.* omitted through 1889. § *1863:* AUREOLUS PARACELSUS, a student.

PARACELSUS

1835

PART I. PARACELSUS ASPIRES

SCENE—*Würzburg; a garden in the environs.* 1512.

FESTUS, PARACELSUS, MICHAL.

PARACELSUS Come close to me, dear friends; still closer; thus!
Close to the heart which, though long time roll by
Ere it again beat quicker, pressed to yours,
As now it beats—perchance a long, long time—
At least henceforth your memories shall make
Quiet and fragrant as befits their home.
Nor shall my memory want a home in yours—
Alas, that it requires too well such free
Forgiving love as shall embalm it there!
For if you would remember me aright,
As I was born to be, you must forget
All fitful strange and moody waywardness
Which e'er confused my better spirit, to dwell
Only on moments such as these, dear friends!
—My heart no truer, but my words and ways
More true to it: as Michal, some months hence,

§ Ed. 1835, 1849, 1863, 1868, 1888, 1889. MS in Forster-Dyce Bequest, Victoria and Albert Museum. For description of MS see Notes. § SCENE| *MS:* 1507 *1849:* 1512 [1]| *MS:* Friends <> closer—thus; *1835:* friends *1849:* closer; thus! [2]| *MS:* which,—tho' *1835:* which, though [3]| *1835:* press'd *1849:* pressed [4]| *MS:* beats . . . perchance <> time . . . *1835:* beats—perchance <> time— [7]| *MS:* yours:— *1835:* yours.— *1849:* yours— [8]| *1835:* Alas! that *1849:* Alas, that [10]| *MS:*—For <> aright . . *1835:* For <> aright— *1863:* aright, [11]| *MS:*— —As <> be . . you *1835:* As <> be—you *1863:* be, you [12]| *MS:* fitful, strange *1835:* strange, and <> waywardness, *1849:* waywardness *1863:* strange and *1868:* fitful strange [13]| *MS:* spirit . . . to *1835:* spirit, to [14]| *MS:* Friends; *1835:* friends; *1849:* friends! [15]| *MS:* My heart no truer . . . but *1835:* truer, but *1849:*—My heart

Will say, "this autumn was a pleasant time,"
For some few sunny days; and overlook
Its bleak wind, hankering after pining leaves.
Autumn would fain be sunny; I would look
Liker my nature's truth: and both are frail,
And both beloved, for all our frailty.

MICHAL Aureole!

PARACELSUS Drop by drop! she is weeping like a child!
Not so! I am content—more than content;
Nay, autumn wins you best by this its mute
Appeal to sympathy for its decay:
Look up, sweet Michal, nor esteem the less
Your stained and drooping vines their grapes bow down,
Nor blame those creaking trees bent with their fruit,
That apple-tree with a rare after-birth
Of peeping blooms sprinkled its wealth among!
Then for the winds—what wind that ever raved
Shall vex that ash which overlooks you both,
So proud it wears its berries? Ah, at length,
The old smile meet for her, the lady of this
Sequestered nest!—this kingdom, limited
Alone by one old populous green wall
Tenanted by the ever-busy flies,
Grey crickets and shy lizards and quick spiders,

17| *MS:* say this Autumn <> time *1835:* say, this autumn *1849:* say, "this <> time," 18| *MS:* days—and *1835:* days; and 19| *MS:* leaves:— *1835:* leaves. 20| *MS:* sunny — — *I* *1835:* sunny—*I* *1863:* sunny; I 21| *MS:* truth . . . and *1835:* truth; and *1863:* truth: and 22| *MS:* beloved for all their frailty! . . / Aureole! . . *1835:* frailty! / Aureole! . . . *1849:* Aureole! *1863:* beloved, for 23| *MS:* by drop! . . . she *1835:* by drop!—she *1863:* by drop! she 24| *MS:* so . . . I am content . . . more than content . . . *1835:* so . . . I am content—more than content— 1849| so! I *1863:* than content; 25| *MS:* Nay Autumn *1849:* Nay, Autumn *1863:* autumn 26| *MS:* decay . . . *1849:* decay! *1863:* decay: 28| *MS:* The stained <> down— *1835:* stain'd *1849:* Your stained <> down, 29| *MS:* Those <> fruit . . . and see *1835:* fruit—and *1849:* Nor blame those <> fruit, 31| *MS:* among— *1835:* among; *1849:* among! 32| *MS:* And for the winds . . what *1835:* winds—what *1849:* Then for 33| *MS:* ash that overlooks the rest *1835:* rest, *1849:* overlooks you both, *1863:* ash which overlooks 34| *MS:* berries . . . Ah! at *1835:* berries. Ah *1849:* berries? Ah 36| *MS:* kingdom limited *1835:* Sequester'd nest! This kingdom, limited *1849:* Sequestered *1863:* nest!—this 37| *1835:* wall, *1863:* wall 39| *MS:* crickets, and shy lizards, and *1863:* crickets and shy lizards and

Each family of the silver-threaded moss—
Which, look through near, this way, and it appears
A stubble-field or a cane-brake, a marsh
Of bulrush whitening in the sun: laugh now!
Fancy the crickets, each one in his house,
Looking out, wondering at the world—or best,
Yon painted snail with his gay shell of dew,
Travelling to see the glossy balls high up
Hung by the caterpillar, like gold lamps.
MICHAL In truth we have lived carelessly and well.
PARACELSUS And shall, my perfect pair!—each, trust me, born
For the other; nay, your very hair, when mixed,
Is of one hue. For where save in this nook
Shall you two walk, when I am far away,
And wish me prosperous fortune? Stay: that plant
Shall never wave its tangles lightly and softly,
As a queen's languid and imperial arm
Which scatters crowns among her lovers, but you
Shall be reminded to predict to me
Some great success! Ah see, the sun sinks broad
Behind Saint Saviour's: wholly gone, at last!
FESTUS Now, Aureole, stay those wandering eyes awhile!
You are ours to-night, at least; and while you spoke

40| *MS:* All families <> moss . . . *1835:* moss— *1849:* Each family 41| *MS:*—Which look thro', near, this way,—and *1835:* Which <> through <> way, and *1849:* Which, look *1863:* through near, this 42| *MS:* stubble-field, or a cane-brake . . . a *1835:* crane-brake—a *1849:* cane-brake *1863:* stubble-field or a cane-brake, a 45| *MS:* out and wondering <> world: . . or best, *1835:* world—or *1849:* out, wondering 46| *MS:* The painted snail, with *1849:* Yon painted *1863:* snail with 48| *1849:* lamps! *1863:* lamps. 49| *MS:* truth, we <> well! *1835:* truth we *1863:* well. 50| *MS:* Pair! . . each *1835:* pair—each *1863:* pair!—each 51| *MS:* other — — nay your very hair when mixed *1835:* other—nay <> hair, when mixed, *1849:* other; nay, your 52| *MS:* hue — — for where beside this *1835:* hue. For *1849:* where save in this 54| *MS:* fortune? — — stay,—that *1835:* fortune? . . . Stay! that *1849:* fortune? Stay! Whene'er *1863:* Stay: that plant 55| *MS:* softly *1835:* softly, *1849:* That plant shall wave *1863:* Shall never wave 56| *MS:* Queen's *1835:* queen's 57| *MS:* lovers, . . but *1835:* lovers, but *1849:* lovers, you *1863:* lovers, but you 58| *MS:* predict some great *1849:* predict to me 59| *MS:* Success to me: . . . Ah, see! the *1835:* to me. Ah *1849:* Some great success! Ah *1863:* see, the *1868:* Ah see 60| *MS:* St. Saviour's — — wholly *1835:* Saviour's . . . wholly *1849:* Saviour's: wholly *1863:* Saint 61| *MS:* awhile— *1835:* awhile: *1849:* awhile! 62| *MS:*—You <> least—and *1835:* You <> to-night at least; and

Of Michal and her tears, I thought that none
Could willing leave what he so seemed to love:
But that last look destroys my dream—that look
As if, where'er you gazed, there stood a star!
How far was Würzburg with its church and spire
And garden-walls and all things they contain,
From that look's far alighting?

PARACELSUS

I but spoke
And looked alike from simple joy to see
The beings I love best, shut in so well
From all rude chances like to be my lot,
That, when afar, my weary spirit,—disposed
To lose awhile its care in soothing thoughts
Of them, their pleasant features, looks and words,—
Needs never hesitate, nor apprehend
Encroaching trouble may have reached them too,
Nor have recourse to fancy's busy aid
And fashion even a wish in their behalf
Beyond what they possess already here;
But, unobstructed, may at once forget
Itself in them, assured how well they fare.
Beside, this Festus knows he holds me one

63| *MS:* tears, § illegible by crossing out § that § replaced by § tears, I thought *1849:* tears, the thought came back *1863:* tears, I thought that none 64| *MS:* love . . . *1835:* seem'd *1849:* That none could leave <> seemed to love: *1863:* Could willing leave 65| *MS:* dream . . . that look! *1835:* dream—that *1863:* look 66| *MS:* if where'er you gazed there *1849:* if, where'er you gazed, there 67| *MS:* — — How *1835:* How <> Wurzburg, with <> spire, *1863:* Wurzburg with <> spire 68| *MS:* all that they *1835:* garden-walls, and *1849:* all things they *1863:* garden-walls and 70| *1835:* look'd <> joy, to *1849:* looked *1863:* joy to 71| *MS:* I best love, so well shut in *1835:* love so *1849:* I love best, shut in so well 72| *1835:* lot; *1849:* lot, 73| *MS:* That, far from them, my <> spirit, disposed *1849:* That, when afar, my <> spirit,—disposed 74| *MS:* cares *1849:* care 75| *MS:* looks, and words — — — *1835:* words, *1849:* words,— *1863:* looks and 76| *MS:* hesitate—nor *1835:* hesitate, nor *1849:* Need *1863:* Needs 77| *MS:* Incroaching <> too, . . . § written over by § too,— *1835:* Encroaching <> reach'd <> too; *1849:* reached <> too, 78| *MS:* Fancy's *1863:* fancy's 79| *MS:* Even to frame a *1849:* To fashion even a *1863:* And fashion 80| *MS:* here, . . . § written over by § here,— 82| *MS:* them,—assured <> they are. *1835:* them—assured *1849:* them, assured *1863:* they fare. 83| *MS:* — — This Festus knows, beside, he *1835:* This <> knows; beside *1849:* Beside, this Festus knows, he thinks me *1863:* knows he holds me

Whom quiet and its charms arrest in vain,
One scarce aware of all the joys I quit,
Too filled with airy hopes to make account
Of soft delights his own heart garners up:
Whereas behold how much our sense of all
That's beauteous proves alike! When Festus learns
That every common pleasure of the world
Affects me as himself; that I have just
As varied appetite for joy derived
From common things; a stake in life, in short,
Like his; a stake which rash pursuit of aims
That life affords not, would as soon destroy;—
He may convince himself that, this in view,
I shall act well advised. And last, because,
Though heaven and earth and all things were at stake,
Sweet Michal must not weep, our parting eve.
FESTUS True: and the eve is deepening, and we sit
As little anxious to begin our talk
As though to-morrow I could hint of it
As we paced arm-in-arm the cheerful town
At sun-dawn; or could whisper it by fits
(Trithemius busied with his class the while)
In that dim chamber where the noon-streaks peer

84| *MS:* vain— *1835:* vain; *1849:* charms attract in vain, *1863:* charms arrest in 85| *MS:* joys he quits . . . *1835:* quits; *1849:* joys I quit, 86| *1835:* fill'd *1863:* filled 87| *MS:* up . . . . *1835:* up: *1849:* delights which free hearts garner *1863:* delights his own heart garners 88| *MS:* . . Whereas *1835:* Whereas, behold *1868:* Whereas behold 89| *MS:* That's beautiful, is one!—and when he learns *1835:* one! And *1849:* That's beauteous proves alike! When Festus learns 90| *MS:* common sight he can enjoy *1849:* common pleasure of the world 91| *MS:* himself—that *1835:* himself; that 92| *MS:* joys *1849:* appetites for joy *1863:* appetite 93| *MS:* things—a *1835:* things; a 94| *MS:* his—and which a rash *1835:* his; and *1849:* his; a stake which rash 95| *MS:* That it affords not would < > destroy——— *1835:* destroy;— *1849:* That life affords not, would 96| *MS:* himself, that, knowing this, *1849:* that, this in view, *1863:* himself that 97| *MS:* advised: and last, because *1835:* because, *1863:* advised. And 98| *MS:* Tho' Heaven < > stake *1835:* Though heaven and earth, and all things, were at stake, *1863:* earth and all things were 99| *MS:* Eve. *1835:* weep our < > eve. *1849:* weep, our < > eve! 100| *MS:* True:—and < > deepening, and *1835:* True: and < > deepening, and 102| *MS:* tho' tomorrow *1835:* though to-morrow *1849:* could open it *1863:* could hint of it 103| *MS:* arm in arm *1863:* arm-in-arm 104| *MS:* sundawn—or *1835:* sun-dawn; or *1849:* sun-dawn; and continue it *1863:* sun-dawn; or could whisper it 105| *1849:* (Old Tritheim *1863:* (Trithemius

Half-frightened by the awful tomes around;
Or in some grassy lane unbosom all
From even-blush to midnight: but, to-morrow!
Have I full leave to tell my inmost mind?
We have been brothers, and henceforth the world
Will rise between us:—all my freest mind?
'Tis the last night, dear Aureole!

PARACELSUS Oh, say on!
Devise some test of love, some arduous feat
To be performed for you: say on! If night
Be spent the while, the better! Recall how oft
My wondrous plans and dreams and hopes and fears
Have—never wearied you, oh no!—as I
Recall, and never vividly as now,
Your true affection, born when Einsiedeln
And its green hills were all the world to us;
And still increasing to this night which ends
My further stay at Würzburg. Oh, one day
You shall be very proud! Say on, dear friends!

FESTUS In truth? 'Tis for my proper peace, indeed,
Rather than yours; for vain all projects seem

107| *MS:* Half frightened < > around— *1835:* frighten'd < > around; *1849:* frightened *1868:* Half-frightened 108| *MS:*—Or *1835:* Or *1849:* And here at home unbosom all the rest *1863:* Or in some grassy lane unbosom all
109| *MS:* midnight . . . . but to-morrow *1835:* midnight . . . but to-morrow! . . . *1849:* midnight: but, to-morrow! . . . *1863:* to-morrow! 110| *MS:* — — I have full *1835:* I *1849:* Have I full 111| *MS:*—We < > brothers and *1835:* We < > brothers, and *1849:* We two were brothers *1863:* We have been brothers 112| *MS:* Will be between us; — — all < > mind? — — *1835:* us . . . . all < > mind? . . . *1849:* Will rise between us:—all < > mind? 113| *MS:* Tis *1835:* 'Tis 114| *MS:*—Devise < > love — — some § written over by § love—some *1835:* Devise *1863:* love, some 115| *MS:* you . . . say on, . . . if § written over by § you—say on,—if *1835:* perform'd for you—say on; if *1849:* performed < > on! If *1863:* you: say 116| *MS:* better: . . . recall § written over by § better:—recall *1835:* better: recall *1849:* better! Recall
117| *1835:* plans, and dreams, and hopes, and fears, *1863:* plans and dreams and hopes and fears 118| *MS:* you . . oh, no! . . as *1835:* you . . . oh, no! . . . as *1863:* you, oh, no!—as 120| *MS:* affection born *1835:* affection, born
121| *MS:* us,— *1835:* us, *1863:* us; 122| *1835:* night, which *1863:* night which 123| *MS:* Würzburg . . . Oh you shall *1849:* Oh, one day *1863:* Würzburg. Oh 124–125| *MS:* Be very proud one day! . . . say < > Friend; / Talk volumes, I shall still be in arrear. / FESTUS In truth? . . . 'tis *1835:* friend; < > truth? 'Tis *1849:* You shall be very proud! Say < > friends! / FESTUS
126| *MS:* yours . . for vain it looks, to seek *1835:* yours—for < > looks to *1849:* yours; for vain all projects seem

To stay your course: I said my latest hope
Is fading even now. A story tells
Of some far embassy despatched to win
The favour of an eastern king, and how
The gifts they offered proved but dazzling dust
Shed from the ore-beds native to his clime.
Just so, the value of repose and love,
I meant should tempt you, better far than I
You seem to comprehend; and yet desist
No whit from projects where repose nor love
Has part.
PARACELSUS Once more? Alas! As I foretold.
FESTUS A solitary briar the bank puts forth
To save our swan's nest floating out to sea.
PARACELSUS Dear Festus, hear me. What is it you wish?
That I should lay aside my heart's pursuit,
Abandon the sole ends for which I live,
Reject God's great commission, and so die!
You bid me listen for your true love's sake:
Yet how has grown that love? Even in a long
And patient cherishing of the self-same spirit
It now would quell; as though a mother hoped
To stay the lusty manhood of the child

127| *MS:* course — — the last hopes I conceived *1835:* course—the *1849:* course: I said my latest hope 128| *MS:* Are fading < > now:—old stories tell *1835:* now. Old *1849:* Is fading < > now. A story tells 129| *1835:* despatch'd *1849:* despatched to buy *1863:* dispatched to win *1888:* despatched
130| *MS:* Eastern king,—and *1835:* eastern king, and 131| *MS:* gifts it proffered were but *1835:* proffer'd *1849:* gifts they offered proved but
132| *MS:* to the clime;— *1835:* clime; *1849:* to his clime; *1863:* clime.
133| *MS:* —Just < > love *1835:* Just < > love, 134| *MS:* you . . better § written over by § you—better *1835:* you, better 135| *MS:* comprehend . . . and still desist *1835:* comprehend—and *1849:* and yet desist *1863:* comprehend; and 136| *MS:* where they have no part: *1835:* part. *1849:* where repose nor love 137–138| *MS:* PARACELSUS Alas! as I forbode; this weighty talk / Has for its end no other than to revive . . . . . . / FESTUS *1835:* forbode, this < > revive . . . *1849:* Have part. PARACELSUS Once more? Alas! as I forbode! FESTUS / *1888:* Has
140| *MS:* me;— — what § edited? to § me.— — What *1835:* me. What
141| *MS:* pursuit— § over §, *1835:* pursuit, 142| *MS:* live— § over §, *1835:* live, 143| *MS:* commission . . . and *1835:* commission—and *1863:* commission, and 144| *MS:* . . And still I listen < > sake. *1835:* And *1849:* sake: 145| *MS:* even *1835:* Even 146| *1835:* selfsame *1888:* self-same 147| *MS:* quell . . . as tho' a mother should hope *1835:* quell—as though *1849:* quell; as < > mother hoped

Once weak upon her knees. I was not born
Informed and fearless from the first, but shrank
From aught which marked me out apart from men:
I would have lived their life, and died their death,
Lost in their ranks, eluding destiny:
But you first guided me through doubt and fear,
Taught me to know mankind and know myself;
And now that I am strong and full of hope,
That, from my soul, I can reject all aims
Save those your earnest words made plain to me,
Now that I touch the brink of my design,
When I would have a triumph in their eyes,
A glad cheer in their voices—Michal weeps,
And Festus ponders gravely!

FESTUS

When you deign
To hear my purpose . . .

PARACELSUS

Hear it? I can say
Beforehand all this evening's conference!
'Tis this way, Michal, that he uses: first,
Or he declares, or I, the leading points
Of our best scheme of life, what is man's end
And what God's will; no two faiths e'er agreed

149| *MS:* knees; I *1835:* knees. I 150| *1835:* Inform'd *1849:* Informed 151| *MS:* Men . . § edited? to § Men. *1835:* mark'd <> men. *1849:* marked 152| *MS:* life, and striven their strife, *1835:* strife— *1849:* life, and died their death, 153| *MS:* Eluding Destiny, if that might be, . . . § written over by § be,— *1835:* be— *1849:* Lost in their ranks, eluding destiny; 154| *MS:* thro' *1835:* through 155| *MS:* And taught <> know them and <> myself; . . . § written over by § myself;— *1835:* myself; *1849:* Taught me to know mankind and 156| *MS:* hope § edited? to § hope— *1835:* hope; *1849:* hope, 157| *MS:*—That I can from my soul reject *1835:* aims, *1849:* That, from my soul, I can reject all aims 158| *MS:* me; . . § written over by § me;— *1835:* me; 159| *MS:* Now, that <> design,— *1835:* design, *1863:* Now that 160| *MS:*—When *1835:* When 161| *MS:* voices . . . Michal *1835:* voices—Michal 162| *MS:* you shall *1849:* you deign 163| *MS:* Have learned my purpose . . . . PARACELSUS Learned it? . . . I *1835:* learn'd my purpose . . . PARACELSUS Learn'd it? I *1849:* To hear my <> PARACELSUS Hear it 164| *MS:* this conference will produce:— *1835:* produce. *1849:* this evening's conference! 165| *MS:* . . 'Tis § written over by § —'Tis <> uses; . . . first, § written over by § uses;—first, *1835:* 'Tis <> uses: first, 167| *MS:* our belief in what is Man's true End *1835:* man's <> end *1849:* our best scheme of life, what is man's end, *1868:* end 168| *MS:* And God's apparent will . . . no <> ever *1835:* will—no *1849:* And what God's will—no <> e'er *1863:* will; no

As his with mine. Next, each of us allows
Faith should be acted on as best we may;
Accordingly, I venture to submit
My plan, in lack of better, for pursuing
The path which God's will seems to authorize.
Well, he discerns much good in it, avows
This motive worthy, that hope plausible,
A danger here to be avoided, there
An oversight to be repaired: in fine
Our two minds go together—all the good
Approved by him, I gladly recognize,
All he counts bad, I thankfully discard,
And nought forbids my looking up at last
For some stray comfort in his cautious brow.
When, lo! I learn that, spite of all, there lurks
Some innate and inexplicable germ
Of failure in my scheme; so that at last
It all amounts to this—the sovereign proof
That we devote ourselves to God, is seen
In living just as though no God there were;

169–170| *MS:* Agreed as ours agree:—next, each allows / These points are no mere visionary truths: / But, once determined, it remains alone / To act upon them straight as <> may:— *1835:* agree: next <> determin'd <> may: *1849:* As his with mine: next, each of us allows / Faith should be acted on as *1863:* mine. Next may; **172**| *1849:* A plan *1863:* My plan **173–174**| *MS:* authorize . . . / . . A broad plan, vague and ill defined enough, / But courting censure and imploring aid: . . . / Well . . . he <> it—avows § written over by § aid:— *1835:* authorize— / A <> aid: Well—he <> it, avows *1849:* authorize: / Well *1863:* Well, he **175**| *MS:* plausible,— *1835:* plausible, **176**| *MS:* —A danger, here, to be avoided—there, *1835:* A danger here *1863:* here to be avoided, there **177**| *MS:* repaired . . in fine, § written over by § repaired—in *1835:* repair'd: in fine *1849:* repaired: at last *1863:* repaired: in fine **178**| *MS:* Our minds go every way together . . all good *1835:* together—all *1849:* Our two minds go together—all the good **179**| *1835:* recognize; *1863:* recognize, **180**| *MS:* discard; *1863:* discard, **181**| *MS:* forbids me to look *1849:* forbids my looking **182**| *MS:* brow—— — *1835:* brow— *1863:* brow. **185**| *MS:* schemes . . so § written over by § schemes—so *1835:* schemes; so *1863:* scheme **186**| *MS:* this . . . the § written over by § this—the **187**| *MS:* ourselves wholly to God *1849:* ourselves to God **188**| *MS:* Is in a life as tho' <> were:— *1835:* though <> were: *1849:* In living just as though there were no God: *1863:* though no God there were;

A life which, prompted by the sad and blind
Folly of man, Festus abhors the most;
But which these tenets sanctify at once,
Though to less subtle wits it seems the same,
Consider it how they may.

MICHAL Is it so, Festus?
He speaks so calmly and kindly: is it so?

PARACELSUS Reject those glorious visions of God's love
And man's design; laugh loud that God should send
Vast longings to direct us; say how soon
Power satiates these, or lust, or gold; I know
The world's cry well, and how to answer it.
But this ambiguous warfare . . .

FESTUS . . . Wearies so
That you will grant no last leave to your friend
To urge it?—for his sake, not yours? I wish
To send my soul in good hopes after you;
Never to sorrow that uncertain words
Erringly apprehended, a new creed
Ill understood, begot rash trust in you,
Had share in your undoing.

PARACELSUS Choose your side,

189| *MS:* . . A <> which prompted *1835:* which, prompted 190| *MS:* Man <> most, *1835:* man <> most— *1849:* Lusts of the world, Festus *1863:* Folly of man, Festus 191| *1835:* once— *1849:* once; *1863:* once, 192| *MS:* Tho' <> same *1835:* Though <> same, 193| *MS:* may: *1835:* may. *1888:* Festus *1889:* Festus? 194| *MS:* kindly . . is *1835:* kindly—is *1863:* kindly: is 196| *MS:* Man's design—laugh <> that he should *1835.* man's design; laugh *1849:* that God should 197| *MS:* us; . . or find out *1835:* us; or *1849:* us; say how soon 198–200| *MS:* How else they may be satiated: . . but § written over by § satiated:—but this / Ambiguous warfare wearies: — FESTUS Not so much *1835:* satiated: but / wearies . . . FESTUS *1849:* Power satiates these, or lust, or gold; I know / The world's cry well, and how to answer it! / But this ambiguous warfare . . . FESTUS . . . Wearies so *1863:* lust or *1868:* lust, or 201| *1835:* friend, *1849:* friend 202| *MS:*—And for his own sake, not for your's? — I *1835:* And <> yours? I *1849:* To urge it?—for his sake, not yours 203| *MS:* you . . . § written over by § you— *1849:* you; 204| *1835:* words, *1868:* words 205| *MS:* apprehended—a *1835:* creed, *1863:* apprehended, a new creed 206| *MS:* you . . . § written over by § you— *1835:* understood—begot *1849:* you, *1863:* understood, begot 207| *MS:* undoing— — — *π* PARACELSUS Choose your party: . . § written over by § party:— *1835:* undoing. *π* PARACELSUS <> party: *1849:* And shared <> your side: *1863:* Had share <> side,

Hold or renounce: but meanwhile blame me not
Because I dare to act on your own views,
Nor shrink when they point onward, nor espy
A peril where they most ensure success.

FESTUS Prove that to me—but that! Prove you abide
Within their warrant, nor presumptuous boast
God's labour laid on you; prove, all you covet
A mortal may expect; and, most of all,
Prove the strange course you now affect, will lead
To its attainment—and I bid you speed,
Nay, count the minutes till you venture forth!
You smile; but I had gathered from slow thought—
Much musing on the fortunes of my friend—
Matter I deemed could not be urged in vain;
But it all leaves me at my need: in shreds
And fragments I must venture what remains.

MICHAL Ask at once, Festus, wherefore he should scorn . . .

FESTUS Stay, Michal: Aureole, I speak guardedly
And gravely, knowing well, whate'er your error,
This is no ill-considered choice of yours,
No sudden fancy of an ardent boy.
Not from your own confiding words alone
Am I aware your passionate heart long since

208| *MS:* renounce: . . but § written over by § renounce:—but *1835:* renounce: but 209| *MS:* views *1835:* views— *1849:* views, 210| *MS:*—Nor <> onward . . nor § written over by § onward—nor spy out *1835:* Nor shrink *1849:* onward, nor espy 211| *MS:* success: . . . § written over by § success:—*1835:* success . . . *1849:* success. 212| *MS:* that:—that you *1835:* that: that *1849:* that! Prove you 213| *MS:* warrant—nor *1849:* warrant, nor 214| *MS:* you; . . . that § written over by § you;—that all *1835:* you; that *1849:* you; prove, all 215| *MS:* expect;—and most of all *1835:* expect; and, most of all,
216| *MS:* That the *1849:* Prove the 217| *MS:* attainment . . . and <> speed! *1835:* attainment—and *1849:* speed, 218| *MS:* And count <> 'till <> forth. *1835:* till *1849:* Nay, count <> forth! 219| *MS:* You will smile,—but <> thought, *1835:* smile; but <> gather'd <> thought— *1849:* You smile; but <> gathered 220| *MS:* friend, *1835:* friend—
221| *1835:* deem'd *1849:* deemed 222| *MS:* need—in *1835:* need: in
223| *MS:* remains: . . . § written over by § remains:— *1835:* remains.
225| *MS:* Michal;—Aureole *1835:* Michal: Aureole 226| *MS:* gravely, . . knowing *1835:* gravely, knowing 227| *MS:* your's, *1835:* ill-consider'd <> yours— *1849:* ill-considered 228| *MS:* boy:— *1835:* boy.
229| *MS:* ——Not *1835:* Not 230| *MS:* heart has long *1849:* heart long since

Gave birth to, nourished and at length matures
This scheme. I will not speak of Einsiedeln,
Where I was born your elder by some years
Only to watch you fully from the first:
In all beside, our mutual tasks were fixed
Even then—'twas mine to have you in my view
As you had your own soul and those intents
Which filled it when, to crown your dearest wish,
With a tumultuous heart, you left with me
Our childhood's home to join the favoured few
Whom, here, Trithemius condescends to teach
A portion of his lore: and not one youth
Of those so favoured, whom you now despise,
Came earnest as you came, resolved, like you,
To grasp all, and retain all, and deserve
By patient toil a wide renown like his.
Now, this new ardour which supplants the old
I watched, too; 'twas significant and strange,
In one matched to his soul's content at length

231–232| *MS:* Nourished, and has at length matured a plan / To give yourself up wholly to one End: . . . . / . . . I <> Einsiedeln,—'twas as *1835:* Nourish'd <> matured, a plan / <> end / I <> Einsiedeln; 'twas *1849:* Gave birth to, nourished, and at length matures / This scheme. I <> Einsiedeln, *1868:* nourished and **233**| *MS:* I had been born *1849:* Where I was born **234**| *MS:* first:— *1835:* first: **235**| *1835:* fix'd *1849:* fixed **236**| *MS:* then . . . 'twas § written over by § then— 'twas **237–238**| *MS:* soul; . . accordingly §written over by § soul;—accordingly / I could go further back, and trace each bough / Of this wide-branching tree even to its birth . . § written over by § birth— / . . Each § written over by §—Each fullgrown passion to its outspring faint, — — / But I shall only dwell upon the intents / Which filled you when *1835:* soul: accordingly // <> birth; / Each full-grown <> faint; // <> fill'd *1849:* soul and those intents / Which filled it when **239**/ *MS:* heart you *1835:* heart, you **240**| *MS:* childhoods' *1835:* favour'd *1849:* childhood's <> favoured **241**| *MS:* Whom famed Trithemius *1849:* Whom, here at Würzburg, Tritheim deigns to *1863:* here, Trithemius condescends to **242**| *MS:* lore . . . . and not the dullest *1835:* lore—and *1849:* lore: and not the best *1863:* not one youth **243**| *MS:* favoured—whom <> despise *1835:* favour'd, whom <> despise, *1849:* favoured **244**| *MS:* Was earnest as you were, . . resolved § written over by § were,—resolved like you *1835:* were; resolved, like you, *1849:* Came earnest as you came; resolved *1863:* you came, resolved **246–247**| *MS:* his: . . . / . . . Now, just as well have I descried the growth / Of this <> old: . . § written over by § old:— *1835:* his. / Now <> / <> old: *1849:* his. / And this <> old, *1863:* Now, this *1888:* old **248**| *MS:* watched it . . 'twas § written over by § it—'twas <> strange *1835:* watch'd <> strange, *1849:* watched, too; 'twas **249**| *MS:* one, matched *1835:* one match'd *1849:* matched

With rivals in the search for wisdom's prize,
To see the sudden pause, the total change;
From contest, the transition to repose—
From pressing onward as his fellows pressed,
To a blank idleness, yet most unlike
The dull stagnation of a soul, content,
Once foiled, to leave betimes a thriveless quest.
That careless bearing, free from all pretence
Even of contempt for what it ceased to seek—
Smiling humility, praising much, yet waiving
What it professed to praise—though not so well
Maintained but that rare outbreaks, fierce and brief,
Revealed the hidden scorn, as quickly curbed.
That ostentatious show of past defeat,
That ready acquiescence in contempt,
I deemed no other than the letting go
His shivered sword, of one about to spring
Upon his foe's throat; but it was not thus:
Not that way looked your brooding purpose then.
For after-signs disclosed, what you confirmed,
That you prepared to task to the uttermost
Your strength, in furtherance of a certain aim

250| *MS:* Wisdom's *1863:* wisdom's 251| *MS:* pause— — the § written over by § pause—the < > change— — — § written over by § change— *1835:* pause, the < > change, *1849:* change; 252| *MS:* contest that transition to repose . . . *1835:* contest, that < > repose— *1849:* contest, the transition 253| *MS:* pressed *1835:* press'd, *1849:* pressed, 254| *1835:* idleness; yet *1863:* idleness, yet 255| *MS:* soul content, *1835:* content— *1849:* soul, content, 256| *MS:* quest; *1835:* foil'd—to *1849:* foiled, to < > quest. 258| *MS:* seek . . . § written over by § seek— 259| *MS:*—Smiling < > much yet *1835:* Smiling < > much, yet 260| *MS:* praise . . yet not *1835:* profess'd to praise . . . yet *1849:* professed to praise—though not 261| *MS:* Secured but < > outbreaks—fierce and brief *1835:* outbreaks, fierce and brief, *1849:* Maintained but < > fierce as brief, *1863:* fierce and brief 262| *MS:* scorn—as < > curbed . . . *1835:* Reveal'd < > curb'd . . . *1849:* Revealed < > scorn, as < > curbed— *1863:* curbed. 263| *MS:* . . That < > defeat— *1835:* That *1849:* defeat, 264| *MS:* contempt . . . . . . § written over by § contempt— — *1835:* contempt— *1849:* contempt, 265| *1835:* deem'd *1849:* deemed 266| *1835:* shiver'd *1849:* shivered 267| *MS:* throat . . . but < > thus: — — § written over by § thus:— *1835:* thus: *1849:* throat; but 268| *MS:* then;— *1835:* look'd *1849:* looked < > then. 269| *MS:* But after-signs disclosed, and you *1835:* confirm'd, *1849:* For after-signs disclosed, what you confirmed, 271| *1835:* aim, *1863:* aim

Which—while it bore the name your rivals gave
Their own most puny efforts—was so vast
In scope that it included their best flights,
Combined them, and desired to gain one prize
In place of many,—the secret of the world,
Of man, and man's true purpose, path and fate.
—That you, not nursing as a mere vague dream
This purpose, with the sages of the past,
Have struck upon a way to this, if all
You trust be true, which following, heart and soul,
You, if a man may, dare aspire to KNOW:
And that this aim shall differ from a host
Of aims alike in character and kind,
Mostly in this,—that in itself alone
Shall its reward be, not an alien end
Blending therewith; no hope nor fear nor joy
Nor woe, to elsewhere move you, but this pure
Devotion to sustain you or betray:
Thus you aspire.

PARACELSUS You shall not state it thus:
I should not differ from the dreamy crew
You speak of. I profess no other share
In the selection of my lot, than this

272| *MS:* Which— § above § , while *1835:* Which—while 273| *MS:* To their most <> efforts, was *1835:* efforts—was *1849:* Their own most 276| *MS:* many—the Secret <> World *1835:* secret <> world— *1849:* many,—the <> world, 277| *MS:* Of Man, and Man's <> path, and fate:— *1835:* Of man, and man's <> fate: *1863:* fate. 278| *MS:* That you, . . not <> as a lovely dream *1835:* you, not *1849:*—That <> a mere vague dream 279| *MS:* Sages of old Time . . . *1835:* sages <> Time, *1845:* of the Past, *1868:* past, 282| *MS:* Know: . . . § in large print; written over by § Know:— *1835:* KNOW: 284| *1835:* kind— *1849:* kind, 285| *MS:* this;—that *1835:* this; that *1849:* this,—to seek its own reward *1863:* this,—that in itself alone, *1868:* alone 286| *MS:* be . . . not *1835:* be—not *1849:* In itself only, not *1863:* Shall its reward be, not 287| *MS:* therewith . . no *1835:* therewith—no hope, nor fear, nor joy, *1849:* To blend therewith; no *1863:* Blending therewith *1868:* hope nor fear nor joy 288| *MS:* woe shall elsewhere *1835:* woe, shall <> you; but *1849:* woe, to elsewhere <> you, but 289| *MS:* Devotion shall sustain or shall undo you,— *1835:* you: *1849:* Devotion to sustain you or betray: 290| *MS:*—This you intend;—PARACELSUS <> thus . . . *1835:* This you intend. PARACELSUS <> thus: *1849:* Thus you aspire. PARACELSUS 291| *MS:* . . I *1835:* I 292| *MS:* of:—I *1835:* of. I 293| *MS:* than in *1849:* than this, *1863:* this

My ready answer to the will of God
Who summons me to be his organ. All
Whose innate strength supports them shall succeed
No better than the sages.

FESTUS Such the aim, then,
God sets before you; and 'tis doubtless need
That he appoint no less the way of praise
Than the desire to praise; for, though I hold
With you, the setting forth such praise to be
The natural end and service of a man,
And hold such praise is best attained when man
Attains the general welfare of his kind—
Yet this, the end, is not the instrument.
Presume not to serve God apart from such
Appointed channel as he wills shall gather
Imperfect tributes, for that sole obedience
Valued perchance! He seeks not that his altars
Blaze, careless how, so that they do but blaze.
Suppose this, then; that God selected you

294| *1835:* God, *1849:* A ready <> God *1863:* My ready 295| *MS:* organ——he § written over in pencil by § organ—he *1835:* organ: he *1849:* organ: all *1863:* His organ. All *1868:* his 296| *MS:* supports him shall *1849:* supports them shall 297| *MS:* Sages;— FESTUS Such the aim § *the* written above the line § *1835:* sages. FESTUS *1849:* than your sages *1868:* than the sages 298| *MS:* you;— § written over by pencil as § you; and 'tis, doubtless, need 299| *MS:* Praise *1835:* praise *1863:* He *1868:* he 300| *MS:* praise;—for, tho' *1835:* praise; for, though 302| *MS:* Man,— *1834:* man— *1849:* man, 303| *MS:* And that such praise seemed best attained when he *1835:* attain'd *1849:* And think such praise is best attained when man *1863:* And hold such 304| *MS:* kind, ... § written over by § Kind, ... *1835:* kind— 305–306| *MS:* Yet, *that,* the *instrument,* is not the *end:*— / There is a curse upon the earth—let Man / Presume *1835:* end. / <> earth; let man *1849:* Yet, this, the end, is not the instrument / Presume 307| *1849:* He *1868:* he 308| *MS:* tributes—for *1863:* tributes, for 309| *MS:* perchance:—He *1835:* perchance. He *1849:* Valued, perchance *1863:* that His altars *1868:* Valued perchance <> that his altars *1888:* perchance! He 310–311| *MS:* Blaze—careless <> but blaze . . . . / Tho' I doubt much if he consent that we / Discover this great secret . . . I § written over by § secret—I know well / You will allege no other comprehends / The work in question save its labourer: / —I shall assume the Aim approved—and you / That I am implicated in the issue / Not simply as your friend, but as yourself— / —As tho' it were my task, that you perform, / And some plague dogged my heels till it were done . . . . / ——Suppose this owned, then,—you are born to Know,— § in large print § *1835:* blaze. / —Though <> / <> secret I <> /// <> aim improved; and you /// As though <> task that you perform, / <> plague dogg'd <> done. / Suppose this own'd then; you <> KNOW.

To KNOW (heed well your answers, for my faith
Shall meet implicitly what they affirm)
I cannot think you dare annex to such
Selection aught beyond a steadfast will,
An intense hope; nor let your gifts create
Scorn or neglect of ordinary means
Conducive to success, make destiny
Dispense with man's endeavour. Now, dare you search
Your inmost heart, and candidly avow
Whether you have not rather wild desire
For this distinction than security
Of its existence? whether you discern
The path to the fulfilment of your purpose
Clear as that purpose—and again, that purpose
Clear as your yearning to be singled out
For its pursuer. Dare you answer this?

PARACELSUS [*after a pause*] No, I have nought to fear! Who will may know
The secret'st workings of my soul. What though
It be so?—if indeed the strong desire
Eclipse the aim in me?—if splendour break
Upon the outset of my path alone,
And duskest shade succeed? What fairer seal
Shall I require to my authentic mission
Than this fierce energy?—this instinct striving

1849: but blaze. / Suppose this, then; that God selected you *1863:* Blaze, careless **312**| *MS:* (You will heed < > answers for *1835:* (You will heed < > answers, for *1849:* To KNOW (heed **313**| *MS:* affirm)— *1849:* affirm) **314**| *MS:* you have annexed *1835:* annex'd *1849:* you dare annex **316**| *MS:* intense purpose . . . gifts § written over by § purpose—gifts that would induce *1849:* intense hope, nor let your gifts create *1863:* hope; nor **318**| *MS:* And instruments of success; no destiny *1849:* Conducive to success—make destiny *1863:* success, make **319**| *MS:* Dispenses with endeavour: . . now § written over by § endeavour:— now *1835:* endeavour. Now *1849:* Dispense with man's endeavour **322**| *MS:* distinction, than a full assurance *1849:* distinction, than security *1868:* distinction than **323**| *MS:* That it exists,—or whether *1835:* exists; or *1849:* Of its existence; whether *1863:* existence? whether **325**| *MS:* purpose, and *1835:* purpose—and **327**| *MS:* For its possessor—— dare *1835:* possessor. Dare *1849:* its pursuer. Dare **328**| *MS: pause*] . . No § written over by § *pause*]—No *1835: pause*] No; I *1849:* No, I **329**| *MS:* of my soul —— what § *my* written above the line § *1835*| *MS:* soul. What **331**| *MS:* Eclipse the true aim § *true* cancelled; *in me* added above the line to read § Eclipse the aim in me? . . if *1835:* me?—if **333**| *MS:* succeed:? What *1835:* succeed? What **335**| *MS:* energy . . . this § written over by § energy—this *1835:* energy?—this

Because its nature is to strive?—enticed
By the security of no broad course,
Without success forever in its eyes!
How know I else such glorious fate my own,
But in the restless irresistible force
That works within me? Is it for human will
To institute such impulses?—still less,
To disregard their promptings! What should I
Do, kept among you all; your loves, your cares,
Your life—all to be mine? Be sure that God
Ne'er dooms to waste the strength he deigns impart!
Ask the geier-eagle why she stoops at once
Into the vast and unexplored abyss,
What full-grown power informs her from the first,
Why she not marvels, strenuously beating
The silent boundless regions of the sky!
Be sure they sleep not whom God needs! Nor fear
Their holding light his charge, when every hour
That finds that charge delayed, is a new death.
This for the faith in which I trust; and hence
I can abjure so well the idle arts
These pedants strive to learn and teach; Black Arts,
Great Works, the Secret and Sublime, forsooth—

336| *MS:* strive . . . enticed § written over by § strive—enticed *1835:* strive?—enticed 337| *MS:* course *1835:* course— *1849:* course, 338| *MS:* Where error is not, but success is sure . . . *1835:* sure. *1849:* With no success forever in its eyes! *1863:* Without success 339| *MS:*—How <> own *1835:* How <> own, 341| *MS:* me—is *1835:* me? Is 342| *MS:* less *1849:* less, 343| *MS:* promptings . . . what *1835:* promptings? What *1868:* Promptings! What 344| *MS:* all—your loves, your cares *1835:* all; your loves, your cares, 345| *MS:* life——all *1835:* life—all 346| *MS:* impart—————— *1835:* impart. *1849:* impart! *1863:* He *1868:* he 347| *MS:* gier-eagle why she stoops § *she* written above the line § *1888:* geier-eagle 348| *MS:* abyss— *1835:* abyss! *1849:* abyss, 349| *MS:* fullgrown *1835:* first! *1849:* full-grown <> first, 351| *MS:* sky! —— § written over by § sky!— *1835:* sky! 352| *MS:* needs;—nor *1835:* needs; nor *1849:* needs! Nor 353| *1863:* His *1868:* his 354| *MS:* delayed is <> death: *1835:* delay'd <> death. *1849:* delayed, is 355| *MS:*——Thus for <> trust;—and *1835:* Thus <> trust; and *1849:* This for 356| *MS:* the secret Arts *1835:* arts *1849:* the idle arts 357| *MS:* learn—the Magic they *1849:* learn and teach: Black Arts, 358| *MS:* So reverence——I shall scarcely seek to know *1835:* reverence. I *1849:* Great Works, the Secret and Sublime, forsooth—

Let others prize: too intimate a tie
Connects me with our God! A sullen fiend
To do my bidding, fallen and hateful sprites
To help me—what are these, at best, beside
God helping, God directing everywhere,
So that the earth shall yield her secrets up,
And every object there be charged to strike,
Teach, gratify her master God appoints?
And I am young, my Festus, happy and free!
I can devote myself; I have a life
To give; I, singled out for this, the One!
Think, think! the wide East, where all Wisdom sprung;
The bright South, where she dwelt; the hopeful North,
All are passed o'er—it lights on me! 'Tis time
New hopes should animate the world, new light
Should dawn from new revealings to a race
Weighed down so long, forgotten so long; thus shall
The heaven reserved for us at last receive
Creatures whom no unwonted splendours blind,
But ardent to confront the unclouded blaze
Whose beams not seldom blessed their pilgrimage,
Not seldom glorified their life below.

359| *MS:* If it exist: too *1849:* Let others prize: too 360| *MS:* God: . . a § written over by § God:—a *1835:* God. A sullen friend *1849:* God! A sullen fiend 361| *MS:* bidding——fallen § written over by § bidding—fallen *1849:* bidding, fallen 362| *MS:* me——what *1835:* me—what 363| *MS:* God every where— § above §, sustaining and directing *1835:* where, sustaining *1849:* God helping, God directing everywhere, 364| *MS:* up *1849:* up, 365| *MS:* object shall be *1863:* object there be 366| *MS:* To teach, to gratify, and to suggest———§ written over by § suggest?— *1835:* suggest? *1849:* Teach, gratify, her master God appoints? *1863:* gratify her 367| *MS:* young, Festus,—happy *1835:* Festus happy *1849:* young, my Festus 368| *MS:* myself—I *1835:* myself; I 369| *MS:* give— I who am singled out for this . . . § written over by § this ——— give; I, who <> this. *1849:* I, singled out for this, the One! 370| *MS:* Think, think,—the <> where old wisdom sprung *1835:* Think, think; the wide east <> Wisdom sprung; *1863:* wide East, where all Wisdom *1888:* Think, think! the 371| *MS:*—The <> South where she dwelt—the populous North *1835:* The <> south, where she dwelt; the <> north, *1849:* dwelt; the hopeful north, *1863:* South <> North, 372| *MS:*——All <> me!—'tis *1835:* All <> me. 'Tis *1849:* me! 'Tis 373| *MS:* world——new § written over by § world—new *1849:* world, new 376| *MS:* The Heaven <> last, receive *1835:* heaven <> last receive *1849:* us, at *1868:* us at 377| *MS:* No creatures whom unwonted *1849:* Creatures whom no unwonted 378| *1888:* blaze. *1889:* blaze 379| *MS:* seldom lit their *1849:* seldom blessed their

FESTUS My words have their old fate and make faint stand
Against your glowing periods. Call this, truth—
Why not pursue it in a fast retreat,
Some one of Learning's many palaces,
After approved example?—seeking there
Calm converse with the great dead, soul to soul,
Who laid up treasure with the like intent
—So lift yourself into their airy place,
And fill out full their unfilled careers,
Unravelling the knots their baffled skill
Pronounced inextricable, true!—but left
Far less confused. A fresh eye, a fresh hand,
Might do much at their vigour's waning-point;
Succeeding with new-breathed new-hearted force,
As at old games the runner snatched the torch
From runner still: this way success might be.
But you have coupled with your enterprise,
An arbitrary self-repugnant scheme

382–383| *MS:* Beside § cancelled by § Against your <> periods I renounce / All hope of learning further on this head, / And what I next advance holds good as well / With one assured that all these things are true; / For might not such seek out a fast retreat *1835:* periods: I <> / <> head; / <> /// <> retreat— *1849:* periods. Call this, truth— / Why not pursue it in a fast retreat, *1863:* a vast retreat *1868:* a fast retreat, 383–385| *MS:* retreat / After <> example, there § written over by § example? there to have *1835:* retreat— / example—there *1849:* retreat, / Some one of Learning's many palaces, / After <> example; seeking there *1863:* example ?—seeking 386| *MS:* Dead *1835:* dead—soul to soul— *1849:* dead, soul to soul, 387| *MS:*—Who <> intent,——— § written over by § intent,— *1835:* Who <> intent? 388| *MS:* To lift himself <> place— *1835:* place, *1849:*—So lift yourself into 389| *MS:* To fill <> careers— *1835:* unfulfill'd careers, *1849:* And fill <> unfulfilled 390| *MS:*——Unraveling *1835:* Unravelling 391| *MS:* inextricable, but surely left *1849:* inextricable, true!—but left 392| *MS:* confused—a fresh eye,<> hand *1835:* confused? A fresh eye *1863:* confused. A fresh eye 393| *MS:* much——at <> waning-point *1835:* much at <> waning-point— *1849:* waning-point; 394| *MS:* new-breathed and untired force *1835:* force— *1849:* and earnest force, *1863:* and untired force, *1868:* new-breathed new-hearted force, 395| *MS:* games a runner *1835:* snatch'd *1849:* snatched *1868:* games the runner 396| *MS:* still:——such one might well do this: *1835:* still? Such <> this. *1849:* still: this way success might be. 397| *MS:*——But you have linked to his your enterprize *1835:* But <> link'd to this, your enterprize, *1849:* have coupled with your enterprise, 398| *MS:* arbitrary and most perplexing scheme *1849:* arbitrary self-repugnant scheme

Of seeking it in strange and untried paths.
What books are in the desert? Writes the sea
The secret of her yearning in vast caves
Where yours will fall the first of human feet?
Has wisdom sat there and recorded aught
You press to read? Why turn aside from her
To visit, where her vesture never glanced,
Now—solitudes consigned to barrenness
By God's decree, which who shall dare impugn?
Now—ruins where she paused but would not stay,
Old ravaged cities that, renouncing her,
She called an endless curse on, so it came:
Or worst of all, now—men you visit, men,
Ignoblest troops who never heard her voice
Or hate it, men without one gift from Rome
Or Athens,—these shall Aureole's teachers be!
Rejecting past example, practice, precept,
Aidless 'mid these he thinks to stand alone:
Thick like a glory round the Stagirite
Your rivals throng, the sages: here stand you!
Whatever you may protest, knowledge is not
Paramount in your love; or for her sake
You would collect all help from every source—

399–415| *MS:* paths,—/ Rejecting *1835:* paths; / <> precept— *1849:* paths. / What books are in the desert? writes the sea / The secret of her yearning in vast caves / Where yours will fall the first of human feet? / Has Wisdom sate there and recorded aught / You press to read? Why turn aside from her / To visit, where her vesture never glanced, / Now—solitudes consigned to barrenness / By God's decree, which who shall dare impugn? / Now—ruins where she paused but would not stay, / Old ravaged cities that, renouncing her, / She called an endless curse on, so it came— / Or, worst of all, now—men you visit, men, / Ignoblest troops that never heard her voice, / Or hate it, men without one gift from Rome / Or Athens,—these shall Aureole's teachers be! / Rejecting <> precept, 400| *1868:* desert? Writes 403| *1863:* sat *1868:* Has wisdom 410| *1863:* came: 411| *1868:* Or worst 412| *1868:* troops who never <> voice 416–418| *MS:* That so you may stand aidless and alone— — § written over by § alone: / —If in this wild rejection you regard / Mankind and their award of fame,—'tis clear *1835:* fame—'tis clear, *1849:* Aidless 'mid these he thinks to stand alone: / Thick like a glory round the Stagyrite / Your rivals throng, the sages: here stand you! *1863:* Stagirite 419| *MS:* Whate'er *1868:* Whatever 420| *MS:* love—or *1835:* love; or 421| *MS:* source; *1835:* source—

Rival, assistant, friend, foe, all would merge
In the broad class of those who showed her haunts,
And those who showed them not.

PARACELSUS

What shall I say?
Festus, from childhood I have been possessed
By a fire—by a true fire, or faint or fierce,
As from without some master, so it seemed,
Repressed or urged its current: this but ill
Expresses what would I convey: but rather
I will believe an angel ruled me thus,
Than that my soul's own workings, own high nature,
So became manifest. I knew not then
What whispered in the evening, and spoke out
At midnight. If some mortal, born too soon,
Were laid away in some great trance—the ages
Coming and going all the while—till dawned
His true time's advent; and could then record
The words they spoke who kept watch by his bed,—
Then I might tell more of the breath so light
Upon my eyelids, and the fingers light
Among my hair. Youth is confused; yet never
So dull was I but, when that spirit passed,

422| *MS:*—Friend, foe assistant, rival, all *1835:* Friend *1849:* Rival or helper, friend, foe, all *1863:* Rival, assistant, friend 423| *MS:* shewed her haunts *1835:* show'd *1849:* showed her haunts, 424| *MS:* shewed it § cancelled by § them not:—PARACELSUS < > say?— — *1835:* show'd them not. PARACELSUS < > say? *1849:* showed 425| *MS:*—Festus *1835:* Festus 426| *MS:* fire— —by § written over by § fire—by < > fire— —or faint or fierce *1835:* true fire, or faint or fierce, 427| *MS:* Master *1835:* master < > seem'd, *1849:* seemed, 428| *MS:* current;—this *1835:* Repress'd < > current: this *1849:* Repressed 429| *MS:* convey— —but *1835:* convey—but *1863:* convey: but *1888:* what would I convey *1889:* what I would convey 430| *MS:* Angel *1835:* angel 431| *MS:* nature *1835:* nature, 432| *MS:* manifest;— —I § written over by § manifest;— *1835:* manifest. I 433| *MS:* evening and *1835:* whisper'd < > evening, and *1849:* whispered
434| *MS:* midnight:— —if § written over by § might:—if *1835:* midnight. I
435| *MS:* trance— § above §, the *1835:* trance—the 436| *MS:* while,—until *1835:* while—until *1849:* while—till dawned 437| *MS:* advent—and *1835:* advent, and *1863:* advent; and 438| *MS:* They < > bed, *1835:* they 1849: bed,— 440| *MS:* eyelids— —and § written over by § eyelids—and *1835:* eyelids, and *1849:* fingers warm *1868:* fingers light 441| *MS:* hair;— —youth § written over by § hair;—youth is confused, yet *1835:* hair. Youth is confused; yet 442| *MS:* I, but when < > Spirit passed *1835:* I but < > pass'd *1849:* but, when < > passed,

I turned to him, scarce consciously, as turns
A water-snake when fairies cross his sleep.
And having this within me and about me
While Einsiedeln, its mountains, lakes and woods
Confined me—what oppressive joy was mine
When life grew plain, and I first viewed the thronged,
The everlasting concourse of mankind!
Believe that ere I joined them, ere I knew
The purpose of the pageant, or the place
Consigned me in its ranks—while, just awake,
Wonder was freshest and delight most pure—
'Twas then that least supportable appeared
A station with the brightest of the crowd,
A portion with the proudest of them all.
And from the tumult in my breast, this only
Could I collect, that I must thenceforth die
Or elevate myself far, far above
The gorgeous spectacle. I seemed to long
At once to trample on, yet save mankind,
To make some unexampled sacrifice
In their behalf, to wring some wondrous good
From heaven or earth for them, to perish, winning

443| *1835:* turn'd *1849:* turned 444| *MS:* sleep:— — § written over by § sleep:— *1835:* sleep: *1849:* sleep. 445| *MS:*—And *1835:* And 446| *MS:* When Einsiedeln, its hills and lakes and plains *1835:* hills, and lakes, and *1849:* While Einsiedeln, its mountains, lakes, and woods *1863:* lakes and 447| *MS:* me, what *1835:* me—what 448| *MS:* plain—and <> thronged *1835:* plain, and <> view'd the throng'd, *1849:* viewed the thronged, 449| *MS:* The evermoving concourse of mankind! . . . *1835:* ever-moving, concourse of mankind! *1849:* ever-moving concourse *1863:* The everlasting concourse 450| *MS:* them,—ere *1835:* join'd them—ere *1849:* joined *1863:* them, ere 451| *MS:* pageant— — —or § written over by § pageant—or *1835:* pageant, or 452| *MS:* Consigned to me within its ranks,—while yet *1835:* Consign'd <> ranks—while *1849:* Consigned *1863:* Consigned me in its <> while, just awake 453| *MS:* pure, . . . *1835:* pure— 454| *MS:* . . . 'Twas *1835:* 'Twas <> appear'd *1849:* appeared 455| *1835:* crowd; *1849:* crowd, 456| *MS:* all!— — *1835:* all! *1863:* all. 457| *MS:* . . And § written over by §—And *1835:* And 458| *MS:* collect . . . that *1835:* collect—that *1863:* collect, that 460| *MS:* spectacle;—what seemed a longing *1835:* spectacle; what seem'd *1849:* spectacle. I seemed to long 461| *MS:* To trample on yet save Mankind at once . . . . . . § written over by § once— *1835:* mankind *1849:* At once to trample on, yet save mankind— *1863:* mankind, 462| *MS:*—To *1835:* To 463| *MS:* behalf—to *1863:* behalf, to 464| *MS:* Heaven <> them . . to § written over by § them—to *1835:* heaven *1863:* them, to

Eternal weal in the act: as who should dare
Pluck out the angry thunder from its cloud,
That, all its gathered flame discharged on him,
No storm might threaten summer's azure sleep:
Yet never to be mixed with men so much
As to have part even in my own work, share
In my own largess. Once the feat achieved,
I would withdraw from their officious praise,
Would gently put aside their profuse thanks.
Like some knight traversing a wilderness,
Who, on his way, may chance to free a tribe
Of desert-people from their dragon-foe;
When all the swarthy race press round to kiss
His feet, and choose him for their king, and yield
Their poor tents, pitched among the sand-hills, for
His realm: and he points, smiling, to his scarf
Heavy with riveled gold, his burgonet
Gay set with twinkling stones—and to the East,
Where these must be displayed!

FESTUS Good: let us hear
No more about your nature, "which first shrank
From all that marked you out apart from men!"

PARACELSUS I touch on that; these words but analyse

465| *MS:* act . . as *1835:* act: as 466| *MS:* cloud *1835:* cloud, 467| *1835:* gather'd *1849:* gathered 468| *MS:* Summer's azure weather . . . : § : added in pencil § *1835:* summer's <> weather— *1849:* azure sleep: 469| *MS:*—Yet <> with them, so *1835:* Yet <> mix'd <> them so *1849:* mixed with men so 470| *MS:* work,—share *1835:* work—share 471| *MS:* largess, . . once § written over by § largess,—once <> achieved *1835:* largess. Once <> achieved, 473| *MS:*—Would <> thanks *1835:* Would <> thanks, *1849:* thanks: *1863:* thanks. 474| *MS:*—Like <> wilderness *1835:* Like <> wilderness, 476| *MS:* Desert-people <> dragon-foe, *1835:* desert-people <> dragon-foe; 477| *MS:* Race *1835:* race 478| *MS:* feet and <> King *1835:* feet and <> king 479| *MS:* tents pitched <> sand-hills for *1835:* tents, pitch'd <> sand-hills, for *1849:* pitched 480| *MS:* realm——and he points smiling to *1835:* realm; and he points, smiling to his scarf, *1863:* scarf 481| *1835:* rivel'd gold—his burgonet, *1849:* riveled gold, his *1863:* burgonet 482| *MS:* East *1835:* east, *1863:* East, 483| *MS:* displayed . . . FESTUS Good: . . let § written over by § Good:— *1835:* display'd . . . FESTUS Good: let us *1849:* displayed! FESTUS 484| *MS:* nature "which *1835:* nature, "which 485| *MS:* men." *1849:* men!" 486| *MS:* on it:—I would but *1835:* it: I *1849:* on that: these words but

The first mad impulse: 'twas as brief as fond,
For as I gazed again upon the show,
I soon distinguished here and there a shape
Palm-wreathed and radiant, forehead and full eye.
Well pleased was I their state should thus at once
Interpret my own thoughts:—"Behold the clue
To all," I rashly said, "and what I pine
To do, these have accomplished: we are peers.
They know and therefore rule: I, too, will know!"
You were beside me, Festus, as you say;
You saw me plunge in their pursuits whom fame
Is lavish to attest the lords of mind,
Not pausing to make sure the prize in view
Would satiate my cravings when obtained,
But since they strove I strove. Then came a slow
And strangling failure. We aspired alike,
Yet not the meanest plodder, Tritheim counts
A marvel, but was all-sufficient, strong,
Or staggered only at his own vast wits;
While I was restless, nothing satisfied,
Distrustful, most perplexed. I would slur over
That struggle; suffice it, that I loathed myself

487| *MS:* That first mad impulse . . 'twas < > fond; *1835:* impulse—'twas *1863:* The first mad impulse: 'twas 488| *MS:* show *1835:* show, 489| *1835:* distinguish'd *1849:* distinguished 490| *MS:* eye:— *1835:* eye.
493| *MS:* all—"I rashly said—" and all I *1835:* all," I rashly said, "and *1849:* and what I 494| *MS:* These < > accomplished—we are peers! *1835:* these < > accomplish'd: we *1849:* accomplished *1863:* peers. 495| *MS:* know § written over by § Know < > rule——I too will know!" § written over by § Know!" *1835:* know, and < > rule . . . I *1849:* rule: I, too, will 496| *MS:*—You < > say—— *1835:* You < > say; 497| *1835:* Fame *1863:* fame
498| *MS:* Lords of Mind, *1835:* lords of mind, *1849:* mind; *1868:* mind,
500| *MS:* obtained . . *1835:* obtain'd— *1849:* obtained— *1863:* obtained,
501| *MS:*——But as they strove, I strove . . then § written over by § strove:—then *1835:* But < > strove I strove: then *1849:* But since they < > I strove. Then
502| *MS:* failure——we < > alike *1835:* failure. We < > alike, 503| *MS:* plodder Tritheim deems *1849:* Tritheim schools *1863:* plodder, Tritheim counts 504| *MS:* all-sufficient, well content, *1849:* But faced me, all-sufficient, all-content *1863:* A marvel, but was all-sufficient, strong, 505| *MS:* And staggered < > own strong wits, *1835:* stagger'd < > wits; *1849:* Or staggered *1863:* own vast wits; 506| *MS:*—While *1835:* While 507| *MS:* perplexed———I *1835:* perplex'd. I *1849:* perplexed 508| *MS:* struggle——suffice *1835:* struggle; suffice

As weak compared with them, yet felt somehow
A mighty power was brooding, taking shape
Within me; and this lasted till one night
When, as I sat revolving it and more,
A still voice from without said—"Seest thou not,
Desponding child, whence spring defeat and loss?
Even from thy strength. Consider: hast thou gazed
Presumptuously on wisdom's countenance,
No veil between; and can thy faltering hands,
Unguided by the brain the sight absorbs,
Pursue their task as earnest blinkers do
Whom radiance ne'er distracted? Live their life
If thou wouldst share their fortune, choose their eyes
Unfed by splendour. Let each task present
Its petty good to thee. Waste not thy gifts
In profitless waiting for the gods' descent,
But have some idol of thine own to dress
With their array. Know, not for knowing's sake,
But to become a star to men for ever;
Know, for the gain it gets, the praise it brings,
The wonder it inspires, the love it breeds:
Look one step onward, and secure that step!"

511| *MS:* me——and § written over by § me—and *1835:* me; and *1849:* me: and *1863:* me; and 512| *MS:* sate *1863:* sat 513| *MS:* said "See'st thou not *1835:* said—"See'st thou not, 514| *MS:* springs *1849:* whence came defeat *1863:* whence spring defeat 515| *MS:*—Even <> strength:—know better: hast *1835:* Even <> strength. Know *1849:* strength. Consider: hast 516| *MS:* Presumptuous on Wisdom's *1849:* Presumptuously *1868:* wisdom's 517–520| *MS:* between, and <> hands / Pursue as well the toil their earnest blinking, / Whom <> distracts, so clear descries? *1835:* between; and *1849:* thy hands which falter / Unguided by thy brain the mighty sight / Continues to absorb, pursue their task / On earth like these around thee—what their sense/ Which radiance ne'er distracted, clear *1863:* thy faltering hands / <> the sight absorbs / Pursue their task as earnest blinkers do / Whom radiance ne'er distracted? Live their life *1868:* by the brain the sight absorbs, 521| *MS:*—If *1835:* If <> eyes *1849:* choose their life, *1863:* choose their eyes 522| *MS:* splendor——let § written over by § splendor;—let *1835:* splendour. Let 523| *MS:* thee . . waste § written over by § thee—waste *1835:* thee. Waste 524| *MS:* God's *1835:* gods' 526| *MS:* array:—Know *1835:* array. Know 527| *MS:* Men *1835:* men for ever. *1868:* ever; 528| *MS:* Know! for *1835:* Know, for 529| *MS:* breeds——— *1835:* breeds. *1868:* breeds: 530| *MS:* onward and <> step"———— § above § step" . . . *1835:* onward, and <> step." *1868:* step!"

And I smiled as one never smiles but once,
Then first discovering my own aim's extent,
Which sought to comprehend the works of God,
And God himself, and all God's intercourse
With the human mind; I understood, no less,
My fellows' studies, whose true worth I saw,
But smiled not, well aware who stood by me.
And softer came the voice—"There is a way:
'Tis hard for flesh to tread therein, imbued
With frailty—hopeless, if indulgence first
Have ripened inborn germs of sin to strength:
Wilt thou adventure for my sake and man's,
Apart from all reward?" And last it breathed—
"Be happy, my good soldier; I am by thee,
Be sure, even to the end!"—I answered not,
Knowing him. As he spoke, I was endued
With comprehension and a steadfast will;
And when he ceased, my brow was sealed his own.
If there took place no special change in me,
How comes it all things wore a different hue
Thenceforward?—pregnant with vast consequence,
Teeming with grand result, loaded with fate?

531| *1835:* once; *1868:* once, 532| *MS:* my aim's extent *1835:* extent, *1849:* my own aim's extent 534| *MS:*—And God himself——and § written over by § himself—and *1835:* And God himself, and 535| *MS:* With our own mind;——and § written over by § mind;—and how such shewed beside *1835:* mind; and <> show'd *1849:* With the human mind; I understood, no less,
536| *MS:* fellow's studies—whose <> saw *1835:* studies, whose <> saw, *1863:* fellows' 537| *MS:* me—— *1835:* me. *1863:* Who *1868:* who
538| *MS:* Voice <> *is* a way— *1835:* voice *1849:* is *1863:* way:
539| *MS:*—Tis *1835:* 'Tis 540| *MS:* With weakness——hopeless *1835:* weakness—hopeless *1849:* With frailty—hopeless 541| *MS:* inborn sins to strength——wilt thou *1835:* ripen'd *1849:* ripened inborn germs of sin to strength: 542| *MS:* Adventure for my sake and for thy kind's § written over by § Kind's *1835:* kind's, *1849:* Wilt thou adventure <> and man's,
543| *MS:* Apart for all reward?"——and <> breathed *1835:* reward?" And <> breathed— *1849:* Apart from all 544| *MS:* soldier—I *1835:* soldier; I 545| *MS:* end!"——I *1835:* end!" . . . I answer'd *1849:* end!"—I answered 546| *MS:* Him——as § written over by § Him:—as he spoke I *1835:* him. As he spoke, I *1849:* Him *1868:* him 547| *MS:* will, *1835:* will; 548| *MS:* ceased, my fate was sealed forever:— *1835:* seal'd for ever. *1849:* He ceased, my brow was sealed His own. *1868:* he <> his 549| *MS:* me *1835:* me, 551| *1835:* consequence— *1863:* consequence,
552| *MS:* results,—loaded with fate,— *1835:* results—loaded <> fate; *1863:* results, loaded <> fate? *1868:* result

So that when, quailing at the mighty range
Of secret truths which yearn for birth, I haste
To contemplate undazzled some one truth,
Its bearing and effects alone—at once
What was a speck expands into a star,
Asking a life to pass exploring thus,
Till I near craze. I go to prove my soul!
I see my way as birds their trackless way.
I shall arrive! what time, what circuit first,
I ask not: but unless God send his hail
Or blinding fireballs, sleet or stifling snow,
In some time, his good time, I shall arrive:
He guides me and the bird. In his good time!
MICHAL Vex him no further, Festus; it is so!
FESTUS Just thus you help me ever. This would hold
Were it the trackless air, and not a path
Inviting you, distinct with footprints yet
Of many a mighty marcher gone that way.
You may have purer views than theirs, perhaps,
But they were famous in their day—the proofs
Remain. At least accept the light they lend.
PARACELSUS Their light! the sum of all is briefly this:
They laboured and grew famous, and the fruits

553| *MS:* when quailing *1868:* when, quailing 554| *MS:* truths yearning *1849:* truths which yearn 555| *MS:* Truth— *1835:* truth, 556| *MS:* alone— § above §, at *1835:* alone, at *1849:* alone—at 557| *MS:* star— *1835:* star, 558| *MS:* Demanding life to be explored alone,— *1835:* alone— *1849:* Asking a life to pass exploring thus, 559| *MS:* craze . . I § written over by § craze:—I *1835:* craze. I 560| *MS:* trackless way *1835:* Trackless way— *1863:* trackless way. 561| *MS:*— — I <> arrive— —what § written over by § arrive!—what time *1835:* I <> arrive! what 562| *MS:* not— —but *1835:* not: but *1863:* His *1868:* his 563| *MS:* fire-balls *1835:* sleet, or *1863:* sleet or *1868:* fireballs 564| *MS:* arrive:— *1835:* time—his <> time—I *1863:* time, His <> time, I *1868:* his 565| *MS:* bird— — — in § written over by § bird—in *1835:* bird. In *1863:* His *1868:* his 566| *MS:* Festus—it *1835:* Festus; it 567| *MS:* you answer ever— —this *1835:* ever. This *1849:* you help me ever. 568| *MS:* it the trackless air and § *the* inserted above the line § *1849:* air, and 569| *MS:* foot-prints *1835:* footprints 570| *MS:* mighty spirit gone <> way— — *1835:* way. *1863:* mighty marcher gone 571| *MS:* views, for aught I know *1835:* know; *1849:* views than theirs, perhaps, 573| *MS:* Remain— —at § written over by § Remain:—at *1835:* Remain. At 574| *MS:* light!—the *1835:* light! the *1863:* this; 575| *MS:* laboured after their own fashion— —the *1835:* labour'd <> fashion; the *1849:* laboured, and grew famous; and the *1863:* laboured and <> famous, and

Are best seen in a dark and groaning earth
Given over to a blind and endless strife
With evils, what of all their lore abates?
No; I reject and spurn them utterly
And all they teach. Shall I still sit beside
Their dry wells, with a white lip and filmed eye,
While in the distance heaven is blue above
Mountains where sleep the unsunned tarns?

FESTUS And yet
As strong delusions have prevailed ere now.
Men have set out as gallantly to seek
Their ruin. I have heard of such: yourself
Avow all hitherto have failed and fallen.

MICHAL Nay, Festus, when but as the pilgrims faint
Through the drear way, do you expect to see
Their city dawn amid the clouds afar?

PARACELSUS Ay, sounds it not like some old well-known tale?
For me, I estimate their works and them
So rightly, that at times I almost dream
I too have spent a life the sages' way,
And tread once more familiar paths. Perchance
I perished in an arrogant self-reliance
Ages ago; and in that act, a prayer
For one more chance went up so earnest, so

576| *1835:* earth, *1863:* earth 578| *MS:* evils their best lore cannot abate—— *1835:* abate. *1849:* evils, which of all you Gods bates? *1863:* evils, what of all their lore bates? 579| *MS:*——No, I *1835:* No; I <> utterly, *1863:* utterly 580| *MS:* teach——shall § written over by § teach:— *1835:* teach. Shall 581| *MS:* with white <> eye *1835:* lips *1849:* with a white lip <> eye, 583| *MS:* tarns——FESTUS § written over by § tarns?—FESTUS *1835:* unsunn'd tarns? FESTUS *1849:* unsunned 584| *MS:* now . . . § written over by § now— *1835:* prevail'd ere now: *1849:* prevailed *1863:* now.
585| *MS:*—Men *1835:* Men 586| *MS:* ruin——I <> such——yourself *1835:* ruin; I <> such—yourself *1863:* ruin. I <> such; yourself 587| *MS:* fallen, . . . § written over by § fallen,— *1835:* fail'd and fallen. *1849:* failed
589| *MS:* For the *1849:* Through the 590| *MS:* afar! *1849:* dawn afar amid the clouds? *1863:* dawn amid the clouds afar? 591| *MS:*—Ay <> well known *1835:* Ay <> well-known 592| *MS:*—For *1835:* For
593| *MS:* I wellnigh dream *1835:* well nigh *1849:* I almost dream
594| *MS:* the selfsame way— § above §, *1835:* way— *1849:* the sages' way,
595| *MS:*—Treat once again an old life's course—perchance *1835:* Tread <> course. Perchance *1849:* And tread once more familiar paths. Perchance 596| *1835:* perish'd *1849:* perished 597| *MS:* And age ago——and *1835:* ago; and *1863:* Ages ago 598| *MS:* earnest,—so *1835:* earnest—so *1849:* earnest, so

Instinct with better light let in by death,
That life was blotted out—not so completely
But scattered wrecks enough of it remain,
Dim memories, as now, when once more seems
The goal in sight again. All which, indeed,
Is foolish, and only means—the flesh I wear,
The earth I tread, are not more clear to me
Than my belief, explained to you or no.
FESTUS And who am I, to challenge and dispute
That clear belief? I will divest all fear.
MICHAL Then Aureole is God's commissary! he shall
Be great and grand—and all for us!
PARACELSUS No, sweet!
Not great and grand. If I can serve mankind
'Tis well; but there our intercourse must end:
I never will be served by those I serve.
FESTUS Look well to this; here is a plague-spot, here,
Disguise it how you may! 'Tis true, you utter
This scorn while by our side and loving us;
'Tis but a spot as yet: but it will break
Into a hideous blotch if overlooked.
How can that course be safe which from the first
Produces carelessness to human love?

599–600| *MS:* Imbued with < > Death, / So free from all past sin— —that it was heard: / —That < > out— —not *1835:* Death— / < > sin—that < > heard . . . / That out—not *1849:* Instinct with < > Death, / That *1863:* death,
601| *MS:* enough remain to wake *1835:* scatter'd *1849:* scattered < > enough of it remain, **602**| *MS:* memories; as *1849:* when seems once more *1863:* memories, as *1868:* when once more seems **603**| *MS:* again: . . All which is foolish *1835:* again: all *1849:* which, indeed, *1863:* again. All **604**| *MS:* Indeed and < > means the form I bear *1835:* indeed, and < > means—the *1849:* Is foolish, and < > the flesh I wear, **605–607**| *MS:* me. / And < > I to *1849:* me / Than my belief, explained to you or no. / And *1863:* I, to
608| *MS:* belief?— —I < > devest *1835:* belief? . . . I *1849:* belief? I put away all *1863:* I will divest all **610**| *MS:* grand— —and *1835:* grand—and *1863:* Sweet! *1868:* sweet! **611**| *MS:* great or grand:—if *1835:* grand. If *1849:* great and grand If *1863:* grand. If **612**| *MS:* Tis well— —but < > end:— *1835:* 'Tis well—but < > end: *1863:* well; but **613**| *MS:* serve! *1835:* serve. **614**| *MS: here* < > plague-spot, veil it, *1835:* this; *here* *1849:* here < > plague-spot, here, **615**| *MS:* you will:—'tis *1835:* will: 'tis *1849:* you may! 'Tis **616**| *MS:* us— — *1835:* us— *1849:* us;
617| *MS:* yet;—but *1835:* yet; but *1863:* yet: but **618**| *MS:* overlooked:— *1835:* overlook'd. *1849:* overlooked.

It seems you have abjured the helps which men
Who overpass their kind, as you would do,
Have humbly sought; I dare not thoroughly probe
This matter, lest I learn too much. Let be
That popular praise would little instigate
Your efforts, nor particular approval
Reward you; put reward aside; alone
You shall go forth upon your arduous task,
None shall assist you, none partake your toil,
None share your triumph: still you must retain
Some one to cast your glory on, to share
Your rapure with. Were I elect like you,
I would encircle me with love, and raise
A rampart of my fellows; it should seem
Impossible for me to fail, so watched
By gentle friends who made my cause their own.
They should ward off fate's envy—the great gift,
Extravagant when claimed by me alone,
Being so a gift to them as well as me.
If danger daunted me or ease seduced,
How calmly their sad eyes should gaze reproach!
MICHAL O Aureole, can I sing when all alone,
Without first calling, in my fancy, both

621| *MS:*—I know:—you *1835:* I know you *1849:* It seems you **623**| *MS:* sought—I *1835:* sought. I *1849:* sought—I *1863:* sought; I **624**| *MS:* much:—let be, *1835:* much: let be *1849:* be, *1863:* much. Let **626**| *MS:* efforts——or particular *1835:* efforts—or *1849:* efforts, nor **627**| *MS:* aside;—you shall *1835:* aside; you *1849:* aside; alone **628**| *MS:* Go <> task alone, *1849:* You shall go <> task, **629**| *MS:* you—none <> toil—— § written over by § toil— *1849:* you, none <> toil, **630**| *MS:* triumph:—still *1835:* triumph—still *1863:* triumph: still **631**| *MS:* to trust your glory to,—to *1835:* to; to *1849:* to cast your glory on, to **632**| *MS:* with;—had I been chosen like you *1835:* with. Had *1849:* with. Were I elect like you, **633**| *MS:* I should encircle me with love—should raise § *me* inserted above the line § *1849:* I would encircle <> love, and raise **634**| *MS:* of kind wishes——it *1835:* wishes; it *1849:* of my fellows; it **635**| *MS:* Impossible for me § *for* inserted above the line § *1835:* watch'd *1849:* watched **636**| *MS:* own; *1863:* own. **637**| *MS:*—They <> envy—the great boon, *1835:* Fate's envy—the *1849:* great gift, *1863:* fate's **638**| *1835:* claim'd *1849:* claimed **639**| *MS:* Being a <> me: . . . § written over by § me:— *1835:* me. *1849:* Being so a **640**| *MS:* If ease seduced or danger <> me, *1849:* If danger <> me or ease seduced, **641**| *MS:* reproach!—— *1835:* reproach! **642**| *MS:* sing, tho' all *1835:* sing though *1849:* sing when all

To listen by my side—even I! And you?
Do you not feel this? Say that you feel this!
PARACELSUS I feel 'tis pleasant that my aims, at length
Allowed their weight, should be supposed to need
A further strengthening in these goodly helps!
My course allures for its own sake, its sole
Intrinsic worth; and ne'er shall boat of mine
Adventure forth for gold and apes at once.
Your sages say, "if human, therefore weak:"
If weak, more need to give myself entire
To my pursuit; and by its side, all else . . .
No matter! I deny myself but little
In waiving all assistance save its own.
Would there were some real sacrifice to make!
Your friends the sages threw their joys away,
While I must be content with keeping mine.
FESTUS But do not cut yourself from human weal!
You cannot thrive—a man that dares affect
To spend his life in service to his kind
For no reward of theirs, unbound to them
By any tie; nor do so, Aureole! No—
There are strange punishments for such. Give up

644| *MS:* side——even I! —and you— — § written over by § you?— *1835:* side—even I! And you? 645| *MS:* this?—say <> this!— *1835:* this! *1863:* this? Say 646| *MS:* pleasant, that *1835:* pleasant that 647| *MS:* Allow'd *1849:* Allowed 648–649| *MS:* helps! / Once more (since I am forced to speak as one / Who has full liberty at his discretion) / My <> sake———its *1835:* sake—its *1849:* helps! / My *1868:* sake, its 650| *MS:* worth, and *1835:* worth; and 651| *MS:* once . . . § written over by § once:— *1835:* once: 652| *MS:* say "if <> weak:"— — § written over by § weak:"— *1835:* weak:" *1849:* say, "if 654| *MS:* pursuit;—and <> else— — § above § . . *1835:* pursuit; and <> else . . . 655| *MS:*——No matter:—I *1835:* No matter: I *1849:* matter! I 656| *MS:* own, *1835:* own— *1863:* own. 657| *MS:* And I regret it;—there's no sacrifice *1835:* it; there's *1849:* Would there were some real sacrifice to make! 658| *MS:* To make:—the sages threw so much away *1835:* make; the *1849:* Your friends the sages threw their joys away, 659| *MS:* with gaining all. *1849:* with keeping mine. 660| *MS:* weal! . . *1835:* weal! *1849:* weal? *1863:* weal! 661| *MS:* . . You <> thrive ———a *1835:* You <> thrive—a 662| *1835:* kind, *1868:* kind 663| *MS:* theirs—nor bound *1835:* theirs, nor *1868:* theirs, unbound 664| *MS:* tie——nor § written over by § tie!—nor <> Aureole! *1835:* tie; nor *1849:* Aureole! No— 665| *MS:* for such . . . although *1835:* such; although *1849:* such. Give up

(Although no visible good flow thence) some part
Of the glory to another; hiding thus,
Even from yourself, that all is for yourself.
Say, say almost to God—"I have done all
For her, not for myself!"

PARACELSUS

And who but lately
Was to rejoice in my success like you?
Whom should I love but both of you?

FESTUS

I know not:
But know this, you, that 'tis no will of mine
You should abjure the lofty claims you make;
And this the cause—I can no longer seek
To overlook the truth, that there would be
A monstrous spectacle upon the earth,
Beneath the pleasant sun, among the trees:
—A being knowing not what love is. Hear me!
You are endowed with faculties which bear
Annexed to them as 'twere a dispensation
To summon meaner spirits to do their will
And gather round them at their need; inspiring
Such with a love themselves can never feel,
Passionless 'mid their passionate votaries.
I know not if you joy in this or no,

666| *MS:* thence, give up some *1849:* (Although no <> thence) some part
667| *MS:* Of your renown to another;—so you shall *1835:* another: so *1849:* Of the glory to another; hiding thus, **668**| *MS:* Hide from yourself that <> yourself: *1835:* for yourself. *1849:* Even from yourself, that **669**| *MS:* Say— § above §, say *1835:* Say, say <> God "I *1849:* God—"I **670**| *MS:* her.— —not for myself!"— — PARACELSUS <> late, *1835:* her—not for myself!" *1849:* who, but lately, *1863:* her, not *1868:* who but lately **672**| *MS:* but you? FESTUS Nay, I *1849:* but both of you? FESTUS I **673**| *MS:* tis *1835:* 'tis *1849:* no wish of *1863:* no will of **674**| *MS:* make *1835:* make;
675| *MS:*—And <> cause . . . I will no *1835:* And <> cause—I *1849:* Although I can no longer seek, indeed, *1863:* And this the cause—I **676**| *MS:* truth . . . that *1835:* truth; that *1849:* truth, that there will be *1863:* there would be **677**| *MS:* earth— — § written over by § earth,— *1835:* earth,
678| *MS:* sun— —among § written over by § sun,—among the trees— *1835:* sun, among the trees, *1849:* trees: **679**| *MS:* A <> is:—hear me;— *1835:* is. Hear me; *1849:*—A <> me! **680**| *MS:* which have *1835:* endow'd *1849:* endowed <> which bear **681**| *1835:* Annex'd *1849:* Annexed
682| *MS:* will, *1868:* will **683**| *MS:* To gather <> need,—inspiring *1835:* need; inspiring *1849:* And gather **684**| *MS:* love which *they* can *1835:* feel— *1849:* love themselves can *1863:* feel, **685**| *MS:* midst <> votaries;— — — *1835:* votaries. *1849:* 'mid

Or ever dream that common men can live
On objects you prize lightly, but which make
Their heart's sole treasure: the affections seem
Beauteous at most to you, which we must taste
Or die: and this strange quality accords,
I know not how, with you; sits well upon
That luminous brow, though in another it scowls
An eating brand, a shame. I dare not judge you.
The rules of right and wrong thus set aside,
There's no alternative—I own you one
Of higher order, under other laws
Than bind us; therefore, curb not one bold glance!
'Tis best aspire. Once mingled with us all . . .
MICHAL Stay with us, Aureole! cast those hopes away,
And stay with us! An angel warns me, too,
Man should be humble; you are very proud:
And God, dethroned, has doleful plagues for such!
—Warns me to have in dread no quick repulse,
No slow defeat, but a complete success:
You will find all you seek, and perish so!
PARACELSUS [*after a pause*] Are these the barren firstfruits of my quest?
Is love like this the natural lot of all?
How many years of pain might one such hour

687| *MS:* men live wholly *1849:* men can live 688| *MS:* you so lightly prize, which *1849:* you prize lightly, but which 689| *MS:* sole wealth:—the soft affections *1835:* wealth: the *1849:* sole treasure; the affections 690| *MS:* which they must *1849:* which we must 691| *MS:* accords *1835:* accords, 692| *MS:* how, with you . . . sits § written over by § you—sits *1835:* you; sits 693| *MS:* brow——tho' in <> it were *1835:* brow: though *1849:* brow, though <> it scowls 694| *MS:* brand—a shame:——I § written over by § shame:—I <> not blame you *1835:* shame. I *1849:* not judge you: *1863:* brand, a 695| *MS:* aside *1835:* aside, 696| *MS:* alternative . . . I judge you *1835:* alternative. I *1849:* alternative—I own you 697| *MS:* order—under *1849:* order, under 698| *MS:* us, . . therefore § written over by § us,—therefore curb *1835:* us; therefore *1849:* therefore, curb 699| *MS:* Tis <> aspire——once <> all . . . . . *1835:* 'Tis <> aspire. Once <> all . . . . *1863:* all . . . 700| *MS:* away *1835:* us Aureole <> away, *1849:* us, Aureole 701| *MS:* us—an *1835:* us; an *1849:* us! An 702| *MS:* humble . . . you <> proud! *1835:* humble; you *1849:* proud: 703| *1835:* God dethroned has *1849:* God, dethroned, has 704| *MS:* Warns <> repulse *1835:* repulse, *1849:* He warns me not to dread a quick *1863:*—Warns me to have in dread no quick 705| *MS:* defeat——but *1835:* defeat, but *1849:* Nor slow *1863:* No slow 707| *MS:*—Are <> first fruits I should fear *1835:* Are *1849:* fruits of my life? *1863:* firstfruits of my quest? 709| *MS:* of hate might *1849:* of pain might

O'erbalance? Dearest Michal, dearest Festus,
What shall I say, if not that I desire
To justify your love; and will, dear friends,
In swerving nothing from my first resolves.
See, the great moon! and ere the mottled owls
Were wide awake, I was to go. It seems
You acquiesce at last in all save this—
If I am like to compass what I seek
By the untried career I choose; and then,
If that career, making but small account
Of much of life's delight, will yet retain
Sufficient to sustain my soul: for thus
I understand these fond fears just expressed.
And first; the lore you praise and I neglect,
The labours and the precepts of old time,
I have not lightly disesteemed. But, friends,
Truth is within ourselves; it takes no rise
From outward things, whate'er you may believe.
There is an inmost centre in us all,
Where truth abides in fulness; and around,
Wall upon wall, the gross flesh hems it in,
This perfect, clear perception—which is truth.

710| *MS:* dearest Michal, dearest § corrected in pencil to § Dearest Michal, dearest 712| *MS:* Well to deserve that love, and will <> Friends, *1835:* friends, *1849:* To merit this your love; and *1863:* To justify your love
713| *MS:* my high resolves: § corrected in pencil to § resolves. *1849:* my first resolves. 714| *MS:* See—the *1835:* See, the <> 'ere *1863:* ere
715–716| *MS:* awake, I should have made all sure / For my departure that remains to do; / So answer not, while I run lightly o'er / The topics you have urged to-night:—it § corrected in pencil to § to-night. It seems / We acquiesce <> all, save only *1849:* awake, I was to go. It seems / You acquiesce <> all save this—
718| *MS:* In the <> chuse *1849:* By the *1863:* choose 720| *MS:* will offer joys *1849:* will yet retain 721| *MS:* soul . . . for § corrected in pencil to § soul—for *1868:* soul: for 722| *MS:* expressed: § corrected in pencil to § express'd. *1849:* expressed. 723| *MS:* first;—the § corrected in pencil to § first; the 724| *MS:* old sages, *1849:* old time, 725| *MS:* not slightly disesteemed— —but § corrected in pencil to § disesteem'd. But *1849:* disesteemed. But, friends, *1863:* not lightly disesteemed 726| *MS:* ourselves—it *1835:* ourselves; it 727| *MS:* believe; § corrected in pencil to § believe *1863:* believe. 728| *MS:* all *1835:* all, 729| *MS:* truth § corrected to § Truth *1835:* truth *1849:* around *1868:* around, 730| *MS:* Wall within wall <> in— *1835:* in, *1849:* Wall upon wall 731| Perfect and true Perception <> Truth;— § corrected in pencil to § Truth; *1835:* perception <> truth; *1849:* This perfect, clear perception *1863:* truth.

A baffling and perverting carnal mesh
Binds it, and makes all error: and to KNOW
Rather consists in opening out a way
Whence the imprisoned splendour may escape,
Than in effecting entry for a light
Supposed to be without. Watch narrowly
The demonstration of a truth, its birth,
And you trace back the effluence to its spring
And source within us; where broods radiance vast,
To be elicited ray by ray, as chance
Shall favour: chance—for hitherto, your sage
Even as he knows, not how those beams are born,
As little knows he what unlocks their fount:
And men have oft grown old among their books
To die case-hardened in their ignorance,
Whose careless youth had promised what long years
Of unremitted labour ne'er performed:
While, contrary, it has chanced some idle day,
To autumn loiterers just as fancy-free
As the midges in the sun, gives birth at last
To truth—produced mysteriously as cape
Of cloud grown out of the invisible air.

733| *MS:* Which blinds it, and makes Error: and, "to *know*" § corrected in pencil to § *to know*" *1835:* error *1849:* Blinds it, and makes all error *1868:* and, to KNOW, *1888:* Binds it 735| *MS:* splendor § corrected in pencil to § splendour may dart forth, *1849:* inprisoned <> may escape, *1863:* imprisoned 736| *MS:* for the light *1849:* for a light 737| *MS:* without; watch § corrected in pencil to § without. Watch 738| *MS:* Truth *1835:* truth 739| *MS:* you shall trace the Effluence *1835:* effluence *1849:* you trace back the 740| *MS:* us, where *1863:* us; where 742| *MS:* favour;—*chance* § corrected in pencil to § favour; *chance*—for hitherto, *1835:* favour: *chance* *1849:* chance—for hitherto, your sage 743| *MS:* as we know *1849:* as he knows 744| *MS:* know we what <> their lair;— § corrected in pencil to § lair; *1849:* knows he what <> their fount; *1863:* fount. *1888:* fount; 745| *MS:* For Men *1835:* men *1849:* And men 746| *MS:* And died, case-hardened § corrected in pencil to § case-harden'd *1849:* To die, case-hardened *1868:* die case-hardened 749| *MS:* day *1835:* day, *1863:* day *1868:* day, 750| *MS:* loiterers just § corrected in pencil to § loiterers, just *1835:* loiterers just *1849:* That autumn *1863:* To autumn 751| *MS:* sun, has § corrected in pencil to § have oft brought forth *1835:* has *1849:* have oft given vent *1863:* sun, gives birth at last 752| *MS:* A Truth, produced § corrected in pencil to § Truth—produced *1835:* truth *1849:* To truth 753| *MS:* invisible mist:— § corrected in pencil to § mist. *1849:* invisible air.

Hence, may not truth be lodged alike in all,
The lowest as the highest? some slight film
The interposing bar which binds a soul
And makes the idiot, just as makes the sage
Some film removed, the happy outlet whence
Truth issues proudly? See this soul of ours!
How it strives weakly in the child, is loosed
In manhood, clogged by sickness, back compelled
By age and waste, set free at last by death:
Why is it, flesh enthrals it or enthrones?
What is this flesh we have to penetrate?
Oh, not alone when life flows still, do truth
And power emerge, but also when strange chance
Ruffles its current; in unused conjuncture,
When sickness breaks the body—hunger, watching,
Excess or languor—oftenest death's approach,
Peril, deep joy or woe. One man shall crawl
Through life surrounded with all stirring things,
Unmoved; and he goes mad: and from the wreck
Of what he was, by his wild talk alone,

754| *MS:* Truth *1835:* truth 755| *MS:* highest?—some *1835:* highest? some 756–758| *MS:* soul,— § corrected in pencil to § soul?— / Some <> removed the *1835:* soul? *1849:* binds it up / And makes the idiot, just as makes the sage / Some <> removed, the *1863:* binds a soul 759–760| *MS:* It issues proudly? seeing that the soul / Is deathless, we know well——but § written over by § deathless (we know well)—but oftener cooped § corrected in pencil to § coop'd / A prisoner and a thrall, than a throned Power,— § corrected in pencil to § Power; / That it <> child—is § corrected in pencil to § child; is *1835:* well) but <> / <> power; / <> child, is *1849:* Truth <> proudly? See this soul of ours! / How it 761| *1835:* clogg'd *1849:* clogged 762–765| *MS:* waste—set § corrected in pencil to § waste, set <> death;——— § written over by § death,— § corrected in pencil to § death— / That not <> still do Truth *1835:* death: / <> truth *1849:* death: / Why is it, flesh enthralls it or enthrones? / What is this flesh we have to penetrate? / Oh, not *1863:* still, do 766| *MS:* Power *1835:* power 767| *MS:* Affects it *1849:* Ruffles its 768| *MS:* hunger—watching, § corrected in pencil to § hunger, watching *1835:* Where sickness *1849:* When sickness 769| *MS:* Excess, or <> approach— *1863:* approach, *1868:* Excess or 770| *MS:* joy or woe;—one § corrected in pencil to § joy, or woe. One *1868:* joy or 771| *MS:* Thro' § corrected in pencil to § Through life, surrounded *1868:* life surrounded 772| *MS:* Unmoved——and § corrected in pencil to § Unmoved—and <> mad—and § corrected in pencil to § mad; and *1868:* unmoved; and <> mad: and

You first collect how great a spirit he hid.
Therefore, set free the soul alike in all,
Discovering the true laws by which the flesh
Accloys the spirit! We may not be doomed
To cope with seraphs, but at least the rest
Shall cope with us. Make no more giants, God,
But elevate the race at once! We ask
To put forth just our strength, our human strength,
All starting fairly, all equipped alike,
Gifted alike, all eagle-eyed, true-hearted—
See if we cannot beat thine angels yet!
Such is my task. I go to gather this
The sacred knowledge, here and there dispersed
About the world, long lost or never found.
And why should I be sad or lorn of hope?
Why ever make man's good distinct from God's,
Or, finding they are one, why dare mistrust?
Who shall succeed if not one pledged like me?
Mine is no mad attempt to build a world

774–775| *MS:* hid— § corrected in pencil to § hid. / —Seeing all this, why should I pine in vain / Attempts to win some day the august form / Of Truth to stand before me, and compel / My dark unvalued frame to change its nature / And straight become suffused with light— — at § corrected in pencil to § light—at best / For my sole good—leaving the world to seek / Salvation out as it best may—or § written over by § may, or follow / The same long thorny course: No § corrected in pencil to § course. No, I will learn / How to set < > All, *1835:* hid. / Seeing all this why < > /// < > nature, /// < > course? No < > / < > in all, *1849:* hid. / Therefore, set **776**| *MS:* By searching out the laws < > Flesh § corrected in pencil to § flesh *1849:* Discovering the true laws **777**| *MS:* Spirit— —we § corrected in pencil to § Spirit. We < > doomed § corrected in pencil to § doom'd *1849:* Bars in the spirit! We < > doomed *1863:* Accloys the **779**| *MS:* us—make < > Giants, God! *1835:* us. Make < > giants *1863:* God, **780**| *MS:* Race at once!—we § corrected in pencil to § once! We *1835:* race **781**| *MS:* But to put forth our *1849:* To put forth just our **782**| *MS:*—All < > equipped § corrected in pencil to § equipp'd alike § corrected in pencil to § alike, *1835:* All *1849:* equipped **783**| *MS:* alike and § corrected in pencil to § alike, and eagle-eyed, true-hearted . . . § corrected in pencil to § true-hearted. *1849:* alike, all eagle-eyed, true-hearted— **784**| *MS:* beat thy angels yet!— § corrected in pencil to § yet! *1863:* beat the angels *1868:* beat thine angels **785**| *MS:*—Such < > task— —I § corrected in pencil to § task. I *1835:* Such **786**| *MS:* Mysterious knowledge *1849:* The sacred knowledge **787**| *MS:* or ever-hidden—§ corrected in pencil to § ever-hidden, *1835:* ever-hidden; *1849:* or never found. **788**| *MS:* sad, or *1868:* sad or **789**| *MS:* Man's < > God's? *1835:* man's *1868:* God's, **790**| *MS:* why have mistrust? *1849:* why dare mistrust?

Apart from his, like those who set themselves
To find the nature of the spirit they bore,
And, taught betimes that all their gorgeous dreams
Were only born to vanish in this life,
Refused to fit them to its narrow sphere,
But chose to figure forth another world
And other frames meet for their vast desires,—
And all a dream! Thus was life scorned; but life
Shall yet be crowned: twine amaranth! I am priest!
And all for yielding with a lively spirit
A poor existence, parting with a youth
Like those who squander every energy
Convertible to good, on painted toys,
Breath-bubbles, gilded dust! And though I spurn
All adventitious aims, from empty praise
To love's award, yet whoso deems such helps
Important, and concerns himself for me,
May know even these will follow with the rest—
As in the steady rolling Mayne, asleep
Yonder, is mixed its mass of schistous ore.
My own affections laid to rest awhile,
Will waken purified, subdued alone
By all I have achieved. Till then—till then . . .
Ah, the time-wiling loitering of a page

793| *1849:* His *1868:* his 795–796| *MS:* dreams / And beauteous fancies, hopes and aspirations / Were born only to wither in *1835:* hopes, and aspirations, *1849:* dreams / Were only born to vanish in 797| *MS:* to curb or moderate their longings, / Or fit them to this narrow sphere, but chose / To figure and conceive another *1849:* to fit <> sphere, / But chose to figure forth another *1863:* to its narrow 799| *MS:* desires, *1849:* desires,— 800| *MS:* dream!—thus *1835:* dream! Thus <> scorn'd *1849:* Still, all <> scorned *1863:* And all 801| *MS:* crowned . . twine <> Priest! *1835:* crown'd: twine <> priest! *1849:* crowned 803| *MS:* existence—parting *1863:* existence, parting 804| *MS:* Like theirs who *1868:* Like those who 805| *MS:* good on *1849:* good, on 806| *MS:* and tho' *1835:* And though 809| *MS:* Important and *1835:* me *1849:* Important, and <> me, 812–813| *MS:* is mingled and involved a mass / Of schistous particles of ore . . and even / My own affections, laid *1835:* ore. And <> / <> awhile— *1849:* is mixed its mass of schistous ore. / My <> awhile, *1888:* affections laid 815| *MS:* achieved, . . till then—till then——— *1835:* achieved; till then—till then . . . *1863:* achieved. Till then—till 816| *MS:* time-wiling . . loitering *1835:* time-wiling loitering

Through bower and over lawn, till eve shall bring
The stately lady's presence whom he loves—
The broken sleep of the fisher whose rough coat
Enwraps the queenly pearl—these are faint types!
See, see, they look on me: I triumph now!
But one thing, Festus, Michal! I have told
All I shall e'er disclose to mortal: say—
Do you believe I shall accomplish this?
FESTUS I do believe!
MICHAL I ever did believe!
PARACELSUS Those words shall never fade from out my brain!
This earnest of the end shall never fade!
Are there not, Festus, are there not, dear Michal,
Two points in the adventure of the diver,
One—when, a beggar, he prepares to plunge,
One—when, a prince, he rises with his pearl?
Festus, I plunge!
FESTUS We wait you when you rise!

817| *MS:* Thro' <> over § illegible word cancelled by § lawn, 'till *1835:* Through *1849:* till 818| *MS:* loves . . . . *1835:* loves— 820| *MS:* pearl——these *1835:* pearl—these 821| *MS:* me—I *1849:* See how they *1863:* See, see they *1888:* See, see, they 822| *MS:* Tell me, Festus, Michal, but one thing—I *1849:* But one thing, Festus, Michal!—I *1863:* Michal! I 823| *MS:* mortal: . . . how, *1835:* mortal . . . now, *1849:* mortal: say— 825| *MS:* believe! MICHAL And I, dear Aureole! *1849:* believe! MICHAL I ever did believe! 826| *MS:* brain: —— *1849:* brain! 827| *MS:* Tis earnest <> end: ——shall *1835:* "Tis <> end—shall *1849:* This earnest <> end shall 828| *MS:* not dear Michal *1835:* Michal, *1849:* not, Festus, are <> not, dear 829| *MS:* diver—— *1835:* diver: *1868:* diver, 830| *MS:* beggar he <> plunge *1835:* when a <> plunge? *1849:* when, a beggar, he *1863:* plunge, 831| *MS:* when a prince he <> pearl,? *1835:* pearl? *1849:* when, a prince, he 832| *MS:* plunge! *1849:* plunge! FESTUS I wait you when you rise! *1863:* plunge! FESTUS We wait

PART II. PARACELSUS ATTAINS.

SCENE—*Constantinople; the house of a Greek Conjurer.* 1521.

PARACELSUS.

Over the waters in the vaporous West
The sun goes down as in a sphere of gold
Behind the arm of the city, which between,
With all that length of domes and minarets,
Athwart the splendour, black and crooked runs
Like a Turk verse along a scimitar.
There lie, sullen memorial, and no more
Possess my aching sight! 'Tis done at last.
Strange—and the juggles of a sallow cheat
Have won me to this act! 'Tis as yon cloud
Should voyage unwrecked o'er many a mountain-top
And break upon a molehill. I have dared
Come to a pause with knowledge; scan for once
The heights already reached, without regard
To the extent above; fairly compute

SCENE| *MS:* "*The House of the Greek.*" *1849:* "*The House of the Greek-conjuror.*" *1863: the House of a Greek conjurer.* *1888: the house of a Greek Conjurer.* 1| *1835:* west *1863:* West 2| *1849:* gold, *1863:* gold 3–5| *MS:* between / Athwart the splendour black *1835:* between, / splendour, black *1849:* the outstretched city < > between, / With all that length of domes and minarets, / Athwart *1863:* the arm of the city 6| *MS:* scimetar—— — *1835:* scimetar. *1863:* scimitar. 7| *1849:* lie, thou saddest writing, and while *1863:* lie, sullen memorial, and no more 8| *MS:* sight:—'tis < > last! *1835:* sight. 'Tis *1849:* Relieve my *1863:* Possess my *1868:* last. 9| *MS:* Strange——and § written over by § !— *1835:* Strange—and 10| *MS:* act—'tis *1835:* act: 'tis *1849:* Could win < > act! 'Tis *1863:* Have won 11| *1835:* unwreck'd *1868:* unwrecked 12| *MS:* molehille;—I *1835:* molehill. I 13| *MS:* pause at last—and scan *1835:* last, and *1849:* pause with knowledge; scan 14| *1835:* reach'd *1863:* reached 15| *MS:* above—fairly *1835:* above; fairly

All I have clearly gained; for once excluding
A brilliant future to supply and perfect
All half-gains and conjectures and crude hopes:
And all because a fortune-teller wills
His credulous seekers should inscribe thus much
Their previous life's attainment, in his roll,
Before his promised secret, as he vaunts,
Make up the sum: and here amid the scrawled
Uncouth recordings of the dupes of this
Old arch-genethliac, lie my life's results!

A few blurred characters suffice to note
A stranger wandered long through many lands
And reaped the fruit he coveted in a few
Discoveries, as appended here and there,
The fragmentary produce of much toil,
In a dim heap, fact and surmise together
Confusedly massed as when acquired; he was
Intent on gain to come too much to stay
And scrutinize the little gained: the whole

16| *MS:* gained, for *1835:* gained; for *1849:* What I *1863:* All I 17| *1849:* My future which should finish and fulfil *1863:* A brilliant future to supply and perfect 18| *MS:* half-gains, and conjectures, and <> hopes— *1849:* conjectures, and mere hopes— *1863:* half-gains and conjectures and crude hopes— *1868:* hopes: 19| *MS:*—And *1835:* And *1849:* And this, because a fortune-teller bids *1863:* And all, because a fortune-teller wills *1868:* all because 20–23| *MS:* much / Within this roll——and *1835:* roll: and here, amid the scrawl'd *1849:* credulous enquirers write thus much, / Their previous life's attainment, in his book, / Before his promised secret, as he vaunts, / Make that life perfect: here, accordingly *1863:* credulous seekers should inscribe thus much, / <> his roll, // Make up the sum: and here, amid the scrawled *1888:* much /// <> here amid 24| *1849:* 'Mid the uncouth recordings of such dupes, *1863:* Uncouth recordings of the dupes of this 25| *1849:*—Scrawled in like fashion, lie *1863:* Old arch-genethliac, lie 26| *1849:* These few *1863:* A few 27| *MS:* long in many *1835:* wander'd *1849:* wandered long through many 28| *1835:* reap'd *1849:* reaped 29| *MS:* Discoveries— § above §, as <> there,— *1835:* Discoveries, as <> there, 30| *MS:* of those toils *1835:* toils, *1849:* of much toil 31| *MS:* to-gether *1835:* together 32| *MS:* acquired—he was *1835:* mass'd, as <> acquired; he *1849:* massed <> acquired; himself *1863:* massed as <> acquired; he was 33| *1849:* Too bent on gaining more to calmly stay *1863:* Intent on gain to come too much to stay 34| *MS:* scrutinize whate'er was gained—the *1835:* gain'd: the *1849:* scrutinize the little which he gained: *1863:* little gained: the whole

Slipt in the blank space 'twixt an idiot's gibber
And a mad lover's ditty—there it lies.

And yet those blottings chronicle a life—
A whole life, and my life! Nothing to do,
No problem for the fancy, but a life
Spent and decided, wasted past retrieve
Or worthy beyond peer. Stay, what does this
Remembrancer set down concerning "life"?
" 'Time fleets, youth fades, life is an empty dream,'
It is the echo of time; and he whose heart
Beat first beneath a human heart, whose speech
Was copied from a human tongue, can never
Recall when he was living yet knew not this.
Nevertheless long seasons pass o'er him
Till some one hour's experience shows what nothing,
It seemed, could clearer show; and ever after,
An altered brow and eye and gait and speech
Attest that now he knows the adage true
'Time fleets, youth fades, life is an empty dream.' "

Ay, my brave chronicler, and this same hour

35| *MS:* twixt an ideot's *1835:* 'twixt *1849:* idiot's 36| *MS:* ditty——there *1835:* ditty—there *1849:* ditty—lies the whole! *1863:* ditty—there it lies. 37| *MS:* life *1835:* life— 38| *MS:*——A <> life! no thing to do, *1835:* A <> nothing *1849:* life,—mine! No thought to turn to act *1863:* life,—and my life! Nothing to do, *1868:* life, and 40| *MS:* decided,—wasted *1835:* decided, wasted <> retrieve— *1849:* past recall, *1863:* past retrieve 41–42| *MS:* beyond a peer——stay <> / <> "life"? § above § ———— *1835:* peer. Stay <> / <> "life?" *1849:* beyond peer. Stay, turn the page / And take its chance,—thus: what, concerning "life" / Does this remembrancer set down?—"We say *1863:* peer. Stay, what does this / Remembrancer set down concerning "life"? 43| *MS:* dream' *1835:* dream,' *1849:* dream.' *1888:* dream,' 44| *MS:* time—he whose heart beat *1835:* time: he *1849:* 'Tis the mere echo of time; and he <> heart *1863:* It is the echo 45| *MS:* First underneath a *1849:* Beat first beneath a 46| *MS:* tongue—can *1835:* tongue, can 47| *MS:* knew it not: *1849:* knew not this. 48| *1835:* him, *1849:* seasons come and go, *1863:* seasons pass o'er him 49| *MS:* Until, one hour's <> nothing *1835:* Until one *1849:* Till some one <> what nought, *1863:* what nothing, 50| *MS:* show—and <> after *1835:* seem'd <> show, and *1849:* He deemed, could <> show; and *1863:* It seemed, could <> after, 51| *1835:* alter'd brow, and eye, and gait, and *1849:* altered *1863:* brow and eye and gait and 52| *MS: now* he *knows* this adage *1849:* now he knows the adage 53| *MS:* dream' " *1835:* dream.' " 54| *1849:* same time *1863:* same hour

As well as any: now, let my time be!

Now! I can go no farther; well or ill,
'Tis done. I must desist and take my chance.
I cannot keep on the stretch: 'tis no back-shrinking—
For let but some assurance beam, some close
To my toil grow visible, and I proceed
At any price, though closing it, I die.
Else, here I pause. The old Greek's prophecy
Is like to turn out true: "I shall not quit
His chamber till I know what I desire!"
Was it the light wind sang it o'er the sea?

An end, a rest! strange how the notion, once
Encountered, gathers strength by moments! Rest!
Where has it kept so long? this throbbing brow
To cease, this beating heart to cease, all cruel
And gnawing thoughts to cease! To dare let down
My strung, so high-strung brain, to dare unnerve
My harassed o'ertasked frame, to know my place,

55| *MS:* any:—now *1835:* any: now *1849:* any: let my hour speak now! *1863:* any: now, let my time be! 56| *MS: Now!*—I <> farther——well or ill *1835:* Now! I <> farther; well or ill— *1849:* Now! I *1863:* ill, 57| *MS:* Tis done——I <> chance— *1835:* 'Tis done. I <> chance; *1863:* chance. 58| *MS:* keep at this—'tis no back-shrinking,— *1835:* this; 'tis no back shrinking— *1849:* keep on the stretch; 'tis no back-shrinking— 59| *1849:* let the least assurance dawn, some end *1863:* let but some assurance beam, some close 60| *MS:* To this my toil appear, and *1849:* To my toil seem possible, and *1863:* toil grow visible, and 61| *MS:* tho' <> die: . . . . *1835:* though <> die . . . *1849:* price, by any sacrifice: *1863:* price, though closing it, I die. 62| *MS:* But here I pause:—the *1835:* pause: the *1849:* Else, here I pause: the *1863:* pause. The 63| *MS:* true—I *1849:* true—"I *1863:* true: "I 64–66| *MS:* desire. / § space § / An end,—a *1835:* 'till <> / § space § / An end, a <> notion, once *1849:* till <> desire!" / Was it the light wind sung it, o'er the sea? / § space § / An *1863:* sang it o'er 67| *MS:* moments—rest! *1835:* Encounter'd <> moments. Rest! *1849:* Admitted, gains strength every moment! Rest! *1863:* Encountered, gathers strength by moments 68| *MS:* long?——this *1835:* long? this *1849:* Where kept that thought so *1863:* Where has it kept so 69| *MS:* cease—this <> cease—all *1849:* heart to cease—its crowd *1863:* cease, this <> cease, all cruel 70| *MS:* cease! to *1835:* cease!—to *1849:* of gnawing <> cease!—To *1863:* And gnawing <> cease! To 71| *MS:* brain—to *1863:* brain, to 72| *MS:* frame——to § written over by § frame—to *1835:* harass'd o'er task'd *1849:* harassed o'er-tasked *1863:* frame, to <> place! *1868:* place,

My portion, my reward, even my failure,
Assigned, made sure for ever! To lose myself
Among the common creatures of the world,
To draw some gain from having been a man,
Neither to hope nor fear, to live at length!
Even in failure, rest! But rest in truth
And power and recompense . . . I hoped that once!

What, sunk insensibly so deep? Has all
Been undergone for this? This the request
My labour qualified me to present
With no fear of refusal? Had I gone
Slightingly through my task, and so judged fit
To moderate my hopes; nay, were it now
My sole concern to exculpate myself,
End things or mend them,—why, I could not choose
A humbler mood to wait for the event!
No, no, there needs not this; no, after all,
At worst I have performed my share of the task:

73| *MS:* reward—even *1835:* reward, even *1849:*—My portion, my reward, my failure even, *1863:* My portion, my reward, even my failure 74| *MS:* Assigned—made <> forever!—to *1835:* Assign'd, made <> for ever *1849:* Assigned <> ever!—To *1863:* ever! To 75| *MS:* world,— *1835:* world— *1863:* world, 76| *MS:* Man,— *1835:* man— *1863:* man, 77| *MS:* fear———to *1835:* fear—to *1863:* fear, to 78–80| *MS:* rest! . . . . but § written over by § rest!—but rest, in Truth / <> recompense———/ § space § / Tis little wonder truly—things go on / And at their worst they end or mend—'tis time / To look about with matters at this pass:— / Have I insensibly sunk as deep . . . has *1835:* power, and recompense . . . / § space § / 'Tis <> truly; things <> // <> about, with <> pass: / <> deep—has *1849:* Oh, were it but in failure, to have rest! / What, sunk insensibly so deep? has *1863:* Even in failure, rest! But rest in truth / And power and recompense . . . I hoped that once! / § space § / What
81| *MS:* this? *this*, the *1835:* this? *this* the *1849:* this? Was this the prayer *1863:* this? This the request 83| *MS:* refusal——had § written over by § refusal?—had *1835:* refusal? Had 84| *MS:* thro' my task and therefore judged *1835:* through my task, and *1849:* Carelessly through <> and so judged fit *1863:* Slightingly through 85| *MS:* It fit to <> hopes,—nay, were it *1835:* hopes; nay *1849:* To moderate <> it now 86| *MS:* myself——— *1835:* myself— *1849:* myself, 87| *MS:*—To flounder thro' the scrape——I § written over by § scrape— I <> chuse *1835:* To *1849:* And lessen punishment,—I *1863:* End things or mend them,—why, I 88| *MS:* An *1849:* the decree! *1863:* A <> the event! 89| *MS:*—No, no <> this—no *1835:* No, no <> this; no 90| *MS: my* *1835:* perform'd <> task. *1849:* performed my <> task: *1863:* task; *1888:* task § only upper half of ; or : printed § *1889:* task:

The rest is God's concern; mine, merely this,
To know that I have obstinately held
By my own work. The mortal whose brave foot
Has trod, unscathed, the temple-court so far
That he descries at length the shrine of shrines,
Must let no sneering of the demons' eyes,
Whom he could pass unquailing, fasten now
Upon him, fairly past their power; no, no—
He must not stagger, faint, fall down at last,
Having a charm to baffle them; behold,
He bares his front: a mortal ventures thus
Serene amid the echoes, beams and glooms!
If he be priest henceforth, if he wake up
The god of the place to ban and blast him there,
Both well! What's failure or success to me?
I have subdued my life to the one purpose
Whereto I ordained it; there alone I spy,
No doubt, that way I may be satisfied.
Yes, well have I subdued my life! beyond
The obligation of my strictest vow,

91| *MS:*—The < > concern——mine, merely, this— *1835:* The < > concern—mine < > this, *1863:* concern; mine 93| *MS:* work——the § written over by § work:—the *1835:* work: the *1849:* work. The 94| *MS:* trod so far the Temple-courts unscathed *1835:* temple-courts unscathed, *1849:* trod, unscathed, the temple-courts so far 96| *MS:* daemons' eyes *1835:* demon's eyes, 97–98| *MS:* Which he < > now / Upon < > power—no—no *1835:* power; no, no, *1849:* Whose wrath he met unquailing, follow sly / And fasten on him, fairly past their power, / If where he stands he dares but stay; no, no— *1863:* Whom he could pass unquailing, fasten now / Upon him, fairly past their power; no, no— 99| *MS:* stagger and fall down *1849:* stagger, faint and fall at *1863:* faint, fall down at 100| *MS:* behold *1835:* behold, *1849:*—Knowing a *1863:* Having a 101| *MS:* front—a *1835:* front: a *1849:* front—a *1863:* front; a 102| *MS:* glooms!— *1835:* beams, and glooms! *1863:* beams and 103| *MS:* Priest henceforth—if *1835:* priest henceforth, if he *1849:* henceforth, or if he wake *1863:* henceforth, if he wake up 104| *MS:* God < > there,— *1835:* god < > there. *1849:* there,— *1863:* there, 105| *MS:* well! . .what's *1835:* well! What's 106| *MS:* one end *1863:* one purpose 107| *MS:* it . . . there *1835:* ordain'd it; there *1849:* Ordained life; there alone I cannot doubt, *1863:* Whereto I ordained it; there < > I spy, 108| *MS:* doubt——that < > satisfied: / § no space § / *1835:* doubt; that < > satisfied. *1849:* That only way < > satisfied. *1863:* No doubt, that way *1888:* satisfied. / § space § / 109| *MS:* life——beyond § written over by § life!—beyond *1835:* life! beyond 110| *MS:* vows, *1868:* vow,

The contemplation of my wildest bond,
Which gave my nature freely up, in truth,
But in its actual state, consenting fully
All passionate impulses its soil was formed
To rear, should wither; but foreseeing not
The tract, doomed to perpetual barrenness,
Would seem one day, remembered as it was,
Beside the parched sand-waste which now it is,
Already strewn with faint blooms, viewless then.
I ne'er engaged to root up loves so frail
I felt them not; yet now, 'tis very plain
Some soft spots had their birth in me at first,
If not love, say, like love: there was a time
When yet this wolfish hunger after knowledge
Set not remorselessly love's claims aside.
This heart was human once, or why recall
Einsiedeln, now, and Würzburg which the Mayne
Forsakes her course to fold as with an arm?

And Festus—my poor Festus, with his praise
And counsel and grave fears—where is he now

112| *MS:* gave, in truth, my nature freely up, *1863:* gave my nature freely up, in truth, 113–115| *MS:* state——consenting fully / All <> formed / To <> wither—but forseeing *1835:* state—consenting <> / <> form'd / <> wither; but *1849:* In what it should be, more than what it was— / Consenting that whatever passions slept, / Whatever impulses lay unmatured, / Should wither in the germ,—but scarce foreseeing *1863:* But in its actual state, consenting fully / All passionate impulses its soil was formed / To rear, should wither; but foreseeing not
116| *MS:* tract doomed <> barrenness *1835:* tract doom'd *1849:* That the soil, doomed thus to perpetual waste, *1863:* The tract, doomed to perpetual barrenness, 117| *MS:* was *1849:* remembered in its youth *1863:* remembered as it was, 118| *MS:* Beside the § *the* inserted above the line § parched sand-tract which *1835:* parch'd *1849:* parched *1863:* sand-waste which 119| *MS:* then . . . *1835:* then. 121| *MS:* not . . yet § written over by § not—yet <> tis *1835:* not, yet <> 'tis *1849:* not; yet
122| *1835:* first— *1863:* first, 123| *MS:* love:—there *1835:* love: there 125| *MS:* remorselessly its claims aside . . . . *1835:* remorselessly its <> aside; *1849:* remorselessly love's claims *1863:* aside. 127| *MS:* Einsiedeln, even now—and Würzburg whom the *1835:* now, and Würzburg, whom *1849:* Einsiedeln, now, and Würzburg, which the *1868:* Würzburg which
128| *MS:* The Mayne § cancelled § Forsakes <> arm——— § written over by § arm? —— *1835:* arm? . . . *1849:* arm? 129| *MS:* Festus——my <> Festus—with his praise, *1835:* Festus—my <> Festus, with *1863:* praise
130| *MS:* fears——where <> now? *1835:* counsel, and <> fears—where *1863:* counsel and <> now

With the sweet maiden, long ago his bride?
I surely loved them—that last night, at least,
When we . . . gone! gone! the better. I am saved
The sad review of an ambitious youth
Choked by vile lusts, unnoticed in their birth,
But let grow up and wind around a will
Till action was destroyed. No, I have gone
Purging my path successively of aught
Wearing the distant likeness of such lusts.
I have made life consist of one idea:
Ere that was master, up till that was born,
I bear a memory of a pleasant life
Whose small events I treasure; till one morn
I ran o'er the seven little grassy fields,
Startling the flocks of nameless birds, to tell
Poor Festus, leaping all the while for joy,
To leave all trouble for my future plans,
Since I had just determined to become
The greatest and most glorious man on earth.
And since that morn all life has been forgotten;
All is one day, one only step between
The outset and the end: one tyrant all-
Absorbing aim fills up the interspace,

131| *MS:* long ago § *ago* inserted above the line § his bride,——— *1835:* bride? *1849:* bride *1863:* bride? 133| *MS:* we——gone! gone! the better:—I *1835:* we . . . gone! gone! the better: I *1863:* better. I 134| *1835:* youth, *1863:* youth 135| *MS:* lusts unnoticed < > birth *1835:* lusts, unnoticed < > birth, 136| *MS:* Which have grown up and wound < > Will *1835:* will *1849:* But let grow up and wind 137| *MS:* destroyed:—No *1835:* destroy'd. No *1849:* destroyed 139| *MS:* such loves: *1835:* loves. *1849:* such lusts. *1889:* lusts 140| *MS:* idea: . . *1835:* idea: 141| *MS:* Ere *that* was master . . up 'till < > born *1835:* E're < > master—up 'till *that* *1849:* Ere that was master—up till that was born— *1863:* master, up < > born, 143| *MS:* I can recall even to *1835:* recall, even *1849:* I treasure; till one morn 144| *MS:* The morn I ran § *I ran* inserted above the line § over the grassy fields *1849:* I ran o'er the seven little grassy fields, 147| *MS:* plans *1835:* plans, *1849:* for futurity *1863:* for my future plans 148| *MS:* For I *1835:* determin'd *1849:* Since I < > determined 149| *MS:* glorious being on earth; *1835:* earth. *1849:* glorious man on 150| *MS:* But since that hour, all < > forgotten:— *1835:* hour all < > forgotten. *1849:* And since that morn all < > forgot; *1863:* forgotten; 151| *MS:* Tis as one day——one *1835:* 'Tis < > day—one *1849:* All is one *1863:* day, one 152| *MS:* all *1835:* all— *1849:* tyrant aim, *1863:* tyrant all— 153| *MS:* the interval: *1835:* interval— *1849:* Absorbing all, fills *1863:* Absorbing aim fills up the interspace,

One vast unbroken chain of thought, kept up
Through a career apparently adverse
To its existence: life, death, light and shadow,
The shows of the world, were bare receptacles
Or indices of truth to be wrung thence,
Not ministers of sorrow or delight:
A wondrous natural robe in which she went.
For some one truth would dimly beacon me
From mountains rough with pines, and flit and wink
O'er dazzling wastes of frozen snow, and tremble
Into assured light in some branching mine
Where ripens, swathed in fire, the liquid gold—
And all the beauty, all the wonder fell
On either side the truth, as its mere robe;
I see the robe now—then I saw the form.
So far, then, I have voyaged with success,
So much is good, then, in this working sea
Which parts me from that happy strip of land:
But o'er that happy strip a sun shone, too!
And fainter gleams it as the waves grow rough,
And still more faint as the sea widens; last
I sicken on a dead gulf streaked with light
From its own putrefying depths alone.

154| *MS:* thought kept *1835:* thought, kept 155| *MS:* Throughout a course apparently *1849:* Through a career or friendly or opposed *1863:* career apparently adverse 156| *MS:* existence—life *1835:* existence: life <> light, and *1849:* light and shade *1863:* light and shadow, 157| *MS:* shews <> world . . were *1835:* shows <> world, were 158| *MS:* thence *1835:* thence, 159–161| *MS:* delight— — / <> which I went: / For *1835:* delight— *1849:* Not instruments of <> delight: / For *1863:* Not ministers of <> / A wondrous natural robe in which she went. / For 163| *MS:* Oer <> snow—and tremble *1835:* O'er <> snow, and 164| *MS:* mine, *1863:* mine 165–170| *MS:* ripens swathed in fire the <> gold, Yet all was then o'erlooked, tho' noted now:— / So <> good then, in *1835:* ripens swathed in fire, the <> gold— / <> o'erlook'd <> now. / <> good, then *1849:* gold— / And all the beauty, all the wonder fell / On either side the truth, as its mere robe; / Men saw the robe—I saw the august form. / So far, then, I have voyaged with success, / So much *1863:* robe; / I see the robe now—then I saw the form. / So far 171| *MS:* land; *1835:* land. *1849:* land— *1863:* land; 172| *MS:* shone too! *1849:* shone, too! 174| *MS:* widens . . last, *1835:* widens. Last, *1849:* widens; last 175| *1835:* gulf, streak'd *1849:* gulph, streaked *1863:* gulf streaked 176| *MS:* putrifying <> alone!— *1835:* alone! *1863:* putrefying

Then, God was pledged to take me by the hand;
Now, any miserable juggle can bid
My pride depart. All is alike at length:
God may take pleasure in confounding pride
By hiding secrets with the scorned and base—
I am here, in short: so little have I paused
Throughout! I never glanced behind to know
If I had kept my primal light from wane,
And thus insensibly am—what I am!

Oh, bitter; very bitter!
                    And more bitter,
To fear a deeper curse, an inner ruin,
Plague beneath plague, the last turning the first
To light beside its darkness. Let me weep
My youth and its brave hopes, all dead and gone,
In tears which burn! Would I were sure to win
Some startling secret in their stead, a tincture
Of force to flush old age with youth, or breed
Gold, or imprison moonbeams till they change
To opal shafts!—only that, hurling it
Indignant back, I might convince myself

177| *MS: Then*—God <> hand,— *1835:* hand; *1849:* Then *1863:* Then, God 178| *MS: Now*—any *1849:* Now <> juggler bends *1863:* Now, any <> juggle can bid 179–180| *MS:* depart—all <> length, God <> confounding us *1835:* depart. All *1849:* pride to him. All seems alike at length: / Who knows which are the wise and which the fools? / God <> confounding pride *1863:* pride depart. All is alike at length: / God 181–182| *MS:* secrets in the <> base— — — / I *1835:* scorn'd and base . . . *1849:* secrets with the scorned and base— / He who stoops lowest may find most—in short, / I am here; and all seems natural; I start not: *1863:* base— / I am here, in short: so little have I paused 183| *MS:* Throughout— —I *1835:* Throughout. I *1849:* And never having glanced *1863:* Throughout. I never glanced *1868:* Throughout! I 185| *MS: 1849:* insensibly grown—what *1863:* insensibly am—what 186| *MS:* bitter, very bitter! / And <> bitter *1835:* bitter; very *1849:* more bitter, 187| *MS: 1835:* ruin— *1863:* ruin, 188| *MS:* plague— —the *1835:* plague—the *1863:* plague, the 189| *MS:* darkness: let *1835:* darkness. Let *1849:* darkness. Better weep *1863:* darkness. Let me weep 190| *MS:* hopes all dead and gone, *1835:* hopes, all 191| *MS:* burn— —would *1835:* burn. Would *1849:* burn! Would 192| *MS:* stead—a *1835:* stead! a *1849:* stead!—a *1863:* stead, a 195| *MS:* opal-shafts— —only *1835:* opal shafts! only *1849:* shafts!—only

My aims remained supreme and pure as ever!
Even now, why not desire, for mankind's sake,
That if I fail, some fault may be the cause,
That, though I sink, another may succeed?
O God, the despicable heart of us!
Shut out this hideous mockery from my heart!

'Twas politic in you, Aureole, to reject
Single rewards, and ask them in the lump;
At all events, once launched, to hold straight on:
For now 'tis all or nothing. Mighty profit
Your gains will bring if they stop short of such
Full consummation! As a man, you had
A certain share of strength; and that is gone
Already in the getting these you boast.
Do not they seem to laugh, as who should say—
"Great master, we are here indeed, dragged forth
To light; this hast thou done: be glad! Now, seek
The strength to use which thou hast spent in getting!"

And yet 'tis much, surely 'tis very much,
Thus to have emptied youth of all its gifts,
To feed a fire meant to hold out till morn
Arrived with inexhaustible light; and lo,

197| *MS:* Aim's *1835:* aims remain'd *1849:* remained as ever supreme and pure! *1863:* remained supreme and pure as ever! **198**| *MS:* Mankind's sake *1835:* mankind's sake, **199**| *MS:* fail, it may be for some fault,— *1835:* fault; *1849:* fail, some fault may be the cause,— *1863:* cause, **200**| *MS:* That tho' <> succeed?— *1835:* That, though <> succeed? **201**| *MS:*—I cannot! O God I am despicable! *1835:* God, I *1849:* O God, the despicable heart of us! **202**| *1835:* heart! . . . *1849:* heart! **204**| *MS:* rewards——to ask <> lump . . . 1835| *MS:* rewards, to <> lump; *1849:* rewards, and ask **205**| *MS:* on; *1835:* launch'd <> on: *1849:* launched **206**| *MS:* nothing—mighty *1835:* nothing. Mighty **208**| *MS:* as *1835:* As **209**| *MS:* strength, and *1863:* strength; and **210**| *MS:* boast . . . *1835:* boast. **211**| *MS:* laugh as <> say *1835:* laugh, as <> say— **212**| *MS:* Master <> here, indeed,—dragged *1835:* master <> indeed; dragg'd *1849:* dragged *1863:* indeed, dragged **213**| *MS:* light—this <> done—be <> now *1835:* light: this <> done: be *1863:* Now **214**| *MS:* use, which *1835:* use which **215**| *MS:* very much *1835:* surely, 'tis very much, *1849:* 'tis surely much, 'tis *1863:* 'tis much, surely 'tis **216**| *MS:* gifts *1835:* gifts, **217**| *MS:* Morn *1835:* morn **218**| *MS:* light—and *1835:* light; and *1849:* Arrive *1863:* Arrived

I have heaped up my last, and day dawns not!
And I am left with grey hair, faded hands,
And furrowed brow. Ha, have I, after all,
Mistaken the wild nursling of my breast?
Knowledge it seemed, and power, and recompense!
Was she who glided through my room of nights,
Who laid my head on her soft knees and smoothed
The damp locks,—whose sly soothings just began
When my sick spirit craved repose awhile—
God! was I fighting sleep off for death's sake?

God! Thou art mind! Unto the master-mind
Mind should be precious. Spare my mind alone!
All else I will endure; if, as I stand
Here, with my gains, thy thunder smite me down,
I bow me; 'tis thy will, thy righteous will;
I o'erpass life's restrictions, and I die;
And if no trace of my career remain
Save a thin corpse at pleasure of the wind
In these bright chambers level with the air,
See thou to it! But if my spirit fail,
My once proud spirit forsake me at the last,
Has thou done well by me? So do not thou!
Crush not my mind, dear God, though I be crushed!

219| *MS:* last——and Day *1835:* heap'd <> last, and day *1849:* heaped **220**| *MS:* hands *1835:* hands, *1849:* While I *1863:* And I **221**| *MS:* brow—ha, have I after all *1835:* furrow'd brow. Ha, have I, after all, *1849:* furrowed **222–224**| *MS:* breast . . . / Was <> nights— *1835:* breast? / <> through <> nights; *1849:* breast? / Knowledge it seemed, and Power, and Recompense! / Was <> nights,— *1868:* power <> recompense! **225**| *MS:* knees, and *1835:* smooth'd *1849:* smoothed *1863:* knees and **226**| *MS:* locks——whose *1835:* locks; whose *1849:* locks,—whose **227**| *MS:* awhile . . . *1849:* awhile— **228**| *MS:* Sleep off, for Death's *1835:* off for *1849:* sake? / § no space § / *1863:* sake? / § space § / *1868:* sleep <> death's **229**| *MS:* Mind!—unto the Master-Mind, *1835:* Mind! Unto the Master-Mind *1868:* mind <> master-mind **230**| *MS:* precious . . . spare *1835:* precious. Spare **231**| *MS:* endure: if, *1863:* endure; if **232**| *MS:* down *1835:* down, *1863:* Thy *1868:* thy **233**| *MS:* me—'tis thy will—thy <> will—— *1835:* me; 'tis thy will, thy <> will; *1863:* Thy <> Thy *1868:* thy <> thy **234**| *MS:* restrictions and I die . . . *1835:* restrictions, and I die: *1863:* die; **235**| *1835:* remain, *1863:* remain **237**| *1835:* chambers, level *1863:* chambers level **238**| *MS:* it: but <> fail— *1835:* fail, *1849:* it! But *1863:* Thou *1868:* thou **240**| *1863:* Thou <> Thou! *1868:* thou <> thou **241**| *MS:* tho' <> crushed . . . *1835:* though <> crush'd: *1849:* crushed!

Hold me before the frequence of thy seraphs
And say—"I crushed him, lest he should disturb
My law. Men must not know their strength: behold
Weak and alone, how he had raised himself!"

But if delusions trouble me, and thou,
Not seldom felt with rapture in thy help
Throughout my toils and wanderings, dost intend
To work man's welfare through my weak endeavour,
To crown my mortal forehead with a beam
From thine own blinding crown, to smile, and guide
This puny hand and let the work so wrought
Be styled my work,—hear me! I covet not
An influx of new power, an angel's soul:
It were no marvel then—but I have reached
Thus far, a man; let me conclude, a man!
Give but one hour of my first energy,
Of that invincible faith, but only one!
That I may cover with an eagle-glance
The truths I have, and spy some certain way
To mould them, and completing them, possess!

Yet God is good: I started sure of that,

242| *MS:* Seraphs *1835:* seraphs, *1863:* Thy seraphs *1868:* thy **243**| *MS:* say "I <> him lest *1835:* say—"I crush'd him, lest *1849:* crushed **244**| *MS:* Law——Men <> behold, *1835:* law, men *1888:* behold § , after *behold* probably dropped in error § **245**| *1849:* how near he raised *1863:* how he had raised **246**| *MS:* Thou,— *1835:* me—and Thou, *1863:* me, and *1868:* thou **247**| *MS:*—Not *1835:* Not *1863:* Thy *1868:* thy **248**| *MS:* And stay, throughout my wanderings — § above § , dost *1835:* wanderings, dost *1849:* Throughout my toil and wanderings **249**| *MS:* Man's <> thro' <> Endeavour . . . *1835:* man's <> through <> endeavour— *1863:* endeavour, **251**| *MS:* crown——to *1835:* crown—to *1863:* Thine <> crown, to *1868:* thine **252**| *MS:* hand, and <> so framed *1863:* so wrought *1868:* hand and **253**| *MS:* styled his § cancelled by § my work— § above § , hear *1835:* work—hear *1849:* work,—hear **254**| *MS:* soul—— *1835:* soul: **255**| *MS:* have gone *1849:* have reached **256**| *MS:* Man——let § written over by § Man—let <> Man! *1835:* man; let me conclude a man! *1849:* far, a man; let me conclude, a **257**| *MS:* energy *1835:* energy, **258**| *MS:*—Of *1835:* Of <> faith—but *1849:* faith—one only hour! *1863:* faith, but only one! **259**| *MS:*——I should go over with *1835:* I *1849:* That I may cover with **261–262**| *MS:* them and complete them and pursue them . . . / § space § / (After a pause) / Yet *1835:* them, and <> them, and <> them! /// Yet <> good: I <> that, *1849:* completing them, possess! / § space § Yet

And why dispute it now? I'll not believe
But some undoubted warning long ere this
Had reached me: a fire-labarum was not deemed
Too much for the old founder of these walls.
Then, if my life has not been natural,
It has been monstrous: yet, till late, my course
So ardently engrossed me, that delight,
A pausing and reflecting joy, 'tis plain,
Could find no place in it. True, I am worn;
But who clothes summer, who is life itself?
God, that created all things, can renew!
And then, though after-life to please me now
Must have no likeness to the past, what hinders
Reward from springing out of toil, as changed
As bursts the flower from earth and root and stalk?
What use were punishment, unless some sin
Be first detected? let me know that first!
No man could ever offend as I have done . . .

[*A voice from within.*]

I hear a voice, perchance I heard
Long ago, but all too low,
So that scarce a care it stirred
If the voice were real or no:

263| *MS:* now——I'll § written over by § now?—I'll *1835:* now? I'll
265–266| *MS:* me . . a labarum < > / Too < > walls:— *1835:* reach'd me: a < > deem'd / < > walls. *1849:* reached me: stars would write his will in heaven, / As once when a labarum was not deemed / Too *1863:* reached me: a fire-labarum was not deemed / Too 267| *MS:*—Then, if my § *my* inserted above the line § life have < > natural *1835:* then < > has < > natural, 268| *MS:* monstruous . . yet till *1835:* monstrous: yet, till 269| *MS:* delight,— *1835:* engross'd < > delight, *1849:* engrossed 270–271| *MS:* joy—'tis plain, / Could < > it: 'tis true, I am worn, *1835:* joy, 'tis < > / < > it. "Tis < > worn; *1849:* plain, / Though such were meant to follow as its fruit, / Could < > it. True, I *1863:* plain, / Could 272–274| *MS:* Life itself? / —And then tho' *1835:* And then, though *1849:* itself? / God, that created all things, can renew! / And *1868:* Who < > Who *1868:* who < > who 276| *MS:* toil § written over by § toil *1835:* toil 277| *1835:* earth, and root, and *1863:* earth and root and
278| *MS:*—What *1835:* What 279–297| *MS:* Were first detected?—let < > first! / No < > done . . . . . . / [*A* < > *within.*] / Lost, Lost!—yet *1835:* detected? let < > first: / < > done . . . / § space § / [*A* < > *within.*] / Lost, lost! yet *1849:* Be first < > first! § space § [Aprile, from within.] I hear a voice, perchance I heard / Long ago, but all too low, / So that scarce a thought was stirred / If really spoke the voice or no: /

I heard it in my youth when first
The waters of my life outburst:
But, now their stream ebbs faint, I hear
That voice, still low, but fatal-clear—
As if all poets, God ever meant
Should save the world, and therefore lent
Great gifts to, but who, proud, refused
To do his work, or lightly used
Those gifts, or failed through weak endeavour,
So, mourn cast off by him for ever,—
As if these leaned in airy ring
To take me; this the song they sing.

"Lost, lost! yet come,
With our wan troop make thy home.
Come, come! for we
Will not breathe, so much as breathe
Reproach to thee,
Knowing what you sink'st beneath.
So sank we in those old years,
We who bid thee, come! thou last
Who, living yet, hast life o'erpast.

I heard it in my youth, when first / The waters of my life outburst: / But now their stream ebbs faint, I hear / The voice, still low, but fatal-clear— / As if all Poets, that God meant / Should save the world, and therefore lent / Great gifts to, but who, proud, refused / To do his work, or lightly used / Those gifts, or failed through weak endeavour, / And mourn, cast off by him forever,— / As if these leaned in airy ring / To call me; this the song they sing. / "Lost, lost § 297–339 § indented farther than 281–296 § 279–281| *1863:* first! / No man could ever offend as I have done . . . / § space § / [A voice from within.] / § space § / I hear a 283| *1863:* a care it stirred 284| *1863:* If the voice was real or *1868:* voice were real 285| *1863:* youth when 287| *1868:* But, now 288| *1863:* That voice, still low but 289| *1863:* Poets, God ever meant *1868:* poets 292| *1863:* His *1868:* his 294| *1863:* So, mourn cast <> Him for ever,— *1868:* him 296| *1863:* To take me 297–339| *1888:* § indentation aligned with 281–296 § 298| *MS:* home *1835:* home: *1863:* home. 299| *MS:* Come, come,—for *1835:* Come, come! for 301–304| *MS:* thee! / Lost one, come! the last *1849:* thee! / Knowing what thou sink'st beneath; / So we sank in those old years, / We who bid thee, come! thou last *1863:* beneath. *1868:* Reproach to thee, 305| *MS:* living, hast <> o'erpast *1835:* o'erpast, *1849:* Who, a living man, hast *1863:* Who, living yet, hast *1868:* o'erpast.

And altogether we, thy peers,
Will pardon crave for thee, the last
Whose trial is done, whose lot is cast
With those who watch but work no more,
Who gaze on life but live no more.
Yet we trusted thou shouldst speak
The message which our lips, too weak,
Refused to utter,—shouldst redeem
Our fault: such trust, and all a dream!
Yet we chose thee a birthplace
Where the richness ran to flowers:
Couldst not sing one song for grace?
Not make one blossom man's and ours?
Must one more recreant to his race
Die with unexerted powers,
And join us, leaving as he found
The world, he was to loosen, bound?
Anguish! ever and for ever;
Still beginning, ending never.
Yet, lost and last one, come!
How couldst understand, alas,
What our pale ghosts strove to say,
As their shades did glance and pass

306| *MS:* And, all together we *1835:* And all *1849:* And all together we, thy peers, **307**| *MS:* Will ask for us and ask for thee *1835:* thee, *1849:* Will pardon ask for thee, the last *1888:* pardon crave for **308**| *MS:* is past whose *1835:* past, whose *1849:* trial is done, whose **309**| *MS:* more, *1835:* more— *1849:* watch, but *1863:* watch but **310–315**| *MS:* Life, but <> more: . . / Yet <> birth-place *1835:* life <> more: *1849:* more: / And yet we trusted thou shouldst speak / God's message which our lips, too weak, / Refused to utter,—shouldst redeem / Our fault: such trust, and all, a dream! / So we <> a bright birth-place *1863:* life but <> more. / Yet we <> / The message // <> all a <> / Yet we <> a birthplace **316**| *MS:* flowers . . . *1849:* flowers— *1863:* flowers; *1888:* flowers: **317**| *MS:* Could'st <> for us? *1849:* Couldst <> for grace? **318**| *MS:* blossom ours, *1835:* ours— *1849:* blossom man's and ours? **319–323**| *MS:* Not one of the sweet race? / Anguish <> for ever, *1835:* for ever; *1849:* Must one more recreant to his race / Die with unexerted powers, / And join us, leaving as he found / The world, he was to loosen, bound? / Anguish **324**| *MS:* never! *1888:* never. **326**| *MS:* could'st *1849:* couldst **327**| *MS:* say *1835:* say,

Before thee night and day?
Thou wast blind as we were dumb:
Once more, therefore, come, O come!
How should we clothe, how arm the spirit
Shall next thy post of life inherit—
How guard him from thy speedy ruin?
Tell us of thy sad undoing
Here, where we sit, ever pursuing
Our weary task, ever renewing
Sharp sorrow, far from God who gave
Our powers, and man they could not save!"

APRILE *enters.*

Ha, ha! our king that wouldst be, here at last?
Art thou the poet who shall save the world?
Thy hand to mine! Stay, fix thine eyes on mine!
Thou wouldst be king? Still fix thine eyes on mine!
PARACELSUS Ha, ha! why crouchest not? Am I not king?
So torture is not wholly unavailing!
Have my fierce spasms compelled thee from thy lair?
Art thou the sage I only seemed to be,
Myself of after-time, my very self
With sight a little clearer, strength more firm,

329–331| *MS:* thee, night and day— / O come, come! *1835:* day . . . *1849:* day? / Thou wert blind, as we were dumb: / Once more, therefore, come, O come! *1863:* Thou wast blind as *1888:* thee night **332**| *MS:* How shall we *1849:* we better arm *1863:* we clothe, how arm *1888:* How should we **333**| *MS:* Who next shall thy post inherit—— *1835:* inherit— *1849:* post of life inherit— *1868:* Shall next thy **334**| *1849:* thy ruin? *1863:* thy speedy ruin? **338–342**| *MS:* from——— / § space § / APRILE *enters* / § space § / Ha, ha, our King <> last? / . . . Thy <> mine . . . stay—fix <> mine, *1835:* from . . . //// <> king <> / Thy <> mine. Stay, fix <> mine. *1849:* from God who gave Our powers, and man they could not save!" // APRILE *enters* / § no space § / A spirit better armed, succeeding me? / Ha, ha <> last? / Art thou the Poet who shall save the world? / Thy *1863: enters.* / Ha, ha *1868: enters* / § space § // <> poet <> / <> mine! Stay **343**| *MS:* King?— still <> mine——— *1835:* king? Still <> mine. **344**| *MS:* Ha, ha, why <> not?—am <> King? *1835:* Ha, Ha! why <> not? am <> king? *1849:* Am **346–352**| *MS:* lair? / Ay, look on me!—shall I be king or no? / I *1835:* compell'd <> / <> me! shall *1849:* compelled <> lair? / Art thou the Sage I only seemed to be, / Myself of after-time, my very self / With sight a little clearer, strength more firm, / Who robs me of my prize and takes my place / For just a fault, a weakness, a neglect? / I *1863:* sage <> // <> firm, / Who robes him in my robe and grasps my crown / For

Who robes him in my robe and grasps my crown
For just a fault, a weakness, a neglect?
I scarcely trusted God with the surmise
That such might come, and thou didst hear the while!
APRILE Thine eyes are lustreless to mine; my hair
Is soft, nay silken soft: to talk with thee
Flushes my cheek, and thou art ashy-pale.
Truly, thou hast laboured, hast withstood her lips,
The siren's! Yes, 'tis like thou hast attained!
Tell me, dear master, wherefore now thou comest?
I thought thy solemn songs would have their meed
In after-time; that I should hear the earth
Exult in thee and echo with thy praise,
While I was laid forgotten in my grave.
PARACELSUS Ah fiend, I know thee, I am not thy dupe!
Thou art ordained to follow in my track,
Reaping my sowing, as I scorned to reap
The harvest sown by sages passed away.
Thou art the sober searcher, cautious striver,
As if, except through me, thou hast searched or striven!
Ay, tell the world! Degrade me after all,
To an aspirant after fame, not truth—
To all but envy of thy fate, be sure!

353| *MS:* That thou would'st come——and thou did'st *1835:* wouldst come, and thou didst *1849:* That such might come 354| *MS:* mine,—my *1835:* mine: my 355| *MS:* silkensoft—to *1835:* silken soft: to 356| *MS:* cheek . . and <> ashy-pale . . . *1835:* cheek, and <> ashy-pale. *1849:* ashy-pale, *1863:* ashy-pale. 357| *MS:* Truly thou <> withstood their lips *1835:* labour'd <> lips, *1849:* True, thou <> laboured <> withstood her lips, *1863:* Truly, thou 358| *MS:*—Their kisses . . . yes *1835:* Their kisses. Yes <> attain'd. *1849:* The siren's! Yes <> attained! 359| *MS:* Master *1835:* master 361| *MS:* after-time—that *1835:* after-time: that 362| *MS:* thee, and <> praise *1835:* praise, *1888:* thee and 364| *MS:* Ah, fiend *1849:* Not so! I know *1863:* Ah, fiend, I know *1868:* Ah fiend 365–366| *MS:* track——— § above § track,——/ To reap <> I disdained to *1835:* ordain'd track, / <> sowing—as I disdain'd *1849:* ordained <> track, / Even as thou sayest, succeeding to my place, / Reaping my sowing—as I scorned to *1863:* track, / Reaping my sowing, as 367–370| *MS:* harvest left by sages long since gone . . . . / I am to be degraded, after all, *1835:* gone. *1849:* harvest sown by sages passed away. / Thou art the sober searcher, cautious striver, / As if, except through me, thou had'st searched or striven! / Ay, tell the world! Degrade me, after all, *1863:* thou hadst searched *1888:* me after 371| *MS:* Fame, not Truth . . . *1835:* fame, not truth— 372| *MS:* . . . To *1835:* To

APRILE Nay, sing them to me; I shall envy not:
Thou shalt be king! Sing thou, and I will sit
Beside, and call deep silence for thy songs,
And worship thee, as I had ne'er been meant
To fill thy throne: but none shall ever know!
Sing to me; for already thy wild eyes
Unlock my heart-strings, as some crystal-shaft
Reveals by some chance blaze its parent fount
After long time: so thou reveal'st my soul.
All will flash forth at last, with thee to hear!
PARACELSUS (His secret! I shall get his secret—fool!)
I am he that aspired to KNOW: and thou?
APRILE I would LOVE infinitely, and be loved!
PARACELSUS Poor slave! I am thy king indeed.
APRILE Thou deem'st
That—born a spirit, dowered even as thou,
Born for thy fate—because I could not curb
My yearnings to possess at once the full
Enjoyment, but neglected all the means
Of realizing even the frailest joy,
Gathering no fragments to appease my want,
Yet nursing up that want till thus I die—
Thou deem'st I cannot trace thy safe sure march

374| *MS:* king—sing thou and *1835:* king. Sing thou, and *1849:* will stand *1863:* will sit 375| *MS:* Beside and *1835:* Beside, and 377| *MS:* throne . . . but <> know: *1835:* throne. But <> know! *1849:* throne—but *1863:* throne: but 378| *1835:* me: for *1863:* me; for 379| *MS:* heartsprings <> chrystal-shaft *1835:* heart-springs <> crystal-shaft 381| *MS:* time——so <> revealest my soul! *1835:* time—so <> reveal'st *1863:* time: so <> soul. 382| *MS:* . . All *1835:* All 383| *MS:* secret . . . fool!)—I am *1835:* secret—fool!) I *1849:* secret! my succesor's secret—fool!) *1863:* secret! I shall get his secret 384| *MS:* The mortal who aspired to KNOW . . . and Thou? *1835:* KNOW—and thou? *1849:* I am he that aspired to KNOW *1863:* KNOW: and 385| *MS:* LOVE *1835:* LOVE 386| *MS:* King indeed: APRILE <> deemest *1835:* king indeed APRILE <> deem'st 387| *MS:* That,—born a spirit dowered *1835:* That—born a spirit, dower'd *1849:* dowered 388| *MS:* fate,—because *1835:* fate—because 390| *MS:* Enjoyment——but *1835:* Enjoyment: but *1849:* Enjoyment: yet neglected *1863:* Enjoyment, but neglected 391| *MS:* joy,— *1835:* joy; *1863:* joy, 392| *MS:* want *1835:* want, 393| *MS:* die . . . . *1835:* die— 394| *MS:* That I cannot conceive thy <> March, *1835:* safe, sure march, *1849:* Thou deem'st I cannot trace thy *1888:* safe sure

O'er perils that o'erwhelm me, triumphing,
Neglecting nought below for aught above,
Despising nothing and ensuring all—
Nor that I could (my time to come again)
Lead thus my spirit securely as thine own.
Listen, and thou shalt see I know thee well.
I would love infinitely . . . Ah, lost! lost!
    Oh ye who armed me at such cost,
    How shall I look on all of ye
    With your gifts even yet on me?

PARACELSUS (Ah, 'tis some moonstruck creature after all!
Such fond fools as are like to haunt this den:
They spread contagion, doubtless: yet he seemed
To echo one foreboding of my heart
So truly, that . . . no matter! How he stands
With eve's last sunbeam staying on his hair
Which turns to it as if they were akin:
And those clear smiling eyes of saddest blue
Nearly set free, so far they rise above
The painful fruitless striving of the brow
And enforced knowledge of the lips, firm-set
In slow despondency's eternal sigh!
Has he, too, missed life's end, and learned the cause?)
I charge thee, by thy fealty, be calm!

395| *MS:* Triumphing o'er the perils that o'erwhelm me, *1849:* O'er perils that o'erwhelm me, triumphing, 397| *MS:* all . . . *1835:* all— 398| *MS:* . . That I could not, my <> again, *1835:* That *1849:* Nor that I could (my <> again) 399| *MS:* Lead my own spirit <> own; *1835:* Lead this my spirit *1849:* Lead thus my *1849:* own: *1863:* own. 400| *MS:* well: *1849:* well. 401–403| *MS:* love § written over by § Love <> Ah— § above § , lost, lost, / How *1835:* love <> Ah, lost! lost! *1849:* lost! lost! / O ye who armed me at such cost, / Your faces shall I bear to see *1863:* cost, / How shall I look on all of ye 404| *MS:* me . . . . *1835:* me . . . *1849:* me?— *1863:* me?
405| *MS:* (Ah,—tis *1835:* (Ah, 'tis 406–418| *MS:* den:——) *1849:* den: / They spread contagion, doubtless: yet he seemed / To echo one foreboding of my heart / So truly, that . . . no matter! How he stands / With eve's last sunbeam staying on his hair / Which turns to it, as if they were akin: / And those clear smiling eyes of saddest blue / Nearly set free, so far they rise above / The painful fruitless striving of that brow / And enforced knowledge of those lips, firm-set / In slow despondency's eternal sigh! / Has he, too, missed life's end, and learned the cause?) / Be calm, I charge thee, by thy fealty! 411| *1868:* it as 414| *1863:* of the brow
415| *1863:* of the lips 418| *1863:* I charge thee, by thy fealty, be calm!

Tell me what thou wouldst be, and what I am.
APRILE I would love infinitely, and be loved.
First: I would carve in stone, or cast in brass,
The forms of earth. No ancient hunter lifted
Up to the gods by his renown, no nymph
Supposed the sweet soul of a woodland tree
Or sapphirine spirit of a twilight star,
Should be too hard for me; no shepherd-king
Regal for his white locks; no youth who stands
Silent and very calm amid the throng,
His right hand ever hid beneath his robe
Until the tyrant pass; no lawgiver,
No swan-soft woman rubbed with lucid oils
Given by a god for love of her—too hard!
Every passion sprung from man, conceived by man,
Would I express and clothe it in its right form,
Or blend with others struggling in one form,
Or show repressed by an ungainly form.
Oh, if you marvelled at some mighty spirit
With a fit frame to execute its will—
Even unconsciously to work its will—
You should be moved no less beside some strong

419| *MS:* be and < > am! *1835:* be, and < > am. 420| *MS:* Love infinitely and be loved! *1835:* love infinitely, and be loved. 421| *MS:* First, I < > stone or < > brass *1835:* First: I < > stone, or < > brass,
422| *MS:* Earth:—no *1835:* earth. No *1849:* hunter, raised *1863:* hunter lifted 423| *MS:* Gods by his renown,—no nymph § written over by § Nymph *1835:* gods < > renown; no nymph *1863:* renown, no 424| *MS:* tree, *1863:* tree 425| *MS:* star *1835:* star, 426| *1835:* shepherd-king, *1863:* shepherd-king 427| *MS:* locks . . no *1835:* locks; no *1849:* Regal with his *1863:* Regal for his 429| *MS:* right-hand < > robe, *1835:* right hand < > robe 430| *MS:* pass,—no law-giver, *1835:* pass; no law-giver; *1863:* lawgiver, 431| *1835:* woman, rubb'd < > oils, *1849:* rubbed *1863:* woman rubbed *1868:* oils 432| *MS:* God < > her,—too hard. *1835:* god < > her—too *1849:* hard! 433| *MS:* Man < > Man *1835:* man < > man, *1849:* Each passion *1863:* Every passion 434–436| *MS:* clothe in its fit form,— / Or show, repressed < > ungainly form,— / Or blend < > one form,— *1835:* clothe in its fit form, / Or show repress'd < > ungainly form, / < > one form. *1849:* clothe it in its right form, / Or blend < > one form, / Or show repressed < > ungainly form. 437| *MS:*—O if you marveled < > Spirit *1835:* Oh, if you marvell'd < > spirit *1849:* For, if you marvelled *1863:* Oh, if 438| *MS:* execute his will, *1835:* will— *1863:* execute its will—
439| *MS:*—Even < > work his will, . . . *1835:* Even < > will— *1849:* Ay, even *1863:* Even < > work its will— 440| *1835:* strong, *1888:* strong

Rare spirit, fettered to a stubborn body,
Endeavouring to subdue it and inform it
With its own splendour! All this I would do:
And I would say, this done, "His sprites created,
God grants to each a sphere to be its world,
Appointed with the various objects needed
To satisfy its own peculiar want;
So, I create a world for these my shapes
Fit to sustain their beauty and their strength!"
And, at the word, I would contrive and paint
Woods, valleys, rocks and plains, dells, sands and wastes,
Lakes which, when morn breaks on their quivering bed,
Blaze like a wyvern flying round the sun,
And ocean isles so small, the dog-fish tracking
A dead whale, who should find them, would swim thrice
Around them, and fare onward—all to hold
The offspring of my brain. Nor these alone:
Bronze labyrinth, palace, pyramid and crypt,
Baths, galleries, courts, temples and terraces,
Marts, theatres and wharfs—all filled with men,
Men everywhere! And this performed in turn,
When those who looked on, pined to hear the hopes
And fears and hates and loves which moved the crowd,

441| *MS: 1835:* fetter'd *1849:* fettered 442| *1835:* it, and *1863:* it and 443| *MS:* splendour!—All <> do, *1835:* splendour! All *1863:* do: 444| *1849:* done, "God's sprites being made, *1863:* done, "His sprites created, 445| *MS:* be his world, *1849:* He grants <> be its world, *1863:* God grants 447| *MS:* satisfy his own <> wants; *1849:* satisfy its spiritual desires; *1863:* satisfy its own peculiar wants; *1868:* want; 450| *MS:*—And at *1835:* And, at 451| *MS:* wastes *1835:* rocks, and plains <> sands, and wastes, *1863:* rocks and plains <> sands and 452| *MS:* which when <> bed *1849:* which, when <> bed, 453| *MS:* sun,— *1849:* sun; *1863:* sun, 454| *MS:*—And ocean-isles *1835:* And *1888:* ocean isles 456| *MS:* onward———all *1835:* onward—all 457| *MS:* brain—nor <> alone . . . *1835:* brain. Nor <> alone— *1863:* alone: 458| *MS:* labyrinths <> pyramid and crypt *1835:* pyramid, and crypt, *1863:* labyrinth <> pyramid and 459| *MS:* temples, and terraces *1835:* terraces, *1863:* temples and 460| *MS:* wharfs——all <> men! § written over by § Men! *1835:* theatres, and wharfs—all fill'd <> men! *1849:* filled *1863:* theatres and *1868:* men, 461| *MS:* every where:—and <> performed, in *1835:* everywhere! And <> perform'd *1849:* performed *1863:* performed in 462| *MS:* on pined *1835:* look'd <> hopes, *1849:* looked on, pined *1863:* hopes 463| *1835:* fears, and hates, and *1849:* crowd,— *1863:* fears and hates and <> crowd,

I would throw down the pencil as the chisel,
And I would speak; no thought which ever stirred
A human breast should be untold; all passions,
All soft emotions, from the turbulent stir
Within a heart fed with desires like mine,
To the last comfort shutting the tired lids
Of him who sleeps the sultry noon away
Beneath the tent-tree by the wayside well:
And this in language as the need should be,
Now poured at once forth in a burning flow,
Now piled up in a grand array of words.
This done, to perfect and consummate all,
Even as a luminous haze links star to star,
I would supply all chasms with music, breathing
Mysterious motions of the soul, no way
To be defined save in strange melodies.
Last, having thus revealed all I could love,
Having received all love bestowed on it,
I would die: preserving so throughout my course
God full on me, as I was full on men:
He would approve my prayer, "I have gone through
The loveliness of life; create for me
If not for men, or take me to thyself,

464| *MS:* chisel *1835:* chisel, 465| *MS:* Speak,—no *1835:* speak: no < > stirr'd *1849:* stirred *1863:* speak; no 466| *MS:* passions *1835:* passions, *1849:* untold; no passions, *1863:* untold; all passions, 467| *MS:* emotions,—from *1835:* emotions, from *1849:* No soft *1863:* All soft
468| *MS:* mine . . . *1835:* mine— *1863:* mine, 469| *1835:* comfort, shutting *1863:* comfort shutting 471| *MS:* wayside-well: . . . § written over by § well:— *1835:* way-side well: *1863:* wayside 472| *MS:* this, in < > be,— *1835:* this in < > be, 473| *MS:* Now,—poured *1835:* Now pour'd *1849:* poured 474| *MS:* Now,—piled < > words:— *1835:* Now piled < > words. 475| *MS:* done— § above § , to *1835:* done, to 476| *MS:* to star *1835:* to star, 477| *MS:* music § written over by § Music,—breathing *1835:* music, breathing 479| *MS:* melodies: *1835:* melodies.
480| —Last *1835:* Last < > reveal'd *1849:* revealed 481| *MS:* on them,— *1835:* bestow'd on it, *1849:* And having < > bestowed *1863:* Having 482| *MS:* die: having preserved throughout *1849:* die: so preserving through my *1863:* die: preserving so throughout my 483| *MS:* Men: *1835:* men. *1849:* men: 484| *MS:* prayer—"I < > thro' *1835:* through *1849:* And he would grant my *1863:* He would approve my prayer, "I 485| *MS:* Life,—create *1835:* life, create *1849:* All loveliness of life; make more for me, *1863:* The loveliness of life; create for me 486| *MS:* Men,—or take *1835:* men—or *1863:* men, or < > Thyself, *1868:* thyself,

Eternal, infinite love!"
                                        If thou has ne'er
Conceived this mighty aim, this full desire,
Thou hast not passed my trial, and thou art
No king of mine.

PARACELSUS Ah me!

APRILE But thou art here!
Thou didst not gaze like me upon that end
Till thine own powers for compassing the bliss
Were blind with glory; nor grow mad to grasp
At once the prize long patient toil should claim,
Nor spurn all granted short of that. And I
Would do as thou, a second time: nay, listen!
Knowing ourselves, our world, our task so great,
Our time so brief, 'tis clear if we refuse
The means so limited, the tools so rude
To execute our purpose, life will fleet,
And we shall fade, and leave our task undone.
We will be wise in time: what though our work
Be fashioned in despite of their ill-service,
Be crippled every way? 'Twere little praise
Did full resources wait on our goodwill
At every turn. Let all be as it is.
Some say the earth is even so contrived
That tree and flower, a vesture gay, conceal
A bare and skeleton framework. Had we means

487| *MS:* Love *1868:* love 488| *MS:* Aim <> Desire *1835:* aim <> desire, 489| *1835:* pass'd *1849:* passed 490| *MS:* mine! PARACELSUS *1835:* mine. PARACELSUS 491| *MS:* did'st <> End *1835:* didst <> end 493| *MS:* glory:—nor *1835:* glory; nor 494| *MS:* claim: *1863:* claim, 495| *MS:* that—and *1835:* that. And 496| *MS:* thou, if that might be; Nay, listen:— *1835:* be; nay, listen— *1849:* thou, a second time: nay *1863:* listen! 497| *MS:* world,—our *1835:* world, our 498| *MS:* brief—'tis *1835:* brief; 'tis *1849:* brief,—'tis *1863:* brief, 'tis 500| *MS:* fleet *1835:* fleet, 501| *MS:* fade and nothing will be done— *1835:* fade, and <> done. *1849:* and leave our task undone. 502| *MS:* tho' *1835:* though *1849:* Rather, grow wise *1863:* We will be wise 503| *MS:* ill service, *1835:* fashion'd <> ill-service, *1849:* fashioned 505| *MS:* good will *1863:* goodwill 506| *MS:* turn: . . let <> is:— *1835:* turn. Let <> is. 507| *MS:* contrived— *1835:* contrived 508| *1835:* tree, and *1863:* tree and 509| *MS:* framework——had § written over by § framework:— *1835:* framework: had *1863:* framework. Had

Answering to our mind! But now I seem
Wrecked on a savage isle: how rear thereon
My palace? Branching palms the props shall be,
Fruit glossy mingling; gems are for the East;
Who heeds them? I can pass them. Serpents' scales,
And painted birds' down, furs and fishes' skins
Must help me; and a little here and there
Is all I can aspire to: still my art
Shall show its birth was in a gentler clime.
"Had I green jars of malachite, this way
I'd range them: where those sea-shells glisten above,
Cressets should hang, by right: this way we set
The purple carpets, as these mats are laid,
Woven of fern and rush and blossoming flag."
Or if, by fortune, some completer grace
Be spared to me, some fragment, some slight sample
Of the prouder workmanship my own home boasts,
Some trifle little heeded there, but here
The place's one perfection—with what joy
Would I enshrine the relic, cheerfully
Foregoing all the marvels out of reach!
Could I retain one strain of all the psalm
Of the angels, one word of the fiat of God,
To let my followers know what such things are!
I would adventure nobly for their sakes:

510| *MS:* mind! . . but *1835:* mind! But *1849:* That answered *1863:* Answering 511| *MS:* isle—how *1835:* Wreck'd <> isle. How *1849:* Wrecked <> isle: how 512| *MS:* palace?—branching *1835:* palace? Branching 513| *MS:* East,— *1835:* east; *1863:* East; 514| *MS:* them: serpent scales *1835:* them. Serpent's scales, *1849:* can waive them *1863:* can pass them. Serpents' 515| *1835:* furs, and *1849:* Birds' feathers, down furs *1863:* And painted birds' down, furs and 517| *MS:* Art *1835:* art 518| *MS:* clime: *1835:* clime. 522| *MS:* laid *1835:* laid, 523| *MS:* blossoming-flag." *1835:* blossoming flag." *1849:* of mere fern *1863:* of fern 526| *MS:* Home *1835:* home *1849:* Of my own land's completer workmanship, *1863:* Of the prouder workmanship my own home boasts, 527| *MS: here* *1849:* here 528| *MS:* The one perfection of the place,—how gladly *1835:* place, how *1849:* The place's one perfection—with what joy 529| *MS:* relic—cheerfully *1863:* relic, cheerfully 530| *1835:* reach— *1849:* reach! 531| *MS:* Psalm *1835:* psalm 532| *MS:* Angels—— —one *1835:* angels—one <> God— *1863:* angels, one <> God, 533| *MS:* are! . . . *1835:* are! 534| *MS:*—I <> sakes; *1835:* I <> sakes:

When nights were still, and still the moaning sea,
And far away I could descry the land
Whence I departed, whither I return,
I would dispart the waves, and stand once more
At home, and load my bark, and hasten back,
And fling my gains to them, worthless or true.
"Friends," I would say, "I went far, far for them,
Past the high rocks the haunt of doves, the mounds
Of red earth from whose sides strange trees grow out,
Past tracts of milk-white minute blinding sand,
Till, by a mighty moon, I tremblingly
Gathered these magic herbs, berry and bud,
In haste, not pausing to reject the weeds,
But happy plucking them at any price.
To me, who have seen them bloom in their own soil,
They are scarce lovely: plait and wear them, you!
And guess, from what they are, the springs that fed them,
The stars that sparkled o'er them, night by night,
The snakes that travelled far to sip their dew!"
Thus for my higher loves; and thus even weakness
Would win me honour. But not these alone
Should claim my care; for common life, its wants
And ways, would I set forth in beauteous hues:
The lowest hind should not possess a hope,
A fear, but I'd be by him, saying better
Than he his own heart's language. I would live

535| *MS:* still and still <> sea *1835:* still, and *1849:* and still, the *1868:* and still the *1888:* sea *1889:* sea, 536| *MS:* Land *1835:* land 537| *MS:* return, . . *1835:* return, 538| *MS:* waves and *1835:* waves, and 539| *MS:* bark and <> back *1835:* bark, and <> back, 540| *MS:* true, *1835:* true. *1849:* gains before them, rich or poor— *1863:* gains to them, worthless or true— *1888:* true. 541| *MS:* them *1835:* them, 542| *MS:* doves—the *1835:* doves, the 546| *1835:* Gather'd *1849:* Gathered 547| *MS:* haste——not <> weeds *1835:* haste—not <> weeds, *1863:* haste, not 548| *MS:* happy, plucking <> price: *1835:* happy plucking <> price. 549| *MS:* soil *1835:* soil, 550| *MS:* lovely:—plait *1835:* lovely: plait <> them you! *1849:* them, you! 551| *MS:* guess from *1835:* are the <> them, *1849:* guess, from <> are, the <> fed— *1863:* fed them, 553| *1835:* travell'd *1849:* travelled 554| *MS:* loves——and *1835:* loves; and 555| *MS:* honour:—but *1835:* honour. But 556| *MS:* care,—for *1835:* care; for 557| *MS:* ways would <> hues,—— *1835:* ways, would <> hues: 558| *MS:* hope *1835:* hope, 560| *MS:* he, his <> Language—I *1835:* he his <> language. I

For ever in the thoughts I thus explored,
As a discoverer's memory is attached
To all he finds; they should be mine henceforth,
Imbued with me, though free to all before:
For clay, once cast into my soul's rich mine,
Should come up crusted o'er with gems. Nor this
Would need a meaner spirit, than the first;
Nay, 'twould be but the selfsame spirit, clothed
In humbler guise, but still the selfsame spirit:
As one spring wind unbinds the mountain snow
And comforts violets in their hermitage.

But, master, poet, who hast done all this,
How didst thou 'scape the ruin whelming me?
Didst thou, when nerving thee to this attempt,
Ne'er range thy mind's extent, as some wide hall,
Dazzled by shapes that filled its length with light,
Shapes clustered there to rule thee, not obey,
That will not wait thy summons, will not rise
Singly, nor when thy practised eye and hand
Can well transfer their loveliness, but crowd
By thee for ever, bright to thy despair?
Didst thou ne'er gaze on each by turns, and ne'er
Resolve to single out one, though the rest
Should vanish, and to give that one, entire

562| *1835:* attach'd *1849:* attached 563| *MS:* finds—they <> be mine henceforth § *mine* inserted above the line § *1835:* finds: they *1863:* finds; they 564| *MS:* before,— *1835:* before; *1863:* before: 565| *MS:* mine *1868:* mine, 566| *MS:* oer <> gems: nor *1835:* o'er *1863:* gems. Nor 567| *MS:* first: *1863:* first; 568| *MS:*—Nay *1835:* Nay 569| *MS:* guise,—but *1835:* guise, but <> spirit— *1863:* spirit: 570| *1835:* snow, *1863:* snow 571| *1863:* hermitage. / § no space § / *1888:* hermitage. / § space § / 572| *MS:* . . . But, Master, Poet *1835:* But master, poet *1849:* But, master 573| *MS:* did'st <> ruin I have met? *1835:* didst *1863:* ruin whelming me? 574| *MS:* Did'st *1835:* Didst 575| *MS:* Hall, *1835:* hall, 576| *1835:* fill'd *1849:* filled 577| *MS:* there, to <> obey,— *1835:* cluster'd there to <> obey— *1849:* clustered *1863:* obey, 578| *MS:* summons—will *1835:* summons, will 579| *MS:* Singly— § above § , nor *1835:* Singly, nor 580| *MS:* loveliness— § above § , but are *1835:* loveliness, but *1849:* but crowd 581| *MS:* despair! *1835:* despair? 582| *MS:* turns,—and *1835:* turns, and 583| *MS: One,*—tho' *1835: one,* though *1863:* one 584| *MS:* One *1835:* one

In beauty, to the world; forgetting, so,
Its peers, whose number baffles mortal power?
And, this determined, wast thou ne'er seduced
By memories and regrets and passionate love,
To glance once more farewell? and did their eyes
Fasten thee, brighter and more bright, until
Thou couldst but stagger back unto their feet,
And laugh that man's applause or welfare ever
Could tempt thee to forsake them? Or when years
Had passed and still their love possessed thee wholly,
When from without some murmur startled thee
Of darkling mortals famished for one ray
Of thy so-hoarded luxury of light,
Didst thou ne'er strive even yet to break those spells
And prove thou couldst recover and fulfil
Thy early mission, long ago renounced,
And to that end, select some shape once more?
And did not mist-like influences, thick films,
Faint memories of the rest that charmed so long
Thine eyes, float fast, confuse thee, bear thee off,
As whirling snow-drifts blind a man who treads

585| *MS:* world—and to forget *1835:* world; and *1849:* world; forgetting, so, 586| *MS:* peers whose < > power;— *1835:* peers, whose < > power? 587| *MS:*—And < > wert *1835:* And *1863:* wast 588| *MS:* love *1835:* memories and regrets, and < > love, *1863:* memories and regrets and 589| *MS:* farewel———and *1835:* farewell? and 591| *MS:* could'st < > feet *1835:* couldst < > feet, 592| *MS:* Man's *1835:* man's *1849:* welfare once *1863:* welfare ever 593| *MS:* them: . . or *1835:* them? Or 594| *MS:* passed, and *1835:* pass'd, and < > possess'd < > wholly; *1849:* passed < > possessed *1863:* passed and < > wholly, 596| *1835:* mortals, famish'd *1849:* famished *1863:* mortals famished 597| *MS:* so hoarded *1835:* so-hoarded 598| *MS:* Did'st < > break their spells . . . *1835:* Didst < > spells, *1849:* break those spells, *1863:* spells 599| *MS:* . . . To prove that even yet thou could'st fulfil *1835:* To < > couldst *1849:* And prove thou couldst recover and fulfil 600| *MS:* renounced,— *1835:* renounced, 601| *MS:* And, to < > more *1835:* more? *1868:* And to 602| *MS:* ———And *1835:* And 603| *MS:* rest, so long before *1849:* rest, that charmed so long *1863:* rest that 604| *MS:* eyes, fast float, confuse < > off *1835:* off, *1849:* eyes, float fast, confuse 605| *MS:* snowdrifts *1835:* snow-drifts

A mountain ridge, with guiding spear, through storm?
Say, though I fell, I had excuse to fall;
Say, I was tempted sorely: say but this,
Dear lord, Aprile's lord!

PARACELSUS Clasp me not thus,
Aprile! That the truth should reach me thus!
We are weak dust. Nay, clasp not or I faint!

APRILE My king! and envious thoughts could outrage thee?
Lo, I forget my ruin, and rejoice
In thy success, as thou! Let our God's praise
Go bravely through the world at last! What care
Through me or thee? I feel thy breath. Why, tears?
Tears in the darkness, and from thee to me?

PARACELSUS Love me henceforth, Aprile, while I learn
To love; and, merciful God, forgive us both!
We wake at length from weary dreams; but both
Have slept in fairy-land: though dark and drear
Appears the world before us, we no less
Wake with our wrists and ankles jewelled still.
I too have sought to KNOW as thou to LOVE—

606–607| *MS:* mountain-ridge < > thro' storm:— / Did'st not perceive, spoiled by the subtle ways / Of intricate but instantaneous thought, / That common speech was useless to its ends, / That language, wedded from the first to Thought / Will strengthen as it strengthens——but, divorced, / Will dwindle while Thought widens more and more? . . / Say < > fell I < > fall,— *1835:* mountain ridge < > through storm? / Didst < > // < > ends— / < > thought, / < > strengthens; but < > / < > thought < > and more? . . . / < > fell, I < > fall; *1849:* storm? / Say **608**| *MS:* Say I < > sorely,—say but this *1835:* sorely. Say but this, *1849:* Say, I < > sorely: say **609**| *MS:* lord § written over by § Lord < > Lord! PARACELSUS < > thus *1835:* lord < > lord! PARACELSUS < > thus,
610| *MS:* Aprile!—that *1835:* Aprile! . . . That *1863:* Aprile! That
611| *MS:* dust . . . nay *1835:* dust. Nay < > not, or *1863:* not or
612| *MS:* King < > thee! *1835:* king *1868:* thee? **613**| *MS:*—Lo < > ruin and *1835:* Lo < > ruin, and **614**| *MS:* thou: let *1835:* thou! Let
615| *MS:* thro' < > last!—what *1835:* through < > last! What **616**| *MS:* Thro' < > breath . . . why,—tears *1835:* Through < > breath . . . why tears? *1849:* why, tears? *1863:* breath. Why **617**| *MS:* darkness——and *1835:* darkness—and *1863:* darkness, and **618**| *MS:* henceforth Aprile < > *I* *1835:* henceforth, Aprile *1849:* I **619**| *MS:* love—and merciful God forgive *1835:* love; and, merciful God, forgive **620**| *MS:* dreams . . but *1835:* dreams; but **621**| *MS:* fairy-land—tho' *1835:* fairy-land. Though *1849:* fairy-land: though **623**| *MS:* ancles < > still: . *1835:* jewell'd still. *1849:* jewelled *1863:* ankles **624**| *MS:* I, too, have < > KNOW < > LOVE *1835:* KNOW < > LOVE— *1868:* I too have

Excluding love as thou refusedst knowledge.
Still thou hast beauty and I, power. We wake:
What penance canst devise for both of us?
APRILE I hear thee faintly. The thick darkness! Even
Thine eyes are hid. 'Tis as I knew: I speak,
And now I die. But I have seen thy face!
O poet, think of me, and sing of me!
But to have seen thee and to die so soon!
PARACELSUS Die not, Aprile! We must never part.
Are we not halves of one dissevered world,
Whom this strange chance unites once more? Part? never!
Till thou the lover, know; and I, the knower,
Love—until both are saved. Aprile, hear!
We will accept our gains, and use them—now!
God, he will die upon my breast! Aprile!
APRILE To speak but once, and die! yet by his side.
Hush! hush!
Ha! go you ever girt about
With phantoms, powers? I have created such,
But these seem real as I.
PARACELSUS Whom can you see
Through the accursed darkness?
APRILE Stay; I know,

625| *MS:* refused'st knowledge: . . *1835:* knowledge. *1849:* refusedst
626| *MS:* I power: we *1835:* power. We wake: *1849:* I, power 628| *MS:* faintly . . the <> even *1835:* faintly . . . the <> Even *1863:* faintly. The
629| *MS:* hid: 'tis <> knew . . I speak *1835:* hid. 'Tis <> knew: I speak,
630| *MS:* die——but *1835:* die. But 631| *MS:* O dear soul, think of me,——and <> me . . . *1835:* O, dear <> me, and <> me . . . *1849:* O, poet, think of me, and <> me! 632| *MS:*——But <> thee, and *1835:* But
633| *MS:* Aprile . . . we <> part . . . *1835:* Aprile: we <> part. *1863:* Aprile! We 634| *MS:* world *1835:* dissever'd world, *1849:* dissevered
635| *MS:* part *1835:* Part 636| *MS:* thou, the Lover, know,—and I, the Knower, *1835:* lover, know; and <> knower, *1868:* thou the lover
637–639| *MS:* Love——until <> saved—Aprile § written over by § saved! Aprile, hear! / God! he <> breast: Aprile! *1835:* Love—until <> saved. Aprile, hear! / God, he <> breast! Aprile! *1849:* hear! / We will accept our gains, and use them—now! / God 640| *MS:* once and die! yet <> side: *1835:* once, and <> side, 641| *MS:* Hush, hush— / Ha, go <> girt *1835:* Hush! hush / Ha! go *1849:* girt about 642| *MS:* Phantoms, Powers? . . . I *1835:* phantoms, powers? I 643| *MS:* I:—— PARACELSUS *1835:* I . . . PARACELSUS *1849:* I! PARACELSUS *1863:* I? PARACELSUS *1868:* I. PARACELSUS 644| *MS:* Thro' <> darkness? . . . APRILE—Stay, I know *1835:* Through <> darkness? APRILE Stay; I know,

I know them: who should know them well as I?
White brows, lit up with glory; poets all!
PARACELSUS Let him but live, and I have my reward!
APRILE Yes; I see now. God is the perfect poet,
Who in his person acts his own creations.
Had you but told me this at first! Hush! hush!
PARACELSUS Live! for my sake, because of my great sin,
To help my brain, oppressed by these wild words
And their deep import. Live! 'tis not too late.
I have a quiet home for us, and friends.
Michal shall smile on you. Hear you? Lean thus,
And breathe my breath. I shall not lose one word
Of all your speech, one little word, Aprile!
APRILE No, no. Crown me? I am not one of you!
'Tis he, the king, you seek. I am not one.
PARACELSUS Thy spirit, at least, Aprile! Let me love!

I have attained, and now I may depart.

645| *1835:* as I?— *1863:* as I? 646| *MS:* brows—lit <> glory—Poets *1835:* brows, lit <> glory; poets 648| *MS:* Yes, I see now—God <> PERFECT POET: *1835:* Yes; I see now—God <> PERFECT POET, *1863:* now. God *1868:* perfect poet, 649–650| *MS:* person, acts <> / <> first! . . hush, hush . . . . . *1835:* person acts <> / <> first! . . . Hush! hush! *1849:* Who in creation acts his own conceptions. / Shall man refuse to be aught less than God? / Man's weakness is his glory—for the strength / Which raises him to heaven and near God's self, / Came spite of it: God's strength his glory is, / For thence came with our weakness sympathy / Which brought God down to earth, a man like us. / Had *1863:* Who in His person acts His own creations. / Had <> first! Hush! hush! *1868:* his <> his 651| *MS:* sake——because <> sin *1835:* sake, because <> sin, 652| *MS:* brain oppressed by your § probably, cancelled by § these wild *1835:* brain, oppress'd *1849:* oppressed 653| *MS:* import——Live <> late,— *1835:* import. Live <> late: *1863:* late. 654| *MS:* home far § probably, cancelled by § for us—and friends,— *1835:* us, and friends.
655| *MS:* you——hear you? lean thus *1835:* you . . . Hear <> Lean thus, *1863:* you. Hear 656| *MS:* breath——I *1835:* breath: I *1863:* breath. I
657| *MS:* speech—one *1835:* speech—one <> Aprile. *1849:* speech—no little <> Aprile! *1863:* speech, one little 658| *MS:* No, no—crown *me*? I *1835:* No, no . . . Crown *1849:* me *1863:* No, no. Crown 659| *MS:* Tis <> King you seek . . I <> one . . . *1835:* 'Tis <> king, you seek. I *1863:* one.
669| *MS:* Aprile!—Let *me* love! . . . *1835:* Aprile, let *1849:* Give me thy <> least! Let me love, too! *1863:* Thy <> least, Aprile! Let me love! 661| *MS:* I HAVE ATTAIN'D, AND NOW I MAY DEPART § small capitals probably a printer's misinterpretation; MS has two lines at end of Parts I and II § *1849:* I have attained, and now I may depart.

PART III. PARACELSUS.

SCENE—*Basil; a chamber in the house of* PARACELSUS. 1526.

PARACELSUS, FESTUS.

PARACELSUS Heap logs and let the blaze laugh out!
FESTUS True, true!
'Tis very fit all, time and chance and change
Have wrought since last we sat thus, face to face
And soul to soul—all cares, far-looking fears,
Vague apprehensions, all vain fancies bred
By your long absence, should be cast away,
Forgotten in this glad unhoped renewal
Of our affections.
PARACELSUS Oh, omit not aught
Which witnesses your own and Michal's own
Affection: spare not that! Only forget
The honours and the glories and what not,
It pleases you to tell profusely out.

SCENE| *MS:* A <> *Paracelsus at Basil.* 1526. *1863: Basil; a* <> *Paracelsus.* 1526. 1| *MS:* out: FESTUS True, true,— *1835:* logs, and <> out. FESTUS True, true; *1849:* out! FESTUS True, true! *1863:* true, true *1868:* logs and <> True, true! 2| *MS:* all Time and Chance *1835:* time, and chance, and *1849:* fit that all, time, chance *1863:* fit all, time and chance and 3| *MS:* sate *1849:* to face, *1863:* sat <> to face 4| *MS:* soul— —all cares,—far-looking fears *1835:* soul—all cares, far-looking fears, 5| *MS:* apprehensions—all *1835:* apprehensions, all 6| *MS:* absence— — —should *1835:* absence, should 8| *MS:* affection: PARACELSUS *1835:* affections. PARACELSUS 9| *MS:* Michals *1835:* Michal's *1849:* Michal's love! *1863:* Michal's own 10| *MS:* Affection—spare not that! forget alone *1835:* Affection; spare *1849:* I bade you not spare that! Forget *1863:* Affection: spare not that! Only forget 11| *MS:* not *1835:* glories, and what not, *1849:* glories, and the rest, *1863:* glories and what not, 12| *MS:* That you § *you* inserted above the line § are pleased to *1849:* You seemed disposed to *1863:* It pleases you to

FESTUS Nay, even your honours, in a sense, I waive:
The wondrous Paracelsus, life's dispenser,
Fate's commissary, idol of the schools
And courts, shall be no more than Aureole still,
Still Aureole and my friend as when we parted
Some twenty years ago, and I restrained
As best I could the promptings of my spirit
Which secretly advanced you, from the first,
To the pre-eminent rank which, since, your own
Adventurous ardour, nobly triumphing,
Has won for you.
PARACELSUS Yes, yes. And Michal's face
Still wears that quiet and peculiar light
Like the dim circlet floating round a pearl?
FESTUS Just so.
PARACELSUS And yet her calm sweet countenance,
Though saintly, was not sad; for she would sing
Alone. Does she still sing alone, bird-like,
Not dreaming you are near? Her carols dropt
In flakes through that old leafy bower built under
The sunny wall at Würzburg, from her lattice
Among the trees above, while I, unseen,
Sat conning some rare scroll from Tritheim's shelves,
Much wondering notes so simple could divert

13| *MS:* honours in a certain sense: . . *1835:* sense. *1849:* honours, in a sense, I waive: **14**| *MS:* Paracelsus—the dispenser *1849:* Paracelsus—Life's dispenser, *1863:* Paracelsus, Life's *1868:* life's **15**| *MS:* Of life—the commissary of fate—the idol *1835:* life, the <> Fate, the *1849:* Fate's commissary, idol of the schools, *1863:* schools **16**| *MS:* Of Princes——is no <> still,— *1835:* princes, is <> still— *1849:* And Courts, shall be no *1863:* courts <> still, **17**| *MS:* friend, as *1868:* friend as **18**| *MS:* ago, when I *1835:* ago, when I restrain'd *1849:* ago, and I restrained **19**| *MS:* As I best could *1835:* spirit, *1863:* As best I could <> spirit **20**| *1835:* you from the first *1849:* you, from the first, **21**| *MS:* which since *1835:* since your *1849:* which, since, your **23**| *MS:* PARACELSUS ——Yes, yes . . . and *1835:* PARACELSUS Yes, Yes; and *1849:* Yes, Yes; and *1863:* Yes, yes. And **24**| *1835:* light, *1863:* light **26**| *MS:* so: PARACELSUS <> countenance *1835:* so. PARACELSUS <> countenance, **27**| *MS:* saintly was not sad—for *1835:* saintly, was not sad; for **28**| *MS:* Alone . . does <> alone? bird-like, *1835:* Alone . . . Does <> alone, bird-like, *1863:* Alone. Does **29**| *MS:* near: her *1835:* near? Her **30**| *MS:* thro' *1835:* through **32**| *MS:* above . . while I unseen *1835:* above, while I, unseen, **33**| *MS:* Sate <> rare roll from <> shelves, *1849:* rare scroll from *1863:* Sat *1888:* shelves

My mind from study. Those were happy days.
Respect all such as sing when all alone!
FESTUS Scarcely alone: her children, you may guess,
Are wild beside her.
PARACELSUS Ah, those children quite
Unsettle the pure picture in my mind:
A girl, she was so perfect, so distinct:
No change, no change! Not but this added grace
May blend and harmonize with its compeers,
And Michal may become her motherhood;
But 'tis a change, and I detest all change,
And most a change in aught I loved long since.
So, Michal—you have said she thinks of me?
FESTUS O very proud will Michal be of you!
Imagine how we sat, long winter-nights,
Scheming and wondering, shaping your presumed
Adventure, or devising its reward;
Shutting out fear with all the strength of hope.
For it was strange how, even when most secure
In our domestic peace, a certain dim
And flitting shade could sadden all; it seemed
A restlessness of heart, a silent yearning,
A sense of something wanting, incomplete—

35| *MS:* study . . . those § corrected in pencil to § study. Those < > days! *1835:* study. Those *1863:* days. 36| *MS:* alone. *1863:* alone! 37| *MS:* alone—her < > guess § corrected in pencil to § guess, *1863:* alone: her 38| *MS:* her . . . PARACELSUS *1863:* her. PARACELSUS 39| *MS:* mind:– § corrected in pencil to § mind. *1835:* mind: *1868:* Unsettled *1888:* Unsettle 40| *MS:* girl—she < > distinct, . . § corrected in pencil to § distinct . . . *1863:* girl, she < > distinct. *1888:* distinct: 41| *MS:* No change, no change!—not § corrected in pencil to § No change, no change! Not 43| *MS:* mother-hood; *1849:* motherhood; 44| *MS:* tis § corrected in pencil to § 'tis a change—and *1863:* change, and 45| *MS:* since: *1849:* since! *1863:* since. 46| *MS:* But Michal . . . you *1849:* So, Michal . . . you *1863:* Michal—you 48| *MS:* sate *1863:* sat 49| *MS:* wondering—shaping *1863:* wondering, shaping 50| *MS:* devising your reward; *1835:* Adventure, or *1849:* Adventures, or devising their reward; *1863:* Adventure, or devising its reward; 51| *MS:* fear as long as hopes might be— § —in pencil § *1849:* fear with all the strength of hope. 52| *MS:* . . . § deleted in pencil § For *1849:* Though it *1863:* For it 54| *MS:* all—it seemed § altered in pencil to § all; it seem'd *1849:* seemed 55| *MS:* heart—a § altered in pencil to § heart, a < > yearning, § , added in pencil § 56| *MS:* incomplete,— *1835:* incomplete—

Not to be put in words, perhaps avoided
By mute consent—but, said or unsaid, felt
To point to one so loved and so long lost.
And then the hopes rose and shut out the fears—
How you would laugh should I recount them now
I still predicted your return at last
With gifts beyond the greatest of them all,
All Tritheim's wondrous troop; did one of which
Attain renown by any chance, I smiled,
As well aware of who would prove his peer.
Michal was sure some woman, long ere this,
As beautiful as you were sage, had loved . . .
PARACELSUS Far-seeing, truly, to discern so much
In the fantastic projects and day-dreams
Of a raw restless boy!
FESTUS Oh, no: the sunrise
Well warranted our faith in this full noon!
Can I forget the anxious voice which said
"Festus, have thoughts like these ere shaped themselves
In other brains than mine? have their possessors
Existed in like circumstance? were they weak

58| *MS:* consent— § above § , § , cancelled in pencil § but felt no less, §, added in pencil § when traced, §, added in pencil § *1849:* but, said or unsaid, felt
59| *MS:* lost. § altered in pencil to § lost— *1835:* lost; *1849:* lost.
60| *MS:* — § cancelled in pencil § Not but, to balance fears, were glowing hopes— — — § altered in pencil to § hopes. *1849:* And then the hopes rose and shut out the fears— 61| *MS:* now! *1888:* now 62| *MS:*— § cancelled in pencil § I <> last, § , added in pencil § *1868:* last 63| *MS:* greatest of them all, *1849:* greatest vaunt of all, *1863:* greatest of them all, 64| *MS:* troop—did *1835:* troop; did 65| *MS:* smiled— § — added in pencil § *1863:* smiled, 66| *MS:* peer: *1835:* peer. 67| *MS:* sure that long ere this some being, § , added in pencil § *1849:* sure some woman, long ere this,
68| *MS:* were brave, had loved . . . . . § altered in pencil to § loved . . . *1849:* were sage, had 69| *MS:* Far-seeing, § , added in pencil § truly, § , added in pencil § to discern as much *1849:* discern so much 71| *MS:* raw, restless boy. FESTUS — — Oh no, the *1835:* FESTUS Oh *1849:* boy! FESTUS Say, one whose sunrise *1863:* FESTUS Oh, no: the sunrise *1868:* raw restless 72| *MS:* Noon; *1835:* noon: *1849:* noon! 73| *MS:* Have I forgotten <> voice that said *1849:* Can I forget <> voice which said, *1868:* said 74| *MS:* e'er *1888:* ere 75| *MS:* mine— —have § altered in pencil to § mine—have § cancelled in pencil to § mine—have *1863:* mine? have 76| *MS:* circumstance— —were § altered in pencil to § circumstance?—were § cancelled in pencil to § circumstance—were *1863:* circumstance? were

As I, or ever constant from the first,
Despising youth's allurements and rejecting
As spider-films the shackles I endure?
Is there hope for me?"—and I answered gravely
As an acknowledged elder, calmer, wiser,
More gifted mortal. O you must remember,
For all your glorious . . .

PARACELSUS Glorious? ay, this hair,
These hands—nay, touch them, they are mine! Recall
With all the said recallings, times when thus
To lay them by your own ne'er turned you pale
As now. Most glorious, are they not?

FESTUS Why—why—
Something must be subtracted from success
So wide, no doubt. He would be scrupulous, truly,
Who should object such drawbacks. Still, still, Aureole,
You are changed, very changed! 'Twere losing nothing
To look well to it: you must not be stolen
From the enjoyment of your well-won meed.

PARACELSUS My friend! you seek my pleasure, past a doubt:
You will best gain your point, by talking, not
Of me, but of yourself.

FESTUS Have I not said

77| *MS:* I—or § altered in pencil to § I?—or § cancelled in pencil to § I—or *1863:* I, or 78| *MS:* allurements and § altered in pencil to § allurements, and *1863:* allurements and 80| *MS:* me?"——and I answered § altered in pencil to § me?"—and I answer'd *1849:* answered grave *1863:* gravely 81| *MS:* wiser *1835:* wiser, 82| *MS:* mortal . . . O § altered in pencil to § mortal. O 82| *MS:* glorious . . . . . PARACELSUS § altered in pencil to § glorious . . . PARACELSUS < > ay, to wit this § altered in pencil to § wit, this *1849:* ay, this hair, 86| *1835:* turn'd you pale, *1849:* turned *1863:* pale 87| *MS:* now:—most glorious are § altered in pencil to § now. Most glorious, are < > Why . . . Why . . . *1835:* Why . . . why . . . *1863:* Why—why— 89| *MS:* doubt:—he < > scrupulous truly § altered in pencil to § doubt. He < > scrupulous, truly, 90| *MS:* drawbacks: . . still . . still § altered in pencil to § drawbacks. Still—still *1835:* Still, still Aureole *1849:* Still, still, Aureole, 91| *MS: are* changed—very changed . . . 'twere § altered in pencil to § very changed. 'Twere *1863:* changed, very 93| *MS:* well won § altered in pencil to § well-won 94| *MS:* My Friend!—you < > doubt; § altered in pencil to § My Friend! you < > doubt. § altered in pencil to § doubt: *1863:* friend 95| *MS:* point by *1849:* By talking, not of me, but of yourself, *1863:* You will best gain your point, by talking, not 96| *1849:* You will best gain your point. FESTUS *1863:* Of me, but of yourself. FESTUS

All touching Michal and my children? Sure
You know, by this, full well how Aennchen looks
Gravely, while one disparts her thick brown hair;
And Aureole's glee when some stray gannet builds
Amid the birch-trees by the lake. Small hope
Have I that he will honour (the wild imp)
His namesake. Sigh not! 'tis too much to ask
That all we love should reach the same proud fate.
But you are very kind to humour me
By showing interest in my quiet life;
You, who of old could never tame yourself
To tranquil pleasures, must at heart despise . . .
PARACELSUS Festus, strange secrets are let out by death
Who blabs so oft the follies of this world:
And I am death's familiar, as you know.
I helped a man to die, some few weeks since,
Warped even from his go-cart to one end—
The living on princes' smiles, reflected from
A mighty herd of favourites. No mean trick
He left untried, and truly well-nigh wormed
All traces of God's finger out of him:
Then died, grown old. And just an hour before,
Having lain long with blank and soulless eyes,

97| *MS:* sure *1835:* Sure 98| *MS:* Annchen *1849:* Aennchen 99| *MS:* hair,— § altered in pencil to § hair; 101| *MS:* lake——small § altered in pencil to § lake.——Small *1835:* lake. Small 102| *MS:* honour,—the wild imp!— *1835:* honour, the wild imp! *1849:* imp, *1863:* honour (the wild imp) 103| *MS:* namesake;——sigh not!—'tis § altered in pencil to § namesake.——Sigh not! 'tis *1835:* namesake. Sigh *1849:* namesake! Sigh *1868:* namesake. Sigh 104| *MS:* fate: § altered in pencil to § fate. 108| *MS:* despise . . . . . § altered in pencil to § despise . . . 109| *MS:* Death, § , added in pencil § *1868:* death 110| *MS:* world: § altered in pencil to § world. *1835:* world: 111| *MS:* I, as you know, am Death's familiar oft: § altered in pencil to § oft. *1849:* And I am Death's familiar, as you know. *1868:* death's 112| *MS:* helped § altered in pencil to § help'd *1849:* helped 113| *MS:* Warped § altered in pencil to § Warp'd *1849:* Warped 114| *MS:* To live on Princes' smiles—reflected § altered in pencil to § smiles, reflected *1835:* prince's *1849:* The living on princes' 115| *MS:* favourites:—no § altered in pencil to § favourites. No 116| *MS:* untried, and < > well nigh wormed § altered in pencil to § worm'd *1849:* untried; and < > wormed *1863:* untried, and < > well-nigh 117| *MS:* him. *1863:* him: 118| *MS:* He died < > old;—and < > before,— § altered in pencil to § old; and < > before— *1849:* Then died *1863:* old. And < > before, 119| *MS:* eyes, § altered in pencil to § eyes— *1863:* eyes,

He sat up suddenly, and with natural voice
Said that in spite of thick air and closed doors
God told him it was June; and he knew well,
Without such telling, harebells grew in June;
And all that kings could ever give or take
Would not be precious as those blooms to him.
Just so, allowing I am passing sage,
It seems to me much worthier argument
Why pansies,* eyes that laugh, bear beauty's prize
From violets, eyes that dream—(your Michal's choice)—
Than all fools find to wonder at in me
Or in my fortunes. And be very sure
I say this from no prurient restlessness,
No self-complacency, itching to turn,
Vary and view its pleasure from all points,
And, in this instance, willing other men
May be at pains, demonstrate to itself
The realness of the very joy it tastes.
What should delight me like the news of friends
Whose memories were a solace to me oft,
As mountain-baths to wild fowls in their flight?
Ofter than you had wasted thought on me

*Citrinula (flammula) herba Paracelso multum familiaris.—Dorn

---

120| *MS:* sate *1863:* sat 121| *MS:* Said, that *1863:* Said that
122| *MS:* well § altered in pencil to § well, 123| *1835:* hare-bells *1863:* harebells 124| *MS:* And that all kings *1835:* And all that kings
125| *MS:* him: . . . . § altered in pencil to § him. 126| *MS:* passing wise, *1863:* passing sage, 128| *MS:* pansies *—eyes <> laugh—are lovelier *1835:* pansies, * eyes <> laugh, are *1849:* laugh, bear beauty's prize 129| *MS:* Than violets—eyes *1835:* violets, eyes *1849:* From violets 130| *1835:* me, *1868:* me 131| *MS:* fortunes: and *1863:* fortunes. And
132| *MS:* restlessness— *1863:* restlessness, 133| *MS:*—No self-complacency itching to vary § altered in pencil to § self-complacency—itching to vary, *1835:* No *1849:* to turn, *1863:* self-complacency, itching 134| *MS:* And turn and § altered in pencil to § turn, and *1849:* Vary, and *1868:* Vary and
135| *MS:* Men *1835:* men *1849:* this matter, willing *1863:* this instance, willing 136| *MS:* Should be at pains to demonstrate to it *1849:* Should argue and demonstrate to itself *1863:* Should be at pains, demonstrate *1888:* May be 137| *MS:* joy it lives on . . . . § altered in pencil to § on. *1849:* it tastes. 138| *MS:* What joy is better than the *1863:* What should delight me like the 141| *MS:* Oftener that you *1849:* Yes, ofter than you wasted *1863:* Ofter than you had wasted

Had you been wise, and rightly valued bliss.
But there's no taming nor repressing hearts:
God knows I need such!—So, you heard me speak?
FESTUS Speak? when?
PARACELSUS When but this morning at my class?
There was noise and crowd enough. I saw you not.
Surely you know I am engaged to fill
The chair here?—that 'tis part of my proud fate
To lecture to as many thick-skulled youths
As please, each day, to throng the theatre,
To my great reputation, and no small
Danger of Basil's benches long unused
To crack beneath such honour?
FESTUS I was there;
I mingled with the throng: shall I avow
Small care was mine to listen?—too intent
On gathering from the murmurs of the crowd
A full corroboration of my hopes!
What can I learn about your powers? but they
Know, care for nought beyond your actual state,
Your actual value; yet they worship you,
Those various natures whom you sway as one!
But ere I go, be sure I shall attend . . .

142| *MS:* been sage, and < > bliss,— § altered in pencil to § bliss; *1849:* If you were sage < > bliss! *1863:* Had you been wise, and *1868:* bliss. 144| *MS:* such! . . . so you *1835:* So *1849:* such!—So *1863:* So, you 146| *MS:* enough—I § altered in pencil to § enough. I < > not: *1849:* not. 148| *MS:* here? that *1849:* here?—that 149| *MS:* thick-sculled § altered in pencil to § thick-scull'd *1849:* thick-sculled *1863:* thick-skulled 150| *MS:* please to throng the theatre § written over by § Theatre each day § altered in pencil to § day, *1849:* please, each day, to throng the theatre, 152| *MS:* Peril of benches, long unused to crack *1849:* Danger of Basil's benches, long unused *1868:* benches long 153| *MS:* Beneath < > there, indeed:— § altered in pencil to § indeed. *1849:* To crack beneath < > there; 155| *MS:* to listen?—I § altered in pencil to § listen? I was intent *1849:* I had small care to listen?—too intent *1863:* Small care was mine to 157| *MS:* hopes: § altered in pencil to § hopes. *1849:* hopes! 158| *MS:* I < > powers?—but § altered in pencil to § powers? but *they* *1849:* I < > they 159| *MS:* state, § altered in pencil to § state— *1863:* state, 160| *MS:* value——yet § altered in pencil to § value. Yet < > you! *1849:* value; and yet worship *1863:* value; yet they worship you, 161| *MS:* one:— § altered in pencil to § one. *1849:* one! 162| *MS:* attend . . . . *1835:* attend . . .

PARACELSUS Stop, o' God's name: the thing's by no means yet
Past remedy! Shall I read this morning's labour
—At least in substance? Nought so worth the gaining
As an apt scholar! Thus then, with all due
Precision and emphasis—you, beside, are clearly
Guiltless of understanding more, a whit,
The subject than your stool—allowed to be
A notable advantage.
FESTUS Surely, Aureole,
You laugh at me!
PARACELSUS I laugh? Ha, ha! thank heaven,
I charge you, if't be so! for I forget
Much, and what laughter should be like. No less,
However, I forego that luxury
Since it alarms the friend who brings it back.
True, laughter like my own must echo strangely
To thinking men; a smile were better far;
So, make me smile! If the exulting look
You wore but now be smiling, 'tis so long
Since I have smiled! Alas, such smiles are born
Alone of hearts like yours, or herdsmen's souls
Of ancient time, whose eyes, calm as their flocks,
Saw in the stars mere garnishry of heaven,

164| *MS:* remedy,—shall § altered in pencil to § remedy. Shall <> labour? *1849:* remedy! Shall <> morning's work *1863:* morning's labour **165**| *MS:* At least, in <> nought § altered in pencil to § Nought *1835:* least in *1849:*—At **166**| *MS:* scholar: thus *1849:* scholar! Thus **167**| *MS:* emphasis;—(you § altered in pencil to § emphasis—(you, besides, are *1863:* emphasis—you *1868:* beside **168**| *MS:* more a whit *1849:* understanding a whit more *1863:* understanding more, a whit, **169**| *MS:* subject, than <> stool,—allowed § altered in pencil to § stool—allowed *1835:* subject than <> allow'd *1849:* allowed **170**| *MS:* advantage:) § altered in pencil to § advantage) . . . FESTUS *1863:* advantage. FESTUS **171**| *MS: I* *1849:* I **173**| *MS:* Much—and <> like: no less, § , added in pencil § *1849:* like! No *1863:* Much, and *1868:* like. No **174**| *MS:* luxury, § , added in pencil § *1863:* luxury **175**| *MS:* it offends the *1849:* it alarms the **176**| *1849:* strange *1863:* strangely **177**| *MS:* men;—a § altered in pencil to § men; a <> far,— § altered in pencil to § far, *1835:* far— *1863:* far; **178**| *MS:* So make me smile!—if § altered in pencil to § smile, if *1849:* smile! If **179**| *MS:* now, be smiling, 'tis § altered in pencil to § smiling. 'Tis *1835:* now be *1849:* smiling, 'tis **180**| *MS:* alas *1849:* Alas **181**| *MS:* yours,—and § altered in pencil to § yours, and those old Herds' *1835:* herds, *1849:* yours, or shepherds old *1863:* or herdsmen's souls **182**| *MS:* eyes—calm <> flocks— § altered in pencil to § eyes, calm <> flocks,

And in the earth a stage for altars only.
Never change, Festus: I say, never change!
FESTUS My God, if he be wretched after all!
PARACELSUS When last we parted, Festus, you declared,
—Or Michal, yes, her soft lips whispered words
I have preserved. She told me she believed
I should succeed (meaning, that in the search
I then engaged in, I should meet success)
And yet be wretched: now, she augured false.
FESTUS Thank heaven! but you spoke strangely: could I venture
To think bare apprehension lest your friend,
Dazzled by your resplendent course, might find
Henceforth less sweetness in his own, could move
Such earnest mood in you? Fear not, dear friend,
That I shall leave you, inwardly repining
Your lot was not my own!
PARACELSUS   And this for ever!
For ever! gull who may, they will be gulled!
They will not look nor think; 'tis nothing new
In them: but surely he is not of them!
My Festus, do you know, I reckoned, you—
Though all beside were sand-blind—you, my friend,

184| *MS:* only:— § altered in pencil to § only. *1849:* In earth < > altars, nothing more. *1868:* And in the earth < > altars only. 185| *MS:* Festus: I say, never § altered in pencil to § Festus, I say: never *1835:* Festus: I say, never 186| *1888:* all *1889:* all! 187| *MS:* declared— — § altered in pencil to § declared— *1835:* declared, 188| *MS:* Or Michal— —yes § altered in pencil to § Michal—yes *her* < > whispered § altered in pencil to § whisper'd what *1835:* yes, *her* *1849:*—Or did your Michal's soft lips whisper words *1863:*—Or Michal, yes, her soft lips whispered words 189| *MS:* preserved: the *1849:* preserved? She *1863:* preserved. She 190| *MS:* succeed, (meaning *1835:* succeed (meaning 191| *1835:* in I < > success), *1849:* in, I *1868:* success) 192| *1835:* augur'd *1849:* augured 193| *MS:* strangely! could *1863:* strangely: could 195| *MS:* course, should find *1849:* course, might find 196| *1849:* own, awakes *1868:* own, could move 197| *MS:* you? fear § altered in pencil to § you? Fear < > Friend, *1835:* friend, 199| *MS:* Such lot < > own . . . . PARACELSUS < > forever! § altered in pencil to § for ever! *1849:* Your lot < > own! PARACELSUS And this, for *1868:* this for 200| *MS:* Forever § altered in pencil to § For ever < > be blind! *1863:* be gulled! 201| *MS:* think—'tis *1863:* think; 'tis 202| *MS:* *them*— —but § altered in pencil to § *them;* but < > *he* *1835:* *them:* but *1849:* them; but < > he *1863:* them: but 203| *MS:* know I reckoned § altered in pencil to § reckon'd *you*— *1849:* know, I reckoned, you— 204| *MS:* Tho' § altered in pencil to § Though

Would look at me, once close, with piercing eye
Untroubled by the false glare that confounds
A weaker vision: would remain serene,
Though singular amid a gaping throng.
I feared you, or I had come, sure, long ere this,
To Einsiedeln. Well, error has no end,
And Rhasis is a sage, and Basil boasts
A tribe of wits, and I am wise and blest
Past all dispute! 'Tis vain to fret at it.
I have vowed long ago my worshippers
Shall owe to their own deep sagacity
All further information, good or bad.
Small risk indeed my reputation runs,
Unless perchance the glance now searching me
Be fixed much longer; for it seems to spell
Dimly the characters a simpler man
Might read distinct enough. Old Eastern books
Say, the fallen prince of morning some short space
Remained unchanged in semblance; nay, his brow
Was hued with triumph: every spirit then
Praising, *his* heart on flame the while:—a tale!
Well, Festus, what discover you, I pray?
FESTUS Some foul deed sullies then a life which else

205| *MS:* eye, § , added in pencil § *1863:* eye **206**| *MS:* by false glare that well confounds *1849:* by the false glare that confounds **207**| *MS:* vision; would *1888:* vision: would **208**| *MS:* Tho' singular, amid <> throng: § altered in pencil to § Though <> throng. *1868:* singular amid **209**| *MS:* this, *1835:* fear'd *1849:* feared <> or had *1863:* or I had **210**| *MS:* Einsiedeln: . . . well,—error § altered in pencil to § Einsiedeln. Well, error **213**| *MS:* 'tis § altered in pencil to § 'Tis **214**| *1835:* vow'd *1849:* vowed long since that my *1863:* long ago my **216**| *MS:* bad: *1835:* bad. *1849:* bad: *1863:* bad. **217**| *MS:* risk, indeed, my <> runs *1835:* risk indeed my <> runs, *1849:* And little risk my *1863:* Small risk indeed my **219**| *MS:* longer . . . for § altered in pencil to § longer—for *1835:* fix'd *1849:* fixed *1863:* longer; for **220**| *1849:* Dimly, the *1863:* Dimly the **221**| *MS:* enough: old § altered in pencil to § enough. Old *1835:* eastern *1888:* Eastern **222**| *MS:* Say the <> Prince of Morning *1835:* prince of morning *1849:* Say, the **223**| *MS:* Remained unchanged in seeming——nay his § altered in pencil to § Remain'd unchang'd in seeming—nay, his *1835:* unchanged *1849:* Remained <> in feature—nay *1863:* in semblance; nay **224**| *1849:* Seemed hued *1863:* Was hued **225**| *MS:* Praising; *his* <> while: a tale! *1835:* while . . . a tale! *1849:* while:—a tale! *1863:* Praising, *his*

Were raised supreme?

PARACELSUS Good: I do well, most well

Why strive to make men hear, feel, fret themselves
With what is past their power to comprehend?
I should not strive now: only, having nursed
The faint surmise that one yet walked the earth,
One, at least, not the utter fool of show,
Not absolutely formed to be the dupe
Of shallow plausibilities alone:
One who, in youth, found wise enough to choose
The happiness his riper years approve,
Was yet so anxious for another's sake,
That, ere his friend could rush upon a mad
And ruinous course, the converse of his own,
His gentle spirit essayed, prejudged for him
The perilous path, foresaw its destiny,
And warned the weak one in such tender words,
Such accents—his whole heart in every tone—
That oft their memory comforted that friend
When it by right should have increased despair:

228| *MS:* raised above— — — PARACELSUS <> well—most well! *1835:* above . . . PARACELSUS *1849:* raised supreme? PARACELSUS *1863:* well, most *1888:* most well 229| *MS:* make them know and § altered in pencil to § know, and feel, and fret *1849:* make men hear, feel, fret themselves 230| *MS:* Themselves with what 'tis <> to know, *1849:* With what 'tis past their power to comprehend? *1888:* what is past 231| *MS:* Or feel, or comprehend? still,—having § altered in pencil to § still, having *1835:* Still *1849:* I would not strive now: only, having *1863:* I should not 232| *1835:* walk'd *1849:* walked 233| *MS: One* <> shew, *1835:* show, *1849:* One 234| *1835:* form'd *1849:* formed 235| *MS:* alone;— § altered in pencil to § alone; *1888:* alone: 236| *MS:* youth found *1888:* youth, found 237| *MS:* That happiness *1849:* The happiness 238| *MS:* sake *1849:* sake, 239| *MS:* That ere his Friend *1835:* friend *1849:* That, ere <> a course *1863:* a mad 240| *1849:* Mad, ruinous, the *1863:* And ruinous course, the 241| *MS:* spirit had already tried *1849:* gentler spirit essayed, prejudged for him *1863:* gentle 242| *MS:* foreseen *1849:* foresaw 243| *MS:* words— § added in pencil § *1849:* words, 244| *MS:*—Such accents . . . his § written over by § accents—his <> every one . . . § written over by § one— *1835:* Such *1849:* every tone— 245| *MS:* That they oft served § altered in pencil to § serv'd to comfort him, in hours *1835:* served *1849:* That oft their memory comforted that friend 246| *MS:* When they, by right, should— —despair;— — § altered in pencil to § despair; *1835:* despair: *1849:* When rather it should *1863:* When it by right should

—Having believed, I say, that this one man
Could never lose the light thus from the first
His portion—how should I refuse to grieve
At even my gain if it disturb our old
Relation, if it make me out more wise?
Therefore, once more reminding him how well
He prophesied, I note the single flaw
That spoils his prophet's title. In plain words,
You were deceived, and thus were you deceived—
I have not been successful, and yet am
Most miserable; 'tis said at last; nor you
Give credit, lest you force me to concede
That common sense yet lives upon the world!
FESTUS You surely do not mean to banter me?
PARACELSUS You know, or—if you have been wise enough
To cleanse your memory of such matters—knew,
As far as words of mine could make it clear,
That 'twas my purpose to find joy or grief
Solely in the fulfilment of my plan
Or plot or whatsoe'er it was; rejoicing
Alone as it proceeded prosperously,
Sorrowing then only when mischance retarded

247| *MS:* Having <> say, such happy One *1835:* one *1849:*—Having <> say, that this one man 248| *1849:* the wisdom from *1863:* the light thus from 249| *MS:* portion,—I § altered in pencil to § portion—I can not refuse *1835:* cannot *1849:* portion—how should I refuse 250–251| *MS:* Even at my <> / Relation,—if <> *me* out the wiser . . . . § altered in pencil to § Relation; <> wiser. *1849:* At even my <> it attest his loss, / At triumph which so signally disturbs / Our old relations, proving me more wise? *1863:* it disturb our old / Relation, if it make me out more 254| *MS:* That seems to cross his title: in <> words *1849:* That spoils his prophet's title *1863:* title. In 255| *MS:* thus were you deceived:— § altered in pencil to § deceived: *1849:* thus were you deceived— 257| *1849:* Most wretched; there—'tis <> last; but give *1863:* Most miserable; 'tis <> last; nor you 258| *MS:* to believe *1849:* No credit <> to concede *1863:* Give credit 259| *MS:* world. *1849:* the earth. *1863:* the world. *1868:* world! 261| *MS:* know,—or,—if § written over by § or, (if § altered in pencil to § or (if *1835:* know, or *1863:* or—if 262| *MS:* matters,—knew, § written over by § matters,) knew, § altered in pencil to § matters) knew, *1863:* matters—knew, 265| *MS:* Alone in <> plan, *1849:* Solely in *1863:* plan 266| *MS:* plot, or <> was:—rejoicing *1835:* was: rejoicing *1849:* was; rejoicing *1863:* plot or 267| *MS:* prosperously;— § altered in pencil to § prosperously; *1849:* prosperously, 268| *MS:* only, when *1849:* Sorrowing alone when any chance retarded *1863:* Sorrowing then only when mischance retarded

Its progress. That was in those Würzburg days!
Not to prolong a theme I thoroughly hate,
I have pursued this plan with all my strength;
And having failed therein most signally,
Cannot object to ruin utter and drear
As all-excelling would have been the prize
Had fortune favoured me. I scarce have right
To vex your frank good spirit late so glad
In my supposed prosperity, I know,
And, were I lucky in a glut of friends,
Would well agree to let your error live,
Nay, strengthen it with fables of success.
But mine is no condition to refuse
The transient solace of so rare a godsend,
My solitary luxury, my one friend:
Accordingly I venture to put off
The wearisome vest of falsehood galling me,
Secure when he is by. I lay me bare,
Prone at his mercy—but he is my friend!

269–270| *MS:* progress: nor § altered in pencil to § progress. Nor was this the scheme of one / Enamoured § altered in pencil to § Enamour'd of a lot unlike the world's, / And thus far sure from common casualty— § —added in pencil § / (Folly of follies!) in § altered in pencil to § follies!)—in that, thus, the Mind / Became the only arbiter of fate:— § altered in pencil to § fate. / No: what § altered in pencil to § No; what I termed, and § altered in pencil to § termed and might conceive my choice, § , added in pencil § / Already had been rooted in my soul— — § altered in pencil to § soul— / Had long been part and portion of my self: § altered in pencil to § self. / Not < > hate,— § altered in pencil to § hate, *1835:* (Folly of follies!) in < > mind // < > term'd < > // < > myself. *1849:* progress. That was in those Würzburg days! / Not 271| *MS:* I have since followed § altered in pencil to § follow'd it with *1849:* have pursued this plan with 272| *MS:* failed § altered in pencil to § fail'd *1849:* failed 273| *MS:* ruin utter § altered in pencil to § ruin, utter *1863:* ruin utter 275| *MS:* favoured me: I § altered in pencil to § favour'd me. I *1849:* favoured < > scarce do right *1863:* scarce have right 276| *1835:* spirit, late *1849:* late rejoiced *1863:* late so glad *1868:* spirit late 277| *MS:* prosperity I know;— § altered in pencil to § prosperity, I know; *1849:* By my < > know, *1863:* In my 278| *MS:* And were < > friends *1849:* And, were < > friends, 280| *MS:* And strengthen < > success;— § altered in pencil to § success: *1835:* success. *1849:* Nay, strengthen < > success: *1863:* success. 281| *MS:* But I'm in no *1849:* But mine is no 282| *MS:* Godsend, *1849:* a chance, *1863:* a godsend, 283| *MS:* friend; *1835:* luxury—my *1849:* luxury, my Festus— *1863:* my one friend: 286| *MS:* by: I § altered in pencil to § by. I < > bare *1849:* bare, 287| *MS:* And at his mercy— — —but § altered in pencil to § mercy—but *1849:* Prone at

Not that he needs retain his aspect grave;
That answers not my purpose; for 'tis like,
Some sunny morning—Basil being drained
Of its wise population, every corner
Of the amphitheatre crammed with learned clerks,
Here Œcolampadius, looking worlds of wit,
Here Castellanus, as profound as he,
Munsterus here, Frobenius there, all squeezed
And staring,—that the zany of the show,
Even Paracelsus, shall put off before them
His trappings with a grace but seldom judged
Expedient in such cases:—the grim smile
That will go round! Is it not therefore best
To venture a rehearsal like the present
In a small way? Where are the signs I seek,
The first-fruits and fair sample of the scorn
Due to all quacks? Why, this will never do!
FESTUS These are foul vapours, Aureole; nought beside!
The effect of watching, study, weariness.
Were there a spark of truth in the confusion
Of these wild words, you would not outrage thus
Your youth's companion. I shall ne'er regard
These wanderings, bred of faintness and much study.

288| *MS:* his grave respect— *1849:* his aspect grave; 290| *MS:* morning,—Basil *1835:* morning—Basil < > drain'd *1849:* drained 291| *MS:* population,—every § altered in pencil to § population, every 292| *MS:* Amphitheatre crammed < > clerks— § altered in pencil to § cramm'd < > clerks, *1835:* amphitheatre *1849:* crammed 293| *MS:* Œcolampadius looking < > wit, § altered in pencil to § Œcolampadius, looking < > wit; *1849:* wit, 294| *MS:* Castellanus as < > he, § altered in pencil to § Castellanus, as < > he; *1849:* he, 295| *MS:* there . . all § altered in pencil to § there; all *1849:* there,—all squeezed, *1863:* there, all *1868:* squeezed 296–298| *MS:* staring;—that < > shew § altered in pencil to § staring—that < > shew, // < > grace not seldom *1835:* show, *1849:* staring, and expectant,—then, I say, / 'Tis like that the poor zany of the show, / Your friend, will choose to put his trappings off / Before them, bid adieu to cap and bells / And motley with a grace but seldom *1863:* staring,—that the zany of the show, / Even Paracelsus, shall put off before them / His trappings with 299| *MS:* cases;—the § altered in pencil to § cases. The *1849:* cases:— 300| *MS:* round!—Is *1835:* round! Is 302| *MS:* way?—where *1835:* way? Where 304| *MS:* Quacks? why § altered in pencil to § Quacks? Why *1835:* quacks 306| *MS:* weariness,—— § altered in pencil to § weariness. 309| *MS:* companion: . . I § altered in pencil to § companion. I 310| *MS:* study———— § altered in pencil to § study.

'Tis not thus you would trust a trouble to me,
To Michal's friend.

PARACELSUS I have said it, dearest Festus!
For the manner, 'tis ungracious probably;
You may have it told in broken sobs, one day,
And scalding tears, ere long: but I thought best
To keep that off as long as possible.
Do you wonder still?

FESTUS No; it must oft fall out
That one whose labour perfects any work,
Shall rise from it with eye so worn that he
Of all men least can measure the extent
Of what he has accomplished. He alone
Who, nothing tasked, is nothing weary too,
May clearly scan the little he effects:
But we, the bystanders, untouched by toil,
Estimate each aright.

PARACELSUS This worthy Festus
Is one of them, at last! 'Tis so with all!
First, they set down all progress as a dream;
And next, when he whose quick discomfiture

311| *MS:* Tis *1835:* 'Tis *1849:* You would not trust a trouble thus to *1863:* 'Tis not thus you would trust a trouble to 312| *MS:* friend: PARACELSUS § altered in pencil to § friend. PARACELSUS <> Festus; *1849:* Festus! 313| *MS:* manner—'tis ungracious, probably— § altered in pencil to § manner—'tis <> probably; *1849:* The manner is *1863:* For the manner, 'tis *1868:* ungracious probably; 314| *MS:*—You *1835:* You *1849:* More may be told *1863:* You may have it told 315| *MS:* long,—I § altered in pencil to § long, I thought it best *1835:* long. I *1849:* long: but I thought best 316| *MS:* possible: . . . . § altered in pencil to § possible. 317| *MS:* No: it § altered in pencil to § No; it 318| *MS:* That he whose <> work *1849:* That one whose <> work, 319| *MS:* worn, that he, *1835:* he *1868:* worn that 320| *MS:* Least of all men, can *1835:* men can *1849:* Of all men least can 321| *MS:* Of that he has accomplished;—he alone, § altered in pencil to § accomplish'd. He alone, *1849:* Of what he has accomplished *1868:* alone 322| *MS:* weary, *he* *1835:* task'd *1849:* tasked <> weary too, 323| *MS:* Can clearly <> he has done:— § altered in pencil to § done: *1849:* he effects: *1863:* May clearly 324| *MS:* we,—the § altered in pencil to § we, the *1835:* untouch'd *1849:* untouched 325| *MS:* We estimate aright . . . . . PARACELSUS This worthy Festus, § altered in pencil to § aright. PARACELSUS This, worthy *1849:* Estimate each aright. PARACELSUS This worthy Festus 326| *MS:* Tis <> all: *1835:* 'Tis *1849:* all! 327| *MS:* First they <> dream, *1849:* First, they *1863:* dream; 328| *MS:* he, whose *1868:* he whose

Was counted on, accomplishes some few
And doubtful steps in his career,—behold,
They look for every inch of ground to vanish
Beneath his tread, so sure they spy success!
FESTUS Few doubtful steps? when death retires before
Your presence—when the noblest of mankind,
Broken in body or subdued in soul,
May through your skill renew their vigour, raise
The shattered frame to pristine stateliness?
When men in racking pain may purchase dreams
Of what delights them most, swooning at once
Into a sea of bliss or rapt along
As in a flying sphere of turbulent light?
When we may look to you as one ordained
To free the flesh from fell disease, as frees
Our Luther's burning tongue the fettered soul?
When . . .
PARACELSUS When and where, the devil, did you get
This notable news?
FESTUS   Even from the common voice;
From those whose envy, daring not dispute
The wonders it decries, attributes them

329| *MS:* on— —accomplishes § altered in pencil to § on, 330| *MS:* career,—behold § altered in pencil to § career, behold *1849:* career,—behold, 332| *1835:* tread—so *1849:* tread, so <> they judge success! *1863:* they spy success! 333| *MS:* Few, doubtful steps / . . . when § altered in pencil to § steps? when *1835:* Few doubtful 334| *MS:* presence,— § altered in pencil to § presence—when 335| *MS:* body, yet untired in spirit, *1849:* body, or subdued in mind, *1863:* body or subdued in soul, 336| *MS:* thro' § altered in pencil to § through 337| *MS:* shattered § altered in pencil to § shatter'd <> stateliness . . . . *1835:* stateliness: *1849:* shattered <> stateliness? 338| *MS:* That men *1835:* When men 339| *MS:* most—swooning *1863:* most, swooning 340| *MS:* bliss—or *1835:* bliss; or *1868:* bliss or 341| *MS:* light— *1835:* light: *1849:* light? 342| *1835:* ordain'd *1849:* ordained 344| *MS:* fettered § altered in pencil to § fetter'd soul,— *1835:* soul: *1849:* fettered soul? 345| *MS:* When . . . . . PARACELSUS And when and § altered in pencil to § When . . . PARACELSUS And when, and where the devil did *1835:* And when and *1849:* PARACELSUS Rather, when and where, friend, did *1863:* PARACELSUS When and where, the devil, did 346| *MS:* FESTUS—Even *1835:* FESTUS Even 348| *MS:* it descries, attributes *1835:* it decries, attributes

To magic and such folly.
PARACELSUS   Folly? Why not
To magic, pray? You find a comfort doubtless
In holding, God ne'er troubles him about
Us or our doings: once we were judged worth
The devil's tempting . . . I offend: forgive me,
And rest content. Your prophecy on the whole
Was fair enough as prophesyings go;
At fault a little in detail, but quite
Precise enough in the main; and hereupon
I pay due homage: you guessed long ago
(The prophet!) I should fail—and I have failed.
FESTUS You mean to tell me, then, the hopes which fed
Your youth have not been realized as yet?
Some obstacle has barred them hitherto?
Or that their innate . . .
PARACELSUS   As I said but now,
You have a very decent prophet's fame,
So you but shun details here. Little matter
Whether those hopes were mad,—the aims they sought,
Safe and secure from all ambitious fools;
Or whether my weak wits are overcome
By what a better spirit would scorn: I fail.
And now methinks 'twere best to change a theme

349| *MS:* folly;— PARACELSUS Folly?— —Why § altered in pencil to § folly. PARACELSUS Folly? Why 350| *MS:* pray—you § altered in pencil to § pray? You 351| *MS:* holding God *1849:* holding, God 352| *MS:* doings:—once § altered in pencil to § doings: once *1863:* Him *1868:* him 353| *MS:* tempting— — —I *1835:* tempting . . . I 354| *MS:* content: your § altered in pencil to § content. Your 355| *MS:* go,— § altered in pencil to § go; 356| *MS:*—At *1835:* At 357| *1849:* main; accordingly *1863:* main; and hereupon 358| *1835:* guess'd *1849:* guessed 359| *MS:* prophet) I <> fail . . . . and § written over by § fail—and *1835:* have fail'd. *1849:* prophet!) I <> have failed. 360| *MS:* then,—the § altered in pencil to § then, the 362| *MS:*—Some <> hitherto,— § altered in pencil to § hitherto, *1835:* Some <> barr'd *1849:* barred <> hitherto? 363| *MS:* now *1835:* now, 364| *MS:* fame *1849:* fame, 365| *MS:* shun these details;—little § altered in pencil to § details. Little matters *1849:* shun details here. Little *1863:* matter 366| *MS:* mad and § altered in pencil to § mad, and what they sought *1849:* mad,—the aims they sought, 367| *MS:* fools,— § altered in pencil to § fools, *1849:* fools; 369| *MS:* scorn:—I § altered in pencil to § scorn—I *1849:* scorn: I 370| *MS:* change the theme. *1849:* change a theme, *1868:* theme

I am a sad fool to have stumbled on.
I say confusedly what comes uppermost;
But there are times when patience proves at fault,
As now: this morning's strange encounter—you
Beside me once again! you, whom I guessed
Alive, since hitherto (with Luther's leave)
No friend have I among the saints at peace,
To judge by any good their prayers effect.
I knew you would have helped me—why not he,
My strange competitor in enterprise,
Bound for the same end by another path,
Arrived, or ill or well, before the time,
At our disastrous journey's doubtful close?
How goes it with Aprile? Ah, they miss
Your lone sad sunny idleness of heaven,
Our martyrs for the world's sake; heaven shuts fast:
The poor mad poet is howling by this time!
Since you are my sole friend then, here or there,
I could not quite repress the varied feelings
This meeting wakens; they have had their vent,
And now forget them. Do the rear-mice still
Hang like a fretwork on the gate (or what

371| *MS:* on it— — § altered in pencil to § on it. *1849:* on. 372| *MS:* uppermost . . . . § altered in pencil to § uppermost— *1835:* uppermost; 373| *MS:* fault,— § altered in pencil to § fault, 374| *MS:* now;—this § altered in pencil to § now; this *1835:* now: this 375| *MS:* guessed *1835:* guess'd *1849:* guessed 376| *MS:* hitherto, (with § altered in pencil to § hitherto (with *1835:* Alive—since *1849:* Alive, since 377–389| *MS:* saints above; § altered in pencil to § above / (The poor <> time:) § altered in pencil to § time.) / I *1835:* above— / <> time)— *1849:* saints at rest, / To judge by any good their prayers effect— / I knew you would have helped me!—So would He, / My strange competitor in enterprise, / Bound for the same end by another path, / Arrived, or ill or well, before the time, / At our disastrous journey's doubtful close— / How goes it with Aprile? Ah, your heaven / Receives not into its beatitudes / Mere martyrs for the world's sake; heaven shuts fast: / The poor <> time! / Since you are my sole friend then, here or there, / I 377| *1863:* saints at peace, 378| *1868:* effect: *1888:* effect. 379| *1863:* me!—Why not He, *1868:* me—why not he, 382| *1888:* time, 384–386| *1863:* Ah, they miss / Your lone, sad, sunny idleness of Heaven, / Our martyrs <> Heaven 385| *1868:* heaven 386| *1868:* heaven 390| *MS:* wakens,—they § altered in pencil to § wakens; they <> their way, *1849:* their vent, 391| *MS:* them:—do §altered in pencil to § them. Do 392| *MS:* fret-work <> gate, (or § altered in pencil to § gate (or *1888:* fretwork

In my time was a gate) fronting the road
From Einsiedeln to Lachen?

FESTUS

Trifle not:
Answer me, for my sake alone! You smiled
Just now, when I supposed some deed, unworthy
Yourself, might blot the else so bright result;
Yet if your motives have continued pure,
Your will unfaltering, and in spite of this,
You have experienced a defeat, why then
I say not you would cheerfully withdraw
From contest—mortal hearts are not so fashioned—
But surely you would ne'ertheless withdraw.
You sought not fame nor gain nor even love,
No end distinct from knowledge,—I repeat
Your very words: once satisfied that knowledge
Is a mere dream, you would announce as much,
Yourself the first. But how is the event?
You are defeated—and I find you here!

393| *MS:* time, was § altered in pencil to § time was 394| *MS:* FESTUS—Trifle § altered in pencil to § FESTUS Trifle *1849:* not! *1863:* not: 395| *MS:* me—for <> alone:—you § altered in pencil to § alone. You *1863:* me, for *1868:* alone! For 396| *MS:* deed § written over by § Deed unworthy *1835:* deed *1849:* deed, unworthy 397| *MS:* Yourself, might <> result . . . . § written over by § result—§ altered in pencil to § yourself might <> result; *1863:* Yourself, might 398–401| *MS:* But if <> pure, / Your earnest will, unfaultering——if § altered in pencil to § will unfaultering; if you still / Remain unchanged, and if in spite of all / You have experienced the defeat you tell . . . § altered in pencil to § tell— / I say not, you <> cheerfully resign *1835:* unfaltering: if <> / <> if, in <> all, *1849:* Yet if <> / <> of this, / <> experienced a defeat that proves / Your aims for ever unattainable—I *1863:* pure, / Your will unfaltering, and in spite of this, / You have <> defeat, why, then / I <> cheerfully withdraw *1868:* why then / I say not you 402| *MS:* The contest——mortal <> fashioned . . . . § altered in pencil to § The contest—mortal <> fashioned— *1835:* fashion'd— *1849:* fashioned— *1863:* From contest 403| *MS:* ne'ertheless resign; § altered in pencil to § resign. *1849:* But sure you would resign it, ne'ertheless. *1863:* But surely you would, ne'ertheless, withdraw. *1868:* would ne'ertheless withdraw. 404| *MS:* fame, nor Gain, nor <> Love— § altered in pencil to § fame, nor gain, nor <> love; *1868:* fame nor gain nor <> love, 405| *MS:* Knowledge:—I § altered in pencil to § Knowledge.—I *1835:* knowledge. I *1849:* knowledge,—I 406| *MS:* words:— once § altered in pencil to § words: once <> Knowledge *1835:* knowledge 407| *1835:* much *1849:* much, 408| *MS:* the first:——but § altered in pencil to § first. But 409| *MS:* defeated . . . and <> *here*!—— § altered in pencil to § defeated—and <> *here*! *1849:* here!

PARACELSUS As though "here" did not signify defeat!
I spoke not of my little labours here,
But of the break-down of my general aims:
For you, aware of their extent and scope,
To look on these sage lecturings, approved
By beardless boys, and bearded dotards worse,
As a fit consummation of such aims,
Is worthy notice. A professorship
At Basil! Since you see much much in it,
And think my life was reasonably drained
Of life's delights to render me a match
For duties arduous as such post demands,—
Be it far from me to deny my power
To fill the petty circle lotted out
Of infinite space, or justify the host
Of honours thence accruing. So, take notice,
This jewel dangling from my neck preserves
The features of a prince, my skill restored
To plague his people some few years to come:
And all through a pure whim. He had eased the earth
For me, but that the droll despair which seized

410| *MS:* tho' *"here"* did § altered in pencil to § though "here" did *1849:* though "here" did 411–412| *MS:* my labours *here:*—§ altered in pencil to § here: past doubt / I am quite competent to answer all / Demands, in any such capacity,— § altered in pencil to § capacity, / But *1835:* here—past <> // <> capacity— *1849:* my little labours here— / But *1863:* here, *1868:* here *1888:* here, 413| *MS:* you—aware <> scope— § altered in pencil to § you, aware <> scope, *1849:* That you *1863:* For you 414| *MS:* lecturings, commended *1849:* Should look <> lecturings, approved *1863:* To look 415| *MS:* By silly beardless boys, and <> dotards, *1849:* By beardless <> dotards,—these *1863:* dotards worse, 416| *MS:* of those aims *1835:* aims, *1849:* of such aims, 417| *MS:* notice:—a § altered in pencil to § notice—a *1849:* notice! A *1868:* notice. A 418| *MS:* Basil! . . . since § altered in pencil to § Basil! Since <> it,— *1835:* it; *1849:* it, 419| *MS:* Since 'tis but just my life should have been drained *1835:* drain'd *1849:* And think my life was reasonably drained 420| *MS:* Of its delights *1849:* Of life's delights 421| *MS:* Post demands; . . . . § altered in pencil to § demands; *1835:* post *1849:* demands,— 422| *MS:* Far be it from *1868:* Be it far from 424| *MS:* or to the *1849:* or justify the 425| *MS:* accruing: so take notice: § altered in pencil to § notice. *1849:* so, take notice, *1863:* accruing. So 427| *MS:* Prince my *1835:* prince *1849:* prince, my 428| *MS:* come: § : added in pencil § 429| *MS:*——And all thro' <> whim—he § altered in pencil to § And all through <> whim. He

The vermin of his household, tickled me.
I came to see. Here, drivelled the physician,
Whose most infallible nostrum was at fault;
There quaked the astrologer, whose horoscope
Had promised him interminable years;
Here a monk fumbled at the sick man's mouth
With some undoubted relic—a sudary
Of the Virgin; while another piebald knave
Of the same brotherhood (he loved them ever)
Was actively preparing 'neath his nose
Such a suffumigation as, once fired,
Had stunk the patient dead ere he could groan,
I cursed the doctor and upset the brother,
Brushed past the conjurer, vowed that the first gust
Of stench from the ingredients just alight
Would raise a cross-grained devil in my sword,
Not easily laid: and ere an hour the prince
Slept as he never slept since prince he was.
A day—and I was posting for my life,
Placarded through the town as one whose spite
Had near availed to stop the blessed effects

431| *MS:* me:— § altered in pencil to § me. 432| *MS:* —I <> see:—here, drivelled the Physician § altered in pencil to § see: here, drivell'd the physician *1835:* I <> physician, *1849:* drivelled *1863:* see. Here 433| *MS:* fault; — — § altered in pencil to § fault; 434| *MS:* There shook the Astrologer § altered in pencil to § astrologer in his shoes, whose grand *1849:* There quaked the astrologer, whose horoscope 435| *MS:* Horoscope promise further score of years;— — § altered in pencil to § years; *1849:* Had promised him interminable years; 436| *MS:* at the sick § *the* inserted above the line § man's nose *1849:* man's mouth 437| *MS:* relic . . . a § altered in pencil to § relic—a 438| *MS:* Virgin;— —while some half-a-dozen § altered in pencil to § Virgin; while some half-dozen knaves *1849:* some other dozen knaves *1863:* while another piebald knave 440| *MS:* Were making active preparations for *1849:* Were actively preparing 'neath his nose *1863:* Was 443| *MS:*—I <> Doctor, and upset the Wiper; *1835:* I <> doctor <> wiper; *1849:* upset the brother; *1868:* brother, 444| *MS:* Brushed <> conjurer—vowed § altered in pencil to § Brush'd <> conjurer;—vow'd *1835:* conjurer; vow'd *1849:* Brushed <> vowed *1868:* conjurer, vowed 446| *MS:* cross-grained § altered in pencil to § cross-grain'd *1849:* cross-grained 447| *MS:* laid:—and <> Prince § altered in pencil to § laid; and <> prince *1849:* hour, the *1863:* laid: *1868:* hour the 448| *MS:* Prince § altered in pencil to § prince 449| *MS:* life *1835:* life, 450| *MS:* thro' the Town § altered in pencil to § through the town 451| *MS:* blessed § altered in pencil to § bless'd *1835:* avail'd *1849:* availed <> blessed

Of the doctor's nostrum which, well seconded
By the sudary, and most by the costly smoke—
Not leaving out the strenuous prayers sent up
Hard by in the abbey—raised the prince to life:
To the great reputation of the seer
Who, confident, expected all along
The glad event—the doctor's recompense—
Much largess from his highness to the monks—
And the vast solace of his loving people,
Whose general satisfaction to increase,
The prince was pleased no longer to defer
The burning of some dozen heretics
Remanded till God's mercy should be shown
Touching his sickness: last of all were joined
Ample directions to all loyal folk
To swell the complement by seizing me
Who—doubtless some rank sorcerer—endeavoured
To thwart these pious offices, obstruct
The prince's cure, and frustrate heaven by help
Of certain devils dwelling in his sword.
By luck, the prince in his first fit of thanks
Had forced this bauble on me as an earnest

452| *MS:* Doctor's § altered in pencil to § doctor's nostrum, which *1868:* nostrum which 453| *MS:* smoke; . . § altered in pencil to § smoke— 454| *MS:*—Not § altered in pencil to § Not 455| *MS:* by, in the Abbey,—raised § altered in pencil to § Abbey—raised the Prince to life . . . . § altered in pencil to § life— *1835:* abbey <> prince to life; *1888:* life: 456| *MS:* of the Sage *1835:* sage, *1849:* of the seer, *1863:* seer 458| *MS:* Doctor's recompense . . . § altered in pencil to § recompense— *1835:* doctor's 459| *MS:* Highness <> Monks,— — § altered in pencil to § Monks— *1835:* highness <> monks— 461| *MS:* increase, § , added in pencil § 462| *MS:* Prince *1835:* prince 463| *MS:* heretics, § , added in pencil § *1868:* heretics 464| *MS:* 'till *1868:* till 465–466| *MS:* all, were joined § altered in pencil to § join'd / Ample *1849:* sickness, as a prudent pledge / To make it surer: last of all were joined / Ample *1863:* sickness: last <> joined / Ample 467| *MS:* To seize myself, to swell the complement, *1849:* To swell the complement, by seizing me *1868:* complement by 468| *MS:* doubless <> sorcerer—had endeavoured § altered in pencil to § endeavour'd *1835:* doubtless *1849:* endeavoured *1868:* sorcerer—endeavoured 469| *MS:* offices— — —obstruct § altered in pencil to § offices, obstruct 470| *MS:* Prince's <> frustrate all by *1835:* prince's *1849:* frustrate Heaven, by *1863:* Heaven by *1868:* heaven 471| *MS:* in his sword: § *my* written in pencil below *his* § sword. 472| *MS:* Prince § altered in pencil to § prince

Of further favours. This one case may serve
To give sufficient taste of many such,
So, let them pass. Those shelves support a pile
Of patents, licences, diplomas, titles
From Germany, France, Spain, and Italy;
They authorize some honour; ne'ertheless,
I set more store by this Erasmus sent;
He trusts me; our Frobenius is his friend,
And him "I raised" (nay, read it) "from the dead."
I weary you, I see. I merely sought
To show, there's no great wonder after all
That, while I fill the class-room and attract
A crowd to Basil, I get leave to stay,
And therefore need not scruple to accept
The utmost they can offer, if I please:
For 'tis but right the world should be prepared
To treat with favour e'en fantastic wants
Of one like me, used up in serving her.
Just as the mortal, whom the gods in part
Devoured, received in place of his lost limb

474| *MS:* favours; this § altered in pencil to § favours. This **476**| *MS:* So let <> pass:———those § altered in pencil to § pass. Those *1835:* pass: those *1863:* pass. Those *1868:* So, let **477–479**| *MS:* Of Patents, Licenses, Diplomas, got § altered in pencil to § Of patents, licenses, diplomas, got / In France and Spain and Italy, as well / As Germany;—they § altered in pencil to § Germany; they authorize my claims / To honour from the world—nevertheless § altered in pencil to § world. Nevertheless *1835:* France, and Spain, and *1849:* diplomas, titles, / From Germany, France, Spain, and Italy: / They authorise some honour: ne'ertheless, *1863:* Italy; / <> authorize <> honour; ne'ertheless, *1868:* Spain and *1888:* Spain, and **480**| *MS:* sends——§ altered in pencil to § sends. *1835:* sends; *1849:* sent; **481**| *MS:* me—our <> friend *1835:* me: our <> friend, *1849:* me; our **482**| *MS:* him I raised (nay <> it) from the dead;——— § altered in pencil to § dead. *1835:* dead . . . *1849:* him "I raised" (nay, read it) "from the dead" . . . *1863:* dead." **483**| *MS:* see——I *1835:* see; I *1863:* see. I **484**| *MS:* show there's *1849:* show, there's **485**| *MS:* That while <> class-room, and attract *1868:* That, while <> class-room and **486**| *MS:* I have leave to stay; *1849:* I get leave *1888:* stay, **487**| *MS:* And that I need *1849:* And therefore need **488**| *MS:* offer . . if § written over by § offer—if I love it: *1849:* I please: *1868:* offer, if **490**| *MS:* To treat especially the several wants *1849:* To treat with favour e'en fantastic wants **491**| *MS:* her;— § altered in pencil to § her; *1849:* her. **492**| *MS:* Gods *1863:* gods **493**| *MS:* Devoured § altered in pencil to § Devour'd *1849:* Devoured

Some virtue or other—cured disease, I think;
You mind the fables we have read together.

FESTUS You do not think I comprehend a word.
The time was, Aureole, you were apt enough
To clothe the airiest thoughts in specious breath;
But surely you must feel how vague and strange
These speeches sound.

PARACELSUS Well, then: you know my hopes;
I am assured, at length, those hopes were vain;
That truth is just as far from me as ever;
That I have thrown my life away; that sorrow
On that account is idle, and further effort
To mend and patch what's marred beyond repairing,
As useless: and all this was taught your friend
By the convincing good old-fashioned method
Of force—by sheer compulsion. Is that plain?

FESTUS Dear Aureole, can it be my fears were just?
God wills not . . .

PARACELSUS Now, 'tis this I most admire—
The constant talk men of your stamp keep up
Of God's will, as they style it; one would swear
Man had but merely to uplift his eye,
And see the will in question charactered
On the heaven's vault. 'Tis hardly wise to moot

494| *MS:* think;— § altered in pencil to § think; 496| *MS:* word: *1863:* word. 497| *MS:* Aureole, when you were not slow *1849:* Aureole, you were apt enough 498| *MS:* specious words;— § altered in pencil to § words; *1849:* specious breath; 501| *MS:* length, they may not be: § altered in pencil to § be; *1849:* length, those hopes were vain; 502| *MS:* Truth <> ever: § altered in pencil to § ever; *1835:* truth 503| *MS:* away——that § altered in pencil to § away; that 504| *MS:* is vain and § altered in pencil to § vain, and *1863:* is idle, and 505| *MS:* repairing *1835:* marr'd *1849:* marred <> repairing, 506| *MS:* taught to me *1868:* taught your friend 507| *MS:* convincing, good oldfashioned § altered in pencil to § oldfashion'd *1835:* old-fashion'd *1849:* old-fashioned *1868:* convincing good 508| *MS:* compulsion:— Is § altered in pencil to § compulsion. Is 509| *MS:* Aureole! can <> just! *1849:* Aureole! you confess my <> just? *1863:* Aureole! can it be my *1868:* Aureole, can 510| *MS:* Now 'tis *1835:* Now, 'tis 512| *MS:* will,—as <> it . . . one § altered in pencil to § will, as <> it—one *1835:* it; one 514| *MS:* To see <> charactered § altered in pencil to § character'd *1849:* charactered *1863:* And see 515| *MS:* vault: . . . . 'tis § altered in pencil to § vault. 'Tis

Such topics: doubts are many and faith is weak.
I know as much of any will of God
As knows some dumb and tortured brute what Man,
His stern lord, wills from the perplexing blows
That plague him every way; but there, of course,
Where least he suffers, longest he remains—
My case; and for such reasons I plod on,
Subdued but not convinced. I know as little
Why I deserve to fail, as why I hoped
Better things in my youth. I simply know
I am no master here, but trained and beaten
Into the path I tread; and here I stay,
Until some further intimation reach me,
Like an obedient drudge. Though I prefer
To view the whole thing as a task imposed
Which, whether dull or pleasant, must be done—
Yet, I deny not, there is made provision
Of joys which tastes less jaded might affect;
Nay, some which please me too, for all my pride—
Pleasures that once were pains: the iron ring
Festering about a slave's neck grows at length
Into the flesh it eats. I hate no longer
A host of petty vile delights, undreamed of

516| *MS:* topics:—doubts <> weak:— § altered in pencil to § topics: doubts <> weak. **517**| *MS:* will of His *1849:* will of God's, *1868:* God
518| *MS:* tortured § altered to § tortur'd brute of what *1849:* tortured brute what Man, **519**| *MS:* lord will <> the bewildering blows *1849:* lord, wills <> the perplexing blows **520**| *MS:* way,—and there *1835:* way, and *1863:* way; but there **521**| *MS:* he will stay— § altered in pencil to § stay: *1849:* he remains— **522**| *MS:* on . . . § altered in pencil to § on— *1849:* on,
523| *MS:* Subdued, but not convinced: I § altered in pencil to § convinced. I *1868:* Subdued but **525**| *MS:* youth . . . . I § altered in pencil to § youth. I
526| *MS:* trained § altered in pencil to § train'd *1849:* trained **527**| *MS:* tread;—and § altered in pencil to § tread; and **528**| *MS:* me, § , added in pencil § **529**| *MS:* drudge;—and though I like *1835:* drudge: and *1849:* drudge: though I prefer *1863:* drudge. Though **530**| *MS:* The best to <> task *1849:* To view <> task imposed, *1868:* imposed **531**| *MS:* Imposed—which, dull <> done; . . . . . § altered in pencil to § done— *1849:* Which, whether dull **533**| *MS:* affect;— § altered in pencil to § affect; **534**| *MS:* pride . . . § altered in pencil to § pride— **535**| *MS:* pains; the iron-ring *1835:* pains: the iron ring **536**| *MS:* neck, grows *1835:* neck grows **537**| *MS:* eats———I § altered in pencil to § eats. I *1849:* no more *1863:* no longer
538| *MS:* petty, vile delights—undreamed § altered in pencil to § undream'd *1835:* delights, undream'd *1849:* undreamed *1868:* petty vile

Or spurned before; such now supply the place
Of my dead aims: as in the autumn woods
Where tall trees used to flourish, from their roots
Springs up a fungous brood sickly and pale,
Chill mushrooms coloured like a corpse's cheek.
FESTUS If I interpret well your words, I own
It troubles me but little that your aims,
Vast in their dawning and most likely grown
Extravagantly since, have baffled you.
Perchance I am glad; you merit greater praise;
Because they are too glorious to be gained,
You do not blindly cling to them and die;
You fell, but have not sullenly refused
To rise, because an angel worsted you
In wrestling, though the world holds not your peer;
And though too harsh and sudden is the change
To yield content as yet, still you pursue
The ungracious path as though 'twere rosy-strewn.
'Tis well: and your reward, or soon or late,
Will come from him whom no man serves in vain.

539| *MS:* spurned, before:—such § altered in pencil to § spurn'd, before: such *1835:* before; such *1849:* spurned 540| *MS:* Aims; as <> Autumn *1835:* aims: as <> autumn 541| *MS:* trees flourished § altered in pencil to § flourish'd—from their very roots *1849:* trees used to flourish, from their roots 542| *MS:* brood, sickly *1868:* brood sickly 543| *MS:* mushrooms, coloured § altered in pencil to § colour'd <> cheek . . . . *1835:* cheek . . . *1849:* coloured <> cheek. *1868:* mushrooms coloured 544| *MS:*—If *1835:* If *1849:* well what words I seize, *1863:* well your words, I own 545| *MS:* Aims, *1835:* aims, 546| *1835:* dawning, and *1868:* dawning and 547| *MS:* have proved abortive:— § altered in pencil to § abortive: *1849:* have baffled you. 548| *MS:* glad—you have the greater *1835:* glad; you <> praise, *1849:* you merit greater praise; 549| *MS:* gained, § altered in pencil to § gain'd, *1835:* gain'd— *1849:* gained, 550| *MS:* You have not <> clung <> and died *1849:* You do not <> cling <> and die; 551| *MS:* With them: you § written over by § them; you have *1835:* them—you *1849:* You fell, but have 553| *MS:* tho' § altered in pencil to § though the world has not <> peer: § altered in pencil to § peer; *1849:* world holds not <> peer *1863:* peer; 554| *MS:* tho' § inserted above the line; altered in pencil to § though 555| *MS:* To yield your pleasure, as yet,—still, you § altered in pencil to § yet—still *1849:* To yield content as *1863:* yet, still you 556| *MS:* rosy-strewn: § altered in pencil to § rosy-strewn. 557| *MS:* Tis <> reward, sooner or later, § , added in pencil § *1835:* 'Tis *1849:* reward, or soon or late, 558| *MS:* Him whom none e'er served *1849:* whom no man serves *1868:* him

PARACELSUS Ah, very fine! For my part, I conceive
The very pausing from all further toil,
Which you find heinous, would become a seal
To the sincerity of all my deeds.
To be consistent I should die at once;
I calculated on no after-life;
Yet (how crept in, how fostered, I know not)
Here am I with as passionate regret
For youth and health and love so vainly lavished,
As if their preservation had been first
And foremost in my thoughts; and this strange fact
Humbled me wondrously, and had due force
In rendering me the less averse to follow
A certain counsel, a mysterious warning—
You will not understand—but 'twas a man
With aims not mine and yet pursued like mine,
With the same fervour and no more success,
Perishing in my sight; who summoned me
As I would shun the ghastly fate I saw,
To serve my race at once; to wait no longer

559| *MS:* Ah! very fine:—for § altered in pencil to § fine: for my part *1849:* Ah, very fine! For my part 561| *MS:* heinous . . would § altered in pencil to § heinous, would be as a *1868:* would become a 562| *MS:* deeds: *1849:* deeds. 563| *MS:* once;— § altered in pencil to § once; 564–565| *MS:* after-life, . . . § altered in pencil to § after-life, / Nay, was assured no such could be for me, / Yet . . . (how § written over by § Yet—(how < > not— § written over by § not) *1835:* after-life; // < > foster'd *1849:* after-life; / Yet (how < > fostered < > not) 567| *MS:* youth, and health, and love < > lavished, § altered in pencil to § lavish'd *1849:* vainly lost, *1863:* youth and health and < > vainly lavished, 569| *MS:* thoughts . . . and § altered in pencil to § thoughts; and 571| *1849:* the more disposed to *1863:* the less averse to
572| *MS:* counsel———a § altered in pencil to § counsel, a < > warning, *1835:* warning— 573–576| *MS:*——You < > understand——but § altered in pencil to § You < > understand—but < > Man / Perishing < > sight, who summoned § altered in pencil to § summon'd me, § , added in pencil § *1835:* man *1849:* man / With aims not mine, but yet pursued like mine, / With the same fervor and no more success, / Who perished < > sight; but summoned me *1863:* mine and < > / < > fervour < > / Perishing < > sight; who summoned 577| *MS:* saw, § , added in pencil § 578| *MS:* Race at once——to § altered in pencil to § once—to *1835:* race at once; to

That God should interfere in my behalf,
But to distrust myself, put pride away,
And give my gains, imperfect as they were,
To men. I have not leisure to explain
How, since, a singular series of events
Has raised me to the station you behold,
Wherein I seem to turn to most account
The mere wreck of the past,—perhaps receive
Some feeble glimmering token that God views
And may approve my penance: therefore here
You find me, doing most good or least harm.
And if folks wonder much and profit little
'Tis not my fault; only, I shall rejoice
When my part in the farce is shuffled through,
And the curtain falls: I must hold out till then.
FESTUS Till when, dear Aureole?
PARACELSUS Till I'm fairly thrust
From my proud eminence. Fortune is fickle
And even professors fall: should that arrive,
I see no sin in ceding to my bent.
You little fancy what rude shocks apprise us
We sin; God's intimations rather fail

579–580| *MS:* behalf, § , added in pencil § / Nor trust to Time——but § altered in pencil to § Time—but to distrust myself, *1835:* behalf— / < > time; but *1849:* 'Till God < > behalf, / And let the next world's knowledge dawn on this; / But to distrust myself, put pride away, *1863:* That God < > behalf, / But 581| *MS:* gains imperfect < > were *1835:* gains, imperfect < > were, 582| *MS:* Men:——I § altered in pencil to § Men. I *1835:* men 583| *MS:* How since *1849:* a strange succession of *1863:* a singular series of *1868:* How, since 586| *MS:* The sad wreck < > past, and to receive *1849:* The mere wreck < > past,—perhaps receive *1863:* Past *1868:* past 588| *MS:* penance—therefore § altered in pencil to § penance; therefore *1835:* penance: therefore 589| *MS:* me——doing § altered in pencil to § me—doing good as best I may, *1835:* may; *1849:* doing most good or least harm: *1863:* me, doing < > harm. 591| *MS:* Tis < > fault——only I § altered in pencil to § 'Tis < > fault; only *1849:* only, I 592| *MS:* thro', § altered in pencil to § through, 593| *MS:* falls;——I § altered in pencil to § falls. I < > 'till *1835:* falls; I *1863:* falls: I < > till 594| *1835:* 'Till < > 'Till *1849:* Till when *1868:* PARACELSUS Till 595| *MS:* eminence:——fortune § altered in pencil to § eminence. Fortune 596| *MS:* Professors < > arrive *1835:* professors < > arrive, 597–598| *MS:* bent / Whatever that may be——but not till then: § altered in pencil to § be—but < > then. / You < > apprize *1835:* bent, *1849:* bent. / You *1863:* apprise 599| *MS:* sin—God's *1835:* sin: God's *1868:* sin; God's

In clearness than in energy: 'twere well
Did they but indicate the course to take
Like that to be forsaken. I would fain
Be spared a further sample. Here I stand,
And here I stay, be sure, till forced to flit.
FESTUS Be you but firm on that head! long ere then
All I expect will come to pass, I trust:
The cloud that wraps you will have disappeared.
Meantime, I see small chance of such event:
They praise you here as one whose lore, already
Divulged, eclipses all the past can show,
But whose achievements, marvellous as they be,
Are faint anticipations of a glory
About to be revealed. When Basil's crowds
Dismiss their teacher, I shall be content
That he depart.
PARACELSUS This favour at their hands
I look for earlier than your view of things
Would warrant. Of the crowd you saw to-day,
Remove the full half sheer amazement draws,
Mere novelty, nought else; and next, the tribe
Whose innate blockish dulness just perceives
That unless miracles (as seem my works)
Be wrought in their behalf, their chance is slight

600| *MS:* energy——'twere § altered in pencil to § energy: 'twere 602| *MS:* forsaken: I § altered in pencil to § forsaken. I 603| *MS:* sample . . . here I am *1835:* Here *1849:* sample! Here I stand, *1868:* sample. Here 605| *MS:* head—long *1835:* head; long *1849:* Remain but *1863:* Be you but *1888:* head! long 607| *MS:* disappeared. § altered in pencil to § disappear'd. *1849:* disappeared. 608| *MS:* At present, I *1835:* present I *1849:* Meantime, I 609| *MS:* Lore § altered to § lore already *1849:* lore, divulged *1863:* lore, already 610| *MS:* Divulged eclipses < > Past can show § altered in pencil to § past can show, *1849:* Already, eclipses *1863:* Divulged, eclipses < > Past *1868:* past 612| *MS:* a light *1849:* a glory 613| *MS:* Which shall hereafter be revealed . . . when They § altered in pencil to § reveal'd. When they *1849:* About to be revealed. When Basil's crowds 615| *MS:* depart—PARACELSUS *1835:* depart. PARACELSUS 617| *MS:* warrant;—of § altered in pencil to § warrant. Of < > to-day *1863:* to-day, 618| *MS:* the herd whom sheer amazement brings, *1849:* the full half sheer amazement draws, 619| *MS:*—The novelty < > else;—and § altered in pencil to § else; and *1835:* The *1863:* Mere novelty 622| *MS:* behalf, they are not like *1849:* behalf, their chance is slight

To puzzle the devil; next, the numerous set
Who bitterly hate established schools, and help
The teacher that oppugns them, till he once
Have planted his own doctrine, when the teacher
May reckon on their rancour in his turn;
Take, too, the sprinkling of sagacious knaves
Whose cunning runs not counter to the vogue
But seeks, by flattery and crafty nursing,
To force my system to a premature
Short-lived development. Why swell the list?
Each has his end to serve, and his best way
Of serving it: remove all these, remains
A scantling, a poor dozen at the best,
Worthy to look for sympathy and service,
And likely to draw profit from my pains.

FESTUS 'Tis no encouraging picture: still these few
Redeem their fellows. Once the germ implanted,
Its growth, if slow, is sure.

PARCELSUS God grant it so!
I would make some amends: but if I fail,
The luckless rogues have this excuse to urge,

623| *MS:* devil: and § altered in pencil to § devil; and a numerous *1849:* devil; next, the numerous 624| *MS:* established § altered in pencil to § establish'd schools and *1835:* schools, and *1849:* established schools, so help *1863:* schools, and help 625| *MS:* A Teacher § altered in pencil to § teacher <> 'till *1849:* The teacher <> them, and o'erthrows, *1863:* them, till he once 626| *MS:* Teacher § altered in pencil to § teacher *1849:* 'Till having <> doctrine, he *1863:* Have <> doctrine, when the teacher 628| *MS:* With a good sprinkling *1849:* Take, too, the sprinkling 629| *1835:* vogue, *1868:* vogue 630| *MS:* seeks by § altered in pencil to § seeks, by *1849:* and nursing craft *1863:* and crafty nursing *1868:* nursing, 632| *MS:* development:—why § altered in pencil to § development—why *1835:* developement . . . Why *1849:* development *1863:* development. Why 634| *MS:* Of pushing it *1849:* Of serving it 635–636| *MS:* scantling—a <> best, § altered in pencil to § best— / Worthy *1849:* best— / That really come to learn for learning's sake; / Worthy *1863:* scantling, a <> best, / Worthy 637| *MS:* pains *1835:* pains. 638| *MS:* Tis *1835:* 'Tis 639| *MS:* fellows—once <> implanted *1835:* fellows. Once *1849:* Once implant the germ *1863:* Once the germ implanted, 640| *MS:* The rest will fail not to succeed: § altered in pencil to § succeed. PARACELSUS God <> it! *1849:* Its growth, if slow, is sure. PARACELSUS God <> it so! 641–642| *MS:* amends . . . the § altered in pencil to § amends—the hate between us / Is of one side: should it prove otherwise, / The *1835:* amends: the <> / Is on one side. Should *1849:* amends: but if I fail, / The

That much is in my method and my manner,
My uncouth habits, my impatient spirit,
Which hinders of reception and result
My doctrine: much to say, small skill to speak!
These old aims suffered not a looking-off
Though for an instant; therefore, only when
I thus renounced them and resolved to reap
Some present fruit—to teach mankind some truth
So dearly purchased—only then I found
Such teaching was an art requiring cares
And qualities peculiar to itself:
That to possess was one thing—to display
Another. With renown first in my thoughts,
Or popular praise, I had soon discovered it:
One grows but little apt to learn these things.
FESTUS If it be so, which nowise I believe,
There needs no waiting fuller dispensation
To leave a labour of so little use.
Why not throw up the irksome charge at once?
PARACELSUS A task, a task!
But wherefore hide the whole

645| *MS:* of its influence and reception *1849:* of reception and result 646–647| *MS:* speak: / ——It is, I fancy, some slight proof my old / Devotion suffered § altered in pencil to § suffer'd *1835:* speak . . . / It <> / <> looking-off, *1849:* speak! / Those old aims suffered *1868:* These old <> looking-off 648| *MS:* Tho' § altered in pencil to § Though <> instant, seeing that then alone *1849:* instant; therefore, only when 649| *MS:* When I renounced it, and *1835:* it and *1849:* I thus renounced them and 650| *MS:* fruit——to § altered in pencil to § fruit—to <> Mankind the truth *1835:* mankind *1849:* mankind some truth 651| *MS:* purchased—then I first discovered § altered in pencil to § discover'd *1849:* purchased—only then I found 653| *MS:* itself;— § altered in pencil to § itself: *1849:* itself; *1888:* itself: 654| *MS:* thing . . . to § altered in pencil to § thing—to *1849:* display, *1868:* display 655–656| *MS:* Another—I had never dreamed § altered in pencil to § Another. I <> dream'd of this; / Had but renown been present in my thoughts / Or <> soon found it out:— § altered in pencil to § out: *1835:* this: / <> thoughts, / <> out. *1849:* Another. / Had renown been in my thoughts, Or <> soon discovered it! *1868:* Another. With renown first in <> / <> it: 658| *MS:* so,—which <> believe— § altered in pencil to § so, which <> believe, 660| *MS:* labour to so <> use: *1863:* use. *1868:* labour of so 662| *MS:* A task, a task! . . . / . . . but *1835:* A task, a task! . . . / But *1849:* hide from you *1863:* A task, a task! / But <> hide the whole

Extent of degradation, once engaged
In the confessing vein? Despite of all
My fine talk of obedience and repugnance,
Docility and what not, 'tis yet to learn
If when the task shall really be performed,
My inclination free to choose once more,
I shall do aught but slightly modify
The nature of the hated task I quit.
In plain words, I am spoiled; my life still tends
As first it tended; I am broken and trained
To my old habits: they are part of me.
I know, and none so well, my darling ends
Are proved impossible: no less, no less,
Even now what humours me, fond fool, as when
Their faint ghosts sit with me and flatter me
And send me back content to my dull round?
How can I change this soul?—this apparatus
Constructed solely for their purposes,
So well adapted to their every want,
To search out and discover, prove and perfect;

663| *1849:* The whole extent of degradation, once *1863:* Extent of degradation, once engaged **664**| *MS:* vein? In spite *1849:* Engaged in the confession? Spite *1863:* In the confessing vein? Despite **665**| *MS:* obedience, and *1868:* obedience and **666**| *1835:* Docility, and *1868:* Docility and **667**| *MS:* performed, § altered in pencil to § perform'd, *1849:* the old task really is performed, *1863:* the task shall really be performed, **668**| *MS:* inclinations < > more . . . § altered in pencil to § more— *1835:* more, *1849:* And my will free once more, to choose a new, *1863:* My inclinations free to choose once more, *1868:* inclination **670**| *MS:* Its nature in the next career they try: § altered in pencil to § try. *1849:* The nature of the hated one I quit. *1863:* hated task I **671**| *MS:* spoiled:—my § altered in pencil to § spoil'd: my *1849:* spoiled *1868:* spoiled; my **672**| *MS:* tended . . . I < > trained § altered in pencil to § tended. I < > train'd *1849:* trained *1868:* tended; I **673**| *MS:* habits—they § altered in pencil to § habits; they < > me: *1849:* me. *1868:* habits: they **674**| *MS:* know——and § altered in pencil to § know, and < > Ends § altered to § ends **675**| *MS:* impossible——no less——no less § altered in pencil to § impossible—no less—no less *1835:* impossible: no less, no less, **677**| *MS:* me, and *1835:* flatter me, *1868:* with me < > me **678**| *MS:* round? . . § altered in pencil to § round? **679**| *MS:* soul . . . this § written over by § soul—this § altered in pencil to § soul?—this *1835:* soul? this *1849:* soul?—this **680**| *MS:* purposes—— § altered in pencil to § purposes— *1835:* purposes? *1868:* purposes, **681**| *MS:* their wants and uses, *1835:* uses— *1849:* their every want, **682**| *MS:* To search, discover, and dissect, and prove . . . § altered in pencil to § prove— *1835:* prove: *1849:* search out and discover, prove and perfect;

This intricate machine whose most minute
And meanest motions have their charm to me
Though to none else—an aptitude I seize,
An object I perceive, a use, a meaning,
A property, a fitness, I explain
And I alone:—how can I change my soul?
And this wronged body, worthless save when tasked
Under that soul's dominion—used to care
For its bright master's cares and quite subdue
Its proper cravings—not to ail nor pine
So he but prosper—whither drag this poor
Tried patient body? God! how I essayed
To live like that mad poet, for a while,
To love alone; and how I felt too warped
And twisted and deformed! What should I do,
Even tho' released from drudgery, but return
Faint, as you see, and halting, blind and sore,
To my old life and die as I began?
I cannot feed on beauty for the sake

683| *MS:* machine whose *1849:* minute, *1863:* machine whose <> minute 684| *1835:* charms *1849:* Least obvious motions <> charm *1863:* And meanest motions 685| *MS:* Tho' § altered in pencil to § Though <> else— —an <> I see— — § written over by § else—an <> I see— *1849:* I seize, 686| *MS:* perceive— *1849:* perceive, a 687| *1835:* explain, *1868:* explain 688| *MS:* alone . . . how <> soul?— *1835:* soul? *1849:* alone:—how 689| *MS:* wronged § altered in pencil to § wrong'd *1835:* task'd *1849:* wronged <> tasked 691| *MS:* Masters § altered in pencil to § masters care, and to subdue *1835:* master's *1849:* and quite subdue *1868:* cares and 692| *MS:* cravings . . not § altered in pencil to § cravings—not to ail nor pine § altered in pencil to § ail, nor pine, *1863:* ail nor *1868:* pine
693| *MS:* He § altered in pencil to § he but prosper— — —whither <> poor, *1835:* prosper—whither *1849:* So the soul prosper *1863:* So he but prosper *1868:* poor 694| *MS:* Tried, patient body? God! how I essayed § altered in pencil to § essay'd *1835:* essay'd *1849:* essayed, *1868:* Tried patient <> essayed
695–696| *MS:* while!— —§ altered in pencil to § while! / To Love alone — —and § written over by § alone!—and § altered in pencil to § alone! and <> warped § altered in pencil to § warp'd *1835:* love *1849:* while, / To catch Aprile's spirit, as I hoped, / And love <> warped *1863:* while, / To love *1868:* alone; and 697| *MS:* deformed § altered in pencil to § deform'd *1849:* deformed 698| *MS:* Released from this sad drudgery but *1835:* drudgery, but *1849:* Even tho' released from drudgery 699| *MS:* Faint as I am and halting— —blind § altered in pencil to § halting, blind *1835:* halting, blind *1849:* Faint, as you see, and halting
700| *MS:* begun! *1835:* life—and *1863:* began! *1868:* life and *1888:* began? 701| *MS:* beauty, for *1868:* beauty for

Of beauty only, nor can drink in balm
From lovely objects for their loveliness;
My nature cannot lose her first imprint;
I still must hoard and heap and class all truths
With one ulterior purpose: I must know!
Would God translate me to his throne, believe
That I should only listen to his word
To further my own aim! For other men,
Beauty is prodigally strewn around,
And I were happy could I quench as they
This mad and thriveless longing, and content me
With beauty for itself alone: alas,
I have addressed a frock of heavy mail
Yet may not join the troop of sacred knights;
And now the forest-creatures fly from me,
The grass-banks cool, the sunbeams warm no more.
Best follow, dreaming that ere night arrive,
I shall o'ertake the company and ride
Glittering as they!

FESTUS I think I apprehend
What you would say: if you, in truth, design
To enter once more on the life thus left,
Seek not to hide that all this consciousness

702| *MS:* only— —not § altered in pencil to § only—nor *1835:* only; nor *1868:* only, nor 703| *MS:* loveliness . . . . § altered in pencil to § loveliness. *1835:* loveliness; 704| *MS:* impress: § altered in pencil to § impress; *1849:* first intent; *1863:* first imprint; 705| *MS:* hoard, and heap, and < > Truths § altered in pencil to § truths *1863:* hoard and heap and 706| *MS:* One § altered in pencil to § one < > purpose—one intent— — § altered in pencil to § intent. *1849:* purpose: I must know! 707| *1863:* His *1868:* his 708| *MS:* Words *1835:* words *1863:* His *1868:* his word 709| *MS:* Aims § altered in pencil to § aims! full well I know *1835:* Full *1849:* aims! For other men, *1868:* aim 710| *MS:* strown *1835:* strewn 711| *MS:* I trample under *1849:* I quench as they 712| *MS:* longing, be content *1863:* longing, and content me 713| *MS:* alone;— —alas! § altered in pencil to § alone; alas! *1835:* alone: alas! *1868:* alas, 714| *MS:* addressed § altered in pencil to § address'd *1835:* mail, *1849:* addressed *1868:* mail 715| *MS:* knights;— § altered in pencil to § knights; 717| *MS:* more! *1863:* more. 718| *MS:*—Best § altered in pencil to § Best < > arrive *1849:* arrives *1863:* arrive, 719| *MS:* company, and *1868:* company and 720| *MS:* FESTUS—I think I *1835:* FESTUS I think I 722| *MS:* enter on such life again, seek not *1849:* enter once more on the life thus left, 723| *MS:* To hide that much of all the § altered in pencil to § this *1849:* Seek not to hide that all

Of failure is assumed!
PARACELSUS My friend, my friend,
I toil, you listen; I explain, perhaps
You understand: there our communion ends.
Have you learnt nothing from to-day's discourse?
When we would thoroughly know the sick man's state
We feel awhile the fluttering pulse, press soft
The hot brow, look upon the languid eye,
And thence divine the rest. Must I lay bare
My heart, hideous and beating, or tear up
My vitals for your gaze, ere you will deem
Enough made known? You! who are you, forsooth?
That is the crowning operation claimed
By the arch-demonstrator—heaven the hall,
And earth the audience. Let Aprile and you
Secure good places: 'twill be worth the while.
FESTUS Are you mad, Aureole? What can I have said
To call for this? I judged from your own words.
PARACELSUS Oh, doubtless! A sick wretch describes the ape
That mocks him from the bed-foot, and all gravely
You thither turn at once: or he recounts
The perilous journey he has late performed,

724| *MS:* assumed——PARACELSUS *1835:* assumed. PARACELSUS *1868:* assumed! PARACELSUS 725| *MS:* I tell . . . you listen;—I explain——perhaps § altered in pencil to § I tell—you listen; I explain—perhaps *1849:* I speak, you < > explain, perhaps *1863:* I tell, you *1888:* I toil, you 726| *MS:* understand:——there § altered in pencil to § understand: there 728| *MS:*—When *1835:* When 729| *MS:* pulse—press § altered in pencil to § pulse, press 730| *MS:* brow—look § altered in pencil to § brow, look 731| *MS:* rest——must § altered in pencil to § rest. Must 732| *MS:* heart—hideous and beating—or § altered in pencil to § heart, hideous and beating, or 734| *MS:* known?—You *1835:* known? You 735| *MS:*—*That* < > claimed § altered in pencil to § claim'd *1835: That* *1849:* That < > claimed 736| *MS:* Arch-demonstrator *1835:* arch-demonstrator 737| *MS:* audience.——Let § altered in pencil to § audience. Let 738| *MS:* places—'twill < > while . . . § altered in pencil to § while. *1863:* places: 'twill be worth the while. 739| *MS:* what *1835:* What 740| *MS:* this . . I < > words.— § altered in pencil to § this? I < > words. 741| *MS:* a *1835:* A *1849:* Oh, true! A fevered wretch *1863:* Oh, doubtless! A sick wretch 742| *MS:* bed-foot . . . and § altered in pencil to § bed-foot, and *1849:* and you turn *1863:* and all gravely 743| *1849:* All gravely thither at *1863:* You thither turn at 744| How sweet the gardens where he slept last night, § cancelled by § The perilous journey he has late performed, § altered in pencil to § perform'd *1849:* performed,

And you are puzzled much how that could be!
You find me here, half stupid and half mad;
It makes no part of my delight to search
Into these matters, much less undergo
Another's scrutiny; but so it chances
That I am led to trust my state to you:
And the event is, you combine, contrast
And ponder on my foolish words as though
They thoroughly conveyed all hidden here—
Here, loathsome with despair and hate and rage!
Is there no fear, no shrinking and no shame?
Will you guess nothing? will you spare me nothing?
Must I go deeper? Ay or no?

FESTUS Dear friend . . .

PARACELSUS True: I am brutal—'tis a part of it;
The plague's sign—you are not a lazar-haunter,
How should you know? Well then, you think it strange
I should profess to have failed utterly,
And yet propose an ultimate return
To courses void of hope: and this, because
You know not what temptation is, nor how
'Tis like to ply men in the sickliest part.

746| *MS:* here—half-stupid § written over by § here; half-stupid § altered in pencil to § here, half-stupid and half mad:— § altered in pencil to § mad: *1835:* half stupid *1863:* mad; 747| *MS:*——It *1835:* it 748| *MS:* things—much § written over by § things; much less to undergo *1835:* things, much *1868:* these matters, much less undergo 749| *MS:* scrutiny;—but *1835:* scrutiny; but 750–751| *MS:* you / As calm, as sincerely as I may,— § altered in pencil to § may; / And *1835:* sincerely, as <> / <> contrast, *1849:* you: / And *1868:* contrast 752| *MS:* tho' § altered in pencil to § though *1835:* words, as *1868:* words as 753| *MS:* conveyed <> *here,* § altered in pencil to § convey'd <> *here—* *1849:* conveyed <> here— 754| *MS: Here*——loathsome § altered in pencil to § *Here*—loathsome *1835: Here,* loathsome <> despair, and hate, and *1849:* Here *1868:* despair and hate and 755| *MS:* shrinking, or no *1863:* shrinking or *1868:* shrinking and no 757| *MS:* Aye or No? FESTUS ———Dear Friend, ... § altered in pencil to § FESTUS Dear Friend . . . *1835:* no <> friend . . . *1863:* Ay 758| *MS:* True:—I § altered in pencil to § True: I am brutal—'tis <> it;— *1835:* it; 759| *MS:* A plague fit:—you § altered in pencil to § plague fit: you *1849:* The plague's sign—you 761| *MS:* failed § altered in pencil to § fail'd *1849:* failed 764| *MS:* temptation § written over by § Temptation *1835:* temptation 765| *MS:* Tis <> to ply me in my sickliest part *1835:* 'Tis <> in the sickliest *1849:* ply men in

You are to understand that we who make
Sport for the gods, are hunted to the end:
There is not one sharp volley shot at us,
Which 'scaped with life, though hurt, we slacken pace
And gather by the wayside herbs and roots
To staunch our wounds, secure from further harm:
We are assailed to life's extremest verge.
It will be well indeed if I return,
A harmless busy fool, to my old ways!
I would forget hints of another fate,
Significant enough, which silent hours
Have lately scared me with.

FESTUS Another! and what?

PARACELSUS After all, Festus, you say well: I am
A man yet: I need never humble me.
I would have been—something, I know not what;
But though I cannot soar, I do not crawl.
There are worse portions than this one of mine.
You say well!

FESTUS Ah!

PARACELSUS And deeper degradation!
If the mean stimulants of vulgar praise,

766| *MS:* . . You § altered in pencil to § You <> understand, that we, who *1835:* we who *1868:* understand that 767| *MS:* Gods *1835:* gods
768| *MS:* us *1835:* us, 768–770| *MS:* 'tho § altered in pencil to § though <> pace / And gather *1835:* way-side *1849:* Which if we manage to escape with life, / Though touched and hurt, we straight may slacken pace / And gather *1863:* Which 'scaped with life, though hurt, we slacken pace / And gather <> wayside 771| *MS:* harm: . . . § altered to § harm . . . *1849:* harm— *1863:* stanch <> harm: *1868:* staunch 772| *MS:* assailed § altered in pencil to § assail'd <> verge: § altered to § verge. *1849:* No; we are chased to *1863:* We are assailed to 774| *MS:* ways! . . . § altered in pencil to § ways! 775| *MS:* fate *1849:* fate, 777| *MS:* with;—FESTUS § altered to § with; FESTUS § altered in pencil to § with. FESTUS 778| *MS:* . . . After § altered to § After *1849:* I stand *1863:* I am 779| *MS:* A Man yet—I need <> me;— — § altered in pencil to § me; *1835:* A man *1849:* me. *1863:* yet: I 780| been— —something I <> what,— § altered in pencil to § been—something I <> what; *1835:* something, I 781| *MS:* tho' § altered in pencil to § though <> crawl: *1863:* crawl. 782| *MS:* mine,— § altered in pencil to § mine; *1863:* mine.
783| *MS:* well . . . FESTUS Ah! . . PARACELSUS . . . And § & altered in pencil to *And* § <> degradation: *1849:* well! FESTUS <> degradation! *1863:* Ah! PARACELSUS 784| *MS:* praise, § , added in pencil §

If vanity should become the chosen food
Of a sunk mind, should stifle even the wish
To find its early aspirations true,
Should teach it to breathe falsehood like life-breath—
An atmosphere of craft and trick and lies;
Should make it proud to emulate, surpass
Base natures in the practices which woke
Its most indignant loathing once . . . No, no!
Utter damnation is reserved for hell!
I had immortal feelings; such shall never
Be wholly quenched: no, no!
My friend, you wear
A melancholy face, and certain 'tis
There's little cheer in all this dismal work.
But was it my desire to set abroach
Such memories and forebodings? I foresaw
Where they would drive. 'Twere better we discuss
News from Lucerne or Zurich; ask and tell
Of Egypt's flaring sky or Spain's cork-groves.
FESTUS I have thought: trust me, this mood will pass away!

785| *MS:* And vanity—should § altered in pencil to § vanity,—should *1835:* vanity, should *1868:* If vanity should **786**| *MS:* mind,—should § altered in pencil to § mind; should *1868:* mind, should **787**| *MS:* true— — § altered in pencil to § true; *1868:* true, **788**| *MS:* life-breath;— § altered in pencil to § life-breath— **789**| *MS:* lies;— § altered in pencil to § lies— *1835:* craft, and trick, and *1849:* lies; *1863:* craft and trick and **790**| *MS:* emulate or surpass *1868:* emulate, surpass **792**| *MS:* once . . . . No, No. *1835:* once . . . No, no: *1849:* No, no! **793**| *MS:* Hell!— § altered in pencil to § Hell! *1868:* hell! **794**| *MS: had* <> feelings—such *1849:* had *1863:* feelings: such *1868:* feelings; such **795**| *MS:* quenched . . No—No— — § altered in pencil to § quench'd—No,—No. *1835:* no, no. *1849:* quenched—no, no! *1863:* quenched: no, no! **796**| *MS:* 'tis, *1849:* and truth to speak, *1863:* and, certain 'tis *1868:* and certain **797**| *MS:* work; *1863:* work. **798**| *MS:* But 'twas not my *1868:* But was it my **799**| *MS:* forbodings . . I § altered in pencil to § forbodings. I *1835:* forebodings *1863:* forebodings: I *1868:* forebodings? I **800**| *MS:* drive— —'twere § altered in pencil to § drive; 'twere better to discuss *1849:* better you detailed *1863:* drive. 'Twere better to discuss *1868:* better we discuss **801**| *MS:* News of Lucerne or Zurich; or to tell *1849:* or I described *1863:* or to tell *1868:* News from Lucerne or Zurich; ask and tell **802**| *MS:* sky, or <> cork-groves: . . § written over by § cork-groves:— § altered in pencil to § cork-groves: *1835:* cork-groves. *1849:* Great Egypt's *1863:* Of Egypt's <> sky or **803**| *MS:* away: § altered in pencil to § away. *1849:* thought now: yes, this *1863:* thought: trust me, this *1868:* away!

I know you and the lofty spirit you bear,
And easily ravel out a clue to all.
These are the trials meet for such as you,
Nor must you hope exemption: to be mortal
Is to be plied with trials manifold.
Look round! The obstacles which kept the rest
From your ambition, have been spurned by you;
Their fears, their doubts, the chains that bind them all,
Were flax before your resolute soul, which nought
Avails to awe save these delusions bred
From its own strength, its selfsame strength disguised,
Mocking itself. Be brave, dear Aureole! Since
The rabbit has his shade to frighten him,
The fawn a rustling bough, mortals their cares,
And higher natures yet would slight and laugh
At these entangling fantasies, as you
At trammels of a weaker intellect,—
Measure your mind's height by the shade it casts!
I know you.

PARACELSUS And I know you, dearest Festus!
And how you love unworthily; and how
All admiration renders blind.

FESTUS You hold

804| *MS:*—I § altered in pencil to § I <> you, and *1868:* you and 805| *MS:* all: *1849:* all. 806| *MS:* you . . . § altered in pencil to § you— *1835:* you, 807| *MS:*—Nor § altered in pencil to § Nor 809| *1835:* round! the obstacles *1849:* round! The obstacles 810| *MS:* ambition have <> spurned by you § altered in pencil to § spurn'd by you: *1849:* Of men from <> ambition, you have spurned; *1863:* From <> ambition, have been spurned by you; 811| *MS:* doubts . . the § altered in pencil to § doubts—the <> them best *1835:* doubts, the <> best, *1863:* them all, 813| *MS:* awe, save *1835:* delusions, bred *1863:* delusions bred *1868:* awe save 814| *MS:* strength—its selfsame *1835:* strength, its <> strength, disguised— *1863:* strength disguised— *1868:* disguised, 815| *MS:* itself—be § altered in pencil to § itself. be <> since *1835:* itself. Be *1849:* Since 817| *MS:* bough,—mortals § altered in pencil to § bough, mortals *1835:* bough; mortals *1849:* bough, mortals 818| *MS:* Natures *1835:* natures *1849:* yet their power to laugh *1863:* yet would slight and laugh 820| *MS:* weaker mind;—but judge *1835:* mind; but *1849:* weaker intellect. *1863:* intellect,— 821| *MS: Your* mind's dimensions by *1849:* Measure your mind's height by 822| *MS:* you: PARACELSUS § altered in pencil to § you. PARACELSUS 823| *MS:* unworthily . . and § altered in pencil to § unworthily; and

That admiration blinds?

PARACELSUS Ay and alas!

FESTUS Nought blinds you less than admiration, friend!
Whether it be that all love renders wise
In its degree; from love which blends with love—
Heart answering heart—to love which spends itself
In silent mad idolatry of some
Pre-eminent mortal, some great soul of souls,
Which ne'er will know how well it is adored.
I say, such love is never blind; but rather
Alive to every the minutest spot
Which mars its object, and which hate (supposed
So vigilant and searching) dreams not of.
Love broods on such: what then? When first perceived
Is there no sweet strife to forget, to change,
To overflush those blemishes with all
The glow of general goodness they disturb?
—To make those very defects an endless source
Of new affection grown from hopes and fears?
And, when all fails, is there no gallant stand
Made even for much proved weak? no shrinking-back
Lest, since all love assimilates the soul
To what it loves, it should at length become
Almost a rival of its idol? Trust me,

825| *MS:* Aye, and *1863:* Ay and 826| *MS:* admiration: *1849:* admiration will. *1868:* admiration, friend! 828| *MS:* degree . . . from Love <> Love § altered in pencil to § degree; from Love <> Love— *1835:* love <> love— 829| *MS:*——Heart <> heart———to that which § altered in pencil to § Heart <> heart—to *1849:* to love which 831| *MS:* mortal—some <> Soul of Souls— *1835:* soul of souls— *1849:* mortal, some <> of souls, 832| *MS:* adored: . . . . § altered in pencil to § adored: *1849:* adored:— *1863:* adored. 833| *MS:* . . I <> blind,—but § altered in pencil to § I <> blind; but 835| *MS:* That mars <> Hate *1835:* hate *1849:* Which mars 836| *MS:* of: *1863:* of. 837| *MS:* then? in § altered in pencil to § then? In the first case *1849:* then? When first perceived *1863:* perceived, *1888:* perceived 840| *MS:* of goodness they cannot disturb? *1849:* of general goodness they disturb? 841| *MS:* To *1849:*—To 843| *MS:*—And § altered in pencil to § And in the last,—is *1835:* last, is *1849:* And, when all fails, is 845| *MS:* Lest, since § written over by § Lest (since *1849:* Lest, rising even as its idol sinks, *1863:* Lest, since all love assimilates the soul 846| *MS:* loves, it § written over by § loves) it *1849:* It nearly reach the sacred place, and stand *1863:* To what it loves, it should at length become 847| *1849:* of that idol *1863:* of its idol

If there be fiends who seek to work our hurt,
To ruin and drag down earth's mightiest spirits
Even at God's foot, 'twill be from such as love,
Their zeal will gather most to serve their cause;
And least from those who hate, who most essay
By contumely and scorn to blot the light
Which forces entrance even to their hearts:
For thence will our defender tear the veil
And show within each heart, as in a shrine,
The giant image of perfection, grown
In hate's despite, whose calumnies were spawned
In the untroubled presence of its eyes.
True admiration blinds not; nor am I
So blind. I call your sin exceptional;
It springs from one whose life has passed the bounds
Prescribed to life. Compound that fault with God!
I speak of men; to common men like me
The weakness you reveal endears you more,
Like the far traces of decay in suns.
I bid you have good cheer!

PARACELSUS *Præclare! Optime!*

848| *MS:* Fiends <> hurt,— § altered in pencil to § hurt, *1835:* fiends **849**| *MS:* Earth's *1835:* earth's <> spirits, *1863:* spirits **850**| *MS:* foot— § above § , twill <> love— § written over by § Love—§ — added in pencil § *1835:* foot, 'twill <> love— *1849:* love, **853**| *MS:* Light *1835:* light **854**| *MS:* Which will have entrance <> *their* hearts; *1849:* their *1863:* Which forces entrance <> hearts: **855**| *MS:* . . For § altered in pencil to § For <> Defender *1835:* defender *1849:* Defender *1863:* defender **856**| *MS:* And show within the heart § *show* inserted above the line § *1849:* within each heart **857**| *MS:* Perfection *1868:* perfection **858**| *MS:* In their despite <> spawned § altered in pencil to § spawn'd *1849:* In hate's despite <> spawned **859**| *MS:* eyes! *1868:* eyes. **860**| *MS:* not: nor *1835:* not; nor **861–862**| *MS:* blind: I know your unexampled sins, / But I know too, what sort of soul is prone / To errors of that stamp;—sins like to spring / From one alone, whose <> passed § altered in pencil to § pass'd *1835:* too what <> / <> stamp—sins <> / <> alone whose *1849:* blind: I call your sin exceptional; / It springs from one whose <> passed *1863:* blind. I **863**| *MS:* life . . . compound § altered in pencil to § life—compound *that* *1835:* life. Compound *1849:* that **864**| *MS:* Men . . to § altered in pencil to § Men; to <> Men *1835:* men <> men **865**| *MS:* you confess endears you more, § altered in pencil to § more— *1863:* more, **866**| *MS:* suns:— § altered in pencil to § suns: *1863:* suns. **867**| *MS: Præclarè! Optimè!* *1868: Præclare! Optime!*

Think of a quiet mountain-cloistered priest
Instructing Paracelsus! yet 'tis so.
Come, I will show you where my merit lies.
'Tis in the advance of individual minds
That the slow crowd should ground their expectation
Eventually to follow; as the sea
Waits ages in its bed till some one wave
Out of the multitudinous mass, extends
The empire of the whole, some feet perhaps,
Over the strip of sand which could confine
Its fellows so long time: thenceforth the rest,
Even to the meanest, hurry in at once,
And so much is clear gained. I shall be glad
If all my labours, failing of aught else,
Suffice to make such inroad and procure
A wider range for thought: nay, they do this;
For, whatsoe'er my notions of true knowledge
And a legitimate success, may be,
I am not blind to my undoubted rank
When classed with others: I precede my age:

868| *MS:* mountain-cloistered Priest § altered in pencil to § mountain-cloister'd Priest *1835:* priest *1863:* mountain-cloistered 869–870| *MS:* so: And that his flittering words should soothe me better § : added in pencil § / Than fulsome tributes . . . not § altered in pencil to § tributes—not that 'tis so § *'tis so* cancelled by *that* § that strange:— / Come *1835:* yet, 'tis so: / < > better / < > tributes: not that that is strange: / Come *1849:* so. / Come *1868:* yet 'tis 870–871| *MS:* lies: / I ne'er supposed that since *I* failed no other / Needs hope success . . . I § altered in pencil to § success. I act as though each one / Who hears me, may aspire; now mark me well:— § altered in pencil to § well: / Tis *1835:* lies. / < > fail'd < > / < > success: I < > / < > me may < > / 'Tis *1849:* lies. / 'Tis 873| *MS:* follow,——as § written over by § follow,—as *1835:* follow—as *1863:* follow; as 874| *MS:* bed, 'till *1868:* bed 'till *1888:* till 875| *MS:* Of all the < > mass extends *1849:* Out of the multitude aspires, extends *1863:* multitudinous mass, extends 878| *MS:* fellows, so long time:—thenceforth § altered in pencil to § time: thenceforth 879| *MS:* once,— § altered in pencil to § once, 880| *MS:* gained: . . . I § altered in pencil to § gained. I 882| *MS:* inroad——to § altered in pencil to § in road—to procure *1849:* inroad, and procure *1863:* inroad and 883| *MS:* Thought < > *do* this,— § altered in pencil to § this; *1835:* thought *1849:* do 884| *MS:* For whatsoe'er *1849:* For, whatsoe'er 885| *MS:* success . . . no § altered in pencil to § success—no less *1835:* success may be, *1849:* success, may 887| classed < > others:—I § altered in pencil to § class'd < > others. I *1849:* others: I

And whoso wills is very free to mount
These labours as a platform whence his own
May have a prosperous outset. But, alas!
My followers—they are noisy as you heard;
But, for intelligence, the best of them
So clumsily wield the weapons I supply
And they extol, that I begin to doubt
Whether their own rude clubs and pebble-stones
Would not do better service than my arms
Thus vilely swayed—if error will not fall
Sooner before the old awkward batterings
Than my more subtle warfare, not half learned.
FESTUS I would supply that art, then, or withhold
New arms until you teach their mystery.
PARACELSUS Content you, 'tis my wish; I have recourse
To the simplest training. Day by day I seek
To wake the mood, the spirit which alone
Can make those arms of any use to men.
Of course they are for swaggering forth at once

888–889| *MS:* wills, is < > to make / That use of me which I disdained § altered in pencil to § disdain'd to make / Of my forerunners—(vanity, perchance: But had I deemed § altered in pencil to § deem'd their learning wonder-worth, / I had been other than I am)——to § altered in pencil to § am)—to mount / Those labours, as < > whence their own *1835:* labours as a platform, whence *1849:* to mount / These labours *1868:* will is < > / < > platform whence his own 890| *MS:* outset;—but § altered in pencil to § outset; but *1863:* outset. But 891| *MS:* followers . . . they § altered in pencil to § followers—they < > heard, *1868:* heard; 892| *MS:* But for intelligence;——the § altered in pencil to § intelligence; the *1835:* intelligence—the *1868:* But, for intelligence, the 893| *MS:* supply, *1835:* supply 894| *MS:* extol,—that § altered in pencil to § extol, that 897| *MS:* swayed,—if § altered in pencil to § swayed—if *1835:* sway'd *1849:* swayed 898| *MS:* before their aukward *1835:* awkward *1849:* the old awkward 899–900| *MS:* warfare! FESTUS In that case, / I < > art and would withold *1835:* art, and < > withhold *1849:* warfare, not half learned. / FESTUS I < > art, then, and withhold *1868:* then, or withhold 901| *MS:* The arms until their mystery was made known. *1849:* Its arms until you have taught their mystery. *1868:* New arms < > you teach their 902| *MS:* you; 'tis § altered in pencil to § you, 'tis 903| *MS:* training: day by *1835:* training. Day by 905| *MS:* to them. *1849:* to men. 906| *MS:*——Of § altered in pencil to § Of *1849:* course, they *1868:* course they

Graced with Ulysses' bow, Achilles' shield—
Flash on us, all in armour, thou Achilles!
Make our hearts dance to thy resounding step!
A proper sight to scare the crows away!
FESTUS Pity you choose not then some other method
Of coming at your point. The marvellous art
At length established in the world bids fair
To remedy all hindrances like these:
Trust to Frobenius' press the precious lore
Obscured by uncouth manner, or unfit
For raw beginners; let his types secure
A deathless monument to after-time;
Meanwhile wait confidently and enjoy
The ultimate effect: sooner or later
You shall be all-revealed.
PARACELSUS   The old dull question
In a new form; no more. Thus: I possess
Two sorts of knowledge; one,—vast, shadowy,
Hints of the unbounded aim I once pursued:
The other consists of many secrets, caught
While bent on nobler prize,—perhaps a few
Prime principles which may conduct to much:
These last I offer to my followers here.

907–910| *MS:* With Hercules' club, Achilles' shield, Ulysses' / Bow—a choice sight *1849:* Graced with Ulysses' club, Achilles' shield— / Flash on us, all in armour, thou Achilles! / Make our hearts dance to thy resounding step! / A proper sight *1863:* Ulysses' bow, Achilles' 911| *MS:* no, then, some *1888:* not then some 912| *MS:* point:—the § altered in pencil to § point. The 913| *1835:* establish'd *1849:* established 915| *MS:* Press *1835:* press 917| *MS:* beginners—let *1849:* beginners; let 918| *MS:* after-times; *1868:* after-time; 919| *MS:* Meanwhile enjoy and confidently wait *1849:* Meanwhile wait confidently and enjoy 920| *1849:* later, *1868:* later 921| *MS:* An ancient question *1835:* all-reveal'd *1849:* all-revealed. PARACELSUS The old dull question 922| *MS:* more: thus § altered in pencil to § more. Thus 923| *MS:* Knowledge,—one § altered in pencil to § Knowledge—one, vast, shadowy hints *1835:* knowledge *1849:* knowledge; one,—vast, shadowy, 924| *MS:* Of <> Aim <> pursued;— § altered in pencil to § pursued— *1835:* aim *1849:* Hints of <> pursued: 925| *MS:* other, many secrets, made my own *1849:* other consists of many secrets, learned *1863:* secrets, caught 926| *MS:* prize, and not a *1849:* prize,—perhaps a 927| *MS:* First principles <> much; § altered in pencil to § much: *1863:* Prime principles 928| *MS:* here:— § altered in pencil to § here: *1835:* here.

Now, bid me chronicle the first of these,
My ancient study, and in effect you bid
Revert to the wild courses just abjured:
I must go find them scattered through the world.
Then, for the principles, they are so simple
(Being chiefly of the overturning sort),
That one time is as proper to propound them
As any other—to-morrow at my class,
Or half a century hence embalmed in print.
For if mankind intend to learn at all,
They must begin by giving faith to them
And acting on them: and I do not see
But that my lectures serve indifferent well:
No doubt these dogmas fall not to the earth,
For all their novelty and rugged setting.
I think my class will not forget the day
I let them know the gods of Israel,
Aetius, Oribasius, Galen, Rhasis,
Serapion, Avicenna, Averröes,
Were blocks!

FESTUS And that reminds me, I heard something
About your waywardness: you burned their books,
It seems, instead of answering those sages.

PARACELSUS And who said that?

FESTUS Some I met yesternight

929| *MS:* Now bid <> these,— § altered in pencil to § these, *1868:* Now, bid 930| *MS:* study— § above § , and <> bid me *1835:* effect you *1868:* bid 931–933| *MS:* course I have abjured:— § altered in pencil to § abjured. / And, for *1849:* courses just abjured: / I must go find them scattered through the world. / Then, for 934| *MS:*—(Being <> sort), § , added in pencil § *1835:* (Being 936| *MS:* other—tomorrow <> class, § , added in pencil § *1835:* to-morrow 937| *MS:* print— *1835:* embalm'd in print; *1849:* embalmed in print: *1863:* print. 938| *MS:* Mankind <> all *1835:* mankind <> all, 939| *1835:* them, *1868:* them 940| *1835:* them; and *1888:* them: and 942| *MS:* earth *1835:* earth, 943| *MS:* setting; § altered in pencil to § setting. 945| *MS:* Gods *1835:* gods 947| *MS:* And Avicenna, and Averröes, *1849:* Serapion, Avicenna, Averröes,— *1868:* Averröes, 948| *MS:* blocks!—FESTUS ——And <> me,—they § altered in pencil to § me, they said something *1835:* blocks! FESTUS And *1849:* me, I heard something 949| *MS:* books *1835:* burn'd <> books, *1849:* burned 950| *MS:* It seems instead <> sages . . . . *1835:* seems, instead <> sages . . . *1849:* sages.

With Œcolampadius. As you know, the purpose
Of this short stay at Basil was to learn
His pleasure touching certain missives sent
For our Zuinglius and himself. 'Twas he
Apprised me that the famous teacher here
Was my old friend.

PARACELSUS Ah, I forgot: you went . . .

FESTUS From Zurich with advices for the ear
Of Luther, now at Wittenberg—(you know,
I make no doubt, the differences of late
With Carolostadius)—and returning sought
Basil and . . .

PARACELSUS I remember. Here's a case, now,
Will teach you why I answer not, but burn
The books you mention. Pray, does Luther dream
His arguments convince by their own force
The crowds that own his doctrine? No, indeed!
His plain denial of established points
Ages had sanctified and men supposed
Could never be oppugned while earth was under
And heaven above them—points which chance or time
Affected not—did more than the array
Of argument which followed. Boldly deny!
There is much breath-stopping, hair-stiffening

952| *MS:* Œcolampadius: as *1835:* Œcolampadius. As **953**| *MS:* Basil, was *1835:* Basil was **955**| *MS:* himself:—'twas § altered in pencil to § himself. 'Twas **956**| *MS:* Apprized *1863:* Apprised **957**| *MS:* friend—— PARACELSUS <> went . . . . *1835:* friend. PARACELSUS <> went . . . **959**| *MS:* Luther now at Wittemburg——(you *1835:* Luther, now at Wittemburg—(you *1888:* Wittenberg **961**| *MS:* Carolostadius-),- and *1835:* Carolostadius)—and **962**| *MS:* and Œcolempadius. PARACELSUS Here's a case now, *1835:* now *1849:* and . . . PARACELSUS I remember. Here's a case, now, **964**| *MS:* mention: Pray *1835:* pray *1888:* mention. Pray **966**| *MS:* indeed: *1888:* indeed! **967**| *MS:* established § altered in pencil to § establish'd *1849:* established **968**| *MS:* sanctified, and none supposed *1835:* sanctified and *1849:* and men supposed **969**| *MS:* Could be oppugned <> under him *1835:* oppugn'd *1849:* Could never be oppugned <> under **970**| *MS:* heaven above——which § written over by § above—which chance or change or § altered in pencil to § change, or time *1849:* above them—points which chance, or time *1863:* chance or time **971**| *MS:* not . . . did § altered in pencil to § not—did **972**| *MS:* followed: boldly § altered in pencil to § followed. Boldly deny!— *1835:* follow'd <> deny! *1849:* followed

Awhile; then, amazed glances, mute awaiting
The thunderbolt which does not come: and next,
Reproachful wonder and inquiry: those
Who else had never stirred, are able now
To find the rest out for themselves, perhaps
To outstrip him who set the whole at work,
—As never will my wise class its instructor.
And you saw Luther?

FESTUS 'Tis a wondrous soul!

PARACELSUS True: the so-heavy chain which galled mankind
Is shattered, and the noblest of us all
Must bow to the deliverer—nay, the worker
Of our own project—we who long before
Had burst our trammels, but forgot the crowd,
We should have taught, still groaned beneath their load:
This he has done and nobly. Speed that may!
Whatever be my chance or my mischance,
What benefits mankind must glad me too;
And men seem made, though not as I believed,
For something better than the times produce.
Witness these gangs of peasants your new lights

974| *MS:* Awhile,—amazed glances—mute *1835:* Awhile, amazed glances, mute *1849:* Awhile; then, amazed 975| *MS:* thunder-bolt <> come,——and next § altered in pencil to § come—and next *1835:* thunderbolt *1849:* come; and next, *1868:* come: and 976| *MS:* inquiry—those § altered in pencil to § inquiry; those *1849:* inquiry: those 977| *MS:* stirred § altered in pencil to § stirr'd *1835:* stirr'd are *1849:* stirred, are 978| *MS:* themselves . . perhaps § altered in pencil to § themselves—perhaps *1868:* find rest for themselves, perhaps *1888:* find the rest out for 979| *MS:* work; . . . § altered in pencil to § work:, *1835:* work, 980| *MS:* . . . As <> instructor:— § altered in pencil to § As <> instructor: *1835:* instructor . . . *1849:*—As <> instructor. 981| *MS:*—And <> Soul! *1835:* And <> soul! 982| *MS:* so heavy <> galled § altered in pencil to § gall'd Mankind *1835:* so-heavy <> mankind 983| *MS:* shattered—and § altered in pencil to § shatter'd, and *1849:* shattered 984| *MS:* Deliverer——, nay § altered in pencil to § deliverer—nay 985| *MS:* projects *1863:* project 986| *MS:* burst its trammels <> crowd *1849:* crowd, *1863:* burst our trammels *1868:* trammels but *1888:* trammels, but 987| *MS:* We would have <> beneath the load:— § altered in pencil to § load: *1835:* groan'd *1849:* should <> taught, still groaned *1889:* beneath their load: 988| *MS:* nobly; speed § altered in pencil to § nobly. Speed 989| *MS:* or my despair, *1835:* despair *1849:* despair, *1863:* or my mischance, 990| *MS:* too: *1888:* too; 991| *MS:* Men <> tho' *1835:* men <> though 992| *MS:* times can show;— § altered in pencil to § show: *1849:* times produce: *1863:* produce. 993| *MS:* Peasants *1835:* peasants

From Suabia have possessed, whom Münzer leads,
And whom the duke, the landgrave and the elector
Will calm in blood! Well, well; 'tis not my world!
FESTUS Hark!
PARACELSUS 'Tis the melancholy wind astir
Within the trees; the embers too are grey:
Morn must be near.
FESTUS Best ope the casement: see,
The night, late strewn with clouds and flying stars,
Is blank and motionless: how peaceful sleep
The tree-tops altogether! Like an asp,
The wind slips whispering from bough to bough.
PARACELSUS Ay; you would gaze on a wind-shaken tree
By the hour, nor count time lost.
FESTUS So you shall gaze:
Those happy times will come again.
PARACELSUS Gone, gone,
Those pleasant times! Does not the moaning wind
Seem to bewail that we have gained such gains
And bartered sleep for them?
FESTUS It is our trust
That there is yet another world to mend
All error and mischance.
PARACELSUS Another world!
And why this world, this common world, to be
A make-shift, a mere foil, how fair soever,

994| *MS:* Munzer *1835:* possess'd *1849:* possessed *1863:* Münzer
995| *MS:* Duke, the Landgrave, and the Elector *1835:* duke <> landgrave <> elector *1868:* landgrave and
996| *MS:* blood— —well, well § altered in pencil to § blood—well, well—'tis *1835:* blood! Well, well <> world. *1849:* world! *1868:* Well, well; 'tis
997| *MS:* PARACELSUS— —Tis *1835:* PARACELSUS 'Tis
998| *MS:* trees— —the § altered in pencil to § trees; the <> grey, *1863:* grey:
999| *MS:*—Morn <> near: FESTUS <> see *1835:* Morn <> near. FESTUS *1849:* see,
1001| *MS:* motionless;—how § altered in pencil to § motionless; how *1835:* motionless: how
1002| *MS:* all together! like an asp *1849:* Like an asp, *1868:* altogether
1004| *MS:*—Ay: you *1835:* Ay; you
1005| *MS:* lost? FESTUS *1835:* lost FESTUS
1006| *MS:* again . . . PARACELSUS Gone! Gone! *1863:* again. PARACELSUS Gone, gone,
1007| *MS:* times! . . . does § altered in pencil to § times! Does
1008| *MS:* gained § altered in pencil to § gain'd *1849:* gained
1009| *1835:* barter'd *1849:* bartered
1011| *MS:* mischance.— — — PARACELSUS *1835:* mischance . . . . PARACELSUS *1849:* mischance. PARACELSUS
1012| *MS:* world to *1849:* world, to
1013| *MS:* make-shift— § above § , a *1835:* make-shift, a

To some fine life to come? Man must be fed
With angels' food, forsooth; and some few traces
Of a diviner nature which look out
Through his corporeal baseness, warrant him
In a supreme contempt of all provision
For his inferior tastes—some straggling marks
Which constitute his essence, just as truly
As here and there a gem would constitute
The rock, their barren bed, one diamond.
But were it so—were man all mind—he gains
A station little enviable. From God
Down to the lowest spirit ministrant,
Intelligence exists which casts our mind
Into immeasurable shade. No, no:
Love, hope, fear, faith—these make humanity;
These are its sign and note and character,
And these I have lost!—gone, shut from me for ever,
Like a dead friend safe from unkindness more!
See, morn at length. The heavy darkness seems
Diluted, grey and clear without the stars;
The shrubs bestir and rouse themselves as if
Some snake, that weighed them down all night, let go

1014| *MS:* to-come *1849:* to come 1015| *MS:* Angels' *1835:* angel's *1868:* angels' 1017| *MS:* Thro' § altered to § Through < > baseness warrant *1849:* baseness, warrant 1018| *MS:* contempt for all *1863:* contempt of all 1019| *MS:* tastes . . . some *1835:* tastes—some 1021| *MS:* gem, would *1835:* gem would 1022| *MS:* bed, a diamond. *1863:* bed, one diamond. 1023| *MS:*—But < > so, . . were § written over by and altered to § so—were Man all mind . . the § written over by § Mind—the station *1835:* But < > man all mind *1849:* mind—he gains 1024| *MS:* he gains is little enviable: . . from § written over by and altered to § enviable. From *1849:* A station little 1025| *MS:* ministrant *1849:* ministrant, 1026| *MS: our* Mind *1835:* mind *1849:* our 1027| *MS:* shade . . No, No:— § altered to § shade. No, No: *1835:* No, no: 1028| *MS:* Love, Hope, Fear, Faith . . . . these § written over by § Faith—These < > Humanity: *1835:* Love, hope, fear, faith—these < > humanity; 1029| *MS:* sign, and note, and character . . . . § altered to § character; *1863:* sign and note and character, 1030| *MS:*— —And § altered to § And < > lost! gone—shut < > for ever *1835:* gone; shut < > for ever, *1849:* lost!—gone, shut 1031| *MS:* friend, safe *1868:* friend safe 1032| *MS:* length— —the § altered to § length. The *1835:* See morn *1863:* See, morn 1033| *MS:* Diluted,—grey < > stars, *1835:* Diluted; grey < > stars; *1888:* Diluted, grey 1034| *MS:*—The < > themselves, as though *1835:* The *1849:* as if *1888:* themselves as 1035| *MS:* snake, that < > night, let § altered to § snake that < > night let *1835:* weigh'd *1849:* snake, that weighed < > night, let

His hold; and from the East, fuller and fuller,
Day, like a mighty river, flowing in;
But clouded, wintry, desolate and cold.
Yet see how that broad prickly star-shaped plant,
Half-down in the crevice, spreads its woolly leaves
All thick and glistering with diamond dew.
And you depart for Einsiedeln this day,
And we have spent all night in talk like this!
If you would have me better for your love,
Revert no more to these sad themes.

FESTUS

One favour,
And I have done. I leave you, deeply moved;
Unwilling to have fared so well, the while
My friend has changed so sorely. If this mood
Shall pass away, if light once more arise
Where all is darkness now, if you see fit
To hope and trust again, and strive again,
You will remember—not our love alone—
But that my faith in God's desire that man
Should trust on his support, (as I must think
You trusted) is obscured and dim through you:
For you are thus, and this is no reward.
Will you not call me to your side, dear Aureole?

1036| *MS:* East § altered to § east, fuller and fuller *1863:* East *1889:* fuller, **1037**| *1849:* river, is flowing *1868:* river, flowing **1038**| *MS:* desolate, and cold: *1863:* desolate and cold. **1039**| *MS:* plant *1835:* broad, prickly, star-shaped plant, *1863:* broad prickly star-shaped **1040**| *MS:* Half down *1835:* leaves, *1868:* half-down < > leaves **1041**| *MS:* dew:— § altered to § dew. **1042**| *1835:* day: *1868:* day, **1043**| *MS:* this!—— § altered to § this! **1044**| *MS:* love *1849:* love, **1045**| *MS:* themes;—FESTUS § altered to § themes. FESTUS **1046**| *MS:* done:—I < > moved: *1835:* done. I < > moved; **1048**| *MS:* Friend < > sorely: if *1835:* friend *1863:* sorely. If **1049**| *MS:* away——if *1835:* away—if *1863:* away, if **1050**| *MS:* now——if *1835:* now—if *1863:* now, if **1051**| *MS:* hope, and < > again,— *1835:* again; *1863:* again, *1868:* hope and **1053**| *MS:* Man *1835:* man *1849:* desire for man *1863:* desire that man **1054**| *MS:* support . . . as *1835:* support, as *1849:* support, (as *1863:* Should trust on His *1868:* his **1055**| *MS:* trusted . . . . is < > thro' you,— *1835:* trusted, is < > through you; *1849:* trusted,) is *1868:* trusted) is *1888:* you: **1056**| *MS:* reward;— *1835:* reward: *1849:* reward. **1057**| *1849:* dear friend? *1863:* dear Aureole?

PART IV. PARACELSUS ASPIRES.

SCENE—*Colmar in Alsatia: an Inn.* 1528.

PARACELSUS, FESTUS.

PARACELSUS [*to* JOHANNES OPORINUS, *his Secretary*]. *Sic itur ad astra!* Dear
Von Visenburg
Is scandalized, and poor Torinus paralysed,
And every honest soul that Basil holds
Aghast; and yet we live, as one may say,
Just as though Liechtenfels had never set
So true a value on his sorry carcass,
And learned Pütter had not frowned us dumb.
We live; and shall as surely start to morrow
For Nuremberg, as we drink speedy scathe
To Basil in this mantling wine, suffused
A delicate blush, no fainter tinge is born
I' the shut heart of a bud. Pledge me, good John—
"Basil; a hot plague ravage it, and Pütter
Oppose the plague!" Even so? Do you too share

SCENE| *MS: A House at Colmar in Alsatia.* 1528. *1863: Colmar in Alsatia: an Inn.* 1528. 1| *MS:* PARACELSUS [to JOHN OPORINUS < > astra! . . . . dear *1835:* astra! Dear *1863:* PARACELSUS [to JOHANNES OPORINUS 4| *MS:* Aghast . . . and < > live—as < > say— § altered in pencil to § Aghast; and < > live, as < > say, 5| *MS:* tho *1835:* though 6| *MS:* carcass . . . § written over by § carcass— § altered in pencil to § carcass, 7| *MS:* dumb; . . . § altered in pencil to § dumb. *1835:* frown'd *1849:* frowned 8| *MS:* live, and § altered in pencil to § live; and < > to-morrow *1888:* to morrow 9| *MS:* Nuremburg, as § altered in pencil to § Nuremburg as *1849:* Nuremburg, as *1888:* Nuremberg 11| *MS:* blush; no *1835:* blush—no *1849:* With a *1863:* A < > blush, no 12| *MS:* th' < > bud;— —pledge < > John,—§ altered in pencil to § John— *1835:* bud: pledge *1863:* bud. Pledge *1868:* the 13| *MS:* "Basil—a § altered in pencil to § "Basil; a *1849:* it, with Pütter 14| *MS:* plague!"—even so! do § altered in pencil to § so? Do *1835:* plague!" Even *1849:* To stop the *1863:* Oppose the

Their panic, the reptiles? Ha, ha; faint through these,
Desist for these! They manage matters so
At Basil, 'tis like: but others may find means
To bring the stoutest braggart of the tribe
Once more to crouch in silence—means to breed
A stupid wonder in each fool again,
Now big with admiration at the skill
Which stript a vain pretender of his plumes:
And, that done,—means to brand each slavish brow
So deeply, surely, ineffaceably,
That henceforth flattery shall not pucker it
Out of the furrow; there that stamp shall stay
To show the next they fawn on, what they are,
This Basil with its magnates,—fill my cup,—
Whom I curse soul and limb. And now despatch,
Despatch, my trusty John; and what remains
To do, whate'er arrangements for our trip
Are yet to be completed, see you hasten
This night; we'll weather the storm at least: to-morrow
For Nuremberg! Now leave us; this grave clerk

15| *MS:* panic . . . the reptiles! Ha § altered in pencil to § panic—the reptiles? Ha, ha, faint thro' *them,* *1835:* Ha, ha; faint through *1863:* panic, the *1868:* through these, 16–18| *MS:* for *them!* . . . they § altered in pencil to § They <> / <> like——but § altered in pencil to § like; but *1835: them!* They <> / <> like; but *1849: them!*—while means enough exist / To bow the stoutest *1863: them!* They manage matters so / At Basil 'tis like: but others may find means / To bring the stoutest *1868:* for these! They 19| *1849:* more in crouching silence *1863:* more to crouch in silence 20| *MS:* again *1835:* again, 22| *MS:* stripped <> plumes,—§ altered in pencil to § plumes;— *1835:* stript <> plumes; *1888:* plumes: 23| *MS:* done, means *1863:* done,—means 24| *MS:* deeply-sure—so § altered in pencil to § deeply-sure, so ineffaceably, *1849:* deeply, surely, ineffaceably, 25| *MS:* That, thenceforth, flattery § altered in pencil to § That thenceforth flattery *1868:* that henceforth flattery 26| *MS:* So well but there the hideous stamp *1835:* stay, *1849:* Out of the furrow of that hideous stamp *1863:* furrow; there that stamp shall stay 27–29| *MS:* To teach the man they <> on, who § altered in pencil to § on who they are / Whom <> limb: and § altered in pencil to § limb. And now dispatch, § , added in pencil § *1849:* Which shows the next they fawn on, what they are, / This Basil with its magnates one and all, / Whom *1863:* To show <> / <> magnates,—fill my cup,— *1888:* despatch, 30| *MS:* Dispatch <> John, and *1835:* John; and *1888:* Despatch 31| *MS:* do—whate'er § altered in pencil to § do; whate'er *1835:* do, whate'er 33| *MS:* night—we'll <> least—to-morrow § altered in pencil to § night: we'll <> least: to-morrow *1835:* night; we'll 34| *MS:* Nuremburg!—Now <> us—this § altered in pencil to § us; this *1835:* Nuremburg! Now *1888:* Nuremberg

Has divers weighty matters for my ear: [OPORINUS *goes out.*
And spare my lungs. At last, my gallant Festus,
I am rid of this arch-knave that dogs my heels
As a gaunt crow a gasping sheep; at last
May give a loose to my delight. How kind,
How very kind, my first best only friend!
Why, this looks like fidelity. Embrace me!
Not a hair silvered yet? Right! you shall live
Till I am worth your love; you shall be proud,
And I—but let time show! Did you not wonder?
I sent to you because our compact weighed
Upon my conscience—(you recall the night
At Basil, which the gods confound!)—because
Once more I aspire. I call you to my side:
You come. You thought my message strange?

FESTUS
So strange
That I must hope, indeed, your messenger
Has mingled his own fancies with the words
Purporting to be yours.

PARACELSUS
He said no more,

35| *MS:* ear——. *1835:* ear, *1863:* ear: 36| *MS:* lungs—at § altered in pencil to § lungs. At *1849:* Festus *1863:* Festus, 37| *MS:* I have got rid <> dogs me *1849:* I am rid <> that follows me *1863:* that dogs my heels 38| *MS:* sheep,—and § altered in pencil to § sheep;—and now *1835:* sheep; and *1849:* sheep; at last 39| *MS:* delight; how § altered in pencil to § delight. How 40| *MS:* kind!—my first, best, only Friend! *1835:* kind, my <> friend! *1868:* first best only friend! 41| *MS:*—Why this <> fidelity:—embrace § altered in pencil to § fidelity. Embrace me,— *1835:* Why <> me: *1863:* Why, this <> me! 42| *MS:*—Not <> Right: you *1835:* Not <> silver'd yet! Right *1849:* silvered *1863:* yet? Right! you 43| *MS:* love—you <> proud § altered in pencil to § love; you <> proud; *1835:* love; you <> proud, 44| *MS:* I——but time will show: did § altered in pencil to § I—but <> show. Did *1849:* but let time show. *1888:* show! Did 45| *MS:* weigh'd *1849:* weighed 46| *MS:* conscience, (you § altered in pencil to § conscience—(you *1849:* recal *1863:* recall 47| *MS:* Gods confound)—beçause *1835:* gods *1863:* confound!)—because 48| *MS:* more, I aspire!——and you are here! all this § altered in pencil to § more I aspire! And you are here! All this *1849:* aspire! I call you to my side; *1863:* aspire. I *1888:* side: 49| *MS:* Is strange;—and § altered in pencil to § strange, and strange my message? FESTUS I confess *1835:* message. FESTUS I confess, *1849:* You come. You thought my message strange? FESTUS So strange 50| *MS:* So strange that I must think your *1849:* That I must hope, indeed, your 52| *MS:* yours . . . . . PARACELSUS *1835:* yours. PARACELSUS

'Tis probable, than the precious folk I leave
Said fiftyfold more roughly. Well-a-day,
'Tis true! poor Paracelsus is exposed
At last; a most egregious quack he proves:
And those he overreached must spit their hate
On one who, utterly beneath contempt,
Could yet deceive their topping wits. You heard
Bare truth; and at my bidding you come here
To speed me on my enterprise, as once
Your lavish wishes sped me, my own friend!
FESTUS What is your purpose, Aureole?
PARACELSUS Oh, for purpose,
There is no lack of precedents in a case
Like mine; at least, if not precisely mine,
The case of men cast off by those they sought
To benefit.
FESTUS They really cast you off?
I only heard a vague tale of some priest,
Cured by your skill, who wrangled at your claim,
Knowing his life's worth best; and how the judge
The matter was referred to, saw no cause
To interfere, nor you to hide your full

53| *MS:* Tis <> folks *1835:* 'Tis *1888:* folk 54| *MS:* Have said more roughly fifty-fold—alack § altered in pencil to § fifty-fold: Alack, *1835:* fifty-fold. Alack, *1849:* Said fifty-fold more roughly. Well-a-day, *1863:* fiftyfold 55| *MS:* Tis true: poor *1835:* 'Tis *1849:* true; poor *1863:* true! poor 56| *MS:* last—a § altered in pencil to § last; a <> quack is he, *1835:* last: a <> he; *1849:* last; a <> quack he proves, *1863:* proves: 57| *1835:* overreach'd *1849:* overreached 58| *MS:* who— § above § , utterly <> contempt,— *1835:* who, utterly <> contempt, 59| *MS:* wits—He said § altered in pencil to § wits. He said *1849:* wits. You heard 60| *MS:* you are here *1849:* you come here 62| *MS:* me; my § altered in pencil to § me, my *1835:* friend? *1863:* friend! 63–64| *MS:* And now, what <> Aureole? / PARACELSUS There *1849:* What <> Aureole? PARACELSUS Oh, for purpose, / There 65| *MS:* mine . . . . at § altered in pencil to § mine; at *1835:* mine, at *1849:* mine; at 67| *MS:* benefit——— FESTUS <> off? . . . *1835:* benefit . . . FESTUS *1849:* off? *1863:* benefit. FESTUS 68| *MS:* I merely heard <> priest, § , added in pencil § *1849:* I only heard 69| *MS:* wrangled at the just *1849:* at your claim, 70| *MS:* Reward you claimed . . . and § altered in pencil to § claimed; and that the Magistrate *1835:* claim'd <> magistrate *1849:* Knowing his life's worth best; and how the judge 71| *MS:* to saw *1835:* referr'd *1849:* referred to, saw 72| *MS:* interfere——nor § altered in pencil to § interfere, nor

Contempt of him; nor he, again, to smother
His wrath thereat, which raised so fierce a flame
That Basil soon was made no place for you.
PARACELSUS The affair of Liechtenfels? the shallowest fable,
The last and silliest outrage—mere pretence!
I knew it, I foretold it from the first,
How soon the stupid wonder you mistook
For genuine loyalty—a cheering promise
Of better things to come—would pall and pass;
And every word comes true. Saul is among
The prophets! Just so long as I was pleased
To play off the mere antics of my art,
Fantastic gambols leading to no end,
I got huge praise: but one can ne'er keep down
Our foolish nature's weakness. There they flocked,
Poor devils, jostling, swearing and perspiring,
Till the walls rang again; and all for me!
I had a kindness for them, which was right;
But then I stopped not till I tacked to that
A trust in them and a respect—a sort

73| *MS:* him——nor § altered in pencil to § him, nor *1835:* him; nor 74| *MS:* wrath which § altered in pencil to § wrath, which raised so hot an opposition *1849:* wrath thereat, which < > so fierce a flame 75| soon became no *1849:* soon was made no 76| *MS:* Liechtenfels? The § altered in pencil to § Liechtenfels! The shallowest pretext, *1835:* Liechtenfels? the *1849:* shallowest cause, *1863:* shallowest fable, 77| *MS:* outrage!——mere § altered in pencil to § outrage—mere *1835:* pretence. *1849:* pretence! 78| *MS:*—I < > it—I first—§ altered in pencil to § it, I < > first: *1835:* I knew < > first, 80| *MS:* loyalty, a *1835:* loyalty—a 81| *MS:* come, would < > pass . . . *1835:* come—would < > pass; 82| *MS:* true—Saul *1835:* true. Saul 83| *MS:* just *1835:* Just 84| *MS:* off all the marvels of my art— *1849:* off the mere marvels *1863:* mere antics of my art, 85| *MS:* end,— *1835:* end— *1863:* end, 86–87| *MS:* I had huge praise, and doubtless might have grown / Grey in the exposition of such antics / Had my stock lasted long enough;—but such / Was not my purpose—one can ne'er keep down / Our < > weakness——there < > flocked *1835:* enough; but such / < > purpose: one < > / < > weakness . . . There < > flock'd, *1849:* I got huge praise; but one can ne'er keep down / Our < > weakness: there < > flocked, *1863:* praise: but < > / < > weakness. There 88| *MS:* perspiring *1835:* swearing, and perspiring, *1863:* swearing and perspiring, 89| *MS:* again——. . . and *1835:* again; and 90| *MS:* for them—§ above § , which was right— *1835:* them, which was right; 91| *MS:* 'till I *1835:* stopp'd not till I tack'd *1849:* stopped < > tacked 92| *MS:* respect——a *1835:* respect—a

Of sympathy for them; I must needs begin
To teach them, not amaze them, "to impart
The spirit which should instigate the search
Of truth," just what you bade me! I spoke out.
Forthwith a mighty squadron, in disgust,
Filed off—"the sifted chaff of the sack," I said,
Redoubling my endeavours to secure
The rest. When lo! one man had tarried so long
Only to ascertain if I supported
This tenet of his, or that; another loved
To hear impartially before he judged,
And having heard, now judged; this bland disciple
Passed for my dupe, but all along, it seems,
Spied error where his neighbours marvelled most;
That fiery doctor who had hailed me friend,
Did it because my by-paths, once proved wrong
And beaconed properly, would commend again
The good old ways our sires jogged safely o'er,
Though not their squeamish sons; the other worthy
Discovered divers verses of St. John,
Which, read successively, refreshed the soul,
But, muttered backwards, cured the gout, the stone,

93| *MS:* them——I, in short, began *1835:* them: I *1849:* I must needs begin *1868:* them; I **94|** *MS:* them; to *1849:* them: "to *1863:* them, "to **96–98|** *MS:* Of truth——forthwith a mighty squadron straight / Filed off:—"the sifted <> said,— *1835:* truth. Forthwith <> / <> off—"the sifted <> sack," I said, *1849:* Of truth:" just what you bade me! I spoke out. / Forthwith <> squadron, in disgust, / Filed *1863:* Of truth," just **100|** *MS:* rest; when *1849:* had stayed thus long *1863:* rest. When <> had tarried so long **102|** *MS:* tenet or the other;—another *1835:* other; another *1849:* tenet of his, or that; another **103–105|** *MS:* judged, / And now was satisfied;—one had all along *1835:* satisfied; one *1849:* judged, / And having heard, now judged; this bland disciple / Passed for my dupe, but all along, it seems, **106–110|** *MS:* marveled most:— / —This doctor set a school up to revive / The good old ways which could content our sires *1835:* marvell'd most: // <> sires, *1849:* marvelled most: / That fiery doctor who had hailed me friend, / Did it because my bye-paths, once proved wrong / And beaconed properly, would commend again / The good old ways our sires jogged safely o'er, *1863:* most; // <> by-paths **111|** *MS:* Tho <> sons;—the *1835:* Though <> sons; the **112|** *MS:* St. John *1835:* St. John, **113|** *MS:* Which read successively refreshed the soul *1835:* refresh'd *1849:* Which, read successively, refreshed **114|** *MS:* But muttered backwards cured the gout, the stone *1835:* mutter'd <> stone, *1849:* But, muttered backwards, cured

The colic and what not. *Quid multa?* The end
Was a clear class-room, and a quiet leer
From grave folk, and a sour reproachful glance
From those in chief who, cap in hand, installed
The new professor scarce a year before;
And a vast flourish about patient merit
Obscured awhile by flashy tricks, but sure
Sooner or later to emerge in splendour—
Of which the example was some luckless wight
Whom my arrival had discomfited,
But now, it seems, the general voice recalled
To fill my chair and so efface the stain
Basil had long incurred. I sought no better,
Only a quiet dismissal from my post,
And from my heart I wished them better suited
And better served. Good night to Basil, then!
But fast as I proposed to rid the tribe
Of my obnoxious back, I could not spare them
The pleasure of a parting kick.

FESTUS

You smile:
Despise them as they merit!

PARACELSUS

If I smile,
'Tis with as very contempt as ever turned
Flesh into stone. This courteous recompense,
This grateful . . . Festus, were your nature fit

115| *MS:* cholic <> not—*quid multa?*—the *1835:* cholic, and <> *multa?* The *1849:* not:—*quid* *1863:* colic <> not. *Quid* *1868:* colic and 116| *MS:* class-room and *1835:* class-room, and *1849:* class-room, with a *1863:* class-room, and a 117| *MS:* reproachful look *1849:* reproachful glance
118| *1835:* chief, who <> install'd *1849:* installed *1863:* chief who
119| *MS:* Professor <> before,— *1835:* professor <> before; 120| *MS:*— —And *1835:* And 122| *MS:* splendour,— *1835:* splendour—
124| *MS:* discomfited *1835:* discomfited, 125| *1835:* recall'd *1849:* recalled 126| *1835:* chair, and *1863:* chair and 127| *MS:* incurred;— —I <> better: *1835:* incurr'd. I <> better— *1849:* incurred *1863:* better, 128| *MS:*—Nought but a <> Post— *1835:* Nought <> post; *1863:* Only a <> post, 129| *1835:* wish'd <> suited, *1849:* While from <> wished *1863:* And from <> suited 130| *MS:* served:—goodnight *1835:* served. Good night 132| *MS:* obnoxious self, I *1849:* obnoxious back, I 133| *MS:* kick: . . . FESTUS You smile:— — *1835:* kick. FESTUS You smile: 134| *MS:* smile *1835:* smile: *1863:* smile, 135| *MS:* Tis *1835:* 'Tis <> turn'd *1849:* turned 136| *MS:* stone: this *1849:* recompense! *1863:* stone. This *1868:* recompense,

To be defiled, your eyes the eyes to ache
At gangrene-blotches, eating poison-blains,
The ulcerous barky scurf of leprosy
Which finds—a man, and leaves—a hideous thing
That cannot but be mended by hell fire,
—I would lay bare to you the human heart
Which God cursed long ago, and devils make since
Their pet nest and their never-tiring home.
Oh, sages have discovered we are born
For various ends—to love, to know: has ever
One stumbled, in his search, on any signs
Of a nature in us formed to hate? To hate?
If that be our true object which evokes
Our powers in fullest strength, be sure 'tis hate!
Yet men have doubted if the best and bravest
Of spirits can nourish him with hate alone.
I had not the monopoly of fools,
It seems, at Basil.

FESTUS But your plans, your plans!
I have yet to learn your purpose, Aureole!

PARACELSUS Whether to sink beneath such ponderous shame,

138| *MS:* defiled——your eyes, the *1835:* defiled, your eyes the 139| *MS:* At festering blotches—eating poisoning *1835:* blotches, eating *1849:* At gangrened blotches, eating poisonous *1863:* gangrene-blotches, eating poison-blains, 140| *1849:* ulcered *1863:* ulcerous 141| *MS:* finds a Man, and leaves a < > Thing *1835:* man and < > thing *1849:* finds—a man, and leaves—a 142–143| *MS:* hell-fire——— / I < > bare the heart of man to you;— *1835:* hell fire, / < > you, *1849:* fire, / —I say that, could you see as I could show, / I would lay bare to you these human hearts *1863:* fire, / —I would < > you the human heart 144| *MS:* ago,—which devils have made *1835:* ago—which *1849:* ago, and devils make since 145| *MS:* pet-nest < > home, ... *1835:* pet nest < > home. 146| *MS:*———O, sages have found out that Man is born *1835:* O < > man *1849:* have discovered we are born *1888:* Oh 147| *MS:* ends,—to love, to know;—has *1835:* ends—to < > know. Has *1849:* know: has 148| *MS:* stumbled in his search on *1849:* stumbled, in his search, on 149| *MS:* in him formed to *Hate?* . . to *Hate?* *1835:* form'd to *hate?* To *hate?* *1849:* formed to hate? To hate? *1863:* in us formed 150| *MS:* . . . If < > be Man's true *1835:* If < > man's *1849:* be our true 151–157| *MS:* His powers < > Hate;— / Yet Men < > bravest / Of < > Hate alone! . . . / I < > fools, / It < > Basil;—FESTUS < > plans—your / I have yet < > Aureole! / Whether < > shame— 151| *1835:* hate: 152| *1835:* men 153| *1835:* hate alone. 155| *1835:* Basil. FESTUS < > plans, your plans: 156| *1835:* Aureole. 151–157| *1849:* Our powers < > hate! / But I have yet < > Aureole! / PARACELSUS What purpose were the fittest now for me? / Decide! To

To shrink up like a crushed snail, undergo
In silence and desist from further toil,
And so subside into a monument
Of one their censure blasted? or to bow
Cheerfully as submissively, to lower
My old pretensions even as Basil dictates,
To drop into the rank her wits assign me
And live as they prescribe, and make that use
Of my poor knowledge which their rules allow,
Proud to be patted now and then, and careful
To practise the true posture for receiving
The amplest benefit from their hoofs' appliance
When they shall condescend to tutor me?
Then, one may feel resentment like a flame
Within, and deck false systems in truth's garb,
And tangle and entwine mankind with error,
And give them darkness for a dower and falsehood
For a possession, ages: or one may mope
Into a shade through thinking, or else drowse
Into a dreamless sleep and so die off.

151–157| *1863:* hate! / Yet men have doubted if the best and bravest / Of spirits can nourish him with hate alone. / I had not the monopoly of fools. / It seems at Basil. FESTUS But your plans, your plans! / I have yet <> Aureole! / PARACELSUS Whether to <> shame, 155| *1868:* seems, at 158| *MS:* shrink in like <> shame— *1835:* crush'd *1849:* shrink up like a crushed snail—undergo *1863:* snail—to endure *1835:* crush'd *1849:* shrink up like a crushed snail—undergo *1863:* snail, undergo 159| *MS:* toil *1835:* toil, *1863:* toil *1888:* toil, 161| *MS:* Or *1835:* blasted; or *1863:* blasted? or 162| *MS:* submissively,—to *1835:* submissively—to *1863:* submissively, to 163| *MS:* as they dictate, *1835:* dictate— *1849:* as Basil dictates— *1863:* dictates, 164| *MS:* rank their wit assigns me, *1849:* rank her wits assign *1863:* me 165| *1863:* prescribe and *1868:* prescribe, and 166| *MS:* Of all my knowledge <> allow— *1849:* Of my poor knowledge *1863:* allow, 168| *MS:* the fit posture *1849:* the true posture 169| *MS:* hoofs *1835:* hoofs' appliance, *1863:* appliance 170| *MS:* me?—— *1835:* me. *1863:* me? 171| *MS:*——Then one *1835:* Then *1849:* flame, *1863:* flame *1868:* Then, one 172| *MS:* Within—and <> garb *1835:* Within, and <> Truth's garb, *1849:* Prompting to deck *1863:* Within, and deck <> truth's 173| *MS:* error *1835:* error; *1849:* error, 174| *MS:* dower, and *1863:* dower and 175| *1849:* possession: or <> mope away *1863:* possession, ages: or <> mope 176| *MS:* shade, for thinking: or may drowse *1835:* shade for thinking; or *1849:* shade through thinking; or else drowse *1863:* thinking, or 177| *MS:* off:— *1835:* sleep, and <> off: *1863:* sleep and <> off.

But I,—now Festus shall divine!—but I
Am merely setting out once more, embracing
My earliest aims again! What thinks he now?
FESTUS Your aims? the aims?—to Know? and where is found
The early trust . . .
PARACELSUS Nay, not so fast; I say,
The aims—not the old means. You know they made me
A laughing-stock; I was a fool; you know
The when and the how: hardly those means again!
Not but they had their beauty; who should know
Their passing beauty, if not I? Still, dreams
They were, so let them vanish, yet in beauty
If that may be. Stay: thus they pass in song! [*He sings.*

Heap cassia, sandal-buds and stripes
Of labdanum, and aloe-balls,
Smeared with dull nard an Indian wipes
From out her hair: such balsam falls
Down sea-side mountain pedestals,
From tree-tops where tired winds are fain,

178| *MS:* But I . . . now <> divine— — but I *1835:* But I—now <> divine—but I *1849:* But I, but I—now <> divine! *1863:* But I,—now <> divine!—but I 179| *MS:* more-embracing *1835:* more, embracing *1849:*—Am <> out in life once more, *1863:* Am <> out once more, embracing 180| *MS:* what *1835:* What *1849:* Embracing my old aims! What *1863:* My earliest aims again! What 181| *MS: The Aims?—to know* § written over by § *Know?*—and *1835: the aims?—to know?*—and *1849:* the aims?—to know? and *1863:* Know 182| *MS:* The trust, the sure belief . . . . PARACELSUS <> fast;— *1835:* belief . . . PARACELSUS <> fast; *1849:* The early trust . . . PARACELSUS <> fast; I say, 183| *MS: The Aims,* . . . but not the Means—you *1835:* The aims—but <> means. You *1849:* The aims—not the old means. You know what made *1863:* know they made 184| *MS:* laughing stock— —I <> fool—you *1835:* laughing-stock: I <> fool; you *1849:* laughing-stock; I 185| *MS:* how—hardly <> Means again! . . . *1835:* how: hardly <> means again; *1849:* again! 186| *MS:* beauty— —who *1835:* beauty—who *1863:* beauty; who 187| *MS:* beauty if not I?—but still *1835:* I? But *1849:* beauty, if *1868:* I? Still, dreams 188| *MS:* They were dreams, so <> vanish!—yet *1835:* vanish: yet in beauty, *1863:* vanish, yet *1868:* They were, so *1888:* beauty 189| *MS:* may be,— —stay— *1835:* be. Stay . . . *1849:* Stay—thus they pass in song! *1863:* Stay: thus 190| *MS:* sandal-buds, and *1863:* sandal-buds and 191| *MS:* aloe-balls *1863:* aloe-balls, 192| *1835:* Smear'd *1849:* Smeared 193–195| *MS:* hair . . . such <> falls / From tall trees where *1835:* hair: such *1849:* hair: (such <> falls / Down sea-side mountain pedestals, / From summits where *1863:* hair: such <> / <> seaside <> / From tree-tops where *1868:* sea-side

Spent with the vast and howling main,
To treasure half their island-gain.

And strew faint sweetness from some old
  Egyptian's fine worm-eaten shroud
Which breaks to dust when once unrolled;
  Or shredded perfume, like a cloud
  From closet long to quiet vowed,
With mothed and dropping arras hung,
Mouldering her lute and books among,
As when a queen, long dead, was young.

Mine, every word! And on such pile shall die
My lovely fancies, with fair perished things,
Themselves fair and forgotten; yes, forgotten,
Or why abjure them? So, I made this rhyme
That fitting dignity might be preserved;
No little proud was I; though the list of drugs
Smacks of my old vocation, and the verse
Halts like the best of Luther's psalms.

FESTUS
But, Aureole,
Talk not thus wildly and madly. I am here—
Did you know all! I have travelled far, indeed,

197| *MS:* island-gain; . . . / § end of page § / And *1835:* island-gain; / § no space § / And *1849:* island-gain.) / § space § / And *1863:* island-gain. 199| *MS:* Egyptians *1835:* Egyptian's <> shroud, *1863:* shroud 200| *MS:* unrolled;—— *1835:* unroll'd; *1849:* unrolled; 201| *MS:* perfume like *1835:* perfume, like *1849:* And shred dim perfume *1863:* Or shredded perfume, like 202| *MS:* closet, long <> vowed *1835:* closet long <> vow'd, *1849:* From chamber long <> vowed, *1863:* From closet long 203| *1835:* moth'd *1849:* mothed 204| *MS:* among *1835:* among, *1849:* Mouldering the lute <> among *1863:* Mouldering her lute <> among, 205| *MS:* Queen *1835:* queen *1849:* Of queen, long dead, who lived there young. *1863:* As when a queen, long dead, was young. 206| *MS:* word!—and *1835:* word; and *1849:* word!—and *1863:* word! And 207| *MS:* fancies—with *1835:* fancies with <> perish'd *1849:* fancies, with <> perished 208| *MS:* forgotten—yes, forgotten *1835:* forgotten; yes 209| *MS:* them?—so I *1835:* them? So *1863:* So, I 210| *MS:* preserved: . . . *1835:* preserved: *1863:* preserved; 211| *MS:* was I——tho' *1835:* I; though 213| *MS:* psalms———FESTUS *1835:* psalms . . . FESTUS *1849:* psalms! FESTUS *1863:* psalms. FESTUS 214| *MS:* madly; I *1835:* madly. I 215| *MS:* all!—but I have travelled far *1835:* all! But <> travell'd *1849:* all, indeed! I <> travelled *1863:* all! I <> far, indeed,

To learn your wishes. Be yourself again!
For in this mood I recognize you less
Than in the horrible despondency
I witnessed last. You may account this, joy;
But rather let me gaze on that despair
Than hear these incoherent words and see
This flushed cheek and intensely-sparkling eye.
PARACELSUS Why, man, I was light-hearted in my prime,
I am light-hearted now; what would you have?
Aprile was a poet, I make songs—
'Tis the very augury of success I want!
Why should I not be joyous now as then?
FESTUS Joyous! and how? and what remains for joy?
You have declared the ends (which I am sick
Of naming) are impracticable.
PARACELSUS Ay,
Pursued as I pursued them—the arch-fool!
Listen: my plan will please you not, 'tis like,
But you are little versed in the world's ways.
This is my plan—(first drinking its good luck)—
I will accept all helps; all I despised
So rashly at the outset, equally
With early impulses, late years have quenched:

216| *MS:* wishes . . Be *1835:* wishes. Be <> again; *1849:* again!
219| *MS:* last: you <> joy, . . . *1835:* witness'd last. You <> this joy; *1849:* witnessed <> this, joy; 220| *MS:* on your despair *1849:* on that despair 221| *MS:* hear your incoherent words, and *1849:* hear these incoherent *1863:* words and 222| *MS:* That flushed cheek, and intensely sparkling eye . . . *1835:* flush'd <> intensely-sparkling eye. *1849:* This flushed <> eye! *1863:* eye. 223| *MS:* lighthearted <> prime,— *1835:* light-hearted <> prime, *1888:* prime 224–226| *MS:* lighthearted now——what <> have? / ——Tis *1835:* light-hearted now; what <> / 'Tis *1849:* have? / Aprile was a poet, I make songs— / 'Tis 227| *MS:* joyous even as *1849:* joyous now as 228| *MS:* Joyous? and *1835:* Joyous! and 229| *MS:* Ends *1835:* ends 230| *MS:* impracticable . . . PARACELSUS Aye, *1835:* impracticable. PARACELSUS *1863:* Ay, 231| *MS:* them——the *1835:* them—the 232| *MS:*—Listen—my *1835:* Listen: my <> like; *1863:* like, 233| *MS:* ways:— *1835:* ways . . . *1849:* ways. 234| *MS:* plan, (first <> luck!)— *1835:* plan—(first <> luck)— 235| *MS:* *all* helps!—all *1835:* helps; all *1849:* accept all helps 237| *MS:* impulses which lately seemed *1835:* impulses, which <> seem'd *1849:* impulses, late years have quenched:

I have tried each way singly: now for both!
All helps! no one sort shall exclude the rest.
I seek to know and to enjoy at once,
Not one without the other as before.
Suppose my labour should seem God's own cause
Once more, as first I dreamed,—it shall not baulk me
Of the meanest earthliest sensualest delight
That may be snatched; for every joy is gain,
And gain is gain, however small. My soul
Can die then, nor be taunted—"what was gained?"
Nor, on the other hand, should pleasure follow
As though I had not spurned her hitherto,
Shall she o'ercloud my spirit's rapt communion
With the tumultuous past, the teeming future,
Glorious with visions of a full success.
FESTUS Success!
PARACELSUS And wherefore not? Why not prefer
Results obtained in my best state of being,
To those derived alone from seasons dark
As the thoughts they bred? When I was best, my youth

238| *MS:* The mere persuasion of fantastic dreams;— *1835:* dreams; *1849:* I have tried each way singly—now for both: *1863:* singly: now **239**| *MS:* helps . . . no <> rest:— *1835:* helps—no <> rest: *1849:* rest. *1863:* helps! no **240–242**| *MS:* Know <> Enjoy:—well then,—§ *know* and *enjoy* in print § / For all my cause should seem the cause of God *1835:* KNOW <> ENJOY *1849:* ENJOY at once, / Not one without the other as before. / Suppose my labour should seem God's own cause *1863:* know <> enjoy **243**| *1835:* dream'd, it *1849:* dreamed *1863:* dreamed,—it **244**| *MS:* meanest, earthliest, sensualest *1868:* meanest earthliest sensualest **245**| *MS:* be realized;—for joy *1835:* realized; for *1849:* be snatched; for every joy **246–248**| *MS:* is gain however small: nor, should / On <> hand those honeyed pleasures *1835:* is gain, however <> nor should, / <> hand, those honey'd *1849:* And why spurn gain, however small? My soul / Can die then, nor be taunted "what was gained?" / Nor, on <> hand, if pleasure meets me *1863:* And gain is gain, however small. My soul / <> taunted—"what <> / <> hand, should pleasure follow **249**| *MS:* tho' <> spurned them hitherto, *1835:* though <> spurn'd *1849:* spurned her hitherto, **250**| *MS:* Shall they o'ercloud my spirits *1835:* spirit's *1849:* Shall she o'ercloud **251**| *MS:* Past <> Future *1835:* past <> future, *1863:* Past <> Future, *1868:* past <> future **252**| *MS:* success . . . . *1835:* success . . . *1849:* success! *1868:* success. **254**| *MS:* The grand results <> state *1835:* obtain'd *1849:* Results obtained in <> state of being, **255**| *MS:* Of being, to <> derived from *1835:* being to *1849:* To those derived alone from **256**| *MS:* best—my *1863:* best, my

Unwasted, seemed success not surest too?
It is the nature of darkness to obscure.
I am a wanderer: I remember well
One journey, how I feared the track was missed,
So long the city I desired to reach
Lay hid; when suddenly its spires afar
Flashed through the circling clouds; you may conceive
My transport. Soon the vapours closed again,
But I had seen the city, and one such glance
No darkness could obscure: nor shall the present—
A few dull hours, a passing shame or two,
Destroy the vivid memories of the past.
I will fight the battle out; a little spent
Perhaps, but still an able combatant.
You look at my grey hair and furrowed brow?
But I can turn even weakness to account:
Of many tricks I know, 'tis not the least
To push the ruins of my frame, whereon
The fire of vigour trembles scarce alive,
Into a heap, and send the flame aloft.
What should I do with age? So, sickness lends
An aid; it being, I fear, the source of all
We boast of: mind is nothing but disease,

257| *MS:* Unwasted—seemed *1835:* seem'd *1849:* seemed *1863:* Unwasted, seemed 258| *MS:* Is it not Darkness' nature to obscure *1835:* darkness' *1849:* It is the nature of darkness to obscure. 259| *MS:*——I am *1835:* I am 260| *MS:* missed,— *1835:* fear'd <> miss'd— *1849:* feared <> missed, 262| *MS:* hid—when *1835:* hid, when *1849:* hid; when
263| *MS:* thro' <> clouds——you *1835:* Flash'd through <> clouds; you *1849:* Flashed <> clouds; conceive my joy! *1863:* clouds; you may conceive
264| *MS:* transport:—soon *1835:* transport: soon *1849:* Too soon the vapours closed o'er it again, *1863:* My transport. Soon the vapours closed again,
266–268| *MS:* obscure:——nor shall sad days / Destroy <> past: *1835:* obscure: nor <> / <> past: *1849:* shall the present / A few dull hours, a passing shame or two, / Destroy <> past. *1863:* Present— // <> Past. *1868:* present— // <> past. 269| *MS:* out!——a § written over by § out!—a *1849:* little tired, *1863:* little spent *1868:* out; a 270| *MS:* Perhaps—but <> combatant: *1835:* combatant. *1863:* Perhaps, but 271| *1835:* furrow'd brow; *1849:* furrowed brow? 272| *MS:* account—— § altered in pencil to § account— *1835:* account: 274| *MS:* frame whereon *1835:* frame, whereon
275| *MS:* alive *1835:* alive, 276| *MS:* aloft! *1868:* aloft.
277| *MS:*—What <> Age?—so sickness *1835:* What <> age? so *1863:* age? So, sickness 278| *MS:* aid;—it *1835:* aid; it 279| *MS:* disease *1835:* disease, *1863:* disease *1868:* disease,

And natural health is ignorance.

FESTUS

I see
But one good symptom in this notable scheme.
I feared your sudden journey had in view
To wreak immediate vengeance on your foes;
'Tis not so: I am glad.

PARACELSUS

And if I please
To spit on them, to trample them, what then?
'Tis sorry warfare truly, but the fools
Provoke it. I would spare their self-conceit,
But if they must provoke me, cannot suffer
Forbearance on my part, if I may keep
No quality in the shade, must needs put forth
Power to match power, my strength against their strength,
And teach them their own game with their own arms—
Why, be it so and let them take their chance!
I am above them like a god, there's no
Hiding the fact: what idle scruples, then,
Were those that ever bade me soften it,
Communicate it gently to the world,
Instead of proving my supremacy,
Taking my natural station o'er their head,
Then owning all the glory was a man's!

280| *MS:* ignorance:—FESTUS There is *1835:* ignorance. FESTUS *1849:* FESTUS I see 281| *MS:* scheme: *1849:* notable plan: *1863:* notable scheme. 282| *MS:* sudden project had *1835:* fear'd *1849:* feared <> sudden journey had 283| *MS:* foes,— *1835:* foes; *1888:* foes 284| *MS:* Tis *1835:* 'Tis *1849:* pleased *1863:* please 285| *MS:* them—to <> them,—what *1835:* them, to <> them, what 287–288| *MS:* it: I ne'er sought to domineer,— / The mere asserting my supremacy / Has little mortified their self-conceit / —I took my natural station and no more; / But if they *will* provoke me,—will not suffer *1835:* domineer; // <> self-conceit; / <> more: / <> more-will *1849:* I had spared their self-conceit, / But if they must provoke me—cannot suffer *1863:* it. I would spare <> / <> provoke me, cannot *1888:* self-conceit 289| *MS:* part,—if I can have *1835:* part—if *1849:* may keep *1863:* part, if 290| *MS:* shade, but must put *1849:* shade, must needs put forth 291| *MS:* Power for power—my <> against theirs— *1835:* for power; my *1849:* Power to match power, my <> against their strength, 292| *MS:* Must teach <> arms . . . *1835:* arms— *1849:* And teach 293| *MS:* Why be it so, and *1863:* Why, be it so and 294| *MS:* God—there's *1849:* God—in vain *1863:* God, there's no *1868:* god 295–300| *MS:* fact—and, had I been but wise, / Had ne'er concerned myself with scruples, nor / Communicated ought to such a race;—But been content to own myself a Man,

—And in my elevation man's would be.
But live and learn, though life's short, learning, hard!
And therefore, though the wreck of my past self,
I fear, dear Pütter, that your lecture-room
Must wait awhile for its best ornament,
The penitent empiric, who set up
For somebody, but soon was taught his place;
Now, but too happy to be let confess
His error, snuff the candles, and illustrate
(Fiat experientia corpore vili)
Your medicine's soundness in his person. Wait,
Good Pütter!
FESTUS He who sneers thus, is a god!
PARACELSUS Ay, ay, laugh at me! I am very glad
You are not gulled by all this swaggering; you
Can see the root of the matter!—how I strive
To put a good face on the overthrow
I have experienced, and to bury and hide
My degradation in its length and breadth;
How the mean motives I would make you think
Just mingle as is due with nobler aims,
The appetites I modestly allow

295–300| *1835:* concern'd < > / < > race; / < > man, *1849:* To hide the fact—what idle scruples, then, / Were those that ever bade me soften it, / Communicate it gently to the world, / Instead of proving my supremacy, / Taking my natural station o'er their heads, / Then owning all the glory was a man's 295| *1863:* Hiding the fact: what 299| *1868:* head, 300| *1863:* man's! 301| *MS:* And < > elevation, Man's < > be . . . *1835:* man's *1849:* be! *1863:*—And < > be. 302–303| *MS:* tho' life's so short: as 'tis,— / ——Tho' no more than the wreck < > self, . . *1835:* Though < > short! as 'tis— / Though < > self— *1849:* life's short; learning, hard! / Still, one thing I have learned—not to despair: / And therefore, though the < > self, *1863:* short, learning, hard! / And 305| *MS:* ornament,— *1835:* ornament, 306| *MS:* Empiric who *1835:* empiric, who 307| *MS:* place . . *1835:* place— *1863:* place; 309–311| *MS:* illustrate / Your tenets' soundness < > person . . . wait, *1835:* person. Wait, *1849:* illustrate / *(Fiat experientia corpore vili)* / Your medicine's soundness 312| *MS:* God! *1868:* god! 313| *MS:* Ay, Ay *1835:* Ay, ay 314| *MS:* swaggering——*you* *1835:* gull'd < > swaggering; *you* *1849:* gulled < > you 317| *MS:* experienced—and to hide and bury *1835:* experienced, and *1849:* to bury and hide 318| *MS:* breadth *1835:* breadth; 319| *MS:*—And how the motives *1835:* And *1849:* How the mean motives 320| *MS:* nobler passions,— *1835:* passions, *1849:* nobler aims, 321| *MS:* The cursed lusts I *1849:* The appetites I

May influence me as being mortal still—
Do goad me, drive me on, and fast supplant
My youth's desires. You are no stupid dupe:
You find me out! Yes, I had sent for you
To palm these childish lies upon you, Festus!
Laugh—you shall laugh at me!

FESTUS The past, then, Aureole,
Proves nothing? Is our interchange of love
Yet to begin? Have I to swear I mean
No flattery in this speech or that? For you,
Whate'er you say, there is no degradation;
These low thoughts are no inmates of your mind,
Or wherefore this disorder? You are vexed
As much by the intrusion of base views,
Familiar to your adversaries, as they
Were troubled should your qualities alight
Amid their murky souls; not otherwise,
A stray wolf which the winter forces down
From our bleak hills, suffices to affright
A village in the vales—while foresters
Sleep calm, though all night long the famished troop
Snuff round and scratch against their crazy huts.

322| *MS:* as I am mortal still,— *1835:* me—as < > still— *1863:* me as being mortal 323| *MS:* Are goading me, and fast supplanting all *1849:* Do goad me, drive me on, and fast supplant 324| *MS:* desires:— —*you* < > dupe, *1835:* desires: you < > dupe; *1849:* you *1863:* desires. You < > dupe: 325| *MS:* out— —yes *1835:* out. Yes *1849:* out! Yes 327| *MS:* Laugh,—*you* < > FESTUS—Dear Aureole, then *1835:* Laugh—*you* < > FESTUS Dear *1849:* you < > FESTUS The past, then, Aureole, *1863:* Past *1868:* past 328| *MS:* The Past is nothing? is our intercourse *1835:* past < > Is *1849:* Proves nothing? Is our interchange of love 329| *MS:* begin—have *1835:* begin? Have 330| *MS:* this or that? Whatever *1849:* this speech or that? For you, 331| *MS:* You be, this is no degradation . . these *1835:* degradation—these *1849:* Whate'er you say, there is no degradation, *1863:* degradation; 332| *MS:* Unworthy thoughts no < > mind; *1849:* These low thoughts are no *1863:* mind, 333| *MS:* you are troubled *1835:* You *1849:* are vexed 334| *MS:* views *1835:* views, 336| *MS:* Would be should your high qualities *1849:* Were troubled should your qualities 337| *MS:* souls: and even so *1849:* souls: not otherwise, *1888:* souls; not 339| *MS:* From the bleak hills suffices *1849:* From our bleak hills, suffices 340| *MS:* vales— —while *1835:* vales—while 341| *MS:* Sleep sound tho' < > troops *1835:* though < > famish'd *1849:* Sleep calm though < > famished *1868:* calm, though *1888:* troop 342| *MS:* huts:— — — *1835:* huts: *1863:* huts.

These evil thoughts are monsters, and will flee.
PARACELSUS May you be happy, Festus, my own friend!
FESTUS Nay, further; the delights you fain would think
The superseders of your nobler aims,
Though ordinary and harmless stimulants,
Will ne'er content you. . . .
PARACELSUS   Hush! I once despised them,
But that soon passes. We are high at first
In our demand, nor will abate a jot
Of toil's strict value; but time passes o'er,
And humbler spirits accept what we refuse:
In short, when some such comfort is doled out
As these delights, we cannot long retain
Bitter contempt which urges us at first
To hurl it back, but hug it to our breast
And thankfully retire. This life of mine
Must be lived out and a grave thoroughly earned:
I am just fit for that and nought beside.
I told you once, I cannot now enjoy,
Unless I deem my knowledge gains through joy;
Nor can I know, but straight warm tears reveal
My need of linking also joy to knowledge:

343| *MS:* evil things are monsters and *1849:* evil thoughts are monsters, and
345| *MS:* further . . . the § altered to § further—the *1835:* further; the
346| *MS:* Have superseded nobler aims,—— §written over by § aims,—the harmless *1835:* aims, the *1849:* The superseders of your nobler aims, 347| *MS:* And ordinary stimulants, will never *1849:* Though ordinary and harmless stimulants, 348| *MS:* Content you——— PARACELSUS Ah, forbear!—I once despised——— *1835:* you . . . PARACELSUS Oh, forbear! I < > despised . . . *1849:* Will ne'er content you . . . PARACELSUS Hush! I < > despised them, 349| *MS:* passes: we *1863:* passes. We 350| *MS:* demands *1868:* demand
351| *MS:* Of their strict value . . . but < > o'er *1835:* value; but *1849:* Of toil's strict < > o'er, 352| *MS:* refuse— *1835:* refuse; *1863:* refuse:
353| *MS:* short when *1835:* short, when 354| *MS:* delights——we *1853:* delights—we *1849:* delights, we 355| *MS:* The bitter *1868:* Bitter
356| *MS:* back——but *1835:* back—but *1849:* back, but
357| retire:—this *1835:* retire. This 358| *MS:* earned;— *1835:* earn'd: *1849:* out, and < > earned: *1863:* out and 360| *MS:*——I told < > Enjoy *1835:* I told < > Enjoy, *1863:* enjoy, 361| *MS:* Knowledge gains thereby,— *1835:* knowledge < > thereby; *1849:* gains through joy;
362| *MS:* Know without warm tears revealing *1835:* know, without *1849:* Know, but straight warm < > reveal *1863:* know 363| *MS:* The need of linking some Delight to Knowledge,— *1835:* delight to knowledge: *1849:* My need of linking also joy to

So, on I drive, enjoying all I can,
And knowing all I can. I speak, of course,
Confusedly; this will better explain—feel here!
Quick beating, is it not?—a fire of the heart
To work off some way, this as well as any.
So, Festus sees me fairly launched; his calm
Compassionate look might have disturbed me once,
But now, far from rejecting, I invite
What bids me press the closer, lay myself
Open before him, and be soothed with pity;
I hope, if he command hope, and believe
As he directs me—satiating myself
With his enduring love. And Festus quits me
To give place to some credulous disciple
Who holds that God is wise, but Paracelsus
Has his peculiar merits: I suck in
That homage, chuckle o'er that admiration,
And then dismiss the fool; for night is come,
And I betake myself to study again,
Till patient searchings after hidden lore
Half wring some bright truth from its prison; my frame

364| *MS:* So on I drive . . . Enjoying < > can *1835:* drive—enjoying *1849:* can, *1863:* So, on I drive, enjoying 365| *MS:* Knowing < > can:—I *1835:* knowing < > can. I 366| *MS:* Confusedly—*this* < > explain . . feel *1835:* Confusedly; *this* < > explain—feel *1849:* this 367| *MS:* not? a fire which must *1849:* not?—a fire of the heart 368| *MS:* Be worked off someway < > any: *1835:* work'd *1849:* To work < > any! *1863:* any. 369| *MS:* So Festus < > launched;—his *1835:* launch'd; his *1849:* So, Festus < > launched 370| *1835:* disturb'd *1849:* disturbed 371| *MS:* invite it—— *1835:* it. *1849:* invite 372| *MS:* I can lament with him, and lay *1849:* What bids me press the closer, lay 373| *MS:* and receive his pity, *1849:* and be soothed with pity; 374| *MS:* And hope < > hope—and believe *1835:* command hope; and *1863:* I hope, if *1868:* command hope, and 375| *MS:* What he would have me;—satiating *1835:* me—satiating *1849:* As he directs me—satiating 376| *MS:* love:—and he shall leave me *1835:* love: and *1849:* and Festus quits me *1863:* love. And 379| *MS:* merits——I *1835:* merits. I *1863:* merits: I 380| *MS:* His homage—chuckle o'er his admiration *1835:* homage, chuckle < > admiration, *1849:* That homage < > o'er that admiration, 381| *MS:* dismiss him in his turn:—night comes, *1835:* turn: night *1849:* dismiss the fool; for night is come, *1863:* come. *1889:* come, 382| *MS:* And I shall give myself to painful study *1835:* study; *1849:* And I betake myself to study again, 383| *MS:* And patient searchings < > lore, *1835:* lore *1849:* Till patient searchings 384| *MS:*—Shall wring *1835:* Shall *1849:* Half wring

Trembles, my forehead's veins swell out, my hair
Tingles for triumph. Slow and sure the morn
Shall break on my pent room and dwindling lamp
And furnace dead, and scattered earths and ores,
When, with a failing heart and throbbing brow,
I must review my captured truth, sum up
Its value, trace what ends to what begins,
Its present power with its eventual bearings,
Latent affinities, the views it opens,
And its full length in perfecting my scheme.
I view it sternly circumscribed, cast down
From the high place my fond hopes yielded it,
Proved worthless—which, in getting, yet had cost
Another wrench to this fast-falling frame.
Then, quick, the cup to quaff, that chases sorrow!
I lapse back into youth, and take again
My fluttering pulse for evidence that God
Means good to me, will make my cause his own.
See! I have cast off this remorseless care
Which clogged a spirit born to soar so free,

385| *MS:* Shall tremble, and my thin lips swell—my *1835:* swell, my *1849:* Trembles, my forehead's veins swell out, my 386| *MS:* Tingle—and all for triumph: and the *1835:* Tingle, and *1849:* Tingles for triumph! Slow and sure the *1868:* triumph. Slow 387| *1835:* room, and *1863:* room and 388| *MS:* And scattered papers and unfinished scrawls, *1835:* scatter'd papers, and unfinish'd scrawls; *1849:* And furnace dead, and scattered earths and ores, *1863:* ores; *1889:* ores, 389| *MS:* And with <> brow *1849:* When, with <> brow, 390–393| I shall review <> truth—and trace / Its end and consequence, its further bearings, / Its true affinities *1835:* captur'd truth, and *1849:* I must review my captured truth, sum up / Its value, trace what ends to what begins, / Its present power with its eventual bearings, / Latent affinities 394| *MS:* The length it goes in <> Scheme, *1835:* scheme, *1849:* And its full length in <> scheme; *1863:* scheme. 395| *MS:* And view it <> circumscribed—cast *1849:* I view <> circumscribed, cast 396| *MS:* it,— *1835:* it, 397| *MS:* worthless— § above § which in getting yet *1835:* worthless—which *1849:* which, in getting, yet 398| *MS:* frame;— *1863:* frame. 399| *MS:* And I shall quaff the cup that <> sorrow *1849:* The, quick, the cup to quaff, that <> sorrow! *1868:* chaces *1888:* chases 400–401| *MS:* And lapse <> youth again—and take / My *1835:* again, and *1849:* I lapse <> youth, and take again / Mere hopes of bliss for proofs that bliss will be, / —My <> pulse, for *1863:* again / My *1868:* pulse for 402| *MS:* me, and see my hopes come true, *1849:* me, will make my cause his own; *1863:* His own. *1868:* his 403| *MS:* And flee away from this *1849:* See! I have cast off this 404| *MS:* clogs <> free *1835:* free, *1849:* clogged

And my dim chamber has become a tent,
Festus is sitting by me, and his Michal . . .
Why do you start? I say, she listening here,
(For yonder—Würzburg through the orchard-bough!)
Motions as though such ardent words should find
No echo in a maiden's quiet soul,
But her pure bosom heaves, her eyes fill fast
With tears, her sweet lips tremble all the while!
Ha, ha!
FESTUS It seems, then, you expect to reap
No unreal joy from this your present course,
But rather . . .
PARACELSUS Death! To die! I owe that much
To what, at least, I was. I should be sad
To live contented after such a fall,
To thrive and fatten after such reverse!
The whole plan is a makeshift, but will last
My time.
FESTUS And you have never mused and said,
"I had a noble purpose, and the strength
To compass it; but I have stopped half-way,
And wrongly given the first-fruits of my toil
To objects little worthy of the gift.
Why linger round them still? why clench my fault?

405| *MS:* chamber shall become *1849:* chamber has become 406–409| *MS:* And Festus shall sit by me, and sweet Michal / Shall make as tho' my ardent *1835:* though *1849:* Festus is sitting by me, and his Michal . . . / Why do you start? I say, she listening here, / (For yonder's Würzburg through the orchard-boughs) Motions as though such ardent *1868:* yonder—Würzburg <> orchard-bough!) 410| *MS:* soul— *1849:* soul, 411| *MS:* bosom shall heave *1849:* bosom heaves, her 412| *MS:* her lips shall tremble, all *1835:* tremble all *1849:* her sweet lips tremble 413| *MS:* FESTUS—It seems then *1835:* FESTUS It <> then you *1849:* seems, then, you 414| *MS:* course; *1849:* course, 415| *MS:* That you expect . . . PARACELSUS To *1849:* But rather . . . PARACELSUS Death! To 416| *MS:* what I *was,* at least——I *1835:* *was* at least. I *1849:* what, at least, I was. I 417| *MS:* fall—— *1835:* fall— *1863:* fall, 420| *MS:* time: FESTUS *1835:* time . . . FESTUS *1849:* time. FESTUS 421| *MS:* purpose—and *1835:* purpose, and *1849:* purpose, and full strength *1863:* and the strength 422| *MS:* halfway *1835:* stopp'd half-way, *1849:* stopped 423| *MS:* And have bestowed the first fruits *1835:* bestow'd *1849:* And wrongly give the *1863:* given the firstfruits *1888:* first-fruits 424| *MS:* On objects <> worthy to receive them: *1849:* To objects <> worthy of the gift: *1863:* gift.

Why seek for consolation in defeat,
In vain endeavours to derive a beauty
From ugliness? why seek to make the most
Of what no power can change, nor strive instead
With mighty effort to redeem the past
And, gathering up the treasures thus cast down,
To hold a steadfast course till I arrive
At their fit destination and my own?"
You have never pondered thus?

PARACELSUS

Have I, you ask?
Often at midnight, when most fancies come,
Would some such airy project visit me:
But ever at the end . . . or will you hear
The same thing in a tale, a parable?
You and I, wandering over the world wide,
Chance to set foot upon a desert coast.
Just as we cry, "No human voice before
Broke the inveterate silence of these rocks!"
—Their querulous echo startles us; we turn:
What ravaged structure still looks o'er the sea?
Some characters remain, too! While we read,
The sharp salt wind, impatient for the last
Of even this record, wistfully comes and goes,
Or sings what we recover, mocking it.
This is the record; and my voice, the wind's. [*He sings.*

Over the sea our galleys went,
With cleaving prows in order brave

426| *MS:* defeat *1835:* defeat— *1863:* defeat, 429| *MS:* change, in place of striving *1849:* change, nor strive instead 430| *MS:* past, *1863:* Past *1868:* past 431| *MS:* To gather < > treasures I cast *1849:* And, gathering < > treasures thus cast 432| *MS:* And hold < > 'till *1849:* To hold *1863:* till 433| *MS:* own:" *1835:* destination—and my own." *1849:* destination, and my own?" *1863:* destination and 434–450| *MS:* this? / § space § / PARACELSUS (sings) Over < > went,— *1835:* ponder'd thus? 434| *1849:* pondered thus? PARACELSUS Have I, you ask? 435–449| § added in 1849; variants from 1889 § 438–439| *1849:* parable? / It cannot prove more tedious; listen then! / You *1863:* parable? / You 440| *1849:* coast: *1863:* coast. 446| *1849:* sharp, salt *1863:* sharp salt 449–450| *1849:* wind's / § space § / (He sings.) / Over *1863:* wind's. [He sings. / § space § / Over 451| *MS:*—Cleaving < > brave, *1835:* Cleaving *1849:* With cleaving *1888:* brave

To a speeding wind and a bounding wave,
A gallant armament:
Each bark built out of a forest-tree
Left leafy and rough as first it grew,
And nailed all over the gaping sides,
Within and without, with black bull-hides,
Seethed in fat and suppled in flame,
To bear the playful billows' game:
So, each good ship was rude to see,
Rude and bare to the outward view,
But each upbore a stately tent
Where cedar pales in scented row
Kept out the flakes of the dancing brine,
And an awning drooped the mast below,
In fold on fold of the purple fine,
That neither noontide nor starshine
Nor moonlight cold which maketh mad,
Might pierce the regal tenement.
When the sun dawned, oh, gay and glad
We set the sail and plied the oar;
But when the night-wind blew like breath,
For joy of one day's voyage more,
We sang together on the wide sea,
Like men at peace on a peaceful shore;
Each sail was loosed to the wind so free,
Each helm made sure by the twilight star,

452| *MS:* With speeding <> wave— *1849:* To a speeding *1863:* wave, 453| *MS:*—A <> Armament *1835:* armament: 454| *1835:* forest-tree, *1888:* forest-tree 455| *MS:* grew *1835:* grew, 456| *MS:* sides *1835:* nail'd <> sides, *1849:* nailed 457| *MS:* without with black-bull hides *1835:* without, with <> hides, *1863:* black bull-hides, 458–460| *MS:* flame,— / So each *1835:* Seeth'd <> flame; *1849:* Seethed <> flame, / To bear the playful billows' game; / So *1863:* game: / So, each 461| *MS:* to outward view,— *1835:* view, *1849:* to the outward 462| *MS:* tent:— *1835:* tent: *1849:* tent; *1863:* tent 463| *MS:* Cedar-pales *1849:* Where cedar-pales *1868:* cedarpales 464| *MS:* flakes of dancing brine;— *1835:* brine: *1849:* of the dancing *1863:* brine, 465–467| *MS:* An <> below, / That <> noon-tide, nor star-shine, *1835:* droop'd <> / <> noon-tide nor *1849:* And an <> drooped <> below, / In fold on fold of the purple fine, That <> noon-tide, nor *1863:* noontide nor star-shine *1868:* starshine 470| *MS:* dawned, gay *1835:* dawn'd *1849:* dawned, oh, gay 473| *MS:* more *1835:* more, 474| *MS:* sea *1835:* sea, 475| *MS:* show;— *1835:* shore; 477| *MS:* twilight-star, *1835:* twilight star,

And in a sleep as calm as death,
We, the voyagers from afar,
   Lay stretched along, each weary crew
In a circle round its wondrous tent
Whence gleamed soft light and curled rich scent,
   And with light and perfume, music too:
So the stars wheeled round, and the darkness past,
And at morn we started beside the mast,
And still each ship was sailing fast.

Now, one morn, land appeared—a speck
Dim trembling betwixt sea and sky:
"Avoid it," cried our pilot, "check
   The shout, restrain the eager eye!"
But the heaving sea was black behind
For many a night and many a day,
And land, though but a rock, drew nigh;
So, we broke the cedar pales away,
Let the purple awning flap in the wind,
   And a statue bright was on every deck!
We shouted, every man of us,
And steered right into the harbour thus,
With pomp and pæan glorious.

478| *MS:* death *1835:* death, 479| *1849:* the strangers from *1863:* the voyagers from 480| *MS:* stretched—each *1835:* stretch'd *1849:* stretched along, each 481| *MS:* round their § cancelled by § its wondrous tent *1835:* tent, *1863:* tent 482| *MS:* scent *1835:* gleam'd <> curl'd <> scent, *1849:* gleamed <> curled 483–485| *MS:* too— — — / At morn, they § cancelled by § we *1835:* too: / At morn we *1849:* too: / So the stars wheeled round, and the darkness past, / And at 486| *MS:* fast! *1835:* fast! / § no space § *1849:* fast! / § space § *1868:* fast. 487| *MS:* Now one more land appeared!— —a *1835:* appeared!—a *1849:* One morn, the land *1863:* Now, one morn, land 488| *MS:* § indented § sky:— *1835:* sky— *1849:* § not indented § *1849:* sky: 489| *MS:*—Not so the Isles our voyage must find *1835:* Not <> isles *1849:* Avoid it, cried our pilot, check *1863:* "Avoid it," cried <> pilot, "check 490| *MS:* Should meet our longing eye: *1835:* eye; *1849:* The shout, restrain the longing eye! *1863:* the eager eye!" 492| *MS:* Many *1849:* For many 493| *MS:* tho' <> rock, was nigh, *1835:* though <> nigh; *1849:* rock, drew nigh; 494| *MS:* So we <> cedar-pales *1835:* cedar pales *1863:* So, we 495| *MS:* And let the purple flap *1835:* wind: *1849:* Let the purple awning flap <> wind, 498| *1835:* steer'd *1849:* steered

A hundred shapes of lucid stone!
All day we built its shrine for each,
A shrine of rock for every one,
Nor paused till in the westering sun
We sat together on the beach
To sing because our task was done.
When lo! what shouts and merry songs!
What laughter all the distance stirs!
A loaded raft with happy throngs
Of gentle islanders!
"Our isles are just at hand," they cried,
"Like cloudlets faint in even sleeping;
Our temple-gates are opened wide,
Our olive-groves thick shade are keeping
For these majestic forms"—they cried.
Oh, then we awoke with sudden start
From our deep dream, and knew, too late,
How bare the rock, how desolate,
Which had received our precious freight:
Yet we called out—"Depart!
Our gifts, once given, must here abide.
Our work is done; we have no heart

500| *MS:* An < > shapes § written over by § Shapes *1835:* shapes *1863:* A 501| *MS:* each— *1863:* each, 502| *MS:*—A < > one,— *1835:* A < > one— *1863:* one, 503| *MS:* 'till *1835:* till *1849:* paused we till *1868:* paused till 504| *MS:* sate *1863:* sat 505| *MS:* done . . . *1835:* sing, because < > done; *1863:* sing because < > done. 508| *MS:* raft and happy *1835:* raft, and *1849:* What raft comes loaded with its throngs *1863:* A loaded raft with happy throngs 509| *MS:* Islanders! *1835:* islanders! *1849:* islanders? *1863:* islanders! 510| *1835:* cried; *1849:* The isles *1863:* Our isles < > cried, 511| *MS:* sleeping, *1849:* faint at even *1863:* faint in even sleeping; *1888:* sleeping; § ; probable; upper half only printed § *1889:* sleeping 512| *1835:* open'd *1849:* opened 513| *MS:* olive groves *1835:* olive-groves 514| *MS:* Forms," they cried: *1835:* forms < > cried. *1849:* For the lucid shapes you bring"—they *1863:* For these majestic forms"—they 515| *MS:* Then we *1849:* Oh, then 516| *MS:* knew too late *1835:* knew, too late, *1849:* dream; we knew *1863:* dream, and knew 518| *MS:* freight *1835:* freight: *1849:* To which we had flung our *1863:* Which had received our 519| *MS:*—Yet < > out "Depart! *1835:* Yet we call'd out—"Depart! *1849:* called 520| *MS:* abide! *1835:* abide: *1863:* abide. 521| *MS:* § not indented § done—we *1835:* § indented § done; we

To mar our work,"—we cried.

FESTUS In truth?

PARACELSUS Nay, wait: all this in tracings faint
On rugged stones strewn here and there, but piled
In order once: then follows—mark what follows!
"The sad rhyme of the men who proudly clung
To their first fault, and withered in their pride."

FESTUS Come back then, Aureole; as you fear God, come!
This is foul sin; come back! Renounce the past,
Forswear the future; look for joy no more,
But wait death's summons amid holy sights,
And trust me for the event—peace, if not joy.
Return with me to Einsiedeln, dear Aureole!

PARACELSUS No way, no way! it would not turn to good.
A spotless child sleeps on the flowering moss—
'Tis well for him; but when a sinful man,
Envying such slumber, may desire to put
His guilt away, shall he return at once
To rest by lying there? Our sires knew well
(Spite of the grave discoveries of their sons)
The fitting course for such: dark cells, dim lamps,

522| *MS:* § indented § work;" we cried! *1835:* § not indented § work," we cried. *1849:* work, though vain"—we *1863:* work,"—we 523–524| *MS:* truth? . . PARACELSUS nay wait,—all <> faint / On <> stones,—strewn <> there—but piled *1835:* truth? PARACELSUS Nay, wait: all <> / <> stones, strewn <> there, but *1849:* faint / May still be read on that deserted rock, / On *1863:* stones strewn *1868:* faint / On 525| *MS:* what follows; ——— *1835:* once; then <> what follows— *1863:* once: then <> what follows: *1868:* what follows! 526| *MS:* § in italics § *Men* *1835:* men *1849:* § in roman § 527| *MS:* § in italics § *pride!"* *1835:* *wither'd* *1849:* § in roman § withered *1868:* pride." 528| *1835:* back, then *1868:* back then 529| *MS:* sin—come back—renounce *1835:* sin; come back: renounce *1863:* back. Renounce the Past, *1868:* back! Renounce the past. 530| *MS:* future . . . look *1835:* future; look *1863:* Future <> more *1868:* future *1888:* more, 531| *MS:* wait for death amid all peaceful sights *1835:* sights, *1849:* wait death's summons amid holy sights, 532| *MS:* went——peace if not joy!— *1835:* event—peace, if not joy! *1863:* joy. 533| *1835:* Aureole. *1863:* Aureole! 534| *MS:* No way, no way!——it <> good—— *1835:* good. *1863:* No way, no way! it 536| *MS:* Tis <> him; and one deformed by sin, *1835:* 'Tis <> deform'd *1849:* him; but when a sinful man, 537| *MS:* slumber may *1835:* slumber, may 538| *MS:* away . . . shall *1835:* away: shall *1849:* away, shall 539| *MS:* To boyhood's carelessness? our *1835:* Our *1849:* To rest by lying there? Our 541| *MS:* such——dark *1835:* such—dark *1849:* such; dark *1888:* such: dark

A stone floor one may writhe on like a worm:
No mossy pillow blue with violets!
FESTUS I see no symptom of these absolute
And tyrannous passions. You are calmer now.
This verse-making can purge you well enough
Without the terrible penance you describe.
You love me still: the lusts you fear will never
Outrage your friend. To Einsiedeln, once more!
Say but the word!
PARACELSUS No, no; those lusts forbid:
They crouch, I know, cowering with half-shut eye
Beside,you; 'tis their nature. Thrust yourself
Between them and their prey; let some fool style me
Or king or quack, it matters not—then try
Your wisdom, urge them to forego their treat!
No, no; learn better and look deeper, Festus!
If you knew how a devil sneers within me
While you are talking now of this, now that,
As though we differed scarcely save in trifles!
FESTUS Do we so differ? True, change must proceed,
Whether for good or ill; keep from me, which!
Do not confide all secrets: I was born

542| *MS:* stone-floor <> worm . . . *1835:* stone floor <> worm; *1863:* worm: 543| *MS:* pillow, blue *1835:* violets. *1849:* violets! *1863:* pillow blue 544| *MS:* these overbearing *1849:* these absolute 545| *MS:* passions:—you <> now:— *1835:* passions. You <> now. 546| *1835:* enough, *1863:* enough 547| *MS:* describe;— *1835:* describe. 548| *MS:* still——the § written over by § still—the *1835:* still: the *1849:* fear, will *1888:* fear will 549| *MS:* friend: to *1835:* friend. To 550| *MS:* No, No: those <> forbid; *1835:* No, no; those <> forbid: 551| *MS:* know,—cowering *1835:* know, cowering 552| *MS:* you—'tis *1835:* you; 'tis 553| *MS:* prey . . . let *1835:* prey; let 554| *MS:* King or Quack <> not— § above § , and let *1835:* king or quack <> not, and *1849:* and try *1888:* not—then try 555| *MS:* wisdom urge *1849:* wisdom then, at urging their retreat! *1863:* wisdom, urge them to forego their treat! 556| *MS:* No, no: learn <> Festus: *1835:* no, no; learn <> Festus. *1849:* Festus! 558| *MS:* that *1835:* that, 559| *MS:* tho' *1835:* though we differ'd *1849:* differed 560| *MS:* I know what you would say:—all change proceeds, *1835:* say: all *1849:* Do we so differ? True, change must proceed, 561–562| *MS:* keep that from me! Do not confide *those* secrets *1849:* keep from me, which! / God made you and knows what you may become— / Do not confide all secrets *1863:* which! / Do

To hope, and you . . .
PARACELSUS   To trust: you know the fruits!
FESTUS Listen: I do believe, what you call trust
Was self-delusion at the best: for, see!
So long as God would kindly pioneer
A path for you, and screen you from the world,
Procure you full exemption from man's lot,
Man's common hopes and fears, on the mere pretext
Of your engagement in his service—yield you
A limitless licence, make you God, in fact,
And turn your slave—you were content to say
Most courtly praises! What is it, at last,
But selfishness without example? None
Could trace God's will so plain as you, while yours
Remained implied in it; but now you fail,
And we, who prate about that will, are fools!
In short, God's service is established here
As he determines fit, and not your way,
And this you cannot brook. Such discontent
Is weak. Renounce all creatureship at once!
Affirm an absolute right to have and use
Your energies; as though the rivers should say—

563| *MS:* hope,—and < > trust: you § altered in pencil to § trust:—you < > the rest. *1835:* hope, and < > trust: you *1849:* the fruits! 564| *MS:* believe the trust you boast, *1835:* boast *1849:* believe, what you call trust
565| *MS:* best; so long *1835:* best. So *1849:* Was self-reliance at the best: for, see! *1863:* Was self-delusion at 566| *MS:* As < > pioneer your path,— *1835:* path— *1849:* So long as < > pioneer 567| *MS:* Would undertake to screen *1835:* world— *1849:* A path for you, and screen < > world,
568| *MS:* from their lot *1835:* lot, *1849:* from man's lot, 569| *MS:* The common *1849:* Man's common 570| *MS:* service,—yield *1835:* service—yield *1863:* His *1868:* his 571| *MS:* license . . . make you God in *1835:* license—make you God, in *1849:* license, make *1863:* license
572| *MS:* slave— § above § , you *1835:* slave—you 573| *MS:* praises: what is it at last *1849:* praises! What is it, at last, 574| *MS:* example?—None *1835:* example? None 576| *MS:* it—but *now,* you *1835:* Remain'd < > it; but *now* you *1849:* Remained < > now 577| *MS:* we who < > will are fools;— *1835:* fools. *1849:* we, who < > will, are fools! 578| *MS:* service must be ordered here *1835:* order'd *1849:* service is established here
579| *1849:* He *1868:* he 580| *MS:* brook: such *1849:* brook! Such *1863:* brook. Such 581| *MS:* weak:—renounce all creatureship—affirm *1835:* weak. Renounce *1849:* creatureship at once! 582| *MS:* An < > and to dispose *1849:* Affirm an < > and use 583| *MS:* energies—as tho' < > say *1835:* energies; as though < > say—

"We rush to the ocean; what have we to do
With feeding streamlets, lingering in the vales,
Sleeping in lazy pools?" Set up that plea,
That will be bold at least!

PARACELSUS

'Tis like enough.
The serviceable spirits are those, no doubt,
The East produces: lo, the master bids,—
They wake, raise terraces and garden-grounds
In one night's space; and, this done, straight begin
Another century's sleep, to the great praise
Of him that framed them wise and beautiful,
Till a lamp's rubbing, or some chance akin,
Wake them again. I am of different mould.
I would have soothed my lord, and slaved for him
And done him service past my narrow bond,
And thus I get rewarded for my pains!
Beside, 'tis vain to talk of forwarding
God's glory otherwise; this is alone
The sphere of its increase, as far as men
Increase it; why, then, look beyond this sphere?
We are his glory; and if we be glorious,

584| *MS:* ocean—what *1835:* ocean; what 585| *MS:* vales *1835:* vales, *1849:* the marshes, *1863:* the vales, 586| *MS:* plea. *1835:* plea, 587| *MS:* least. PARACELSUS Tis *1835:* 'Tis *1849:* least! PARACELSUS Perhaps, perhaps! *1863:* PARACELSUS 'Tis like enough! *1868:* enough. 588| *1849:* Your only servicable spirits are those *1863:* The serviceable <> those, no doubt, 589| *MS:* produces;—lo, the Master nods— *1835:* east produces. Lo, the master nods, *1849:* produces:—lo *1863:* The East produces: lo *1888:* master bids,— 590| *MS:* And they raise *1849:* terraces, spread garden-grounds *1863:* terraces and garden-grounds *1888:* They wake, raise 591| *MS:* space,—and this done, straight relapse *1835:* space; and, this *1849:* straight begin 592| *MS:* Into a century's sleep———to the great honour *1835:* sleep, to *1849:* Another century's <> great praise 593| *MS:* beautiful; *1835:* beautiful, 594| *MS:* akin *1835:* akin, 595| *MS:* Release their limbs:——I *1835:* limbs. I *1849:* Wake them again. I 596| *MS:* Lord and *1835:* Lord, and <> him, *1849:* lord *1888:* him 599| *MS:* Beside 'tis *1835:* Beside, 'tis 600| *MS:* His glory otherwise—*this* is the sphere *1835:* otherwise; *this* *1849:* God's glory <> this is alone 601| *MS:* Alone of <> far as we *1849:* The sphere of <> far as men 602| *MS:* Can be concerned, or I am much deceived;—— *1835:* concern'd <> deceived: *1849:* Increase it; why, then, look beyond this sphere? 603| *MS:* glory, and if *we* be glorious *1835:* glory; and <> glorious, *1849:* We are His <> we *1868:* his

Is not the thing achieved?

FESTUS

Shall one like me
Judge hearts like yours? Though years have changed you much,
And you have left your first love, and retain
Its empty shade to veil your crooked ways,
Yet I still hold that you have honoured God.
And who shall call your course without reward?
For, wherefore this repining at defeat
Had triumph ne'er inured you to high hopes?
I urge you to forsake the life you curse,
And what success attends me?—simply talk
Of passion, weakness and remorse; in short,
Anything but the naked truth—you choose
This so-despised career, and cheaply hold
My happiness, or rather other men's.
Once more, return!

PARACELSUS

And quickly. John the thief
Has pilfered half my secrets by this time:
And we depart by daybreak. I am weary,
I know not how; not even the wine-cup soothes
My brain to-night . . .
Do you not thoroughly despise me, Festus?
No flattery! One like you needs not be told
We live and breathe deceiving and deceived.

605| *MS:* your's?——tho *1835:* yours? Though 607| *MS:* to gild your *1849:* to veil your 608| *MS:* *have* <> God— *1835:* honour'd God; *1849:* have honoured *1863:* God. 609| *MS:* And has your course been all without *1849:* And who shall call your course without 610| *MS:* For wherefore <> defeat, *1849:* For, wherefore *1868:* defeat 612| *MS:*——I <> curse *1835:* I <> curse, 613| *1835:* me? simply *1849:* me?—simply 614| *MS:* weakness, and remorse——in short *1835:* remorse; in short, *1863:* weakness and 615| *MS:* Any thing *1835:* truth: you *1863:* Anything <> truth—you 616| *MS:* so despised *1835:* so-despised *1849:* and rather praise *1863:* and cheaply hold 617| *MS:* Men's:—— *1835:* men's. *1849:* Than take my happiness *1863:* My happiness, or rather other 618| *MS:* more return! PARACELSUS—And quickly—Oporinus *1835:* PARACELSUS And quickly. Oporinus *1849:* And soon. Oporinus *1863:* And quickly. Oporinus *1888:* quickly. John the thief 619| *MS:* time— *1835:* pilfer'd *1849:* pilfered <> time: 620| *MS:* day-break:—I am weary *1835:* day-break. I am weary, 621| *MS:* how——not *1835:* how; not 622| *MS:* to-night——— *1835:* to-night . . . 624| *MS:*——No flattery! . . one *1835:* No flattery! One *1849:* you, needs *1863:* you needs 625| *MS:* and deceived——— *1835:* deceived.

Do you not scorn me from your heart of hearts,
Me and my cant, each petty subterfuge,
My rhymes and all this frothy shower of words,
My glozing self-deceit, my outward crust
Of lies which wrap, as tetter, morphew, furfair
Wrapt the sound flesh?—so, see you flatter not!
Even God flatters: but my friend, at least,
Is true. I would depart, secure henceforth
Against all further insult, hate and wrong
From puny foes; my one friend's scorn shall brand me:
No fear of sinking deeper!

FESTUS   No, dear Aureole!
No, no; I came to counsel faithfully.
There are old rules, made long ere we were born,
By which I judge you. I, so fallible,
So infinitely low beside your mighty
Majestic spirit!—even I can see
You own some higher law than ours which call
Sin, what is no sin—weakness, what is strength.
But I have only these, such as they are,
To guide me; and I blame you where they bid,

626| *MS:* of hearts? *1863:* of hearts, **627**| *MS:* Me—and my cant—my petty subterfuges— *1835:* Me and *1863:* cant, my <> subterfuges, *1868:* cant, each petty subterfuge, **628**| *MS:* These rhymes *1835:* rhymes, and <> words— *1849:* My rhymes *1863:* rhymes and <> words, **629**| *1835:* self-deceit—my *1863:* self-deceit, my **630**| *MS:* tetter morphew furfair *1835:* lies; which wrap, as tetter, morphew, furfair *1863:* lies which **631**| *MS:* Wrap <> flesh . . so see <> not!— *1835:* flesh?—so <> not! *1849:* so, see *1888:* Wrapt **632**| *MS:* flatters——but § written over by § flatters!—but *1835:* flatters! but *1849:* Why, even *1863:* Even *1868:* flatters: but **633**| *MS:* true: I <> depart secure *1835:* true. I <> depart, secure **634**| *1835:* hate, and *1863:* hate and **635**| *MS:* foes: my <> me! *1835:* me— *1863:* foes; my **636**| *MS:* deeper!—FESTUS *1835:* deeper. FESTUS *1849:* deeper! FESTUS **637**| *MS:* No, No—I <> faithfully:—— *1835:* No, no; I <> faithfully: *1863:* faithfully. **638**| *MS:* rules made <> born *1835:* rules, made <> born, **639**| *MS:* you—I, so fallible *1835:* you. I, so fallible, **640**| *1849:* your spirit *1863:* beside your mighty, *1868:* mighty **641**| *MS:* spirit:———even *1835:* spirit—even *1849:* Mighty, majestic!—even *1863:* Majestic spirit!—even **642**| *MS:* law——they make that out *1835:* law. They *1849:* law than ours which call *1863:* calls *1868:* call **643**| *MS:* Sin—which is no sin——weakness—which is strength, *1835:* Sin which <> sin—weakness which is strength; *1849:* Sin, what is <> weakness, what is strength; *1863:* strength. **644**| *MS:* are *1835:* are, **645**| *MS:* me—§ above §, and <> bid *1835:* me; and <> bid, *1849:* they blame, *1863:* they bid,

Only so long as blaming promises
To win peace for your soul: the more, that sorrow
Has fallen on me of late, and they have helped me
So that I faint not under my distress.
But wherefore should I scruple to avow
In spite of all, as brother judging brother,
Your fate is most inexplicable to me?
And should you perish without recompense
And satisfaction yet—too hastily
I have relied on love: you may have sinned,
But you have loved. As a mere human matter—
As I would have God deal with fragile men
In the end—I say that you will triumph yet!
PARACELSUS Have you felt sorrow, Festus?—'tis because
You love me. Sorrow, and sweet Michal yours!
Well thought on: never let her know this last
Dull winding-up of all: these miscreants dared
Insult me—me she loved:—so, grieve her not!
FESTUS Your ill success can little grieve her now.
PARACELSUS Michal is dead! pray Christ we do not craze!
FESTUS Aureole, dear Aureole, look not on me thus!
Fool, fool! this is the heart grown sorrow-proof—

646| *MS:* As long as any chance remains of winning *1849:* Only so long as blaming promises 647| *MS:* Your troubled soul to peace . . the more that *1835:* peace; the *1849:* To win peace for your soul; the more, that *1863:* soul: the 648| *1835:* help'd *1849:* helped 649| *MS:* distress: *1835:* distress. 650| *MS:* to confess *1849:* to avow 651| *MS:* That spite *1835:* That, spite *1849:* In spite 652| *MS:* me: *1835:* fate to me is most inexplicable: *1863:* inexplicable? *1888:* fate is most inexplicable to me? 653| *MS:* perish yet without reward *1835:* reward— *1849:* perish without recompense 654| *MS:*—Some great reward—I have too *1835:* Some *1849:* And satisfaction yet—too 655| *MS:* Relied on love's effect . . you <> sinned *1835:* effect. You <> sinn'd, *1849:* I have relied on love: you <> sinned, 656| *MS:* loved: as <> matter, *1849:* loved. As <> matter— 657| *MS:*—As <> Men *1835:* As <> men 658| *MS:* end . . I *1835:* end—I 659| *MS:* You have felt <> Festus? 'tis *1835:* Have you felt <> Festus? 'tis *1849:* Festus?—'tis 660| *MS:* me——sorrow <> your's? *1835:* me. Sorrow <> yours! 661| *MS:* on . . never *1835:* on; never *1868:* on: never 662| *MS:* winding up of all—these *1835:* winding-up of all: these 663| *MS:* loved;—so grieve *1835:* loved; so <> not. *1863:* loved: so, grieve *1868:* loved:—so 664| *MS:* now——— *1835:* now. 665| *MS:* dead!——pray § written over by § dead!—pray *1835:* dead! pray 666| *MS:* Aureole——dear Aureole— § above §. look <> thus!—— *1835:* Aureole, dear Aureole, look <> thus! 667| *MS:* Fool,—fool <> sorrow-proof!— *1835:* Fool, fool <> sorrow-proof—

I cannot bear those eyes.
PARACELSUS Nay, really dead?
FESTUS 'Tis scarce a month.
PARACELSUS Stone dead!—then you have laid her
Among the flowers ere this. Now, do you know,
I can reveal a secret which shall comfort
Even you. I have no julep, as men think,
To cheat the grave; but a far better secret.
Know, then, you did not ill to trust your love
To the cold earth: I have thought much of it:
For I believe we do not wholly die.
FESTUS Aureole!
PARACELSUS Nay, do not laugh; there is a reason
For what I say: I think the soul can never
Taste death. I am, just now, as you may see,
Very unfit to put so strange a thought
In an intelligible dress of words;
But take it as my trust, she is not dead.
FESTUS But not on this account alone? you surely,
—Aureole, you have believed this all along?
PARACELSUS And Michal sleeps among the roots and dews,
While I am moved at Basil, and full of schemes
For Nuremberg, and hoping and despairing,
As though it mattered how the farce plays out,
So it be quickly played. Away, away!

668| *MS:* eyes;—— PARACELSUS *1835:* eyes. PARACELSUS 669| *MS:* a year——PARACELSUS Stone-dead? then *1835:* year . . . PARACELSUS Stone dead! then *1849:* a month . . . PARACELSUS dead!—then *1863:* month. PARACELSUS
670| *MS:* this——now *1835:* this . . . Now *1849:* this. Now 672| *MS:* you . . I <> julep as they think *1835:* you. I <> julep, as <> think, *1849:* as men think, 673| *MS:* grave—but <> secret;—— *1835:* grave; <> secret.
674| *MS:* Know then *1863:* Know, then 675| *MS:* earth——I <> it— *1835:* earth: *1849:* it: 676| *MS:* die:— *1835:* die. 677| *MS:* Aureole . . . PARACELSUS Nay <> laugh—there *1835:* laugh; there *1863:* Aureole! PARACELSUS 678| *MS:* say—I *1835:* say: I 679| *MS:* death——I am just <> see *1835:* death. I am, just <> see, 681| *MS:* words——— *1835:* words; 682| *MS:* dead! *1835:* dead. 683| *MS:* alone? O you surely . . *1835:* alone? you surely, 684| *MS:* . . . Aureole *1835:* Aureole *1849:*—Aureole 685| *MS:*——And *1835:* And 686| *MS:* and wondering *1849:* and full of schemes 687| *MS:* With Nuremburg <> despairing *1835:* Nuremberg <> despairing, *1849:* For Nuremberg
688| *MS:* tho' <> out *1835:* though it matter'd <> out, *1849:* mattered
689| *MS:* played——Away, Away! *1835:* play'd. Away, away! *1849:* played

Have your will, rabble! while we fight the prize,
Troop you in safety to the snug back-seats
And leave a clear arena for the brave
About to perish for your sport!—Behold!

690| *MS:* prize *1835:* prize, 691| *MS:* back-seats, *1868:* back-seats 692| *MS:* Brave *1835:* brave 693| *MS:* sport:—Behold! *1835:* sport . . . Behold! *1849:* sport!—Behold!

PART V. PARACELSUS ATTAINS.

SCENE—*Salzburg; a cell in the Hospital of St. Sebastian.* 1541.

FESTUS, PARACELSUS.

FESTUS No change! The weary night is well-nigh spent,
The lamp burns low, and through the casement-bars
Grey morning glimmers feebly: yet no change!
Another night, and still no sigh has stirred
That fallen discoloured mouth, no pang relit
Those fixed eyes, quenched by the decaying body,
Like torch-flame choked in dust. While all beside
Was breaking, to the last they held out bright,
As a stronghold where life intrenched itself;
But they are dead now—very blind and dead:
He will drowse into death without a groan.

My Aureole—my forgotten, ruined Aureole!
The days are gone, are gone! How grand thou wast!
And now not one of those who struck thee down—

SCENE| *MS:* A <> *Sebastian at Salzburg.* 1541. *1863: Salzburg; a* <> *Sebastian.* 1541. 1| *MS:* change!—the <> well nigh *1835:* change! The *1863:* well-nigh 3| *MS:* The grey morn <> feebly——yet *1835:* feebly—yet *1849:* Grey morning *1863:* feebly: yet 4| *1835:* stirr'd *1849:* stirred 5| *MS:* fall'n *1835:* discolour'd *1849:* fallen discoloured 6| *MS:* body *1835:* quench'd <> body, *1849:* quenched 7| *MS:* dust;—while *1835:* dust: while *1863:* dust. While 8| *MS:* bright *1835:* bright, 9| *MS:* strong-hold <> itself . . . *1835:* intrench'd itself; *1849:* intrenched *1863:* stronghold 10| *MS:* now—very <> dead:—— *1835:* now—very <> dead. *1863:* and dead: 11| *MS:*——He <> groan! *1835:* He *1868:* groan. 12| *MS:* Aureole, my *1835:* Aureole; my <> ruin'd *1849:* Aureole—my <> ruined 13| *MS:* how <> thou wert,—— *1835:* How <> wert: *1863:* thou wast! 14| *MS:* down *1835:* down—

Poor glorious spirit—concerns him even to stay
And satisfy himself his little hand
Could turn God's image to a livid thing.

Another night, and yet no change! 'Tis much
That I should sit by him, and bathe his brow,
And chafe his hands; 'tis much: but he will sure
Know me, and look on me, and speak to me
Once more—but only once! His hollow cheek
Looked all night long as though a creeping laugh
At his own state were just about to break
From the dying man: my brain swam, my throat swelled,
And yet I could not turn away. In truth,
They told me how, when first brought here, he seemed
Resolved to live, to lose no faculty;
Thus striving to keep up his shattered strength,
Until they bore him to this stifling cell:
When straight his features fell, an hour made white
The flushed face, and relaxed the quivering limb,
Only the eye remained intense awhile
As though it recognized the tomb-like place,

15| *MS:* Poor, glorious Spirit! concerns *1835:* spirit—concerns *1868:* Poor glorious 17| *MS:* thing! *1835:* thing. *1849:* thing. § end of page § *1863:* thing. § no space § *1868:* thing. / § space § 18| *MS:* change!—'tis *1835:* change! 'Tis 19| *MS:* should look on § cancelled by § sit by him and < > brow *1835:* him, and < > brow, 20| *MS:* hands——'tis much—but *1835:* hands—'tis much; but *1863:* hands; 'tis much: but 21| *MS:* me and *1835:* me, and 22| *MS:* once!—his § written over by § His *1835:* once! His 23| *MS:* Looked, all < > tho' *1835:* Look'd all < > though *1849:* Looked 25| *MS:* man . . . my < > swam and my throat *1835:* man: my *1849:* swam, my throat swelled, 26| *MS:* Swelled thick, and yet I § cancelled by § Swelled yet for all I < > away! *1835:* Swell'd, yet *1849:* And yet I < > away. In truth, 27| *MS:* In truth they < > how he seemed at first *1835:* truth, they < > seem'd *1849:* They < > how, when first brought here, he seemed 28| *MS:* live—to let no power forsake him;— *1835:* him; *1849:* live—to lose no faculty; *1863:* live, to 29| *MS:* strength *1835:* shatter'd strength, *1849:* shattered 30| *MS:* they brought him < > cell *1835:* cell: *1849:* they bore him 31| *MS:*——At once his features fell——an *1835:* At < > fell—an *1849:* When straight his *1863:* fell, an 32| *MS:* limb— *1835:* flush'd face and relax'd < > limb; *1849:* flushed < > relaxed *1863:* limb, 33| *1835:* remain'd < > while, *1849:* remained *1863:* awhile 34| *MS:* tho' *1835:* though < > place; *1863:* place,

And then he lay as here he lies.
Ay, here!
Here is earth's noblest, nobly garlanded—
Her bravest champion with his well-won prize—
Her best achievement, her sublime amends
For countless generations fleeting fast
And followed by no trace;—the creature-god
She instances when angels would dispute
The title of her brood to rank with them.
Angels, this is our angel! Those bright forms
We clothe with purple, crown and call to thrones,
Are human, but not his; those are but men
Whom other men press round and kneel before;
Those palaces are dwelt in by mankind;
Higher provision is for him you seek
Amid our pomps and glories: see it here!
Behold earth's paragon! Now, raise thee, clay!

God! Thou art love! I build my faith on that.
Even as I watch beside thy tortured child
Unconscious whose hot tears fall fast by him,
So doth thy right hand guide us through the world

35| *MS:* lay, as < > lies:—/ Ay *1835:* lay as < > lies . . . / Ay, here: *1849:* lies. / Ay, here! 36| *MS:* garlanded! *1835:* noblest nobly garlanded— *1849:* noblest, nobly 37| *MS:* well-won meed! *1835:* champion, with < > meed— *1863:* champion with *1868:* well-won prize— 38| *MS:* best production—all that makes amends *1849:* best achievement, her sublime amends 39| *1835:* generations, fleeting *1863:* generations fleeting
40| *MS:* trace—the all-surpassing *1835:* follow'd *1849:* followed < > trace:—the creature-god 41| *MS:* Creature she cites when Angels *1835:* angels *1849:* She instances when 42| *MS:* them . . *1835:* them . . . *1849:* them— *1863:* them. 43–45| *MS:* Angel! those < > forms / Are the man——but not his,—those < > Men *1835:* angel!—those < > / Are human, but not his: those < > men *1849:* forms / We clothe with purple, crown and call to thrones, / Are *1863:* angel! Those < > // Are human; but *1868:* human, but not his; those
46| *MS:* the rest press around < > before— *1849:* Whom other men press round and *1863:* before; 47| *MS:* Mankind— *1835:* mankind;
48–50| *MS:*——Other provision < > seek——/ Behold < > paragon!—Now < > Clay! *1835:* Other < > seek. / < > paragon! Now < > clay! *1849:* Higher provision < > seek / Amid our pomps and glories: see it here! / Behold *1863:* clay! § end of page § *1868:* clay! § no space § *1888:* clay! / § space § 51| *MS:* Love < > that: *1849:* that! *1868:* love *1888:* that *1889:* that.
52| *1835:* child, *1863:* Thy < > child *1868:* thy 54| *MS:* right-hand < > thro' *1835:* right hand < > through *1863:* Thy *1868:* thy

Wherein we stumble. God! what shall we say?
How has he sinned? How else should he have done?
Surely he sought thy praise—thy praise, for all
He might be busied by the task so much
As half forget awhile its proper end.
Dost thou well, Lord? Thou canst not but prefer
That I should range myself upon his side—
How could he stop at every step to set
Thy glory forth? Hadst thou but granted him
Success, thy honour would have crowned success,
A halo round a star. Or, say he erred,—
Save him, dear God; it will be like thee: bathe him
In light and life! Thou art not made like us;
We should be wroth in such a case; but thou
Forgivest—so, forgive these passionate thoughts
Which come unsought and will not pass away!
I know thee, who hast kept my path, and made
Light for me in the darkness, tempering sorrow
So that it reached me like a solemn joy;
It were too strange that I should doubt thy love.
But what am I? Thou madest him and knowest
How he was fashioned. I could never err

---

[55]| *MS:* stumble:—God *1835:* stumble. God [56]| *MS:*— —How <> sinned—how *1835:* How <> sinn'd—how *1849:* sinned? How [57]| *1863:* Thy <> Thy *1868:* thy <> thy [58]| *MS:* be wedded to the <> so well *1849:* be busied by the <> so much [59]| *MS:* As to forget <> end— — *1835:* end . . . *1849:* end. *1868:* As half forget [60]| *MS:* Lord? . . . Thou *1835:* Lord? Thou [61]| *MS:* side . . . *1849:* side— [63]| *MS:* forth?—hadst Thou *1835:* forth? Hadst *1868:* thou [64]| *MS:* crowned his triumph— *1835:* crown'd *1849:* have crowned success, *1863:* Thy *1868:* thy [65]| *MS:* star— —or § written over by § star!—or say he erred, *1835:* star . . . Or <> err'd: *1849:* star. Or, say he erred,— [66]| *MS:* God—it <> thee—bathe *1835:* God; it <> thee: bathe *1863:* Thee *1868:* thee [67]| *MS:* life! . Thou <> us— *1835:* life! Thou <> us: *1849:* us; [68]| *MS:* be wrath in <> case—but thou § written over by § Thou *1835:* case; but *1849:* be wroth in *1868:* thou [69]| *MS:* Will smile on him! . . . forgive these *1835:* him. Forgive <> thoughts, *1849:* Forgivest—so, forgive *1863:* thoughts [70]| *1835:* unsought, and <> away. *1849:* away! *1863:* unsought and [71]| *MS:* thee—who <> path and *1835:* thee, who <> path, and *1863:* Thee *1868:* thee [72]| *MS:* darkness— —tempering *1835:* darkness—tempering sorrow, *1863:* darkness, tempering sorrow [73]| *MS:* joy— — *1835:* reach'd <> joy; *1849:* reached [74]| *MS: I* <> love . . . *1835:* love: *1849:* I *1863:* Thy love. *1868:* thy [75]| *MS: I* *1835:* him, and *1849:* I *1863:* him and [76]| *MS:* fashioned; *I* *1835:* fashion'd. *I* *1849:* fashioned. I

That way: the quiet place beside thy feet,
Reserved for me, was ever in my thoughts:
But he—thou shouldst have favoured him as well!

Ah! he wakens! Aureole, I am here! 'tis Festus!
I cast away all wishes save one wish—
Let him but know me, only speak to me!
He mutters; louder and louder; any other
Than I, with brain less laden, could collect
What he pours forth. Dear Aureole, do but look!
Is it talking or singing, this he utters fast?
Misery that he should fix me with his eye,
Quick talking to some other all the while!
If he would husband this wild vehemence
Which frustrates its intent!—I heard, I know
I heard my name amid those rapid words.
Oh, he will know me yet! Could I divert
This current, lead it somehow gently back
Into the channels of the past!—His eye
Brighter than ever! It must recognize me!

I am Erasmus: I am here to pray

77| *MS:* way—the <> feet *1835:* way: the *1849:* feet, *1863:* Thy *1868:* thy 78| *MS:* me was <> thoughts;— *1835:* thoughts; *1849:* me, was <> thoughts: 79| *MS:* He—Thou *1835:* he—Thou <> favour'd *1849:* favoured *1863:* well! § end of page § *1868:* well! § no space § *1888;* well! / § space § 80| *MS:* Ah! he wakens—Aureole <> here,—'tis *1835:* wakens! Aureole <> here—'tis *1849:* wakes *1863:* here! 'tis *1868:* wakens 81| *MS:*——I <> wish—— *1835:* I <> wish— 82| *MS:* me, only <> me!—— *1835:* me—only <> me! *1863:* me, only 83| *MS:* mutters—louder and louder:——Any *1835:* mutters—louder and louder; any *1863:* mutters; louder and 84| *MS:* I—with <> laden—would collect *1835:* I, with <> laden, would *1849:* laden, could collect 85| *MS:* forth;—dear Aureole do *1835:* forth. Dear Aureole, do 86| *MS:* singing this *1868:* singing, this 87| *MS:* Misery! that *1835:* Misery, that <> eye— *1863:* eye, *1888:* Misery that 88| *MS:* talking——to *1835:* talking to 89| *1835:* vehemence, *1863:* vehemence 90| *MS:* intent:—I heard . . . I *1835:* intent . . . I heard, I *1849:* intent!—I heard 91| *MS:* words:— *1835:* words: *1863:* words. 92| *MS:* O he will <> could *1835:* Could *1863:* Oh, he 93| *MS:* current——lead *1835:* current—lead *1863:* current, lead 94| *MS:* past . . his *1835:* past . . . His *1849:* past!—His *1863:* Past *1868:* past 95–96| *MS:* ever—it <> me! / § space § / I am Erasmus,—I *1835:* ever, it <> / § space § / <> Erasmus: I *1849:* ever! It <> recognise! / § space § / Let me speak to him in another's name. / I am Erasmus *1863:* recognize me! *1868:* me! / § space § / I am Erasmus

That Paracelsus use his skill for me.
The schools of Paris and of Padua send
These questions for your learning to resolve.
We are your students, noble master: leave
This wretched cell, what business have you here?
Our class awaits you; come to us once more!
(O agony! the utmost I can do
Touches him not; how else arrest his ear?)
I am commissioned . . . I shall craze like him.
Better be mute and see what God shall send.

PARACELSUS Stay, stay with me!

FESTUS I will; I am come here
To stay with you—Festus, you loved of old;
Festus, you know, you must know!

PARACELSUS Festus! Where's
Aprile, then? Has he not chanted softly
The melodies I heard all night? I could not
Get to him for a cold hand on my breast,
But I made out his music well enough,
O well enough! If they have filled him full
With magical music, as they freight a star
With light, and have remitted all his sin,
They will forgive me too, I too shall know!

97| *MS:* That Eremita use his wondrous skill . . . . *1835:* skill: *1849:* That Paracelsus use his skill for me. 98| *MS:* . . The *1835:* The 99| *MS:* resolve . . . *1835:* resolve. 100| *MS:* Master:—leave *1835:* master. Leave *1849:* master: leave 101| *MS:* cell,—what *1835:* cell; what *1863:* cell, what 102| *MS:* you— —come *1835:* you; come < > more. *1863:* more! 103| *MS:*— § written over by § (O Agony!—the *1835:* (O agony! the 104| *MS:* not . . . how *1835:* not; how 105| *MS:* commissioned . . . . (I < > him— *1835:* commission'd . . . I *1849:* commissioned *1863:* him! *1868:* him. 106| *MS:* I will be *1835:* mute, and *1849:* Better be mute *1863:* mute and 107| *MS:* Stay—stay < > me! . . . FESTUS —I will—I *1835:* Stay, stay < > me! FESTUS I will; I 108| *MS:* you . . . . Festus you < > old— — § written over by § old— *1835:* you—Festus < > old; *1849:* Festus, you 109| *MS:* Festus—you know—you < > know . . PARACELSUS Festus . . . where's *1835:* Festus, you know, you < > know. PARACELSUS Festus! Where's *1849:* must know! 110| *MS:* Aprile then? has < > chaunted *1835:* Has *1863:* chanted 111| *MS:* night— —I *1835:* night? I 113| *MS:* enough— *1835:* enough, 114| *MS:* enough . . . . if *1835:* enough. If < > fill'd *1849:* O, well enough! If < > filled *1868:* O well 115| *MS:* music as *1849:* music, as 117| *MS:* too— —I shall Know too!— — *1835:* too, I < > know too . . . *1849:* I too shall know!

FESTUS Festus, your Festus!
PARACELSUS Ask him if Aprile
Knows as he Loves—if I shall Love and Know?
I try; but that cold hand, like lead—so cold!
FESTUS My hand, see!
PARACELSUS Ah, the curse, Aprile, Aprile!
We get so near—so very, very near!
'Tis an old tale: Jove strikes the Titans down,
Not when they set about their mountain-piling
But when another rock would crown the work.
And Phaeton—doubtless his first radiant plunge
Astonished mortals, though the gods were calm,
And Jove prepared his thunder: all old tales!
FESTUS And what are these to you?
PARACELSUS Ay, fiends must laugh
So cruelly, so well! most like I never
Could tread a single pleasure underfoot,
But they were grinning by my side, were chuckling
To see me toil and drop away by flakes!
Hell-spawn! I am glad, most glad, that thus I fail!
Your cunning has o'ershot its aim. One year,

118| *MS:* Festus—Festus!— — PARACELSUS —I would have asked if he *1835:* Festus, Festus! PARACELSUS I < > ask'd *1849:* Festus, your Festus! PARACELSUS Ask him if Aprile 119| *MS:* Loves . . . if < > Love as well § capitalized initials in print § *1835:* KNOWS as he LOVES—if < > LOVE *1849:* Knows < > Loves < > Love and Know? 120| *MS:* As Know § capitalized initial in print § — —but < > cold— — —. *1835:* KNOW: but < > cold. *1849:* I try; but < > cold! 121| *MS:* Dear Aureole— — PARACELSUS Ah the *1835:* Dear Aureole . . . PARACELSUS Ah, the *1849:* My hand, see! PARACELSUS 122| *MS:* near— —so *1835:* near—so *1849:* near! 123| *MS:*—Tis tale—Jove < > down *1835:* 'Tis < > tale: Jove *1888:* down, 124| *1835:* mountain-piling, *1868:* mountain-piling 125| *MS:* crown their work!— *1835:* work! *1868:* crown the work. 126| *MS:*— —And Phaeton . . . doubtless *1835:* And Phæton—doubtless 127| *MS:* Mortals—but the Gods < > calm *1835:* Astonish'd mortals; but the gods < > calm, *1849:* Astonished mortals; though the *1868:* mortals, though 128| *MS:* thunder—all *1835:* thunder: all old tales. *1849:* tales! 129| *MS:* Ay, they must *1849:* Ay, fiends must 130| *MS:* well— — —most *1835:* well; most *1888:* well! most 131| *MS:* underfoot *1835:* under foot *1849:* foot, *1863:* underfoot, 132| *MS:* side— —were *1835:* side, were 133| *MS:* flakes:— *1835:* toil, and < > flakes. *1849:* flakes! *1863:* toil and 134–135| *MS:* glad— —most glad that < > fail! / —Your < > aim;—one year *1835:* glad, most glad, that < > / Your < > aim. One year, *1849:* fail! / You that hate men and all who wish their good— / Your *1863:* fail! / Your

One month, perhaps, and I had served your turn!
You should have curbed your spite awhile. But now,
Who will believe 'twas you that held me back?
Listen: there's shame and hissing and contempt,
And none but laughs who names me, none but spits
Measureless scorn upon me, me alone,
The quack, the cheat, the liar,—all on me!
And thus your famous plan to sink mankind
In silence and despair, by teaching them
One of their race had probed the inmost truth,
Had done all man could do, yet failed no less—
Your wise plan proves abortive. Men despair?
Ha, ha! why, they are hooting the empiric,
The ignorant and incapable fool who rushed
Madly upon a work beyond his wits;
Nor doubt they but the simplest of themselves
Could bring the matter to triumphant issue.
So, pick and choose among them all, accursed!
Try now, persuade some other to slave for you,
To ruin body and soul to work your ends!
No, no; I am the first and last, I think.

136| *MS:* month perhaps and *1835:* month, perhaps, and <> turn: *1849:* turn! **137**| *MS:*—You <> awhile:——but now *1835:* You <> curb'd <> awhile. But now, *1849:* curbed **138**| *MS:* You *1835:* you **139**| *MS:* contempt—— *1835:* shame, and hissing, and contempt, *1868:* shame and hissing and **140**| *MS:* me——none *1835:* me—none *1863:* me, none
141| *MS:* me . . . 'tis on *me* *1835:* me; 'tis on *me,* *1849:* me—me alone, *1863:* me, me **142**| *MS:* quack, the liar, the arch-cheat—all on *me!* *1835: me.* *1849:* quack, the cheat, the liar,—all on me! **143**| *MS:* Mankind *1835:* mankind **144**| *MS:* In uttermost despair by *1835:* despair, by *1849:* In silence and despair **145**| *MS:* truth *1835:* truth, **146**| *MS:* Man <> failed in all . . *1835:* man <> fail'd in all— *1849:* failed no less—
147| *MS:*——Your plan has proved abortive——*They* despair? *1835:* Your <> abortive. *They* *1849:* Your wise plan proves abortive. Men despair?
148| *MS:* Ha ha, why they <> empiric *1835:* Ha, ha! why <> empiric, *1863:* why, they **149**| *MS:* who thrust *1849:* who rushed **150**| *MS:* Himself upon <> wits, *1849:* Madly upon <> wits; **151**| *MS:* doubt but the the § cancelled by § doubting but the *1849:* doubt they but the **152**| *MS:* issue! *1863:* issue. **153**| *MS:* So pick <> Accursed! *1835:* accursed! *1849:* Accursed! *1863:* choose, among <> accursed! *1868:* So, pick and choose among **154**| *MS:* now,—persuade <> you *1835:* now, persuade <> you, **155**| *1835:* ends: *1863:* ends! **156**| *MS:* No—no! I am <> think! *1835:* No, no; I am <> think. *1849:* think! *1863:* think.

FESTUS Dear friend, who are accursed? who has done . . .
PARACELSUS What have I done? Fiends dare ask that? or you,
Brave men? Oh, you can chime in boldly, backed
By the others! What had you to do, sage peers?
Here stand my rivals; Latin, Arab, Jew,
Greek, join dead hands against me: all I ask
Is, that the world enrol my name with theirs,
And even this poor privilege, it seems,
They range themselves, prepared to disallow.
Only observe! why, fiends may learn from them!
How they talk calmly of my throes, my fierce
Aspirings, terrible watchings, each one claiming
Its price of blood and brain; how they dissect
And sneeringly disparage the few truths
Got at a life's cost; they too hanging the while
About my neck, their lies misleading me
And their dead names browbeating me! Grey crew,
Yet steeped in fresh malevolence from hell,
Is there a reason for your hate? My truths
Have shaken a little the palm about each prince?
Just think, Aprile, all these leering dotards
Were bent on nothing less than to be crowned

157| *MS:* Sweet friend——who < > done——— *1835:* friend; who < > done . . . *1849:* Dear friend *1863:* friend, who 158| *MS:* done? you dare < > *You* *1835: you,* *1849:* done? Fiends dare < > you, 159| *MS:* Brave Ones——Oh, *you* *1835:* ones? Oh < > back'd *1849:* Brave men? Oh, you < > backed 160–166| *MS:* By them——and what had *you* to do, wise Peers? / —Only observe——why fiends may learn of them § cancelled by § learn from them! *1835:* them; and < > peers? / Only observe: why *1849:* By the others! What had you to do, sage peers? / Here stand my rivals, truly—Arab, Jew, / Greek, join dead hands against me: all I ask / Is, that the world enrol my name with theirs, / And even this poor privilege, it seems, / They range themselves, prepared to disallow! / Only 161| *1863:* rivals; Latin, Arab 166| *1888:* observe! why 167| *MS:* throes— my *1863:* throes, my 168| *MS:* Aspirings—terrible watchings each *1835:* Aspirings, terrible watchings—each *1863:* watchings, each 169| *MS:* brain—how *1835:* brain; how 171| *MS:* cost—they *1835:* cost; they 172| *MS:* neck——their *1835:* neck, their < > me, *1863:* me 173–175| *MS:* Their < > me——Damned § written over by § me!—Damned Crew / Is < > hate?——my *1835:* brow-beating me. Wretched crew! / Is < > hate? My *1849:* And their < > me! Grey crew, / Yet steeped in fresh malevolence from hell, / Is *1863:* browbeating 176| *MS:* each brow? *1849:* each head? *1863:* each prince? 177| *MS:* Aprile——all *1835:* Aprile, all 178| *MS:* be Kings *1835:* kings *1849:* than being crowned *1863:* than to be crowned

As we! That yellow blear-eyed wretch in chief
To whom the rest cringe low with feigned respect,
Galen of Pergamos and hell—nay speak
The tale, old man! We met there face to face:
I said the crown should fall from thee. Once more
We meet as in that ghastly vestibule:
Look to my brow! Have I redeemed my pledge?
FESTUS Peace, peace; ah, see!
PARACELSUS Oh, emptiness of fame!
Oh Persic Zoroaster, lord of stars!
—Who said these old renowns, dead long ago,
Could make me overlook the living world
To gaze through gloom at where they stood, indeed,
But stand no longer? What a warm light life
After the shade! In truth, my delicate witch,
My serpent-queen, you did but well to hide
The juggles I had else detected. Fire
May well run harmless o'er a breast like yours!
The cave was not so darkened by the smoke
But that your white limbs dazzled me: oh, white,
And panting as they twinkled, wildly dancing!
I cared not for your passionate gestures then,

179| *MS:* that <> wretch, in chief *1835:* That <> wretch in chief, *1863:* chief 180| *MS:* respect— *1835:* feign'd *1849:* feigned *1863:* respect, 181| *MS:* Galen—of <> Hell——nay *1835:* Galen, of <> hell; nay *1863:* Galen of <> hell—nay 182–192| *MS:* man—how we met face to face . . . ° § footnote § °—He did in effect affirm that he had disputed with Galen in the vestibule of Hell. / Peace, peace—ah see! PARACELSUS —In truth my *1835:* to face . . . ° § footnote § °He <> hell. / Peace, peace; ah, see! PARACELSUS In *1849:* tale, old man! We met there face to face; § footnote dropped § / I said the crown should fall from thee; once more / We meet as in that ghastly vestibule: / Look to my brow! Have I redeemed my pledge? / FESTUS Peace, peace <> see! PARACELSUS Oh, emptiness of fame! / Oh Persic Zoroaster, lord of stars! / —Who said these old renowns, dead long ago, / Could make me overlook the living world / To gaze through gloom at where they stood, indeed, / But stand no longer? What a warm light life / After the shade! In truth, my 183| *1863:* thee. Once 194| *MS:* detected———fire *1835:* detected. Fire 196| *MS:* not so darkened § *so* inserted above the line § *1835:* darken'd *1849:* darkened 197| *MS:* me——O white, *1835:* me. O *1849:* Oh, white, *1863:* oh 199| *MS:* then,— *1835:* then,

But now I have forgotten the charm of charms,
The foolish knowledge which I came to seek,
While I remember that quaint dance; and thus
I am come back, not for those mummeries,
But to love you, and to kiss your little feet
Soft as an ermine's winter coat!

FESTUS A light
Will struggle through these thronging words at last,
As in the angry and tumultuous West
A soft star trembles through the drifting clouds.
These are the strivings of a spirit which hates
So sad a vault should coop it, and calls up
The past to stand between it and its fate.
Were he at Einsiedeln—or Michal here!

PARACELSUS Cruel! I seek her now—I kneel—I shriek—
I clasp her vesture—but she fades, still fades;
And she is gone; sweet human love is gone!
'Tis only when they spring to heaven that angels
Reveal themselves to you; they sit all day
Beside you, and lie down at night by you
Who care not for their presence, muse or sleep,
And all at once they leave you, and you know them!
We are so fooled, so cheated! Why, even now
I am not too secure against foul play;

200–202| *MS:* now, I <> Charm of Charms / While <> dance;—and *1835:* now I <> charm of charms / <> dance; and *1849:* of charms, / The foolish knowledge which I came to seek, / While **204|** *1835:* feet, *1863:* feet **205|** *MS:* winter-coat! FESTUS—A *1835:* winter coat! FESTUS A *1849:* A sense *1863:* A light **206|** *MS:* thro <> last, *1835:* through *1888:* last. **207|** *MS:* West *1835:* west *1863:* West **208|** *MS:* thro' <> clouds—— *1835:* through <> clouds: *1849:* clouds. **209|** *MS:*——These are the § *are* inserted above the line § *1835:* These **211|** *MS:* fate: *1863:* Past <> fate. *1868:* past **212|** *MS:* Einsiedeln—or <> here . . . . *1835:* Einsiedeln—or <> here . . . *1849* here! **213|** *MS:* Cruel——I seek *1835:* Cruel . . . I seek *1849:* Cruel! I seek **214|** *MS:* vesture——but she fades—still fades *1835:* vesture—but she fades, still fades; **215|** *MS:* gone—sweet Human Love *1835:* gone; sweet human love **216|** *MS:* Tis <> Angels *1835:* 'Tis <> angels **217|** *MS:* you——they *1835:* you; they **218|** *MS:* you and *1835:* you, and <> you, *1863:* by you **219|** *MS:* presence—muse or sleep— *1863:* presence, muse or sleep, **220|** *MS:* you and *1888:* you, and **221|** fooled—so cheated!—even *1835:* fool'd, so cheated! Even *1849:* fooled, so cheated! Why, even **222|** *MS:* play— *1835:* play: *1868:* play;

The shadows deepen and the walls contract:
No doubt some treachery is going on.
'Tis very dusk. Where are we put, Aprile?
Have they left us in the lurch? This murky loathsome
Death-trap, this slaughter-house, is not the hall
In the golden city! Keep by me, Aprile!
There is a hand groping amid the blackness
To catch us. Have the spider-fingers got you,
Poet? Hold on me for your life! If once
They pull you!—Hold!
'Tis but a dream—no more!
I have you still; the sun comes out again;
Let us be happy: all will yet go well!
Let us confer: is it not like, Aprile,
That spite of trouble, this ordeal passed,
The value of my labours ascertained,
Just as some stream foams long among the rocks
But after glideth glassy to the sea,
So, full content shall henceforth be my lot?
What think you, poet? Louder! Your clear voice
Vibrates too like a harp-string. Do you ask
How could I still remain on earth, should God
Grant me the great approval which I seek?

223| *MS:* deepen—and < > contract— *1835:* deepen, and *1863:* deepen and *1868:* contract: 224| *MS:* on! *1868:* on. 225| *MS:* Tis < > dusk——where *1835:* 'Tis < > dusk. Where 226| *MS:* this *1835:* This *1849:* murky, loathsome *1868:* murky loathsome 227| *MS:* Death-trap—this slaughter-house——is *1835:* slaughter-house—is *1863:* Death-trap, this slaughter-house, is 228| *MS:* City! . . keep < > Aprile *1835:* city! Keep < > Aprile, *1849:* me, Aprile! 229| *MS:*——There *1835:* There 230| *MS:* us——have < > you *1835:* us. Have < > you, 231| *MS:* Dearest?—hold < > life——if *1835:* hold < > life; if *1849:* Poet? Hold *1863:* life! if *1868:* If 232| *MS:* you . . Hold——/ Tis < > dream!—no more. *1835:* you . . . Hold . . . / 'Tis < > dream—no 233| *MS:* still——the < > again *1835:* still—the < > again; *1849:* you!—Hold! *1863:* still; the 234| *MS:* happy——all *1835:* happy—all *1863:* happy: all 235| *MS:* confer—is *1835:* confer: is 236| *MS:* of gone-by trouble, this *1835:* pass'd, *1849:* of trouble < > passed, 237| *1835:* ascertain'd, *1849:* ascertained, 239| *MS:* sea *1835:* sea, 241| *MS:* Poet—Louder! your *1835:* poet? Louder! Your 242| *MS:* harp-string:——is it so? *1835:* harp-string. Is *1849:* harp-string. Do you ask 243| *MS:* "How couldst thou still *1849:* How could I still 244| *MS:* Grant thee the < > approval thou dost seek? *1849:* Grant me the < > approval which I seek?

I, you, and God can comprehend each other,
But men would murmur, and with cause enough;
For when they saw me, stainless of all sin,
Preserved and sanctified by inward light,
They would complain that comfort, shut from them,
I drank thus unespied; that they live on,
Nor taste the quiet of a constant joy,
For ache and care and doubt and weariness,
While I am calm; help being vouchsafed to me,
And hid from them.—'Twere best consider that!
You reason well, Aprile; but at least
Let me know this, and die! Is this too much?
I will learn this, if God so please, and die!

If thou shalt please, dear God, if thou shalt please!
We are so weak, we know our motives least
In their confused beginning. If at first
I sought . . . but wherefore bare my heart to thee?
I know thy mercy; and already thoughts
Flock fast about my soul to comfort it,
And intimate I cannot wholly fail,
For love and praise would clasp me willingly

245| *MS:* I, thou and God, can *1835:* thou, and God can *1849:* I, you, and 246| *MS:* Men <> murmur and <> enough;— *1835:* men <> murmur, and <> enough; 247| *MS:* saw thee stainless *1835:* thee, stainless *1849:* saw me, stainless 249| *MS:* complain 'a comfort shut from us *1835:* complain—' a <> us, *1849:* complain that comfort, shut from them, 250| *MS:* He drinketh unespied——for we live on *1835:* unespied; for <> on, *1849:* I drank thus unespied; that they live 251| *MS:* joy *1835:* joy, 252| *MS:* For ache, and care <> weariness,— *1835:* care, and doubt, and weariness, *1863:* ache and care and doubt and 253| *MS:* While He is calm! Help is vouchsafed to Him *1835:* he <> him, *1849:* While I am calm; help being vouchsafed to me, 254| *MS:* from us!' "—twere <> that *1835:* us!' " 'Twere <> that: *1849:* from them!—'Twere <> that! *1868:* them.—'Twere 255| *MS:*—You <> Aprile,—but *1835:* You <> Aprile; but 256| *MS:* die!—is that too *1835:* die! Is *1849:* Is this too 258| *1863:* Thou <> Thou *1868:* thou <> thou 259| *MS:* . . . . We are so weak we *1835:* We are *1849:* weak, we 260| *MS:* beginning; . . . if *1835:* beginning: if *1863:* beginning. If 261| *MS:* sought . . but *1835:* sought . . . But *1863:* but <> bear <> Thee? *1868:* bare <> thee? 262| *MS:* mercy—and *1835:* mercy; and *1863:* Thy *1868:* thy 263| *1863:* it *1868:* it, 264| *MS:* To intimate <> fail,— *1835:* fail, *1849:* And intimate 265| *MS:* That love *1849:* For love

Could I resolve to seek them. Thou art good,
And I should be content. Yet—yet first show
I have done wrong in daring! Rather give
The supernatural consciousness of strength
Which fed my youth! Only one hour of that
With thee to help—O what should bar me then!

Lost, lost! Thus things are ordered here! God's creatures,
And yet he takes no pride in us!—none, none!
Truly there needs another life to come!
If this be all—(I must tell Festus that)
And other life await us not—for one,
I say 'tis a poor cheat, a stupid bungle,
A wretched failure. I, for one, protest
Against it, and I hurl it back with scorn.

Well, onward though alone! Small time remains,
And much to do: I must have fruit, must reap
Some profit from my toils. I doubt my body
Will hardly serve me through; while I have laboured
It has decayed; and now that I demand
Its best assistance, it will crumble fast:
A sad thought, a sad fate! How very full

266| *MS:* them:—Thou art good *1835:* them . . . Thou art good, *1849:* them: Thou *1863:* them. Thou 267| *MS:* content, yet,——yet *1835:* content; yet—yet *1863:* content. Yet—yet 268| *MS:* daring!—rather *1835:* daring! Rather 270| *MS:* That fed my youth——one only hour *1835:* youth . . . one *1849:* youth—one *1863:* youth! One *1868:* Which fed my youth! Only one hour 271| *MS:* Thee to help—O <> then!——— *1835:* thee to help—O <> then! *1863:* Thee *1868:* thee 272| *MS:* Lost, lost!—thus *1835:* Lost, lost! thus <> order'd <> creatures! *1849:* Thus <> ordered <> creatures, 273| *MS:* none! none! *1835:* none, none! *1863:* He *1868:* he 275| *MS:* that— § written over by § that) *1835:* that) 276| *MS:* not . . . for one *1835:* not—for *1849:* one, 277| *MS:* cheat—a <> bungle *1835:* cheat, a <> bungle, 278| *MS:* failure . . I *1835:* failure. I 279| *MS:* it——and <> scorn! . . . *1835:* it—and <> scorn! *1863:* it, and *1868:* scorn. 280| *MS:* well—onward tho' alone: small *1835:* Well, onward though *1868:* alone! Small 281| *MS:* do:—I <> fruit—must *1835:* do: I <> fruit, must 282| *MS:* toils——I *1835:* toils. I 283| *MS:* through——while *1835:* through: while <> labour'd *1849:* laboured *1863:* through; while 284| *MS:* decayed——and *1835:* decay'd; and *1849:* decayed 285| *MS:* fast—— *1835:* fast: 286| *MS:* thought—a sad fate!—how *1835:* fate! How *1863:* thought, a

Of wormwood 'tis, that just at altar-service,
The rapt hymn rising with the rolling smoke,
When glory dawns and all is at the best,
The sacred fire may flicker and grow faint
And die for want of a wood-piler's help!
Thus fades the flagging body, and the soul
Is pulled down in the overthrow. Well, well—
Let men catch every word, let them lose nought
Of what I say; something may yet be done.

They are ruins! Trust me who am one of you!
All ruins, glorious once, but lonely now.
It makes my heart sick to behold you crouch
Beside your desolate fane: the arches dim,
The crumbling columns grand against the moon,
Could I but rear them up once more—but that
May never be, so leave them! Trust me, friends,
Why should you linger here when I have built
A far resplendent temple, all your own?
Trust me, they are but ruins! See, Aprile,
Men will not heed! Yet were I not prepared
With better refuge for them, tongue of mine
Should ne'er reveal how blank their dwelling is:

287| *MS:* Altar-service, *1835:* altar-service, 288| *MS:*—The *1835:* The 289| *MS:* dawns, and < > best,— *1835:* best— *1863:* dawns and *1868:* best, 290| *1835:* faint, *1849:* flicker, and *1863:* flicker and < > faint 291| *MS:* die———for *1835:* die, for *1863:* die for 293| *MS:* overthrow:—well—well— *1835:* pull'd < > overthrow: well, well— *1849:* pulled *1863:* overthrow. Well, well— 294| *MS:* Men < > word—let < > lose nothing *1835:* men *1849:* lose nought *1863:* word, let 295| *MS:* say . . something < > done:——— *1835:* say; something < > done. 296| *MS:* trust *1849:* Trust 297| *MS:* ruins——glorious once but < > now—— *1835:* ruins—glorious once, but < > now: *1849:* now. *1863:* ruins, glorious 298| *MS:* crouching *1849:* crouch 299| *MS:* fane——its arches dim *1835:* fane; its *1849:* fane; the arches *1863:* fane: the 300| *MS:* Its crumbling < > moon—— *1835:* moon: *1849:* The crumbling *1863:* moon— *1868:* moon, 301| *MS:* more——but *1835:* more—but 302| *MS:* be—so < > me Friends! *1835:* be, so < > friends, *1849:* me, friends, 304| *MS:* Temple < > own *1835:* temple < > own? 305| *MS:* me—they < > ruins!——see—Aprile *1835:* me, they < > ruins! see Aprile, *1849:* See, Aprile, 306| *MS:* They will < > yet *1835:* prepar'd *1849:* Men will < > Yet < > prepared 307| *MS:* them, never should tongue *1849:* them, tongue of mine 308| *MS:* Of mine reveal < > is——— *1835:* is; *1849:* Should ne'er reveal *1863:* is:

I would sit down in silence with the rest.

Ha, what? you spit at me, you grin and shriek
Contempt into my ear—my ear which drank
God's accents once? you curse me? Why men, men,
I am not formed for it! Those hideous eyes
Will be before me sleeping, waking, praying,
They will not let me even die. Spare, spare me,
Sinning or no, forget that, only spare me
The horrible scorn! You thought I could support it,
But now you see what silly fragile creature
Cowers thus. I am not good nor bad enough,
Not Christ nor Cain, yet even Cain was saved
From Hate like this. Let me but totter back!
Perhaps I shall elude those jeers which creep
Into my very brain, and shut these scorched
Eyelids and keep those mocking faces out.

Listen, Aprile! I am very calm:
Be not deceived, there is no passion here
Where the blood leaps like an imprisoned thing:
I am calm: I will exterminate the race!

309| *MS:* rest! *1835:* rest. 310| *MS:* Ha——what? spit at me——and grin *1835:* Ha, what <> me, and *1849:* what? you spit at me, you grin 312| *MS:* once—and curse <> why Men, Men, *1835:* once, and <> Why men, men, *1849:* once? you 313| *MS:* it——those *1835:* form'd for it; those *1849:* formed for it! Those 314| *MS:* praying *1835:* praying; *1849:* Follow me sleeping <> praying God, *1863:* Will be before me sleeping <> praying, 315| *MS:* die——spare, spare me *1835:* die: spare, spare me, *1849:* And will <> me. *1863:* They will <> die. Spare, spare me, 316| *MS:*—Sinning <> that— § above § , only *1835:* Sinning <> that, only 317| *MS:* That horrible scorn——you <> it *1835:* scorn; you <> it, *1863:* scorn! You *1888:* it. 319| *MS:* I am——I <> enough—— *1835:* am. I <> enough, *1849:* Cowers thus. I 320| *MS:* Not Christ——nor Cain——yet *1835:* Not Christ, nor Cain, yet *1863:* Christ nor 321| *MS:* hate <> this——let <> back—— *1835:* this: let <> back, *1863:* this. Let <> back! *1888:* Hate 322| *MS:* shall forget those *1849:* shall elude those 323| *1835:* scorch'd *1849:* scorched 324| *MS:* out——— *1835:* Eyelids, and <> out. *1863:* out. § end of page § *1868:* out. § end of page § *1888:* out. / § space § 325| *MS:* Listen Aprile <> calm— *1835:* calm: *1849:* Listen, Aprile 326| *MS:*—Be not deceived—there *1835:* Be not deceived, there <> here, *1863:* here 327| *MS:* thing——— *1835:* imprison'd thing. *1849:* imprisoned *1863:* thing:

Enough of that: 'tis said and it shall be.
And now be merry: safe and sound am I
Who broke through their best ranks to get at you.
And such a havoc, such a rout, Aprile!
FESTUS Have you no thought, no memory for me,
Aureole? I am so wretched—my pure Michal
Is gone, and you alone are left me now,
And even you forget me. Take my hand—
Lean on me thus. Do you not know me, Aureole?
PARACELSUS Festus, my own friend, you are come at last?
As you say, 'tis an awful enterprise;
But you believe I shall go through with it:
'Tis like you, and I thank you. Thank him for me,
Dear Michal! See how bright St. Saviour's spire
Flames in the sunset; all its figures quaint
Gay in the glancing light: you might conceive them
A troop of yellow-vested white-haired Jews
Bound for their own land where redemption dawns.
FESTUS Not that blest time—not our youth's time, dear God!
PARACELSUS Ha—stay! true, I forget—all is done since,
And he is come to judge me. How he speaks,
How calm, how well! yes, it is true, all true;

329| *MS:* be: *1835:* be . . . *1849:* be. **330**| *MS:* merry——safe <> I, *1835:* merry—safe *1863:* merry: safe <> I **331**| *MS:* thro' <> you, *1835:* through *1849:* you; *1863:* you. **332**| *MS:* rout Aprile!——— *1835:* Aprile! . . . *1849:* rout, Aprile! **333**| *MS:* me *1849:* me, **334**| *MS:* Aureole?—I <> wretched . . . my *1835:* Aureole? I <> wretched—my **335**| *MS:* gone——and <> left to me, *1835:* gone, and *1868:* left me now, **336**| *MS:* me——take my hand *1835:* me—take my hand— *1849:* me: take *1863:* me. Take **337**| *MS:* thus . . do <> me Aureole? *1835:* thus. Do *1849:* me, thus <> me, Aureole? *1868:* me thus **338**| *MS:* Festus,—my own friend—you <> last?——— *1835:* Festus, my own friend, you <> last? **339**| *MS:* enterprise——— *1835:* enterprise— *1863:* enterprise; **340**| *MS:* thro' <> it:— *1835:* through <> it: **341**| *MS:* Tis <> thank you;——thank <> me *1835:* 'Tis <> thank you; thank <> me, *1863:* thank you. Thank **342**| *MS:* Michal!——see *1835:* Michal! See **343**| *MS:* sunset—all *1835:* sunset; all **344**| *MS:* light—you *1835:* light: you **345–347**| *MS:* yellow-vested, white-haired Jews . . . . . / Not <> blessed *1835:* white-hair'd Jews . . . *1849:* white-haired Jews, / Bound for their own land where redemption dawns! / Not <> blest *1863:* yellow-vested white-haired Jews *1868:* dawns. **348**| *MS:* Ha——stay—true I forget——all <> since! *1835:* Ha—stay! true, I forget—all *1868:* since, **349**| *MS:* me:—how he speaks,— *1835:* me: how he speaks, *1863:* me. How **350**| *MS:* calm—how <> true—all true: *1835:* How calm, how <> true, all true;

All quackery; all deceit; myself can laugh
The first at it, if you desire: but still
You know the obstacles which taught me tricks
So foreign to my nature—envy and hate,
Blind opposition, brutal prejudice,
Bald ignorance—what wonder if I sunk
To humour men the way they most approved?
My cheats were never palmed on such as you,
Dear Festus! I will kneel if you require me,
Impart the meagre knowledge I possess,
Explain its bounded nature, and avow
My insufficiency—whate'er you will:
I give the fight up: let there be an end,
A privacy, an obscure nook for me.
I want to be forgotten even by God.
But if that cannot be, dear Festus, lay me,
When I shall die, within some narrow grave,
Not by itself—for that would be too proud—
But where such graves are thickest; let it look
Nowise distinguished from the hillocks round,
So that the peasant at his brother's bed
May tread upon my own and know it not;
And we shall all be equal at the last,
Or classed according to life's natural ranks,
Fathers, sons, brothers, friends—not rich, nor wise,

351| *MS:* quackery—all deceit! myself *1835:* quackery; all *1868:* deceit; myself 352| *MS:* desire——but *1835:* desire: but 354| *MS:* nature——envy and hate,— *1835:* nature—envy, and hate— *1863:* envy and hate, 355| *MS:* opposition,—brutal prejudice— *1835* opposition—brutal *1863:* opposition, brutal prejudice, 356| *MS:* ignorance——what *1835:* ignorance—what 357| *MS:* humour them the *1849:* humour men the 358| *MS:* you *1835:* palm'd <> you, *1849:* palmed 359| *MS:* Festus . . . I *1835:* Festus. I *1849:* Festus! I 362| *MS:* will:— *1835:* will: 363| *MS:* up!—let <> end,— *1835:* up! let <> end, *1868:* up: let 364| *MS:* privacy— § above § , an <> me—— *1835:* privacy, an <> me. 365| *MS:* God! *1868:* God. 366| *MS:* be,——dear <> me *1835:* be, dear *1849:* me, 367| *MS:* grave *1835:* grave, 368| *MS:*—Not by itself——for <> proud:—— *1835:* Not by itself—for <> proud— 369| *MS:* thickest; see it *1849:* thickest; let it 370| *MS:* round *1835:* distinguish'd <> round, *1849:* distinguished 372| *MS:* Shall tread *1849:* May tread 373| *MS:* So we *1849:* And we 374| *1835:* class'd *1849:* classed 375| *MS:* friends——not rich nor wise *1835:* friends—not rich, nor wise,

Nor gifted: lay me thus, then say, "He lived
Too much advanced before his brother men;
They kept him still in front: 'twas for their good
But yet a dangerous station. It were strange
That he should tell God he had never ranked
With men: so, here at least he is a man."
FESTUS That God shall take thee to his breast, dear spirit,
Unto his breast, be sure! and here on earth
Shall splendour sit upon thy name for ever.
Sun! all the heaven is glad for thee: what care
If lower mountains light their snowy phares
At thine effulgence, yet acknowledge not
The source of day? Their theft shall be their bale:
For after-ages shall retrack thy beams,
And put aside the crowd of busy ones
And worship thee alone—the master-mind,
The thinker, the explorer, the creator!
Then, who should sneer at the convulsive throes
With which thy deeds were born, would scorn as well
The sheet of winding subterraneous fire
Which, pent and writhing, sends no less at last
Huge islands up amid the simmering sea.
Behold thy might in me! thou hast infused

376| *MS:* thus,—then say "He *1835:* thus, then *1863:* say, "He 377| *MS:* Men:— *1835:* men: *1863:* men; 378| *MS:* Front——'twas <> good, *1835:* front; 'twas *1863:* front: 'twas <> good 379| *MS:* But still a <> station——strange it were *1835:* station. Strange *1849:* But yet a <> station. It were strange 380| *1835:* rank'd *1849:* ranked 381| *MS:* Men:——so here <> "Man!" *1835:* men: so <> man!" *1849:* so, here 382| *MS:* PARACELSUS That <> Spirit, *1835:* FESTUS That *1863:* His <> spirit, *1868:* his 383| *MS:*—Unto <> sure!——and *1835:* Unto <> sure! and *1863:* His *1868:* his 384| *MS:* forever! *1835:* for ever! *1868:* ever. 385| *MS:*—Sun!—all <> thee!——what *1835:* Sun! all <> thee: what 387| *MS:* effulgence yet *1835:* effulgence, yet 388| *MS:* day?——their <> bale, *1835:* day? their <> bale, *1849:* day? Men look up to the sun: *1863:* day? Their theft shall be their bale: 389| *MS:* retrack the beams, *1835:* after ages *1849:* after-ages <> retrack thy beams, 390| *1835:* ones, *1863:* ones 391| *MS:* alone——the Master mind *1835:* alone—the master-mind, 392| *MS:* Thinker <> Explorer <> Creator— *1835:* thinker <> explorer <> creator; *1849:* creator! 393| *MS:* And who *1849:* Then, who 394| *MS:* born— § above § , would *1835:* born would *1849:* born, would 395| *MS:* The winding sheet of subterraneous *1868:* winding-sheet *1888:* The sheet of winding subterraneous 397| *MS:* sea! *1868:* sea. 398| *MS:*—Behold *1835:* Behold

Thy soul in mine; and I am grand as thou,
Seeing I comprehend thee—I so simple,
Thou so august. I recognize thee first;
I saw thee rise, I watched thee early and late,
And though no glance reveal thou dost accept
My homage—thus no less I proffer it,
And bid thee enter gloriously thy rest.

PARACELSUS Festus!

FESTUS I am for noble Aureole, God!
I am upon his side, come weal or woe.
His portion shall be mine. He has done well.
I would have sinned, had I been strong enough,
As he has sinned. Reward him or I waive
Reward! If thou canst find no place for him,
He shall be king elsewhere, and I will be
His slave for ever. There are two of us.

PARACELSUS Dear Festus!

FESTUS Here, dear Aureole! ever by you!

PARACELSUS Nay, speak on, or I dream again. Speak on!
Some story, anything—only your voice.
I shall dream else. Speak on! ay, leaning so!

FESTUS Thus the Mayne glideth
Where my Love abideth.

399| *MS:* mine——and <> thou *1835:* mine; and <> thou, 400| *MS:* thee——I so simple *1835:* thee—I so simple, 401| *MS:* august! I <> thee, first! *1835:* thee first; *1868:* august. I 402| *MS:* rise and I have watched thee well *1835:* rise, and <> watch'd <> well, *1849:* rise, I watched thee early and late, 403| *MS:* tho' <> reveal that thou acceptest *1835:* though *1849:* reveal thou dost accept 404| *MS:* homage——thus <> it *1835:* homage—thus <> it, 405| *MS:* Rest! *1835:* rest! *1868:* rest. 406| *MS:*—Festus!—— FESTUS ——I *1835:* Festus! FESTUS I 407| *MS:* woe! *1868:* woe. 408| *MS:* mine!—He <> well! *1835:* mine! He *1868:* mine. He <> well. 409| *MS:*—I *1835:* I <> sinn'd *1849:* sinned 410| *MS:* sinned! Reward *1835:* sinn'd *1849:* sinned *1868:* sinned. Reward 411| *MS:* Reward!—if *1835:* Reward! If *1863:* Thou *1868:* thou 412| *MS:* King *1835:* king 413| *MS:* ever!———there <> us!— *1835:* ever! . . . There <> us! *1849:* ever! There *1868:* ever. There 414| *MS:* FESTUS—Here *1835:* FESTUS Here 415| *MS:* Nay speak <> again——speak *1835:* Nay, speak <> again. Speak 416| *MS:*—Some story—anything . . only <> voice— *1835:* Some story, any thing—only <> voice. *1863:* anything 417| *MS:* else—speak on *1835:* else. Speak on! *1849:* on! ay, leaning so! 418| *1849:* Softly the Mayne river glideth *1863:* Thus the Mayne glideth 419| *1835:* love abideth; *1849:* Close by where my love abideth; *1863:* Where my Love abideth.

Sleep's no softer: it proceeds
On through lawns, on through meads,
On and on, whate'er befall,
Meandering and musical,
Though the niggard pasturage
Bears not on its shaven ledge
Aught but weeds and waving grasses
To view the river as it passes,
Save here and there a scanty patch
Of primroses too faint to catch
A weary bee.

PARACELSUS More, more; say on!

FESTUS And scarce it pushes
Its gentle way through strangling rushes
Where the glossy kingfisher
Flutters when noon-heats are near,
Glad the shelving banks to shun,
Red and steaming in the sun,
Where the shrew-mouse with pale throat
Burrows, and the speckled stoat;
Where the quick sandpipers flit
In and out the marl and grit
That seems to breed them, brown as they:
Nought disturbs its quiet way,
Save some lazy stork that springs,
Trailing it with legs and wings,

421| *MS:* thro' <> thro' meads *1835:* through <> through meads, 422| *MS:* and on whate'er *1835:* and on, whate'er 423| *MS:* musical *1835:* musical, 424| *MS:* Tho' *1835:* Though *1849:* pasture's edge *1863:* pasturage 425| *MS:* shaven edge *1849:* shaven ledge 427| *MS:* To behold it as *1849:* To view the river as 429| *1835:* primroses, too *1868:* primroses too 430| *MS:* bee—— *1835:* bee . . . *1863:* bee. 431| *MS:* More,—more—say *1835:* More, more; say *1849:* FESTUS The river pushes *1863:* FESTUS And scare it pushes 432| *MS:* thro' *1835:* through <> rushes, *1888:* rushes 433| *MS:* king-fisher *1863:* kingfisher 434| *MS:* near *1835:* near, 435| *MS:* shun *1835:* shun, 436| *MS:* sun *1835:* sun, 438| *MS:* Burrows—and <> stoat— *1835:* Burrows, and <> stoat, *1863:* stoat; 439| *MS:* sand-pipers *1863:* sandpipers 440| *MS:* the soft and wet *1849:* the marl and grit 441| *MS:* Clay that breeds *1835:* they. *1849:* That seems to breed them *1863:* they: 442| *MS:*—Nought <> way *1835:* Nought <> way, *1849:* disturbs the river's way, *1863:* disturbs its quiet way, 443| *MS:* springs *1835:* springs, 444| *MS:* wings *1835:* wings,

Whom the shy fox from the hill
Rouses, creep he ne'er so still.
PARACELSUS My heart! they loose my heart, those simple words;
Its darkness passes, which nought else could touch:
Like some dark snake that force may not expel,
Which glideth out to music sweet and low.
What were you doing when your voice broke through
A chaos of ugly images? You, indeed!
Are you alone here?
FESTUS All alone: you know me?
This cell?
PARACELSUS An unexceptionable vault:
Good brick and stone: the bats kept out, the rats
Kept in: a snug nook: how should I mistake it?
FESTUS But wherefore am I here?
PARACELSUS Ah, well remembered!
Why, for a purpose—for a purpose, Festus!
'Tis like me: here I trifle while time fleets,
And this occasion, lost, will ne'er return.
You are here to be instructed. I will tell
God's message; but I have so much to say,
I fear to leave half out. All is confused
No doubt; but doubtless you will learn in time.
He would not else have brought you here: no doubt

446| *MS:* Arouses— — *1835:* Arouses . . . *1849:* Rouses, creep he ne'er so still. 447| *MS:* heart—they <> heart those <> words— *1835:* heart! they <> heart, those <> words; 448| *MS:* passes which <> touch— *1835:* passes, which <> touch; *1863:* touch: 449| *MS:* expel *1835:* expel, 450| *MS:* low:— *1835:* low. 451| *MS:* thro' *1835:* through 452| *MS:* images . . . . It is you indeed! *1835:* images? . . . It is you, indeed! *1849:* images? You 453| *MS:*—Are <> alone:—you *1835:* Are <> alone: you 454| *MS:*—This <> vault— *1835:* This *1863:* vault: 455| *MS:* stone—the *1863:* stone: the 456| *MS:* in— —a <> nook:—how *1835:* in—a <> nook: how *1863:* in: a 457| *MS:* PARACELSUS—Ah!— —well remembered:— *1835:* PARACELSUS Ah! well remember'd: *1849:* remembered: *1863:* remembered! 458| *MS:* purpose— —for *1835:* purpose—for 459| *MS:* Tis <> me . . . here *1835:* 'Tis <> me: here 460| *MS:* return! *1868:* return. 461| *MS:* instructed— —I *1835:* instructed. I 462| *MS:* Their message— —but <> say *1835:* message; but <> say, *1849:* God's message 463| *MS:* out—all *1835:* out: all *1863:* out. All 464| *MS:* Within—but <> time *1835:* Within; but <> time. *1849:* No doubt; but 465| *MS:*— —They would not have despatched me else— —no *1835:* dispatch'd me else: no *1849:* He would not else have brought you here: no

I shall see clearer soon.
FESTUS Tell me but this—
You are not in despair?
PARACELSUS I? and for what?
FESTUS Alas, alas! he knows not, as I feared!
PARACELSUS What is it you would ask me with that earnest
Dear searching face?
FESTUS How feel you, Aureole?
PARACELSUS Well:
Well. 'Tis a strange thing: I am dying, Festus,
And now that fast the storm of life subsides,
I first perceive how great the whirl has been.
I was calm then, who am so dizzy now—
Calm in the thick of the tempest, but no less
A partner of its motion and mixed up
With its career. The hurricane is spent,
And the good boat speeds through the brightening weather;
But is it earth or sea that heaves below?
The gulf rolls like a meadow-swell, o'erstrewn
With ravaged boughs and remnants of the shore;
And now some islet, loosened from the land,
Swims past with all its trees, sailing to ocean;
And now the air is full of uptorn canes,

466| *MS:* soon:——FESTUS <> this,— *1835:* soon. FESTUS <> this— 467| *MS:* PARACELSUS ——I?—and *1835:* PARACELSUS I? and 468| *MS:* Alas, alas,—he <> not as I feared——— *1835:* Alas, alas! he <> not, as I fear'd . . . *1849:* feared! 469| *1835:* earnest, *1868:* earnest 470| *MS:* Dear, searching <> PARACELSUS —— Well; *1835:* PARACELSUS Well; *1849:* PARACELSUS Well! *1868:* Dear searching <> Well: 471| *MS:* Well:—'tis <> thing;—I *1835:* Well: 'tis <> thing. I *1868:* Well. 'Tis <> thing: I 472| *MS:* now the storm of life is fast subsiding *1849:* now that fast the storm of life subsides, 473| *MS:* how swift the <> been: *1849:* how great the *1863:* been. 474| *MS:* now,— *1835:* now— 476| *1835:* motion, and mix'd *1849:* mixed *1863:* motion and 477| *MS:* career: the *1835:* career. The 478| *MS:* thro' <> weather *1835:* through the bright'ning weather; *1849:* brightening 480| *MS:* meadow-swell—o'erstrewn *1835:* meadow-swell, o'erstrewn *1849:* For the <> a meadow, overstrewn *1863:* The <> meadow-swell, o'erstrewn 481| *MS:* shore *1835:* shore. *1849:* shore; 482| *MS:*——And <> islet loosened *1835:* And <> islet, loosen'd *1849:* loosened *1888:* slet *1889:* islet 483| *MS:* ocean, *1835:* ocean. *1849:* ocean; 484| *MS:*——And canes *1835:* And <> up-torn canes, *1863:* uptorn

Light strippings from the fan-trees, tamarisks
Unrooted, with their birds still clinging to them,
All high in the wind. Even so my varied life
Drifts by me; I am young, old, happy, sad,
Hoping, desponding, acting, taking rest,
And all at once: that is, those past conditions
Float back at once on me. If I select
Some special epoch from the crowd, 'tis but
To will, and straight the rest dissolve away,
And only that particular state is present
With all its long-forgotten circumstance
Distinct and vivid as at first—myself
A careless looker-on and nothing more,
Indifferent and amused, but nothing more.
And this is death: I understand it all.
New being waits me; new perceptions must
Be born in me before I plunge therein;
Which last is Death's affair; and while I speak,
Minute by minute he is filling me

485| *MS:* fan-trees— —tamarisks *1835:* Like strippings < > fan-trees; tamarisks *1849:* Light strippings < > fan-trees, tamarisks 486| *MS:* Unrooted with < > them,— — *1835:* Unrooted, with < > them, 487| *MS:* wind:—even *1835:* wind. Even 488| *MS:* me— —I < > sad *1835:* me. I < > sad, *1863:* me; I 489| *MS:* rest *1835:* rest, 490| *MS:* once!—that is,—those *1835:* once: that is, those 491| *MS:* Flock back upon me . . . if I choose to single *1835:* me. If *1849:* Float back at once on me. If I select 492| *MS:* Some certain epoch < > crowd— § above § , 'tis *1835:* crowd, 'tis *1849:* Some special epoch 493| *MS:* will—and < > away *1835:* will, and < > away, *1863:* away *1868:* away, 494| *MS:* And that < > present only, *1849:* And only that < > present, *1863:* present 495| *MS:* its circumstance forgotten long *1835:* long, *1849:* its long-forgotten circumstance, *1863:* circumstance 496| *MS:* But now distinct < > first,— *1835:* first— *1849:* Distinct < > first—myself 497| *MS:* I being a < > looker-on—nought more! *1835:* looker-on, nought *1849:* A < > looker-on, and nothing more! *1863:* looker-on and *1868:* more, 498| *MS:* amused— —but < > more! *1835:* amused, but *1863:* amused but *1868:* more. *1888:* amused, but 499| *MS:* Death;—I < > all: *1835:* death: I < > all. 500| *MS:* There is new Being waiting me— § above § , and new *1835:* being < > me, and *1849:* New being waits me; new perceptions must 501| *MS:* Perceptions must be < > before *1849:* Be < > before I plunge therein; 502| *MS:* I plunge therein,—this last is Deaths affair, *1835:* therein; this < > Death's *1849:* Which last < > affair; and while I speak, 503| *MS:* And he is filling me, minute by minute, *1835:* me minute by minute *1849:* Minute by minute he is filling me

With power; and while my foot is on the threshold
Of boundless life—the doors unopened yet,
All preparations not complete within—
I turn new knowledge upon old events,
And the effect is . . . but I must not tell;
It is not lawful. Your own turn will come
One day. Wait, Festus! You will die like me.
FESTUS 'Tis of that past life that I burn to hear.
PARACELSUS You wonder it engages me just now?
In truth, I wonder too. What's life to me?
Where'er I look is fire, where'er I listen
Music, and where I tend bliss evermore.
Yet how can I refrain? 'Tis a refined
Delight to view those chances,—one last view.
I am so near the perils I escape,
That I must play with them and turn them over,
To feel how fully they are past and gone.
Still, it is like, some further cause exists
For this peculiar mood—some hidden purpose;
Did I not tell you something of it, Festus?
I had it fast, but it has somehow slipt
Away from me; it will return anon.
FESTUS (Indeed his cheek seems young again, his voice
Complete with its old tones: that little laugh

504| *MS:* With Power— § above § , and *1835:* With power, and *1849:* power; and 505| *MS:* Life—the portals yet unopened— *1835:* life—the < > unopen'd— *1849:* the doors unopened yet, 507| *MS:* Knowledge < > Events *1835:* knowledge < > events, 508| *MS:* is— — —but < > tell *1835:* is . . . But < > tell; *1863:* but 509| *MS:*—It is not fair— —you < > will arrive *1835:* It < > fair. Your < > arrive *1849:* not lawful. Your < > will come 510–511| *MS:* Some day— —dear Festus you < > me,— / Your turn will come so that you do but wait!— — / Tis < > hear . . . . *1835:* day. Dear < > me— / < > wait! / 'Tis < > hear . . . *1849:* One day. Wait, Festus! You < > me! / 'Tis < > hear! *1868:* me. / < > hear. 513| *MS:* too—what's *1835:* too. What's 514| *MS:* fire—where'er *1835:* fire, where'er 516| *MS:* Yet I can not refrain:— —'tis *1835:* refrain: 'tis *1849:* Yet how can I refrain? 'Tis 517| *MS:* chances once again;— *1835:* again. *1849:* chances,—one last view. 518| *MS:* escape *1835:* escape, 519| *MS:* over *1835:* over, 520| *MS:* gone:— *1835:* gone. 521| *1835:* Still it is like some *1868:* Still, it is like, some 522| *MS:* mood— —some < > purpose— — *1835:* mood—some < > purpose; 524| *MS:* fast— — —but *1835:* fast, but 525| *MS:* me— —it < > anon.— — *1835:* me; it < > anon. 526| *MS:* again—his *1835:* again, his 527| *MS:* tones!—that *1835:* tones—that *1849:* tones:that

Concluding every phrase, with upturned eye,
As though one stooped above his head to whom
He looked for confirmation and approval,
Where was it gone so long, so well preserved?
Then, the fore-finger pointing as he speaks,
Like one who traces in an open book
The matter he declares; 'tis many a year
Since I remarked it last: and this in him,
But now a ghastly wreck!)
And can it be,
Dear Aureole, you have then found out at last
That worldly things are utter vanity?
That man is made for weakness, and should wait
In patient ignorance, till God appoint . . .
PARACELSUS Ha, the purpose: the true purpose: that is it!
How could I fail to apprehend! You here,
I thus! But no more trifling: I see all,
I know all: my last mission shall be done
If strength suffice. No trifling! Stay; this posture
Hardly befits one thus about to speak:
I will arise.
FESTUS Nay, Aureole, are you wild?

528| *MS:* phrase—with <> eye *1835:* phrase; with up-turn'd eye, *1849:* phrase, with up-turned *1863:* upturned 529| *1835:* stoop'd <> head, to *1849:* stooped *1863:* head to 530| *MS:* approval—— *1835:* look'd <> approval: *1849:* looked <> and applause,— *1863:* and approval, 531| *MS:* preserved? . . *1835:* preserved? *1849:* long, being kept so well? *1863:* long, so well preserved? 532| *MS:* And the forefinger <> speaks *1835:* fore-finger <> speaks, *1849:* Then, the fore-finger 534| *MS:* declares——'tis *1835:* declares; 'tis 535| *MS:* last:—and <> him *1835:* remark'd it last: and <> him . . . *1849:* remarked <> him, 536| *MS:* wreck!— § written over by § wreck!) / —And <> be *1835:* wreck!) / And <> be, 537| *MS:* Aureole? you *1835:* Aureole, you 538| *MS:* The utter vanity of worldly things? *1849:* That worldly things are utter vanity? 539| *MS:* Man *1835:* man 540| *MS:* ignorance till God appoint . . . . *1835:* appoint . . . *1888:* ignorance, till 541| *MS:* purpose! the <> purpose! that *1835:* purpose; the <> purpose: that *1863:* purpose, the <> it *1863:* it! 542| *MS:*——How <> apprehend!——you *1835:* How <> apprehend! You 543| *MS:* thus——but § written over by § thus!—but <> trifling;—I see all— *1835:* thus! But <> trifling; I see all, *1868:* trifling: I 544| *MS:* all;—my *1835:* all: my 545| *MS:* suffice:—no trifling!—stay—this *1835:* suffice. No trifling! Stay; this 546| *MS:* speak— *1835:* speak: 547| *MS:* arise.— FESTUS Dear Aureole——are you wild? . . *1835:* arise. FESTUS <> Aureole, are you wild? *1849:* FESTUS Nay, Aureole

You cannot leave your couch.
PARACELSUS No help; no help;
Not even your hand. So! there, I stand once more!
Speak from a couch? I never lectured thus.
My gown—the scarlet lined with fur; now put
The chain about my neck; my signet-ring
Is still upon my hand, I think—even so;
Last, my good sword; ah, trusty Azoth, leapest
Beneath thy master's grasp for the last time?
This couch shall be my throne: I bid these walls
Be consecrate, this wretched cell become
A shrine, for here God speaks to men through me.
Now, Festus, I am ready to begin.
FESTUS I am dumb with wonder.
PARACELSUS Listen, therefore, Festus!
There will be time enough, but none to spare.
I must content myself with telling only
The most important points. You doubtless feel
That I am happy, Festus; very happy.
FESTUS 'Tis no delusion which uplifts him thus!
Then you are pardoned, Aureole, all your sin?
PARACELSUS Ay, pardoned: yet why pardoned?
FESTUS 'Tis God's praise

548| *MS:* couch— — PARACELSUS —No help! No help! *1835:* couch. PARACELSUS No help; no help; 549| *MS:* hand!— —so!— —there *1835:* hand. So! there 550| *MS:* couch?—why I ne'er < > thus!— *1835:* couch? why < > thus. *1849:* couch? I never 551| *MS:* gown— —the < > fur:— —now *1835:* gown—the scarlet, lined < > fur; now *1863:* scarlet lined 552| *MS:* neck—my *1835:* neck; my 553| *MS:* think—even so. *1835:* think—even so; 554| *MS:*— —Last my < > sword, —ha trusty Azoth? leapest *1835:* Last, my < > sword; ha, trusty Azoth, leapest *1868:* sword; ah, trusty 555| *MS:* masters *1835:* master's 556| *MS:* bid this cell *1849:* bid these walls 557| *MS:* consecrate . . this wretched bed become *1835:* consecrate; this *1849:* wretched cell become *1863:* consecrate, this 558| *MS:* shrine— —for < > Men thro' me! *1835:* shrine; for < > men through *1863:* shrine, for *1868:* me. 560| *MS:* am blind with wonder! PARACELSUS *1835:* wonder. PARACELSUS *1849:* am dumb with 561| *MS:* spare . . *1835:* spare. 563| *MS:* points: you *1835:* points. You *1868:* doubtlsss *1888:* doubtless 564| *MS:* Festus?—very happy? *1835:* Festus; very happy. 565| *MS:* Tis < > thus!— *1835:* 'Tis < > thus . . . *1849:* thus! 566| *MS:* you are pardoned § *are* inserted above the line § *1835:* pardon'd *1849:* pardoned 567| *MS:* Pardon?— —and wherefore pardon?— — FESTUS —Tis *1835:* Pardon? and < > pardon? FESTUS 'Tis *1849:* Ay, pardoned! yet why pardoned? FESTUS *1868:* pardoned: yet

That man is bound to seek, and you . . .
PARACELSUS Have lived!
We have to live alone to set forth well
God's praise. 'Tis true, I sinned much, as I thought,
And in effect need mercy, for I strove
To do that very thing; but, do your best
Or worst, praise rises, and will rise for ever.
Pardon from him, because of praise denied—
Who calls me to himself to exalt himself?
He might laugh as I laugh!
FESTUS But all comes
To the same thing. 'Tis fruitless for mankind
To fret themselves with what concerns them not;
They are no use that way: they should lie down
Content as God has made them, nor go mad
In thriveless cares to better what is ill.
PARACELSUS No, no; mistake me not; let me not work
More harm than I have worked! This is my case:
If I go joyous back to God, yet bring
No offering, if I render up my soul
Without the fruits it was ordained to bear,
If I appear the better to love God

568| *MS:* Man <> to seek,—and you . . . PARACELSUS ——Have *1835:* man <> seek, and you . . . PARACELSUS Have 569| *MS:* live, alone, to *1835:* live alone to 570| *MS:* praise: 'tis <> thought— *1835:* praise. 'Tis <> sinn'd <> thought, *1849:* sinned 571| *MS:* And, in effect, need mercy——for *1835:* And in effect need mercy, for 572| *MS:* thing . . but *1835:* thing; but 573| *MS:* worst—praise rises and <> ever! *1835:* worst, praise rises, and <> ever. *1888:* ever *1889:* ever. 574| *MS:* Him?——who call me to Himself *1835:* Him, who *1849:* Him, because of praise denied— *1868:* him 575| *MS:* To teach me better, and exalt me higher? . . . . *1835:* better and <> higher! *1849:* Who calls me to Himself to exalt Himself? *1868:* himself <> himself? 576| *MS:* laugh, as <> all this comes *1835:* laugh as I laugh. FESTUS *1849:* I laugh! FESTUS Then all comes *1863:* FESTUS But all 577| *MS:* thing——'tis <> Mankind *1835:* thing. 'Tis <> mankind 578| *MS:* not: *1835:* not; 579| *MS:* way——they *1835:* way: they 581| *MS:* better their condition:— *1835:* condition. *1849:* better what is ill. 582| *MS:* No, No! mistake me not——let *1835:* No, no; mistake me not; let 583| *MS:* have done!—this <> case:—— *1835:* done. This <> case: *1849:* done! This *1868:* have worked! This 585| *MS:* offering—if *1835:* offering; if *1849:* offering, if 586| *MS:* bear,— *1835:* ordain'd to bear; *1849:* ordained to bear, 587| *MS:* appear to love God better for *1849:* appear the better to love God

For sin, as one who has no claim on him,—
Be not deceived! It may be surely thus
With me, while higher prizes still await
The mortal persevering to the end.
Beside I am not all so valueless:
I have been something, though too soon I left
Following the instincts of that happy time.
FESTUS What happy time? For God's sake, for man's sake,
What time was happy? All I hope to know
That answer will decide. What happy time?
PARACELSUS When but the time I vowed myself to man?
FESTUS Great God, thy judgments are inscrutable!
PARACELSUS Yes, it was in me; I was born for it—
I, Paracelsus: it was mine by right.
Doubtless a searching and impetuous soul
Might learn from its own motions that some task
Like this awaited it about the world;
Might seek somewhere in this blank life of ours
For fit delights to stay its longings vast;
And, grappling Nature, so prevail on her
To fill the creature full she dared thus frame
Hungry for joy; and, bravely tyrannous,

588| *MS:* My sins— —as *1835:* sins, as < > him, *1849:* For sin < > him,— *1863:* Him,— *1868:* him,— 589| *MS:* deceived;—it may be only thus *1835:* deceived: it *1849:* be surely thus 590| *MS:* me— —or higher prizes may await *1835:* me; or *1849:* me, while higher prizes still await 591–593| *MS:* end:— / Beside < > valueless / I have < > tho' *1835:* end. / Beside, I < > valueless; / < > though *1849:* end. / For I too have been something, though too soon *1863:* end. / Beside I am not all so valueless: / I have been something, though too soon I left 594| *MS:* time . . . . *1835:* time . . . *1849:* I left the < > time! *1863:* Following the *1868:* time. 595| *MS:* time?— —for < > sake— —for Man's sake *1835:* time? For < > sake, for man's sake, 596| *MS:* all *1835:* All 597| *MS:* decide . . . what *1835:* decide. What 598| *MS:* Man? *1835:* vow'd < > man. *1849:* vowed my help to man? *1863:* vowed myself to 599| *1863:* Thy *1868:* thy 600| *MS:* Yes— —it < > me— —I < > it:— *1835:* Yes, it < > me; I < > it— 601| *MS:* I . . . Paracelsus:—it < > right:— *1835:* I, Paracelsus: it < > right. 602| *MS:* impetuous spirit *1849:* impetuous soul 604| *MS:* world— — — *1835:* world; 606| *MS:* vast, *1835:* vast; 607| *MS:* grappling strenuously with Fate, compel her *1849:* grappling Nature, so prevail on her 608| *MS:* full, whom she dared frame *1835:* full whom *1849:* full she dared to frame *1868:* dare thus frame 609| *MS:* joy:—and—bravely tyrannous— *1835:* joy, and, bravely tyrannous,

Grow in demand, still craving more and more,
And make each joy conceded prove a pledge
Of other joy to follow—bating nought
Of its desires, still seizing fresh pretence
To turn the knowledge and the rapture wrung
As an extreme, last boon, from destiny,
Into occasion for new covetings,
New strifes, new triumphs:—doubtless a strong soul,
Alone, unaided might attain to this,
So glorious is our nature, so august
Man's inborn uninstructed impulses,
His naked spirit so majestical!
But this was born in me; I was made so;
Thus much time saved: the feverish appetites,
The tumult of unproved desire, the unaimed
Uncertain yearnings, aspirations blind,
Distrust, mistake, and all that ends in tears
Were saved me; thus I entered on my course.
You may be sure I was not all exempt
From human trouble; just so much of doubt
As bade me plant a surer foot upon
The sun-road, kept my eye unruined 'mid

610| *MS:* demand—still <> and more— — — *1835:* demand, still <> and more, **611**| *MS:* make the joy *1849:* make each joy **612**| *MS:* Of further joy to follow— — —bating nothing *1835:* follow—bating *1849:* Of other joy <> bating nought **613**| *MS:* desires, but seizing all pretence *1849:* desires, still seizing fresh pretence **615**| *MS:* From Destiny as an extreme, last boon, *1849:* As an extreme, last boon, from Destiny, *1863:* destiny, **617**| *MS:* triumphs: doubtless a strong spirit *1835:* triumphs. Doubtless *1849:* triumphs:—doubtless a strong soul *1888:* soul, **618**| *MS:* Might do all this unaided and alone, *1849:* Alone, unaided might attain to this, **619**| *MS:* nature— —so *1835:* nature, so **620**| *MS:* impulses— — — *1835:* impulses— *1849:* impulses, **622**| *MS:*—But it was <> me! I <> so: *1835:* But <> me: I <> so: *1849:* But this was <> me; I <> so;
623| *MS:* saved—the <> appetites— *1835:* saved: the <> appetites,
624| *MS:* desire—the aimless *1835:* desire, the *1849:* desire, the unaimed
625| *MS:* yearnings—near-sighted ambition, *1835:* yearnings, near-sighted *1849:* yearnings, aspirations blind, **626**| *MS:* mistake—and *1835:* mistake, and **627–628**| *MS:* me, tho' the lion-heart repines not / At working thro' such lets its purpose out: / . . . . You *1835:* though the lion heart <> / <> through <> out. / You *1849:* me; thus I entered on my course! / You *1868:* course.
629| *MS:* trouble,—just *1835:* trouble: just **631**| *MS:* sun-road— —kept *1835:* sun-road—kept <> unruin'd mid *1849:* unruined *1863:* sun-road, kept <> 'mid

The fierce and flashing splendour, set my heart
Trembling so much as warned me I stood there
On sufferance—not to idly gaze, but cast
Light on a darkling race; save for that doubt,
I stood at first where all aspire at last
To stand: the secret of the world was mine.
I knew, I felt, (perception unexpressed,
Uncomprehended by our narrow thought,
But somehow felt and known in every shift
And change in the spirit,—nay, in every pore
Of the body, even,)—what God is, what we are,
What life is—how God tastes an infinite joy
In infinite ways—one everlasting bliss,
From whom all being emanates, all power
Proceeds; in whom is life for evermore,
Yet whom existence in its lowest form
Includes; where dwells enjoyment there is he:
With still a flying point of bliss remote,
A happiness in store afar, a sphere
Of distant glory in full view; thus climbs
Pleasure its heights for ever and for ever.
The centre-fire heaves underneath the earth,
And the earth changes like a human face;

632| *MS:* splendour—set *1863:* splendour, set **633**| *1835:* warn'd *1849:* warned **634**| *MS:* sufferance— —not <> but have *1835:* sufferance—not *1849:* but cast **635**| *MS:* Remembrance of a darkling Race— —save that, *1835:* race; save *1849:* Light on a darkling race; save for that doubt,
637| *MS:* To reach: the secret *1835:* To reach—the *1849:* To stand: the
638–639| *MS:* felt . . not as one knows or feels / Aught else— —a vast perception unexpressed, / Uncomprehended *1835:* felt, not <> / <> else; a <> unexpress'd, *1849:* felt, perception unexpressed, / Uncomprehended
641–642| *MS:* spirit I bear— —nay, dare I say / In every pore of this fast-fading frame / I felt, I knew what God <> are° § footnote § °"Paracelse faisait profession du Pantheisme le plus grossier." *Renauldin.* *1835:* bear—nay <> say, // <> are,° °Panthéisme *1849:* spirit,—nay, in every pore / Of the body, even,)—what <> are, § footnote dropped § **643**| *MS:* Life is . . . how *1835:* life is—how
644| *MS:* ways— —one <> Bliss *1835:* ways—one <> bliss, **645**| *MS:* Being <> Power *1835:* being <> power **646**| *MS:* Proceeds— —in <> Life *1835:* Proceeds; in <> life **647**| *MS:* Existence *1835:* existence **648**| *MS:* Includes— —where <> Enjoyment <> He! *1835:* Includes; where <> enjoyment *1868:* he: **649**| *MS:* remote— *1849:* remote, **650**| *MS:* afar—a *1849:* afar, a **651**| *MS:* view— —thus *1835:* view; thus **652**| *MS:* forever and forever! *1835:* for ever and for ever! *1868:* ever.

The molten ore bursts up among the rocks,
Winds into the stone's heart, outbranches bright
In hidden mines, spots barren river-beds,
Crumbles into fine sand where sunbeams bask—
God joys therein. The wroth sea's waves are edged
With foam, white as the bitten lip of hate,
When, in the solitary waste, strange groups
Of young volcanos come up, cyclops-like,
Staring together with their eyes on flame—
God tastes a pleasure in their uncouth pride.
Then all is still; earth is a wintry clod:
But spring-wind, like a dancing psaltress, passes
Over its breast to waken it, rare verdure
Buds tenderly upon rough banks, between
The withered tree-roots and the cracks of frost,
Like a smile striving with a wrinkled face;
The grass grows bright, the boughs are swoln with blooms
Like chrysalids impatient for the air,
The shining dorrs are busy, beetles run
Along the furrows, ants make their ado;
Above, birds fly in merry flocks, the lark
Soars up and up, shivering for very joy;
Afar the ocean sleeps; white fishing-gulls
Flit where the strand is purple with its tribe

655| *MS:* rocks *1835:* rocks— *1849:* rocks, 656| *MS:* heart——outbranches *1835:* heart-outbranches *1849:* heart, outbranches 657| *MS:* mines . . spots <> river-beds . . *1835:* mines—spots <> river-beds— *1849:* mines, spots <> river-beds, 658| *MS:* bask——. *1835:* bask— 659| *MS:* therein!—the *1835:* therein! The *1868:* therein. The 660| *MS:* foam white *1835:* foam, white <> Hate: *1849:* Hate, *1863:* hate, 661| *MS:* When in <> waste strange *1849:* When, in <> waste, strange 662| *MS:* cyclops-like *1835:* cyclops-like, 663| *MS:* flame . . . *1835:* flame, *1849:* flame;— *1863:* flame— 664| *MS:* pride! *1868:* pride. 665| *MS:* still: earth <> clod, *1835:* clod; *1863:* still; earth <> clod: 667| *MS:* it——rare *1835:* it; rare *1863:* it, rare 668| *MS:* Buds here and there upon *1849:* Buds tenderly upon 669| *MS:* frost *1835:* wither'd <> frost, *1849:* withered 670| *MS:* face, *1835:* face; 671| *MS:* swollen *1835:* swoln <> blooms, *1863:* blooms 672| *MS:* air: *1835:* air; *1863:* air, 673| *MS:* busy——beetles *1835:* busy; beetles *1863:* busy, beetles 674| *MS:* furrows . . ants <> ado . . *1835:* furrows, ants <> ado; 675| *MS:* Above birds <> flocks——the *1835:* flocks—the *1849:* Above, birds *1863:* flocks, the 677| *MS:* sleeps . . . white fishing gulls *1835:* sleeps; white fishing-gulls

Of nested limpets; savage creatures seek
Their loves in wood and plain—and God renews
His ancient rapture. Thus he dwells in all,
From life's minute beginnings, up at last
To man—the consummation of this scheme
Of being, the completion of this sphere
Of life: whose attributes had here and there
Been scattered o'er the visible world before,
Asking to be combined, dim fragments meant
To be united in some wondrous whole,
Imperfect qualities throughout creation,
Suggesting some one creature yet to make,
Some point where all those scattered rays should meet
Convergent in the faculties of man.
Power—neither put forth blindly, nor controlled
Calmly by perfect knowledge; to be used
At risk, inspired or checked by hope and fear:
Knowledge—not intuition, but the slow
Uncertain fruit of an enhancing toil,
Strengthened by love: love—not serenely pure,
But strong from weakness, like a chance-sown plant
Which, cast on stubborn soil, puts forth changed buds

679| *MS:* limpets: savage *1835:* limpets; savage **680**| *MS:* plain:— —and *1835:* plain; and *1863:* plain—and **681**| *MS:* rapture! Thus He *1868:* rapture. Thus he **682**| *MS:* Life's *1835:* life's **683**| *MS:* Man < > Scheme *1835:* man < > scheme **684**| *MS:* Being—the < > Sphere *1835:* being < > sphere *1849:* being, the **685**| *MS:* Life *1835:* life **686**| *1835:* scatter'd *1849:* scattered **687**| *MS:* combined . . . dim *1835:* combin'd—dim *1849:* combined *1863:* combined, dim **688**| *MS:* Whole,— *1835:* whole— *1863:* whole, **689**| *MS:* Creation *1835:* creation, **690–693**| *MS:* Creature < > make . . . / —(So would a Spirit deem, intent on watching / The purpose of the world from its faint rise / To its mature development)—some point / Whereto those wandering rays should all converge— — — § written over by § converge— / Might: neither *1835:* creature < > make— / (So < > // < > developement)—some < > // < > controll'd *1849:* make— / Some point where all those scattered rays should meet / Convergent in the faculties of man. / Power; neither < > controlled **690**| *1863:* make, **693**| *1863:* Power—neither **694**| *MS:* knowledge—to *1849:* knowledge; to **695**| *MS:* risk—inspired < > fear:— *1835:* inspir'd or check'd < > fear— *1849:* risk, inspired or checked < > fear: **696**| *MS:* Knowledge:—not *1835:* Knowledge: not *1849:* Knowledge; not *1863:* Knowledge—not **697**| *MS:* inhancing toil *1835:* enhancing toil, **698**| *MS:* love; Love:—not *1835:* Strengthen'd by love—love: not *1849:* Strengthened by love: love; not *1863:* love: love—not **699**| *MS:* But power from *1849:* But strong from **700**| *MS:* Which cast < > soil puts *1835:* Which, cast < > soil, puts < > buds, *1863:* buds

And softer stains, unknown in happier climes;
Love which endures and doubts and is oppressed
And cherished, suffering much and much sustained,
And blind, oft-failing, yet believing love,
A half-enlightened, often-chequered trust:—
Hints and previsions of which faculties,
Are strewn confusedly everywhere about
The inferior natures, and all lead up higher,
All shape out dimly the superior race,
The heir of hopes too fair to turn out false,
And man appears at last. So far the seal
Is put on life; one stage of being complete,
One scheme wound up: and from the grand result
A supplementary reflux of light,
Illustrates all the inferior grades, explains
Each back step in the circle. Not alone
For their possessor dawn those qualities,
But the new glory mixes with the heaven
And earth; man, once descried, imprints for ever
His presence on all lifeless things: the winds
Are henceforth voices, wailing or a shout,

701| *MS:* stains unknown < > climes . . . *1835:* stains, unknown < > climes: *1849:* climes; **702**| *MS:* endures, and doubts, and *1835:* oppress'd *1849:* oppressed, *1863:* endures and doubts and is oppressed **703**| *MS:* cherished—suffering < > sustained,— *1835:* cherish'd—suffering much, and < > sustain'd— *1849:* cherished, suffering < > sustained, *1863:* much and much **704**| *MS:* A blind, unfailing and devoted Love:— *1835:* unfailing, and < > love: *1849:* blind, oft-failing, yet believing love, *1868:* And blind **705**| *MS:* And half-enlightened < > Trust:—— *1835:* half-enlighten'd, often-chequer'd trust: *1849:* A half-enlightened, often-chequered trust:— **706**| *MS:* Anticipations, hints of these and more *1849:* Hints and previsions of which faculties, **707**| *MS:* everywhere—all seek *1849:* everywhere about **708**| *MS:* An object to possess and stamp their own, *1835:* own; *1849:* The inferior natures; and all lead up higher, *1863:* natures, and **709**| *MS:* the forthcoming race, § written over by § Race, *1835:* race, *1849:* the superior race, **711**| *MS:* Man < > last: so *1863:* man < > last. So **712**| *MS:* Life: one < > Being *1835:* life < > being *1849:* life; one **713**| *MS:* Scheme *1835:* scheme < > up; and *1863:* up: and **714**| *MS:* light *1835:* light, **716**| *MS:* circle:—not *1835:* circle: not *1849:* circle. Not **717**| *MS:* The clear dawn of those qualities shines out, *1849:* For their possessor dawn those qualities, **719**| *MS:* earth—Man *1835:* earth. Man *1849:* earth: Man *1863:* earth; man **720**| *MS:* things—the *1849:* things; the *1863:* things: the **721**| *MS:* voices—wailing *1835:* voices, wailing, or *1849:* voices, in a wail or shout, *1868:* voices, wailing or a shout,

A querulous mutter or a quick gay laugh,
Never a senseless gust now man is born.
The herded pines commune and have deep thoughts,
A secret they assemble to discuss
When the sun drops behind their trunks which glare
Like grates of hell: the peerless cup afloat
Of the lake-lily is an urn, some nymph
Swims bearing high above her head: no bird
Whistles unseen, but through the gaps above
That let light in upon the gloomy woods,
A shape peeps from the breezy forest-top,
Arch with small puckered mouth and mocking eye.
The morn has enterprise, deep quiet droops
With evening, triumph takes the sunset hour,
Voluptuous transport ripens with the corn
Beneath a warm moon like a happy face:
—And this to fill us with regard for man.
With apprehension of his passing worth,
Desire to work his proper nature out,
And ascertain his rank and final place,
For these things tend still upward, progress is
The law of life, man is not Man as yet.
Nor shall I deem his object served, his end
Attained, his genuine strength put fairly forth,

722| *MS:* laugh,— *1835:* mutter, or <> laugh— *1863:* laugh, *1868:* mutter or **723**| *MS:* Man is born: *1835:* man *1849:* born! *1868:* born. **724**| *MS:* commune, and *1863:* commune and *1888:* thoughts *1889:* thoughts, **725**| *MS:* discuss *1835:* discuss, *1863:* discuss **728**| *MS:* urn some *1835:* urn, some **730**| *MS:* thro' *1835:* through **731**| *MS:* woods *1835:* woods, **732**| *MS:* Shape *1835:* shape **733**| *MS:* eye: pucker'd *1849:* puckered *1868:* eye. **734**| *MS:* enterprise—deep *1863:* enterprise, deep **735**| *MS:* evening;— —triumph when the sun takes rest,— *1835:* evening—triumph <> rest— *1849:* evening; triumph takes the sun-set hour, *1863:* evening, triumph <> sunset **736**| *MS:* transport when the cornfields ripen *1835:* corn-fields *1849:* transport ripens with the corn **737**| *MS:* face:— — — *1835:* face: **738**| *MS:* And <> Man, *1835:* man, *1849:*—And *1868:* man. **739**| *MS:* Deep apprehension *1849:* With apprehension **741**| *MS:* To ascertain <> place— *1835:* place, *1849:* And ascertain <> place; *1863:* place, **742**| *MS:* For all these <> tend upward—progress *1849:* For these things tend still upward *1863:* upward, progress **743**| *MS:* Life—Man is not Man as yet: *1835:* man <> man *1849:* man's self is not yet Man! *1863:* life, man's *1868:* man is not Man as yet. **745**| *MS:* fairly out, *1835:* Attain'd *1849:* Attained <> fairly forth,

While only here and there a star dispels
The darkness, here and there a towering mind
O'erlooks its prostrate fellows: when the host
Is out at once to the despair of night,
When all mankind alike is perfected,
Equal in full-blown powers—then, not till then,
I say, begins man's general infancy.
For wherefore make account of feverish starts
Of restless members of a dormant whole,
Impatient nerves which quiver while the body
Slumbers as in a grave? Oh long ago
The brow was twitched, the tremulous lids astir,
The peaceful mouth disturbed; half-uttered speech
Ruffled the lip, and then the teeth were set,
The breath drawn sharp, the strong right-hand clenched stronger,
As it would pluck a lion by the jaw;
The glorious creature laughed out even in sleep!
But when full roused, each giant-limb awake,
Each sinew strung, the great heart pulsing fast,
He shall start up and stand on his own earth,
Then shall his long triumphant march begin,
Thence shall his being date,—thus wholly roused,

747| *MS:* darkness—here <> Mind *1835:* mind *1849:* darkness, here 748| *MS:* its crawling fellows:—when the host § written over by § Host *1835:* fellows: when the host *1849:* its prostrate fellows 749| *MS:* night,— *1835:* night; *1849:* night, 750| *MS:* Mankind is perfected alike, *1835:* mankind *1849:* mankind alike is perfected, 751| *MS:* then—not <> then *1835:* then, not <> then, 752| *MS:* Begins the general infancy of Man; *1835:* man; *1849:* I say, begins man's general infancy! *1868:* infancy. 754| *MS:* Whole *1835:* whole— *1863:* whole, 755| *MS:* Body *1835:* body 756| *MS:* O *1849:* O, long *1868:* Oh long 757| *MS:* twitched—the <> astir— *1835:* twitch'd, the <> astir, *1849:* twitched 758| *MS:* disturbed—half uttered *1835:* disturb'd—half-utter'd *1849:* disturbed; half-uttered 759| *MS:* lip . . . sometimes the teeth set hard *1835:* lip; sometimes the teeth were set, *1849:* lip, and then the 760| *MS:* right hand *1835:* right-hand clench'd stronger— *1849:* clenched stronger, 761| *MS:* the maw . . . *1835:* maw: *1849:* the jaw; 762| *1835:* laugh'd *1849:* laughed 763| *MS:* when aroused—each <> awake— *1835:* arous'd <> awake, *1849:* when full roused 764| *MS:* strung—the <> fast— *1835:* strung, the *1849:* fast, 765| *MS:* up, and <> earth *1835:* earth— *1849:* earth, *1863:* up and 766| *MS:* begin— *1849:* And so begin his <> march, *1863:* Thence shall his <> march begin, 767| *MS:* date—what thus collected *1835:* date; what *1849:* And date his being thence,—thus wholly roused, *1863:* Thence shall his being date,—thus

What he achieves shall be set down to him.
When all the race is perfected alike
As man, that is; all tended to mankind,
And, man produced, all has its end thus far:
But in completed man begins anew
A tendency to God. Prognostics told
Man's near approach; so in man's self arise
August anticipations, symbols, types
Of a dim splendour ever on before
In that eternal circle life pursues.
For men begin to pass their nature's bound,
And find new hopes and cares which fast supplant
Their proper joys and griefs; they grow too great
For narrow creeds of right and wrong, which fade
Before the unmeasured thirst for good: while peace
Rises within them ever more and more.
Such men are even now upon the earth,
Serene amid the half-formed creatures round
Who should be saved by them and joined with them.
Such was my task, and I was born to it—
Free, as I said but now, from much that chains
Spirits, high-dowered but limited and vexed
By a divided and delusive aim,

768| *MS:* He shall achieve, shall <> him! *1849:* What he achieves shall *1868:* him. 770| *MS: Man* <> is:—all <> Mankind *1835: man* <> is: all <> mankind *1849:* Man <> mankind, *1863:* is; all *1868:* man 771| *MS:* Man <> § *all* <> *end* inserted above the line § <> far; *1835:* man *1863:* far: 772| *MS:* Man *1835:* man 773| *MS:* God: prognostics *1835:* God. Prognostics 774| *MS:* Man's *1835:* man's 776| *1835:* before, *1863:* before 777| *MS:* In the eternal <> Life pursues: *1835:* life *1849:* In that eternal circle run by life: *1863:* life. *1868:* circle life pursues. 778| *MS:* bound *1835:* bound, 779| *MS:* To have new *1849:* And find new 780| *MS:* griefs—they *1835:* griefs; they *1849:* griefs; and outgrow all *1863:* griefs; they outgrow *1868:* they grow too great 781| *MS:* wrong which *1835:* wrong, which *1849:* The narrow *1868:* For narrow 782| *MS:* Before unmeasured <> good, while *1835:* unmeasur'd <> good; while *1849:* Before the unmeasured *1863:* good: while 783| *MS:* more *1835:* more. 784| *MS:*—Such *1835:* Such <> earth— *1849:* earth, 785| half-form'd <> round, *1849:* half-formed *1863:* round 786| *MS:* Whom they should save and join with them at last; *1835:* last: *1849:* Who should be saved by them and joined with them. 787| *MS:* Task <> it *1835:* task <> it— 789| *MS:* Spirits high-dowered *1835:* high-dower'd, but <> vex'd *1849:* Spirits, high-dowered <> vexed *1863:* high-dowered but
790| *MS:* Aim, *1835:* aim— *1849:* aim,

A shadow mocking a reality
Whose truth avails not wholly to disperse
The flitting mimic called up by itself,
And so remains perplexed and nigh put out
By its fantastic fellow's wavering gleam.
I, from the first, was never cheated thus;
I never fashioned out a fancied good
Distinct from man's; a service to be done,
A glory to be ministered unto
With powers put forth at man's expense, withdrawn
From labouring in his behalf; a strength
Denied that might avail him. I cared not
Lest his success ran counter to success
Elsewhere: for God is glorified in man,
And to man's glory vowed I soul and limb.
Yet, constituted thus, and thus endowed,
I failed: I gazed on power till I grew blind.
Power; I could not take my eyes from that:
That only, I thought, should be preserved, increased
At any risk, displayed, struck out at once—
The sign and note and character of man.
I saw no use in the past: only a scene

793| *MS:* mimic which itself has bred, *1849:* mimic called up by itself, 794| *1835:* perplex'd *1849:* perplexed 795| *MS:* gleam . . . *1835:* gleam; *1849:* gleam. 796| *MS:* But, from the first the cheat could lure me not: *1835:* But, from the first, the *1849:* I, from the first, was never cheated so; *1863:* cheated thus; 797| *1835:* fashion'd *1849:* fashioned 798| *MS:* Man's—a < > done *1835:* man's; a < > done— *1849:* done, 799| *MS:*—A *1835:* A < > minister'd unto, *1849:* ministered *1868:* unto. *1888:* unto 800| *MS:* Man's expence *1835:* man's expense 801| *MS:* behalf a *1835:* behalf; a 802| *MS:* Reserved that < > him: I ne'er cared *1849:* Denied that < > him! I cared not *1863:* him. I 804| *MS:* Elsewhere—for < > Man, *1835:* Elsewhere: for < > man, 805| *MS:* And thereto I devoted soul and limb. *1835:* And to man's glory vow'd I soul *1849:* glory, vowed *1868:* glory vowed 806| *1835:* endow'd, *1849:* endowed, 807| *MS:* Power < > blind *1835:* fail'd < > power < > blind. *1849:* failed < > blind— *1863:* blind. 808| *MS:* Power: I < > that *1835:* that— *1849:* On power; I *1863:* that: *1868:* Power 809| *MS:*—That only was to be preserved—increased *1835:* That < > preserved, increased *1849:* That only, I thought, should be preserved 810| *MS:* once *1835:* risk, display'd < > once— *1849:* risk, displayed 811| *MS:* Man *1835:* The sign, and note, and < > man. *1863:* sign and note and 812| *MS:* Past— —only *1835:* past: only *1863:* Past *1868:* past

Of degradation, ugliness and tears,
The record of disgraces best forgotten,
A sullen page in human chronicles
Fit to erase. I saw no cause why man
Should not stand all-sufficient even now,
Or why his annals should be forced to tell
That once the tide of light, about to break
Upon the world, was sealed within its spring:
I would have had one day, one moment's space,
Change man's condition, push each slumbering claim
Of mastery o'er the elemental world
At once to full maturity, then roll
Oblivion o'er the work, and hide from man
What night had ushered morn. Not so, dear child
Of after-days, wilt thou reject the past
Big with deep warnings of the proper tenure
By which thou hast the earth: for thee the present
Shall have distinct and trembling beauty, seen
Beside that past's own shade when, in relief,
Its brightness shall stand out: nor yet on thee
Shall burst the future, as successive zones

813| *MS:* tears *1835:* ugliness, and tears; *1849:* degradation, imbecility— *1863:* imbecility, *1868:* degradation, ugliness and tears, 814| *MS:*—The < > forgotten; *1835:* The *1849:* forgotten, 816| *MS:* To be erased: I < > Man *1835:* man *1849:* Fit to erase *1863:* erase. I 817| *MS:* not be all-sufficient *1835:* now; *1868:* not stand all-sufficient < > now, 819| *1835:* light about *1849:* light, about 820–821| *MS:* world was < > spring, / Although my own name led the brightness in: / I < > have had § had inserted above the line § one night— § above § , one § cancelled by § one day—one *1835:* seal'd < > // < > day, one < > space, *1849:* world, was sealed < > spring: / I *1863:* spring: 822| *MS:* Man's condition—push *1835:* man's condition, push 823| *MS:* To mastery *1863:* Of mastery 824| *MS:* maturity,—then *1835:* maturity: then *1849:* maturity, then 825| *MS:* o'er its work and < > Man *1835:* work, and < > man *1849:* o'er the tools, and *1888:* the work, and 826| *MS:* morn—not < > child § written over by § Child *1835:* usher'd morn. Not < > child *1849:* ushered 827| *MS:* Past *1835:* Past, *1868:* past 829| *MS:* earth——for < > Present *1835:* earth: for *1849:* earth: the Present for thee *1868:* present *1888:* earth: for thee the present 831| *MS:* Beside its shadow whence in strong relief *1835:* shadow—whence, in < > relief, *1849:* Beside that Past's own shade, whence, in relief, *1863:* shade whence *1868:* past's own shade when, in 832| *MS:* Its features shall stand out—nor *1835:* out: nor *1849:* Its brightness shall stand out: nor on thee yet *1888:* nor yet on thee 833| *MS:* Future as *1835:* Future, as *1866:* future

Of several wonder open on some spirit
Flying secure and glad from heaven to heaven:
But thou shalt painfully attain to joy,
While hope and fear and love shall keep thee man!
All this was hid from me: as one by one
My dreams grew dim, my wide aims circumscribed,
As actual good within my reach decreased,
While obstacles sprung up this way and that
To keep me from effecting half the sum,
Small as it proved; as objects, mean within
The primal aggregate, seemed, even the least,
Itself a match for my concentred strength—
What wonder if I saw no way to shun
Despair? The power I sought for man, seemed God's.
In this conjuncture, as I prayed to die,
A strange adventure made me know, one sin
Had spotted my career from its uprise;
I saw Aprile—my Aprile there!
And as the poor melodious wretch disburthened
His heart, and moaned his weakness in my ear,
I learned my own deep error; love's undoing
Taught me the worth of love in man's estate,
And what proportion love should hold with power

834| *MS:* Spirit *1835:* spirit 835–837| *MS:* to heaven, / But Hope and Fear and Love < > Man! *1835:* to heaven: / But hope, and fear, and love, shall < > man! *1849:* to heaven: / But thou shalt painfully attain to joy, / While hope *1863:* to heaven: // < > hope and fear and 839| *1835:* circumscribed— *1849:* circumscribed, 840| *MS:* The actual < > decreased *1835:* As actual < > decreased, 841| *1835:* that, *1863:* that 842| *MS:* sum *1835:* sum, 843| *MS:* proved: as *1849:* proved; as 844–845| *MS:* aggregate, remained alone / Of all the company, and, even the least, / More than a < > strength———— *1835:* remain'd alone // < > strength . . . *1849:* aggregate, seemed, even the least, / Itself a < > strength— 847| *MS:* Despair? § above §—for Power seemed shut from Man forever. *1835:* Despair? for power seem'd < > man for ever. *1849:* Despair? The power I sought for man, seemed God's! *1863:* God's. 848| *1835:* pray'd *1849:* prayed 849| *MS:* know one sin *1835:* One Sin *1849:* know, One Sin *1863:* one sin 850–852| *MS:* uprise / And *1835:* uprise; / < > disburthened *1849:* uprise; / I saw Aprile—my Aprile there! / And < > disburthened 853| *MS:* heart and < > ear *1835:* heart, and moan'd < > ear, *1849:* moaned 854| *MS:* error: Love's *1835:* learn'd < > love's *1849:* learned 855| *MS:* Love in Man's estate *1835:* love in man's estate, 856| *MS:* Love < > Power *1835:* love < > power

In his right constitution; love preceding
Power, and with much power, always much more love;
Love still too straitened in his present means,
And earnest for new power to set love free.
I learned this, and supposed the whole was learned:
And thus, when men received with stupid wonder
My first revealings, would have worshipped me,
And I despised and loathed their proffered praise—
When, with awakened eyes, they took revenge
For past credulity in casting shame
On my real knowledge, and I hated them—
It was not strange I saw no good in man,
To overbalance all the wear and waste
Of faculties, displayed in vain, but born
To prosper in some better sphere: and why?
In my own heart love had not been made wise
To trace love's faint beginnings in mankind,
To know even hate is but a mask of love's,
To see a good in evil, and a hope
In ill-success; to sympathize, be proud
Of their half-reasons, faint aspirings, dim
Struggles for truth, their poorest fallacies,
Their prejudice and fears and cares and doubts;

857| *MS:* constitution . . . . Love *1835:* constitution: love *1849:* constitution; love 858| *MS:* Power——with <> Power always <> Love *1835:* Power—with <> power <> love; *1849:* Power, and with <> power, always 859| *MS:* in its present means *1835:* straiten'd <> means, *1849:* straitened *1868:* in his present 860| *MS:* Power to set it free. *1835:* power *1888:* set love free. 861| *1835:* learn'd <> learn'd: *1849:* learned <> learned: 862| *MS:* thus when Men *1835:* thus, when men 863| *MS:* revealings and would worship me *1835:* revealings—would have worshipp'd me— *1849:* revealings, would <> worshipped me, 864| *MS:*—And *1835:* And <> proffer'd praise; *1849:* proffered praise— 865| *MS:*—When *1835:* When awaken'd *1849:* awakened 867| *MS:* knowledge—and <> them . . . . *1835:* them— *1849:* knowledge, and 868| *MS:* Man *1835:* man, 870| *1835:* display'd *1849:* displayed 872| *MS:* Love *1835:* love 873| *MS:* Love's <> Mankind; *1835:* love's <> mankind— *1849:* mankind, 874| *MS:* Hate <> Love's; *1835:* hate <> love's; *1849:* love's, 876| *MS:* In ill success——to sympathize—be *1835:* In ill-success. To *1849:* ill-success; to sympathize, be 877| *MS:* aspirings, struggles *1849:* aspirings, dim 878| *MS:* Dimly for *1835:* truth—their *1849:* Struggles for truth, their 879| *MS:* And prejudice, and <> doubts— *1835:* fears, and cares, and doubts; *1849:* Their prejudice *1863:* prejudice and fears and cares and

All with a touch of nobleness, despite
Their error, upward tending all though weak,
Like plants in mines which never saw the sun,
But dream of him, and guess where he may be,
And do their best to climb and get to him.
All this I knew not, and I failed. Let men
Regard me, and the poet dead long ago
Who loved too rashly; and shape forth a third
And better-tempered spirit, warned by both:
As from the over-radiant star too mad
To drink the life-springs, beamless thence itself—
And the dark orb which borders the abyss,
Ingulfed in icy night,—might have its course
A temperate and equidistant world.
Meanwhile, I have done well, though not all well.
As yet men cannot do without contempt;
'Tis for their good, and therefore fit awhile
That they reject the weak, and scorn the false,
Rather than praise the strong and true, in me:
But after, they will know me. If I stoop
Into dark tremendous sea of cloud,
It is but for a time; I press God's lamp

880| *MS:* nobleness for all *1835:* nobleness, for *1849:* Which all touch upon nobleness, despite *1868:* All with a touch of nobleness **881|** *MS:* error, all ambitious, upward tending *1835:* tending, *1849:* all tend upwardly though weak, *1868:* error, upward tending all though **882|** *MS:* sun *1835:* sun, **884|** *1835:* him: *1849:* him. **885|** *MS:* not and I failed:—let Men *1835:* not, and I fail'd; let men *1849:* failed. Let **886|** *MS:* Poet *1835:* poet **887|** *MS:* rashly——and <> Third *1835:* rashly; and <> third, *1849:* Who once loved rashly *1863:* Who loved too rashly <> third **888|** *MS:* better tempered spirit warned by both, *1835:* temper'd spirit, warn'd by both; *1849:* tempered <> warned by both: *1863:* better-tempered **889|** *MS:* overradiant *1835:* over-radiant **890|** *MS:* the light-springs *1868:* the life-springs **891|** *MS:* abyss *1835:* abyss, **892|** *MS:* Ingulphed <> night— § above § , might *1835:* Ingulf'd <> night, might *1849:* Ingulfed <> night,—might **893|** *MS:* World: *1835:* world: *1849:* world. **894|** *MS:* Meanwhile I <> tho' <> well:— *1835:* Meanwhile, I <> though <> well. **895|** *MS:* Men <> contempt *1835:* men <> contempt— *1863:* contempt; **896|** *MS:*—'Tis <> good,—tis § cancelled by § good, and therefore *1835:* 'Tis **897–899|** *MS:* reject me and speak scorn of me, / But <> well: I stoop *1835:* me, and <> of me; *1849:* reject the weak, and scorn the false, / Rather than praise the strong and true, in me. / But <> know me! If I *1863:* me: / <> me. If **900|** *MS:* cloud *1835:* cloud, **901|** *MS:* But tis but *1835:* 'tis *1849:* It is but

Close to my breast; its splendour, soon or late,
Will pierce the gloom: I shall emerge one day.
You understand me? I have said enough?

FESTUS Now die, dear Aureole!

PARACELSUS Festus, let my hand—
This hand, lie in your own, my own true friend!
Aprile! Hand in hand with you, Aprile!

FESTUS And this was Paracelsus!

902| *MS:* breast,—its splendour soon or late *1835:* breast—its splendour, soon or late, *1863:* breast; its 903| *MS:* gloom . . I < > day *1835:* gloom: I < > day. *1849:* day! *1863:* day. 904| *MS:* me,—I § written over by § me?—I < > enough! § written over by § enough? *1835:* me? I 905| *MS:* Festus—let *1835:* Festus, let 906| *MS: This* hand—lie < > own— —my own *1835:* hand, lie < > own . . . my *1849:* This < > own—my *1863:* own, my

NOTE

The liberties I have taken with my subject are very trifling; and the reader may slip the foregoing scenes between the leaves of any memoir of Paracelsus he pleases, by way of commentary. To prove this, I subjoin a popular account, translated from the "Biographie Universelle, Paris," 1822, which I select, not as the best, certainly, but as being at hand, and sufficiently concise for my purpose. I also append a few notes, in order to correct those parts which do not bear out my own view of the character of Paracelsus; and have incorporated with them a notice or two, illustrative of the poem itself.

"PARACELSUS (Philippus Aureolus Theophrastus Bombastus ab Hohenheim) was born in 1493 at Einsiedeln,[1] a little town in the canton of Schwyz, some leagues distant from Zurich. His father, who exercised the profession of medicine at Villach in Carinthia, was nearly related to George Bombast de Hohenheim, who became afterward Grand Prior of the Order of Malta: consequently Paracelsus could not spring from the dregs of the people, as Thomas Erastus, his sworn enemy, pretends.[2] It appears that his elementary education was much neglected, and that he spent part of his youth in pursuing the life common to the travelling *literati* of the age; that is to say, in

---

1| *MS:* trifling and § ? § *1835:* trifling; and 2| *MS:* the foregoing scenes § *foregoing* inserted above the line § 4| *MS:* Account translated <> *Biographie Universelle, Paris 1822,* *1835:* "Biographie <> Paris, 1822." *1863:* 'Biographie Universelle, Paris, 1822.' *1888:* "Biographie <> Paris," 1822, 6| *MS:* hand and *1835:* hand, and 7| *MS:* notes in <> § *correct* <> *not* inserted above the line § *1835:* notes, in 8| *MS:* Paracelsus, and *1835:* Paracelsus; and 9| *MS:* two illustrative *1835:* two, illustrative 10–11| *MS: (Philippus* <> *Hohenheim)* § *Aureolus* inserted above the line § *1863:* (Philippus <> Hohenheim) 12| *MS:* Schwitz *1888:* Schwyz 13| *MS:* Medecine *1835:* medicine at Villach, in *1868:* Villach in 14–15| *MS:* became in the event Grand *1849:* became afterward Grand 15| *1835:* Malta; consequently *1868:* Malta: consequently 16–17| *MS:* Erastus his <> enemy pretends *1835:* Erastus, his <> enemy, pretends 18–19| *MS:* the § inserted above the line § 19| *MS:* Literati <> age, that *1835:* literati <> age; that wandering from country to country, predicting the future by astrology and cheiromancy, evoking apparitions, and practising the different operations of magic and alchemy, in which he had been initiated whether by his father or by various ecclesiastics, among the number of whom he particularizes the Abbot Tritheim,[3] and many German bishops.

"As Paracelsus displays everywhere an ignorance of the rudiments of the most ordinary knowledge, it is not probable that he ever studied seriously in the schools: he contented himself with visiting the Universities of Germany, France and Italy; and in spite of his boasting himself to have been the ornament of those institutions, there is no proof of his having legally acquired the title of Doctor, which he assumes. It is only known that he applied himself long, under the direction of the wealthy Sigismond Fugger of Schwatz, to the discovery of the Magnum Opus.

"Paracelsus travelled among the mountains of Bohemia, in the East, and in Sweden, in order to inspect the labours of the miners, to be initiated in the mysteries of the oriental adepts, and to observe the secrets of nature and the famous mountain of loadstone.[4] He professes also to have visited Spain, Portugal, Prussia, Poland, and Transylvania; everywhere communicating freely, not merely with the physicians, but the old women, charlatans and conjurers of these several lands. It is even believed that he extended his journeyings as far as Egypt and Tartary, and that he accompanied the son of the Khan of the Tartars to Constantinople, for the purpose of obtaining the secret of the tincture of Trismegistus from a Greek who inhabited that capital.

20–21| *MS:* future from § *from* inserted above the line § the inspection of the stars and the lines of the hand, evoking apparitions and repeating the *1835:* apparitions, and <> alchemy in *1849:* future by astrology and cheiromancy, evoking apparitions, and practising the 22| *MS:* alchemy in *1835:* alchemy, in 23| *MS:* father, or <> ecclesiastics, *1835:* father or <> ecclesiastics, 24| *MS:* Tritheim and *1835:* Tritheim, and 25| *MS:* Bishops. *1835:* bishops. 27| *MS:* he should have ever *1849:* he ever 28| *MS:* Schools *1835:* schools 29| *MS:* France, and Italy *1868:* France and Italy 33| *1835:* Fugger, of *1868:* Fugger of 37| *MS:* Oriental Adepts, and § , probable; concealed by binding § *1835:* oriental adepts, and 39–40| *MS:* Transsylvania— § above § where he communicated freely not *1835:* Transylvania, where <> freely, not *1849:* Transylvania; everywhere communicating 47| *MS:* but with the *1835:* charlatans, and conjurors, of *1849:* but the <> conjurers *1868:* charlatans and conjurers of 44| *MS:* Constantinople for *1835:* Constantinople, for 45| *MS:* Trismegistus, from *1868:* Trismegistus from

"The period of his return to Germany is unknown: it is only certain that, at about the age of thirty-three, many astonishing cures which he wrought on eminent personages procured him such a celebrity, that he was called in 1526, on the recommendation of Œcolampadius,[5] to fill a chair of physic and surgery at the University of Basil. There Paracelsus began by burning publicly in the amphitheatre the works of Avicenna and Galen, assuring his auditors that the latchets of his shoes were more instructed than those two physicians; that all Universities, all writers put together, were less gifted than the hairs of his beard and of the crown of his head; and that, in a word, he was to be regarded as the legitimate monarch of medicine. 'You shall follow me,' cried he, 'you, Avicenna, Galen, Rhasis, Montagnana, Mesues, you, gentlemen of Paris, Montpellier, Germany, Cologne, Vienna,[6] and whomsoever the Rhine and Danube nourish; you who inhabit the isles of the sea; you, likewise, Dalmatians, Athenians; thou, Arab; thou, Greek; thou, Jew: all shall follow me, and the monarchy shall be mine.'[7]

"But at Basil it was speedily perceived that the new Professor was no better than an egregious quack. Scarcely a year elapsed before his lectures had fairly driven away an audience incapable of comprehending their emphatic jargon. That which above all contributed to sully his reputation was the debauched life he led. According to the testimony of Oporinus, who lived two years in his intimacy, Paracelsus scarcely ever ascended the lecture-desk unless half drunk, and only dictated to his secretaries when in a state of intoxication: if summoned to attend the sick, he rarely proceeded thither without previously drenching himself with wine. He was accustomed to retire

---

47| *MS:* unknown; it *1835:* unknown: it 48| *MS:* 33 *1849:* thirty-three 49| *MS:* personages, procured *1835:* personages procured 51| *MS:* Physic and Surgery *1835:* physic and surgery 52| *MS:* Amphitheatre *1835:* amphitheatre 54–55| *MS:* Physicians—that all the Universities, all the writers *1835:* physicians; that *1849:* all Universities, all writers 55| *MS:* together were *1835:* together, were 56| *MS:* crown of his head, and that, finally, he § *crown of his head* replaces four illegible words § *1849:* that, in a word, he 58–59| *MS:* me' cried he 'you <> Mesue,—you, Gentlemen *1835:* me,' cried he, 'you <> Mesue; you *1849:* Mesues, you *1863:* gentlemen 60| *MS:* and all soever whom the *1840:* and whomsoever the 61| *MS:* sea—you likewise, <> Arab— *1835:* sea; you, likewise, <> Arab, 62| *MS:* Greek—thou Jew—all *1835:* Greek; thou, Jew; all *1888:* Jew: all 65| *MS:* Quack: scarcely had a *1835:* quack. Scarcely *1849:* Scarcely a 67| *MS:* their § cancels *his* § 69| *MS:* Oporinus *1835:* Oporinus, 70| *MS:* lecture— § inserted above the line § 72| *MS:* sick he *1835:* sick, he to bed without changing his clothes; sometimes he spent the night in pot-houses with peasants, and in the morning knew no longer what he was about; and, nevertheless, up to the age of twenty-five his only drink had been water.[8]

"At length, fearful of being punished for a serious outrage on a magistrate,[9] he fled from Basil towards the end of the year 1527, and took refuge in Alsatia, whither he caused Oporinus to follow with his chemical apparatus.

"He than entered once more upon the career of ambulatory theosophist.[10] Accordingly we find him at Colmar in 1528; at Nuremberg in 1529; at St. Gall in 1531; at Pfeffers in 1535; and at Augsburg in 1536: he next made some stay in Moravia, where he still further compromised his reputation by the loss of many distinguished patients, which compelled him to betake himself to Vienna; from thence he passed into Hungary; and in 1538 was at Villach, where he dedicated his 'Chronicle' to the States of Carinthia, in gratitude for the many kindnesses with which they had honoured his father. Finally, from Mindelheim, which he visited in 1540, Paracelsus proceeded to Salzburg, where he died in the Hospital of St. Stephen (*Sebastian* is meant), Sept. 24, 1541."—(Here follows a criticism on his writings, which I omit.)

[1]*Paracelsus* would seem to be a fantastic version of *Von Hohenheim;* Einsiedeln is the Latinized Eremus, whence Paracelsus is sometimes called, as in the correspondence of Erasmus, Eremita; Bombast, his proper name, probably acquired, from the characteristic phraseology of his lectures, that unlucky signification which it has ever since retained.

75| *MS:* peasants and *1835:* peasants, and 76| *MS:* and nevertheless <> 25 *1835:* and, nevertheless *1849:* twenty-five 79| *MS:* Basil, towards <> year 27 and *1835:* Basil towards <> year 27, and *1849:* year '27 *1863:* year 1527 81| *MS:* chymical *1863:* chemical 82| *MS:* Theosophist *1835:* theosophist 83–84| *MS:* 1528: at <> 1529: *1835:* 1528/ at <> 1529; *1868:* 1529: at Nuremburg *1888:* 1529; at Nuremberg 84| *MS:* 1531: at <> 1535: at Augsburg *1835:* 1531; at <> 1535; at Augsburg *1849:* 1535; and at Augsburg 88| *MS:* Hungary, and *1849:* Hungary; and 89| *MS:* Chronicle <> Carinthia, in § ? § *1835:* 'Chronicle' <> Carinthia, in 91| *MS:* Mindelheim, where he was in *1849:* Mindelheim, which he visited in 92–93| *MS:* (*Sebastian,* he means.) Sept. 24, 151. (Here *1835:* means), Sept. 24, 1541"—(Here § MS does not put translation in quotes § *1849:* (*Sebastian,* is meant) 95–99| *MS:* § Complete Note 1 § Hohenheim, Einsiedeln and the latin § *the latin* inserted above the line § Eremus, (whence Paracelsus is sometimes called, as in the correspondence of Erasmus, § *in* <> *Erasmus,* inserted above the line § Eremita,) are I suppose one and the same town. *1835:* Einsiedeln, and the Latin Eremus (whence <> are, I suppose, one *1849:* § as in 1888 except § Latin <> name, originally acquired *1863:* name probably acquired *1868:* Latinized

[2]I shall disguise M. Renauldin's next sentence a little. "Hic (Erastus sc.) Paracelsium trimum a milite quodam, alii a sue exectum ferunt: constat imberbem illum, mulierumque osorem fuisse." A standing High-Dutch joke in those days at the expense of a number of learned men, as may be seen by referring to such rubbish as Melander's "Jocoseria," etc. In the prints from his portrait by Tintoretto, painted a year before his death, Paracelsus is *barbatulus*, at all events. But Erastus was never without a good reason for his faith—*e.g.* "Helvetium fuisse (Paracelsum) vix credo, vix enim ea regio tale monstrum ediderit." (De Medicina Nova.)

[3]Then Bishop of Spanheim, and residing at Würzburg in Franconia; a town situated in a grassy fertile country, whence its name, Herbipolis. He was much visited there by learned men, as may be seen by his "Epistolæ Familiares," Hag. 1536: among others, by his staunch friend Cornelius Agrippa, to whom he dates thence, in 1510, a letter in answer to the dedicatory epistle prefixed to the treatise De Occult. Philosoph., which last contains the following ominous allusion to Agrippa's sojourn: "Quum nuper tecum, R. P. in cœnobio tuo apud Herbipolim aliquamdiu conversatus, multa de chymicis, multa de magicis, multa de cabalisticis, cæterisque quæ adhuc in occulto delitescunt, arcanis scientiis atque artibus una contulissemus," etc.

[4]"Inexplebilis illa aviditas naturæ perscrutandi secreta et reconditarum supellectile scientiarum animum locupletandi, uno eodemque loco diu persistere non patiebatur, sed Mercurii instar, omnes terras, nationes et urbes perlustrandi igniculos supponebat, ut cum viris naturæ scrutatoribus, chymicis præsertim, ore tenus conferret, et quæ diuturnis laboribus nocturnisque vigiliis invenerant una vel altera communicatione obtineret." (Bitiskius in Præfat.) "Patris auxilio primum, deinde propria industria doctissimos viros in Germania, Italia, Gallia, Hispania, aliisque Europæ regionibus, nactus est præceptores; quorum liberali

100| *MS:* disguise <> a § cancel illegible words § 101| *MS:* à <> à *1863:* a <> a 102| *MS:* illum et § illegible cancelled by § μισογυταιων fuisse." <> joke of those *1835:* μισογυταιων <> joke in those *1849:* illum fuisse." A *1863:* illum, mulierumque osorem fuisse." A 103| *MS:* days at the expence of a vast number of learned men as § *at* <> *men*, inserted above the line § *1835:* expense *1849:* of a number 104| *MS:* Jocoseria, &c &c. *1845:* Jocoseria, &c. &c. *1863:* 'Jocoseria," etc. *1888:* "Jocoseria," 105| *MS:* painted a year before his death § inserted above the line § 107| *MS:* fuisse (P) vix <> ediderit." *1835:* fuisse (P.) vix <> ediderit."— *1849:* fuisse (Paracelsum) vix *1863:* ediderit: *1868:* ediderit." 108| *MS: De Med. Novâ.* *1835:* (De Medicina Nova.) 109| *MS:* Franconia,—a *1835:* Franconia, a *1849:* Franconia: a 110| *MS:* its Latin name Herbipolis. He *1849:* its name, Herbipolis. He 111–112| *MS: Epistolae familiares. Hag. 1536.* *1835:* 1536: *1863:* 'Epistolae Familiares, Hag. *1888:* "Epistolae Familiares." 112–113| *MS:* Among others by <> Cor. <> dates from thence *1849:* others, by <> Cornelius <> dates thence, *1863:* among 113| *MS:* 1510 a *1849:* 1510, a 114| *MS:* de Occult. Phil. which last § *last* inserted above the line § *1863:* De Occult. Philosoph., 115| *MS:* to his sojourn: <> P, in *1835:* P. in *1849:* to Agrippa's sojourn: 118| *MS:* contulissemus" &c &c *1835:* contulissemus," &c &c. *1863:* contulissemus," etc. 120| *MS:* loco, diu *1868:* loco diu 121| *MS:* mercurii *1868:* Mercurii 122| *MS:* supponebat et cum *1868:* supponebat, ut cum 123| *1849:* unâ *1863:* una 124| *MS: Bitiskius in praefat.* *1835:* Praefat. *1849:* alterâ *1863:* altera <> (Bitiskius in Praefat.) 125| *MS:* primùm <> propriâ industriâ <> Germaniâ, Italiâ, Galliâ, *1863:* primum <> propria industria <> Germania, Italia, Gallia, doctrina, et potissimum propria inquisitione ut qui esset ingenio acutissimo ac fere divino, tantum profecit, ut multi testati sint, in universa philosophia, tam ardua, tam arcana et abdita eruisse mortalium neminem." (Melch. Adam. in Vit. Germ. Medic.) "Paracelsus qui in intima naturæ viscera sic penitus introierit, metallorum stirpiumque vires et facultates tam incredibili ingenii acumine exploraverit ac perviderit, ad morbos omnes vel desperatos et opinione hominum insanabiles percurandum; ut cum Theophrasto nata primum medicina perfectaque videtur." (Petri Rami Orat. de Basilea.) His passion for wandering is best described in his own words: "Ecce amatorem adolescentem difficillimi itineris haud piget, ut venustam saltem puellam vel fœminam aspiciat: quanto minus nobilissimarum artium amore laboris ac cujuslibet tædii pigebit?" etc. ("Defensiones Septem adversus æmulos suos." 1573. Def. 4ta. "De peregrinationibus ex exilio.")

[5]The reader may remember that it was in conjunction with Œcolampadius, then Divinity Professor at Basil, that Zuinglius published in 1528 an answer to Luther's Confession of Faith; and that both proceeded in company to the subsequent conference with Luther and Melanchthon at Marpurg. Their letters fill a large volume.—"D.D. Johannis Œcolampadii et Huldrichi Zuinglii Epistolarum lib. quatuor." Bas. 1536. It must be also observed that Zuinglius began to preach in 1516, and at Zurich in 1519, and that in 1525 the Mass was abolished in the cantons. The tenets of Œcolampadius were supposed to be more evangelical than those up to that period maintained by the glorious German, and our brave Bishop Fisher attacked them as the fouler heresy:—"About this time arose out of Luther's school one Œcolampadius, like a mighty and fierce giant; who, as his master had gone beyond the Church, went beyond his master (or else it had been impossible he could have been reputed the better scholar), who denied the real presence; him, this worthy champion (the Bishop) sets upon, and with five books (like so many smooth stones taken out of the river that doth always run with living water) slays the Philistine; which five books were written in the year of our Lord 1526, at which time he had governed the see of Rochester twenty years." (Life of Bishop Fisher, 1655.) Now, there is no doubt of the Protestantism

---

127| *MS:* doctrinâ, et potissimùm propriâ *1863:* doctrina, et potissimum propria 128| *MS:* tantùm <> philosophiâ *1849:* universâ *1863:* tantum <> universa philosophia 129| *MS:* neminem," *Melch.* <> *Vit.* *1863:* neminem," (Melch. <> Vit. 130| *MS: Medic.* "Paracelsus <> penitùs *1863:* Medic.) "Paracelsus <> penitus 132| *MS:* perviderit; ad <> disperatos *1849:* desperatos *1868:* perviderit, ad 133| *MS:* primùm *1863:* primum 134| *MS:* videtur." Petri <> Basileâ. His *1863:* videtur." (Petri <> Basilea.) His 135| *MS:* words. "Ecce *1835:* words: "Ecce 137–139| *MS:* pigebit? &c. *Defensiones* <> *exilio.*" *1835:* pigebit?" &c.— <> 1573. *Def. 4ta.* "*De* *1863:* pigebit?" etc. ('Defensiones <> suos.' 1573. Def. 4ta. 'De <> exilio.') *1888:* ("Defensiones <> suos." <> "De <> exilio.") 140| *MS:* reader will remember *1849:* reader may remember 141| *MS:* Divinity-Professor *1868:* Divinity Professor 142| *MS:* Faith, and that he accompanied him to *1849:* Faith; and that both proceeded in company to 144| *MS:* volume— *1835:* volume.— 144–145| *MS: D D Johannis* <> *Bas. 1536.* *1835:* D. D. Johannis <> 1536. *1863:* D. D. Johannis <> Epistolarum' <> Bas. *1888:* "D. D. Johannis <> Epistolarum lib. quatuor." Bas. 148| *MS:* those at that *1849:* those up to that 151| *MS:* church *1849:* Church 152| *MS:* scholar) who *1863:* scholar), who 156| *MS:* 20 *1888:* twenty 157| *MS:* years."—*Life of Bp. Fisher. 1655.* Now there *1835:* 1655. *1849:* Now, there *1863:* years." (Life of Bishop Fisher. 1655.)

of Paracelsus, Erasmus, Agrippa, etc., but the nonconformity of Paracelsus was always scandalous. L. Crasso ("Elogj d'Huomini Letterati," Ven. 1666) informs us that his books were excommunicated by the Church. Quenstedt (de Patr. Doct.) affirms "nec tantum novæ medicinæ, verum etiam novæ theologiæ autor est." Delrio, in his Disquisit. Magicar., classes him among those "partim atheos, partim hæreticos" (lib. i. cap. 3). "Omnino tamen multa theologica in ejusdem scriptis plane atheismum olent, ac duriuscule sonant in auribus vere Christiani." (D. Gabrielis Clauderi Schediasma de Tinct. Univ. Norimb. 1736.) I shall only add one more authority:—"Oporinus dicit se (Paracelsum) aliquando Lutherum et Papam, non minus quam nunc Galenum et Hippocratem redacturum in ordinem minabatur, neque enim eorum qui hactenus in scripturam sacram scripsissent, sive veteres, sive recentiores, quenquam scripturæ nucleum recte eruisse, sed circa corticem et quasi membranam tantum hærere." (Th. Erastus, Disputat. de Med. Nova.) These and similar notions had their due effect on Oporinus, who, says Zuingerus, in his "Theatrum," "longum vale dixit ei (Paracelso), ne ob præceptoris, alioqui amicissimi, horrendas blasphemias ipse quoque aliquando pœnas Deo Opt. Max. lueret."

[6]Erastus, who relates this, here oddly remarks, "mirum quod non et Garamantos, Indos et *Anglos* adjunxit." Not so wonderful neither, if we believe what another adversary "had heard somewhere,"—that all Paracelsus' system came of his pillaging "Anglum quendam, Rogerium Bacchonem."

[7]See his works *passim.* I must give one specimen:—Somebody had been styling him "Luther alter." "And why not?" (he asks, as he well might). "Luther is abundantly learned, therefore you hate him and me; but we are at least a match for you.—Nam et contra vos et vestros universos principes Avicennam,

158| *MS:* Agrippa &c but < > of P was *1835:* Agrippa, &c. but < > of Paracelsus was *1868:* Agrippa, etc., but 159| *MS: (Elogj d'Huomini Letterati. Ven. 1666)* *1835:* 1666 *1863:* ('Elogj < > Letterati.' Ven. 1666) *1888:* ("Elogj < > Letterati," Ven. 1666) 160–161| *MS:* church. Quenstedt *(de Patr. Doct.)* *1835:* Church *1868:* (de Patr. Doct.) 161| *MS:* Medicinae < > Theologia *1835:* tantùm < > medicinae < > theologiae *1863:* tantum 162| *MS:* Delrio in his *Disquisit. Magicar.* *1835:* Delrio, in *1863:* Disquisit. Magicar., 163| *MS: (lib 1. cap 3).* < > Theologica *1835:* 1. *cap.* 3.) < > theologica *1863:* (lib. 1. cap. 3). *1888:* lib. i. cap. 3). 164| *MS:* Scriptis < > Atheismum < > Christiani"— *1835:* scriptis planè < > atheismum < > Christiani." *1863:* plane 165| *MS: D. Gabrielis* < > *1736.* *1835:* 1736. *1863:* (D. Gabrielis < > 1736.) 166| *MS:* se (P) aliquando *1835:* se (Paracelsum) aliquando 167| *MS: 1835:* minùs *1863:* minus 169| *MS:* rectè *1863:* recte 170–171| *MS: Th. Erastus. Disputat. de Med. Novâ.* *1863:* (Th. Erastus, Disputat. de Med. Nova.) 172| *MS:* Zuingerus in his "*Theatrum,*" < > ei (P) ne *1835:* Zuingerus, in his *Theatrum,* < > ei (Paracelso) ne *1863:* 'Theatrum,' *1888:* "Theatrum," 173| *MS:* praeceptoris alioqui *1835:* praeceptoris, alioqui 175| *MS:* Erastus who < > remarks "mirum *1835:* Erastus, who < > remarks, "mirùm *1863:* mirum 176–178| *MS:* adjunxit." *1849:* § adds § Not < > Bacchonem." 179| *MS:* specimen: somebody *1835:* specimen:—Somebody 1888: specimen: Somebody *1889:* specimen:—Somebody 180| *MS:* not?" he asks, as he will might,—"Luther *1835:* alter:" "and < > might; "Luther *1849:* not?" (he < > might), "Luther *1863:* might,) "Luther *1868:* might.) "Luther *1888:* alter." "And < > might), "Luther 182| *MS:* you"—"Nam < > Principes *1835:* you." < > principes *1849:* you.—Nam

Galenum, Aristotelem, etc. me satis superque munitum esse novi. Et vertex iste meus calvus ac depilis multo plura et sublimiora novit quam vester vel Avicenna vel universæ academiæ. Prodite, et signum date, qui viri sitis, quid roboris habeatis? quid autem sitis? Doctores et magistri, pediculus pectentes et fricantes podicem." (Frag. Med.)

[8]His defenders allow the drunkenness. Take a sample of their excuses: "Gentis hoc, non viri vitiolum est, a Taciti seculo ad nostrum usque non interrupto filo devolutum, sinceritati forte Germanæ coævum, et nescio an aliquo consanguinitatis vinculo junctum." (Bitiskius.) The other charges were chiefly trumped up by Oporinus: "Domi, quod Oporinus amanuensis ejus sæpe narravit, numquam nisi potus ad explicanda sua accessit, atque in medio conclavi ad columnam τετυφωμένος adsistens, apprehenso manibus capulo ensis, cujus κοίλωμα hospitium præbuit, ut aiunt, spiritui familiari, imaginationes aut concepta sua protulit:—alii illud quod in capulo habuit, ab ipso Azoth appellatum, medicinam fuisse præstantissimam aut lapidem Philosophicum putant." (Melch. Adam.) This famous sword was no laughing-matter in those days, and it is now a material feature in the popular idea of Paracelsus. I recollect a couple of allusions to it in our own literature, at the moment.

Ne had been known the Danish Gonswart,
Or Paracelsus with his long sword.

'Volpone' act ii. scene 2.

Bumbastus kept a devil's bird
Shut in the pummel of his sword,
That taught him all the cunning pranks
Of past and future mountebanks.

'Hudibras,' part ii. cant. 3.

This Azoth was simply "*laudanum suum.*" But in his time he was commonly believed to possess the double tincture—the power of curing diseases and transmuting metals. Oporinus often witnessed, as he declares, both these effects, as did also Franciscus, the servant of Paracelsus, who describes, in a letter to Neander, a successful projection at which he was present, and the results of

---

183| *MS:* Aristotelem &c *1835:* Aristotelem, &c. *1863:* etc. 184| *MS:* quàm *1863:* quam 185| *MS:* Academiae *1835:* academiae 187| *MS:* podicem." *1835:* podicem."—*Frag. Med.* *1863:* podicem." (Frag. Med.)
188| *MS:* allow this:— take § cancelled by § allow the drunkenness:—take *1835:* drunkenness. Take 191| *MS: Bitiskius.* *1863:* junctum." (Bitiskius.)
192| *MS:* Oporinus: § two thirds of a line cancelled § Domi *1835:* saepè *1863:* saepe 195| *MS:* praebuit ut aiunt spiritui *1888:* praebuit, ut aiunt, spiritui 196| *MS:* appellatum *1888:* appellatum, 197–198| *MS:* Medicinam <> *Melch. Adam.* *1835:* Putant."—*Melch.* *1863:* medicinam <> putant." (Melch. Adam.) 198| *MS:* laughing matter <> days and *1835:* days, and *1863:* laughing-matter 201| *MS:* Gonswart *1835:* Gonswart,
203| *MS: Volpone, Act 2. sc. 2* *1835: Act* 2. sc. 2. *1849: Act* ii, *sc.* 2. *1863:* 'Volpone,' Act ii. Scene 2. *1888:* 'Volpone, act ii, scene 2. 204| *MS:* Devil's *1868:* devil's 206| *MS:* Pranks *1835:* pranks, *1868:* pranks 208| *MS: Hudibras. Part 2. Cant. 3.* *1835: Part* 2. *Cant.* 3. *1849: Part* ii, *Cant.* 3. *1863:* 'Hudibras,' Part ii. Cant. 3. *1888:* part ii, cant. 3. 209| *MS:* § no ¶ § <> *suum:"* But *1835: suum."* But 210| *MS:* Double Tincture *1835:* double tincture <> diseases, and *1868:* diseases and 212–213| *MS:* Franciscus the <> Paracelsus who <> Neander a *1835:* Franciscus, the <> Paracelsus, who <> Neander, a

which, good golden ingots, were confided to his keeping. For the other quality, let the following notice vouch among many others:—"Degebat Theophrastus Norimbergæ procitus a medentibus illius urbis, et vaniloquus deceptorue proclamatus, qui, ut laboranti famæ subveniat, viros quosdam authoritatis summæ in Republica illa adit, et infamiæ amoliendæ, artique suæ asserrendæ, specimen ejus pollicetur editurum, nullo stipendio vel accepto pretio, horum faciles præbentium aures jussu elephantiacos aliquot, a communione hominum cæterorum segregatos, et in valetudinarium detrusos, alieno arbitrio eliguntur, quos virtute singulari remediorum suorum Theophrastus a fœda Græcorum lepra mundat, pristinæque sanitati restituit; conservat illustre harum curationum urbs in archivis suis testimonium." (Bitiskius.)* It is to be remarked that Oporinus afterwards repented of his treachery: "Sed resipuit tandem, et quem vivum convitiis insectatus fuerat defunctum veneratione prosequutus, infames famæ præceptoris morsus in remorsus conscientiæ conversi pœnitentia, heu nimis tarda, vulnera clausere exanimi quæ spiranti inflixerant." For these "bites" of Oporinus, see Disputat. Erasti, and Andreæ Jocisci "Oratio de Vit. ob. Opora;" for the "remorse," Mic. Toxita in pref. Testamenti, and Conringius (otherwise an enemy of Paracelsus), who says it was

*The premature death of Paracelsus casts no manner of doubt on the fact of his having possessed the Elixir Vitæ: the alchemists have abundant reasons to adduce, from which I select the following, as explanatory of a property of the Tincture not calculated on by its votaries:—"Objectionem illam, quod Paracelsus non fuerit longævus, nonnulli quoque solvunt per rationes physicas: vitæ nimirum abbreviationem fortasse tallibus accidere posse, ob Tincturam frequentiore ac largiore dosi sumtam, dum a summe efficaci et penetrabili hujus virtute calor innatus quasi suffocatur." (Gabrielis Clauderi Schediasma.)

214| *MS:* his trust: for <> quality *1835:* trust. For <> quality, *1849:* his keeping. For 215| *MS:* following vouch <> others: "Degebat *1835:* others:—"Degebat *1849:* following notice vouch 216| *MS:* prociscus à Medentibus *1863:* procitus a medentibus 218| *MS:* Reipublicâ illâ *1835:* Rei publicâ *1863:* Republica illa 220| *MS:* à *1863:* a 222| *MS:* à fœdâ <> leprâ *1863:* a foeda <> lepra 223–224| *MS:* Urbs in Archivis <> testimonium."—*Bitiskius.* *1839:* urbs in archivis *1863:* testimonium." (Bitiskius.) 225| *MS:* treachery "Sed *1835:* treachery: "Sed 226–227| *MS:* fuerat, defunctum <> conversi, pœnitentiâ heu <> tarda vulnerâ *1835:* fueratu defunctum <> conversi pœnitentiâ *1863:* pœnitentia <> tarda, vulnera 227| *MS:* clausêre *1863:* clausere 228| *MS:* Oporinus see "*Disputat Erasti*"— *1835:* Oporinus, see "*Disputat. Erasti,*" *1863:* Disputat. Erasti, 229–230| *MS:* Andreas Jociscus "*Oratio de vit. et. ob. Opi:*—for <> Toxitus *in praef. Testamenti* *1835:* Opori;" for <> Toxites *1849:* Toxita *1863:* 'Oratio de vit. et ob. Opori, <> in pref. Testamenti, *1868:* Andreae Jocisci *1888:* "Oratio de Vit ob. Opori;"

*1| *MS:* of P. casts *1835:* of Paracelsus casts 2| *MS:* Alchemists *1835:* alchemists 3| *MS:* adduce—from *1835:* adduce, from 4| *MS:* votaries. "Objectionem *1863:* votaries:—'Objectionem 5| *MS:* Physicas *1835:* physicas 8| *MS: Gabrielis Clauderi Schediasma* *1835:* suffocatur."—*Gabrielis* <> *Schediasma.* *1863:* suffocatur." (Gabrielis Clauderi Schediasma.)

contained in a letter from Oporinus to Doctor Vegerus.†

Whatever the moderns may think of these marvellous attributes, the title of Paracelsus to be considered the father of modern chemistry is indisputable. Gerardus Vossius, "De Philosa et Philosum sectis," thus prefaces the ninth section of cap. 9, "De Chymia"—"Nobilem hanc medicinæ partem, diu sepultam avorum ætate, quasi ab orco revocavit Th. Paracelsus." I suppose many hints lie scattered in his neglected books, which clever appropriators have since developed with applause. Thus, it appears from his treatise "De Phlebotomia," and elsewhere, that he had discovered the circulation of the blood and the sanguification of the heart; as did after him Realdo Colombo, and still more perfectly Andrea Cesalpino of Arezzo, as Bayle and Bartoli observe. Even Lavater quotes a passage from his work "De Natura Rerum," on practical Physiognomy, in which the definitions and axioms are precise enough: he adds, "though an astrological enthusiast, a man of prodigious genius." See Holcroft's translation, vol. iii. p. 179—"The Eyes." While on the subject of the writings of Paracelsus, I may explain a passage in the third part of the Poem. He was, as I have said, unwilling to publish his works, but in effect did publish a vast number. Valentius (in Præfat. in Paramyr.) declares "quod ad librorum Paracelsi copiam attinet,

†For a good defence of Paracelsus I refer the reader to Olaus Borrichius' treatise—"Hermetis etc. Sapientia vindicata," 1674. Or, if he is no more learned than myself in such matters, I mention simply that Paracelsus introduced the use of Mercury and Laudanum.

231| *MS:* from O. to *1835:* from Oporinus to 232–234| *MS:* attributes they have confirmed P's title to <> chymistry. Gerardus *1835:* attributes, they <> P.'s *1849:* attributes, the title of Paracelsus to be considered the father of modern chemistry, is indisputable. Gerardus *1888:* Chemistry is 234| *MS:* Vossius *"De Philosâ. et Philosum. sectis* *1835: sectis,"* *1863:* Vossius, 'De Philosa et Philosum sectis,' *1888:* "De <> sectis," 235| *MS: Cap.* 9 "De Chymia."—Nobilem <> sepultam, avorum *1835:* Cap. 9, *"De Chymiâ"*—"Nobilem <> sepultam avorum *1863:* cap. 9, 'De Chymia' *1888:* "De Chymia" 236| *MS:* aetate quasi ab Orco *1835:* orco *1888:* aetate, quasi 238| *MS:* applause: thus <> *"De Phlebotamiâ"* *1835:* applause. Thus <> Phlebotamiâ," *1863:* 'De Phlebotamia,' *1888:* "De Phlebotamia," 240–241| *MS:* heart: as did after him Andreas Cesalpinus of Arezzo, who died 1603 aged 83, as Bayle observes. Even *1835:* heart; as <> 1603, aged *1849:* after him Realdo Columbo, and still more perfectly Andrea Cesalpino of Arezzo, as Bayle and Bartoli observe. Even 242| *MS: "De naturâ Rerum,"* *1835:* work, *"De* *1863:* 'De Natura Rerum,' *1868:* work 'De *1888:* "De Natura Rerum," 243| *MS:* enough <> tho' *1835:* enough: <> though 244–245| *MS: Translation Vol. 3. p 179. "The eyes."* *1835:* Translation, vol. iii. p. 179—*"The Eyes."* 245| *MS:* of P, I *1835:* of Paracelsus, I 246| *MS:* Part *1835:* part 248| *MS: (in præfat. In Paramyr.)* <> Pi. *1835: (in Præfat in Paramyr)* *1849:* (in Præfat. in Paramyr.) <> Paracelsi *1863:* (in Praefat. in Paramyr.)

†2| *MS:* treatise "Hermetis &c sapientia vindicata. 167." *1835:* Treatise—"Hermetis &c. *1863:* 'Hermetis etc. Sapientia vindicata,' 1674. *1888:* "Hermetis <> vindicata." 1674.

audio, a Germanis prope trecentos recenseri." "O fœcunditas ingenii!" adds he, appositely. Many of these, were, however, spurious; and Fred. Bitiskius gives his good edition (3 vols. fol. Gen. 1658) "rejectis suppositis solo ipsius nomine superbientibus quorum ingens circumfertur numerus." The rest were "charissimum et pretiosissimum authoris pignus, extorsum potius ab illo quam obtentum." "Jam minime eo volente atque jubente hæc ipsius scripta in lucem prodisse videntur; quippe quæ muro inclusa ipso absente, servi cujusdam indicio, furto surrepta atque sublata sunt," says Valentius. These have been the study of a host of commentators, amongst whose labours are most notable, Petri Severini, "Idea Medicinæ Philosophiæ. Bas. 1571"; Mic. Toxetis, "Onomastica. Arg. 1574"; Dornei, "Dist. Parac. Franc. 1584"; and "Pi Philosæ Compendium cum scholiis auctore Leone Suavio. Paris." (This last, a good book.)

[9]A disgraceful affair. One Liechtenfels, a canon, having been rescued *in extremis* by the "*laudanum*" of Paracelsus, refused the stipulated fee, and was supported in his meanness by the authorities, whose interference Paracelsus would not brook. His own liberality was allowed by his bitterest foes, who found a ready solution of his indifference to profit in the aforesaid sword-handle and its guest. His freedom from the besetting sin of a profession he abhorred—(as he curiously says somewhere, "Quis quæso deinceps honorem deferat professione tali, quæ a tam facinorosis nebulonibus obitur et administratur?")—is recorded in his epitaph, which affirms—"Bona sua in pauperes distribuenda collocandaque erogavit," *honoravit,* or *ordinavit*—for accounts differ.

[10]"So migratory a life could afford Paracelsus but little leisure for application to books, and accordingly he informs us that for the space of ten years he never opened a single volume, and that his whole medical library was not composed of six sheets: in effect, the inventory drawn up after his death states that the only books which he left were the Bible, the New Testament, the Commentaries of St. Jerome on the Gospels, a printed volume on Medicine, and seven manuscripts."

250| *MS:* he appositely: Many of these were *1835:* appositely. Many *1849:* he, appositely *1888:* these, were 251| *MS: (3 vols. fol. Gen. 1658)* *1835:* (3 vols. fol. Gen. 1658) *1849:* suppositas *1863:* suppositis 252| *1835:* ingeus *1849:* ingens 253| *MS:* Authoris <> quam *1835:* authoris piguus <> potiùs *1849:* pignus *1863:* potius <> quam 255| *MS:* absente servi *1888:* absente, servi 257| *MS:* among *1888:* amongst 257–260| *MS: Idea Medicinæ Philosophiæ. Bas. 1571.* Mic. Toxetis *Onomastica. Arg.* 1574. Dornei *Dict. Parac. Franc.* 1584. and *Pi. Philosæ Compendium um scholiis auctore Leone Suavio. Paris.* *1835:* Severini, *Idea* <> 1571; Mic. Toxetis, *Onomastica.* Arg. 1574: Dornei, *Dict.* <> 1584; and *1863:* 'Idea Medicinæ Philosophiæ Bas. 1571;' Mic. Toxetis, 'Onomastica. Arg. 1574;' Dornei, 'Dict. Parac. Franc. 1584;' and 'Pi Philosæ Compendium cum scholiis auctore Leone Suavio. Paris.' *1888:* "Idea <> 1571;" <> "Onomastica. Arg. 1574;" <> "Dict. <> 1584:" and "Pi <> Paris." 261| *MS:* Liechtenfels a canon, having *1835:* Liicetenfels, a 262| *MS:* of P, refused to come down with the stipulated *1835:* of Paracelsus, refused *1849:* refused the stipulated 263| *MS:* Authorities <> interference P *1835:* authorities <> interference Paracelsus 266| *MS:* guest: his <> abhorred (as *1835:* guest. His <> abohorred—(as 268| *MS:* à <> administratur?) is § written over by § administratur?") is *1849:* administratur?",—is *1863:* a 269| *MS:* epitaph which affirms *1835:* epitaph, which affirms— 270| *MS:* erogavit"—honoravit—or ordinavit *1835:* erogavit" honoravit, or *1849:* erogavit," honoravit *1863:* *honoravit,* or *ordinavit*

Editorial Notes

PAULINE

Pauline; A Fragment of a Confession was written in 1832 and published in March, 1833, London: Saunders and Otley, Conduit Street. At the end of the poem appears the note "Richmond, October 22, 1832." John Forster's copy of the poem has a note in B's hand explaining his presence in Richmond and suggesting that as the date of his conception of the poem: "Kean was acting there: I saw him in Richard III that night, and conceived the childish scheme already mentioned: there is an allusion to Kean, page 47 [11. 669–75]. I don't know whether I had not made up my mind to *act,* as well as to make verses, music, and God knows what,—*que de châteaux en Espagne* [what castles in Spain]!"

The John Forster copy, originally owned by John Stuart Mill, is now in the Forster Collection at the Library of the Victoria and Albert Museum, South Kensington. It contains notes which Mill wrote in anticipation of a review which he either never finished or failed to publish. Mill's annotated copy found its way back to B who responded to Mill's comments by remarks of his own. B later gave the book to Forster.

After its initial publication, the poem did not appear again until 1868. In the introductory note to the 1868 edition Browning felt it necessary to apologize for *Pauline* [See prefatory material to the editions of 1868, 1888, and 1889 included in this edition].

Title Page] *"Plus ne* . . . The quotation is from a poem called "De lui-même". Because of its thematic relevance to *Pauline,* it is translated here in its entirety:

I am no longer that which I was,
Nor will I ever know how to be so again;
My beautiful springtime and my summer
Have gone out the window.
Love, thou hast been my master,
I have served thee above all the gods.
O if I could be born a second time
How much better would I serve thee!

Title Page] *Marot* Clément Marot (c. 1496–1544), a French court poet of the early Renaissance, was born at Cohors in Quercy. His career would have held some interest for B. He lived for a time in Italy (and died there), he was critical of the established theology, the friars, and the papacy. His early collection of poetry, *Adolescence Clementine* (1532), bears some resemblance to *Pauline* in its confessional tone.

Reverse Title Page] *Non dubito* . . . I am sure that the title of my book, because of its rarity, will entice very many to read it. Among those will be some whose opinions are hostile, whose minds are weak—many of these are even malicious—, who are unable to accept my genius, and who, rash in their ignorance, will create a clamor after scarcely even glancing at the title. They will say that I teach forbidden things, lay the seeds of heresies, offend pious ears, and corrupt pure minds. . . . They are so full of care for their consciences that neither Apollo, nor all the Muses, nor even an Angel from heaven could free me from their curses. Now I too am full of care for them—that they not read my book, nor understand it, nor remember it; for it is harmful and very poisonous. In this book is the gateway to hell; it speaks hard words. Let them beware that it not shake their understanding out of them. But you, who come to read it with fair minds, if only you use as much discretion and prudence as bees use in gathering honey, go ahead and read it free from anxiety. I think that you will obtain from it no little utility and much pleasure. If you find anything which displeases you, reject it and do not use it. FOR I AM NOT SAYING THAT THESE THINGS ARE GOOD FOR YOU, I AM ONLY SAYING THEM. But do not reject the others. . . . So, if anything has been said too freely, forgive my youth since I, the writer of this work, am less than a youth.

Reverse Title Page] *H. Cor Agrippa,* . . . Henry Cornelius Agrippa of Nettesheim (1486–1535), writer and physician, wrote on occult philosophy, particularly that ascribed to the tradition of Hermes Trismegistus. His *De occulta philosophia* was written around 1510 and published in revised form in Antwerp in 1531. The work is a mixture of Neoplatonic and Christian belief in which magic emerges as the means by which man most readily achieves knowledge of God.

Reverse Title Page] *V.A. XX Vixi annos viginti.* I was twenty years old.

48] *Northern night* In northern latitudes, as in Lapland, unbroken daylight in summer and darkness in winter last for several months each.

142] *His award* A note in B's hand found in John Forster's copy of *Pauline* reads "The award of fame to him—the late acknowledgement of Shelley's genius."

151] *Sun-treader* Undoubtedly a reference to Percy Bysshe Shelley. In the John Forster copy, Mill wrote in the margin along side the lines beginning "I ne'er had ventured . . ." (141) the comment "Only at the fourth reading of this poem I found out what this meant." B replied at the bottom of the page (ending with line 153) with the comment quoted above (l. 142n). For young B's indebtedness to Shelley, see F. A. Pottle, *Shelley and Browning: A Myth and Some Facts* (Chicago, 1923).

321-322] *a god/Wandering after beauty* . . . Possibly a reference to Apollo whose love for and pursuit of Daphne is the most famous of his many amours. Ovid in his *Metamorphoses* tells the story of his pursuit of Daphne who, a devotee of Artemis and thus vowed to chastity, was changed into a laurel tree in order to avoid the embraces of her lover. The passage might also refer to Pan who pursued many nymphs, one of whom, Syrinx, was transformed into a bed of reeds from which Pan cut the first Pan-pipe. It is conceivable that B left the reference intentionally ambiguous so as to suggest recurring classical themes.

322] *a giant* Perhaps Atlas whom Homer describes as one who kept the pillars which hold heaven and earth asunder. The pillars which he supported were thought to rest in the sea beyond the most Western horizon. Hence, the image which B employs.

323] *an old hunter* P-C suggests that the old hunter is possibly Peleus on the grounds that he participated in the Calydonian boar hunt and that the gods were present for his marriage to the sea nymph Thetis. He appears in conversation with Thetis as an old man at the end of Euripides' *Andromache*. Orion, on the other hand, is identified primarily as a hunter and was in constant converse with the gods. He was beloved of the dawn goddess Eos and is most frequently associated with Artemis (or Diana), goddess of wild animals and the hunt. According to the most popular account of his death, Artemis, who loved him, was tricked by the jealous Apollo into shooting him with arrows. It is true that he appears nowhere in Greek legend as a particularly old man but then Browning may be using the word less to describe the hunter's age than to emphasize that he is a hunter from the remote past. Moreover, age was a very relative thing in Greek myth.

324] *high crested chief* In Book III of Homer's *Odyssey*, old Nestor, king of Pylos, tells Telemachus, son of Odysseus, that following the downfall of Troy the Argive army was divided among those who remained in Troy with Agamemnon, hoping by sacrifice to appease the wrath of Athene, and those who departed immediately for home. The latter sailed first to the island of Tenedos. Among the most illustrious of the crew, in addition to Nestor himself, were Odysseus, Diomedes, and Menelaus.

325] *Tenedos* An island about seven miles in length situated in the Aegean Sea off the Troad. The island is called Bozcaada today.

331] *Dim clustered isles* Islands in the Aegean Sea, east of Greece.

334] *Swift-footed* Hermes, messenger of the gods.

335] *Proserpine's* The daughter of Zeus and Demeter, who with the consent of Zeus was abducted by Hades and became his wife. Because of Demeter's anger Zeus sent Hermes to rescue Proserpine from Hades.

403] *White way* Milky way.

479] *Arab birds* Whether or not B had a specific bird in mind is not clear. Of all the possible identifications of a particular bird that have been offered that of the pelican is most convincing. The pelican is found in Arabia and also fits B's description in its habits of flight.

488] *vanity of vanities! Ecclesiastes* 1:2.

527-528] *One branch from the gold forest, like the knight/Of old tales,* At the command of the Cumaean sybil, Aeneas must find and pluck a golden bough if he wishes to visit Anchises in the Underworld. The story appears in Vergil's *Aeneid,* IV.

567-568] *that king/Treading the purple calmly to his death* On page 30 in the John Forster copy of *Pauline,* B prints in Greek the following quotation from Aeschylus' *Agamemnon,* lines addressed by Agamemnon to Clytemnestra: "Since I have been overbourn to harken to thee in this, I will tread upon the purple pathway as I pass to my palace halls." (The translation is from The Loeb Classical Library, Aeschylus II, *Agamemnon,* ll. 956-957.)

572] *And him sitting alone in blood* On page 40 in the John Forster copy of the poem, B prints in Greek the following quotation from Sophocles' *Ajax,* indicating that it elucidates line 572:

> But now, confounded in his [Ajax'] abject woe,
> Refusing food or drink, he sits there still,
> Just where he fell amid the carcases
> Of the slain sheep and cattle . . .
> Ho Teucer! [Brother of Ajax] where is Teucer? Will his raid
> End never? And the while I am undone!

(The translation is from The Loeb Classical Library, Sophocles II, *Ajax,* 11.322-324, 342-343.)

573] *and the boy* Orestes who says in the *Libation Bearers,* "But—since I would have you known—for I know not how 'twill end. . . . But while I still retain reason, I proclaim to those who hold me dear and declare that not without justice did I slay my mother, polluted murderess of my father, and a thing loathed of Heaven." (The translation is from The Loeb Classical Library, Aeschylus II, *The Libation Bearers,* ll. 1021–23, 1026–27.)

656] *Andromeda* In Greek legend the daughter of Cepheus and Cassiopeia. Cepheus, in order to appease the anger of Poseidon, chained Andromeda to a rocky cliff at the edge of the sea. Perseus rescued her. According to Mrs. Sutherland Orr (*Hbk.,* London, 1896, p. 21) "The 'Andromeda' described . . . is that of Polidori di Caravaggio, of which Mr. Browning possessed an engraving, which was always before his eyes as he wrote his earlier poems. The original was painted on the wall of a garden attached to the Palazzo Bufalo—or del Bufalo—in Rome."

669-675] *I will . . . through decay*. A reference to Edmund Kean (1787-1833). See note on text. Kean was one of the most famous tragic actors of all times, known particularly for his Shakespearean roles. He scored his first important public triumph when he played with great emotional fervor the part of Shylock at Drury Lane in 1814. In March, 1833, shortly after B saw him at Richmond, he collapsed on the stage of Covent Garden where he was playing Othello.

811] *aims** **Je crains* . . . I fear indeed that my poor friend may not always be perfectly understood in what remains to be read of this strange fragment, but he is less suitable than any other to make clear that which of its very nature can never be any more than dream and confusion. Moreover, I do not know whether in trying better to coordinate certain parts, one would not run the risk of destroying the only merit which such a unique work might claim, that of giving a fairly precise idea of the genre of which it is only a rough sketch. This unpretentious beginning, this stirring of passion, which at first increases and then by degrees subsides, these transports of the soul, the sudden return upon the self, and above all, that way of thinking which is peculiar to my friend, make changes almost impossible. Reasons which he has caused to be esteemed elsewhere, and others even more powerful, have won my indulgence for this work which I would otherwise have advised him to throw in the fire. I do not believe less, because of this, in the great principle of all composition, a principle of Shakespeare, of Raphael, of Beethoven, from which it follows that the concentration of ideas is due much more to their conception than to their execution. I have every reason to fear that the first of these qualities is still alien to my friend, and I doubt very strongly that a redoubling of effort would cause him to acquire the second. The best thing would be to burn this—but what am I to do?

I think that in that which follows he alludes to a particular examination which he once made of the soul, or rather his own soul, to discover the sequence of objects that it would be possible for him to achieve, each of which, having been obtained, was to form a kind of plateau, from which he could perceive other ends, other projects, other pleasures, which, in their turn, were to be surmounted. What resulted was that unconsciousness and sleep would put an end to everything. This conception, which I do not fully understand, is perhaps as unintelligible to him as it is to me.

851] *Olivet* The mountain facing Jerusalem on the east. At the foot of the mount of Olives in the garden of Gethsemane, the place where Jesus went with his disciples the night before the crucifixion. A tradition identifies Olivet with the Mount of Transfiguration. Luke 22: 39.

920] *And the crew wandered in its bowers* In Book IX of Homer's *Odyssey,* Odysseus and his men stop at the island of the Lotos Eaters where part of the men eat of the lotus and, because of its narcotic effect, lose their will to return home.

964] *the fair pale sister, went to her chill grave* Antigone, whose story is told in Sophocles' play of that name, chose to be put to death rather than accept Creon's arbitrary decree that her slain brother be denied the customary rites of burial.

1020] *Sun-treader* See l. 151n.

Editorial Notes

PARACELSUS

The Manuscript

The MS is in the Victoria and Albert Museum Library, in the Forster collection. It is now bound in reddish-brown leather, in rather good condition, elaborately decorated in gold. John Forster's bookplate is attached to the inside of the front cover. The cover measures 11⅜″ by 8¼″. The pages are 10¾″ by 8¼″. Compressed, the MS is about ½″ thick. The paper is watermarked "J. Whatman" and the date "1834." The obverse of the first used leaf is blank; on the reverse is pasted a print of the full-length portrait of Paracelsus. Above the print is written, almost certainly in B's hand, "Parturiunt madido quae nixu proela, recepta: Sed quis scripta manu sunt—veneranda magis." "The offspring which issued forth out of intoxicated effort, has been accepted; but whatever is written by hand ought to be venerated." At the side is "To *John Forster Esq* (my early understander) with true thanks for his generous and seasonable public Confession of Faith in me. RB. *Hatcham, Surrey,* 1842." The next leaf, obverse and reverse, headed PARACELSUS: by RBT. BROWNING, contains the preface cancelled after the first edition. It is followed by the "Persons." The next 103 pages contain the poem itself. The Note and notes follow, in considerable disorder, with numerous interleavings.

The MS presents several puzzling features. It is written throughout in B's very clear hand, but the punctuation is corrected in both pencil and ink, as follows. In Act I, the leaf containing lines 704–792 has been corrected in pencil, not, it would seem, in B's hand; on the upper left-hand corner of the obverse is written in pencil "Stock." This leaf is reversed in the present condition of the MS. The second page of Part III is the obverse of its leaf. At this point the corrections in pencil are resumed. In the upper left-hand corner is written in ink "J. Riggs." "J. Riggs" appears twice more in this Part, as does "Stock." The pencil corrections continue through the page that ends with l. 1009, the obverse of its leaf. The next page is corrected in ink, and "Stock" is written in the upper right-hand corner. The first leaf, i.e., the first two pages, of Part IV is corrected in pencil, possibly in B's hand. As the variants indicate, there are punctuation corrections throughout the MS in what is evidently B's hand. A small number of substantive corrections are obviously in B's hand, but the corrections described above are exclusively of punctuation. Another oddity of the MS is that B has pasted in portraits of Paracelsus not only as a Frontispiece, but also at the ends of Parts III and IV. Although we have not been able to reproduce B's discriminations among dashes of differing length we have attempted to indicate in the variants other oddities of punctuation that occur in the MS. The effect of the original punctuation is to give the poetry a spontaneity, a feeling of rapidity of thought not to be found in the 1835 text. It is hoped that something of this effect survives in the conventionalized approximation adopted for the variants; but a reading of *Paracelsus* in the Forster MS is an instructive and vivifying experience.

The Text

B's principal source was Frederick Bitiskius' edition of the works of Paracelsus (Note: l. 119n), and the article on Paracelsus in the *Biographie Universelle,* which B is said to have read through. Most of the information about the various proper names in both text and B's notes is taken from the latter work. For additional information, the principal source has been Walter Pagel, *Paracelsus: An Introduction To Philosophical Medicine in the Era of the Renaissance,* (S. Karger: Basel and New York, 1958). For translations from the Latin we are indebted to Professor K. Don Morris of the University of South Carolina.

Dedication] Comte Amédée de Ripert-Monclar, who was a quasi-official representative of the Bourbons to the French exiles in England, met B through B's half-uncle, William Shergold Browning, of Rothschild's bank in Paris. De Ripert-Monclar suggested Paracelsus to B as the subject for a poem.

Persons] *Paracelsus* See B's Note, which follows the text of the poem, and the present annotations to the poem and the Note.

PART I

Scene] *Würzburg* A town in central Germany on the Main River. In 1512 it was the seat of the Prince-Bishop of Würzburg, an independent principality, part of the Holy Roman Empire. Since 1815 it has been part of the kingdom and then the State of Bavaria.

1512] 1507, the date B first used, is as probable for Paracelsus' association with Trithemius (l. 241n) as 1512.

60] *Saint Saviour's.* Probably the Cathedral. The first Cathedral, begun in 788, was dedicated to the Holy Savior; the second, begun in the latter half of the ninth century, was dedicated to St. Kilian; the third, begun in the eleventh century, is a Romanesque building with two towers, badly damaged in World War II and currently being restored.

120] *Einsiedeln* A town in Switzerland, twenty mi. SE of Zurich and five mi. S of Lake Zurich, in the Canton of Schwyz. Since the early middle ages it has been a famous place of pilgrimage.

241] *Trithemius* John Tritheim, historian, theologian, and writer on alchemy and secret writing. He was born in 1462 at Trittenheim, in the Electorate of Trier, a town in W Germany near the border of Luxembourg. In the sixteenth century it was part of the Rhenish Palatinate and was ruled by an archbishop. Tritheim learned to read at the age of fifteen and studied at Trier. In 1482, returning to Trittenheim, he spent the night at the Benedictine abbey at Spanheim, or Sponheim. He decided to take orders and shortly after was elected abbot. Finding the abbey in a deplorable condition, he set the monks to copying and caring for MSs, and formed a remarkable library of more than 2000 volumes, in many languages, especially Greek, Hebrew, and Latin. He rapidly acquired considerable fame. In 1505, returning from a visit to Heidelberg, the seat of the Prince Palatine, he learned that the monks had rebelled against his discipline and had deposed him. His prince appointed him abbot of the Abbey of St. James in Würzburg, and he entered on his appointment October 15, 1506. He died there December 26, 1516. He was one of the most voluminous of all writers, as famous for his piety as for his learning, and contributed greatly to the revival of learning in Germany.

347] *geier-eagle* Leviticus 11:18 (King James version) mentions the giereagle (see variants). The Revised Standard uses "vulture;" *geier* is German for hawk.

357–358] *Black Arts, Great Works, the Secret and Sublime* The first refers to Black Magic, or sorcery; the other terms are from alchemy. The Great Work or *Magnum Opus,* was the process by which the Philosopher's Stone was formed, which could turn base metals into gold or silver. The materials used for the Stone were sublimed in the course of the Magnum Opus, which was the ultimate ambition and secret of the alchemists. The historical Paracelsus was deeply learned in alchemy, and his important achievements were made in an alchemical context. The alchemists used a veiled and allegorical language in their writings.

417] *Stagirite* Aristotle, the Greek philosopher (384–323 B.C.) was born at Stagira, Macedon.

481] *riveled* Shriveled, or wrinkled, as by heat.

609] *commissary* One to whom some charge, duty, or office has been committed.

651] *gold and apes* Solomon "had at sea a navy of Tharshish with the navy of Hiram; once in three years came the navy of Tharshish, bringing gold, and silver, ivory, and apes, and peacocks." I Kings 10:22.

811] *Mayne* River flowing through N. Bavaria, generally in a western direction. It flows into the Rhine at Mainz. Würzburg is built on both sides of it.

812 *schistous* Schistose.

Part II

25] *arch-genethliac* An astrologer in the modern sense; one who foretells the course of a life by studying the influences of the stars at the moment of birth. Here, *arch* means "of the highest eminence."

265] *fire-labarum . . . old founder of these walls* Eusebeius of Caesarea (270–340), the biographer of the Roman Emperor Constantine, relates that the latter saw a fiery cross in the sky during one of his marches in the campaign against his rival Emperor, Maxentius, whom he defeated in 312 B.C. He subsequently adopted as his banner the labarum, a long streamer of silk hanging from the cross-pole of a long staff. The banner displayed images of the reigning emperor and his children, and the summit of the staff was crowned with a monogram consisting of the first two letters, in Greek, of the name of Christ. Constantine delayed his baptism until he was near death, but established Christianity as the official religion of the Empire. He decided to make the ancient Byzantium the capital of the Empire in 324, and dedicated the city in 330 or 334.

471] *tent-tree* A tall screw pine, confined to Lord Howe Island, between Australia and New Zealand.

Part III

Scene] *Basel* A city in N Switzerland, situated on both sides of the Rhine. In 1526 a center of humanism, publishing, and religious reform, with an important university, it was one of the most cultivated of German cities.

1526 The historical Paracelsus was in Basel by November, 1526, having gone there from Strassburg by way of Tübingen and Freiburg. His students followed him to Basel. Oecolampadius (l. 293n) seems to have been responsible for his appointment, which was a difficult one for Paracelsus, since it was a municipal and not a University appointment, yet carried with it the right to lecture at the University. Oecolampadius was a friend of the reformers at Strassburg whom Paracelsus had known there. The appointment took place in March, 1527, and Paracelsus left in January or February 1528. See annotations to B's Note.

128] *pansies* *Citrinula* . . . Dorn. "Citrinula (flammula), a herb very familiar to Paracelsus." Gerhard Dorn, a German chemist and alchemist lived in the middle of the sixteenth century. He was an early Paracelsean and was one of the group who published their master's works, very few of which had been printed during Paracelsus' lifetime. Perhaps Dorn's most important achievement was his *Dictionary of the Chemistry of Theophrastus,* Frankfurt, 1583, in which he attempted to define and explain Paracelsus' obscure terminology.

211] *Rhasis* Razes, Rhazes, or Rasis. Arabian physician of the tenth century, principally in Bagdad. His various treatises were translated into Latin and used throughout the middle ages and after. His treatise on small-pox and measles was still considered valuable in the nineteenth century.

222] *fallen prince of morning* Lucifer, or morning-star, the leader of the rebellion of the angels against God.
293] *Oecolampadius* John Oecolampadius or, in German, Hausschien. Born in 1482 at Weinsberg in Franconia, Germany, his family was originally from Basel. His interest in theology led him to study Greek and Hebrew, and in 1515 he went to preach at Basel, where he became acquainted with Erasmus, then publishing his edition of the New Testament in Greek (l. 480). After an interim as a monk, his interest in the new theological opinions of the oncoming Reformation led him back to Basel, where, given a chair of theology at the University, he openly attacked the dogma and the rites of Roman Catholicism. He thus became one of the leaders of the Reformation, signalizing his freedom by marrying in 1521. He took part in the great quarrel between Carlstadt and Luther (l. 295n) and declared himself on the side of Zwingli (l. 956n), towards whom he had the same relation as that of Melancthon to Luther, a kind of lieutenant or chief assistant. After further successes, against both Catholics and Anabaptists (l. 993n), he died in 1531.
294] *Castellanus* Pierre Duchatel, born towards the end of the fifteenth century, he eventually became Bishop of Orleans, Grand Almoner of France, and favorite of Francis I of France. He was educated at the then famous College of Dijon. He taught himself Greek and began publishing at the age of sixteen. Attracted to Basel by the reputation of Erasmus (l. 480n), he became an assistant to Frobenius, the printer-publisher (l. 295n), as corrector of the press; thus he had an important and honorable position in the publication of the Greek and Latin editions Erasmus was bringing out. He left Basel in 1529, when Catholicism was officially suppressed.
295] *Munsterus* Sebastian Munster, born in 1489 at Ingelheim in the Palatinate, was a Hebrew scholar, a geographer, and a mathematician. He completed his studies at the University of Tübingen in SW Germany and became a Franciscan in order to work in quiet. Luther's writings led him to break with the Roman Catholic church, and in 1529 he went to Basel, where he taught theology and Hebrew in the University. He died in 1552.
295] *Frobenius* Johannes Froben, born in the last half of the fifteenth century at Hermelburg in Franconia, Germany, went to the University of Basel and established himself there as a printer. He was one of the first German printers to use roman type. He was learned and connected with the principal scholars of the day, especially Erasmus (l. 294n, and l. 480n). He printed a series of the Latin Fathers of the Church and Erasmus' New Testament, which appeared in 1516. In 1526 Paracelsus cured him of an illness, but his sudden death in October, 1527, seriously undermined Paracelsus' position in Basel.
344] *Luther* By 1526 the great Reformer (1483–1546) had abandoned the traditional interpretation of the Bible in favor of the new grammatical-historical interpretation, had developed his new concept of grace as a force that operated not through the sacraments but through the individ-

ual, had made his attack on indulgences, in his ninety-five theses had published his belief that man is justified, or attains to value before God, by his joyous belief in God and in Christ, had been condemned, in 1521, at the Imperial Diet, or Council, at Worms, had been placed under the Imperial Ban, and had gone into hiding at the Wartburg, the ancient castle near Eisenach, in central Germany, had returned to Wittenberg, and had definitely broken with the Roman Catholic church.

391] *rear-mice* Rere-mice, or bats.

394] *Lachen* A village on the shore of Lake Zürich, NE of Einsiedeln.

437] *sudary* A square of linen carried by the upper classes of ancient Rome to wipe sweat off one's face.

441] *suffumigation* The medical application of smoke to the body.

480] *Erasmus* The great Humanist of Northern Europe, he contributed powerfully to the Renaissance in the North, and to the Reformation, though he never accepted it. He was probably born in or near Rotterdam in 1467. In 1514–1516 he was in Basel to publish his Greek New Testament. In 1521 he settled there to supervise the publication of his work by Frobenius (l. 295n). In 1526 he consulted Paracelsus by letter, on the recommendation of Frobenius, asking for advice about how to treat his bladder stones. In 1529, when Roman Catholicism was suppressed in Basel, he left for Freiburg, Germany, some thirty-five mi. N of Basel. In 1535, in the hopes of recovering his health, which had been permanently damaged by his poverty when he was a student in Paris, he returned to Basel, where he died in July, 1836. Erasmus' request and Paracelsus' reply are to be found in Bitiskius (Note: l. 119n).

714] *addressed* Made ready.

801] *News from Lucern or Zurich* Such news would have to do with the growing Reformation in Switzerland.

867] *Praeclare! Optime!* "Excellent! Very well (said)!"

907] *Ulysses' bow, Achilles' shield* The bow is proverbially efficacious because with it Ulysses slew Penelope's many suitors; the shield was the most splendid, since it was forged by *Hephaeistos,* the god of fire and smiths. (*Odyssey,* xxi; *Iliad,* xviii.)

915] *Frobenius' press* See l. 295n.

946] *Aetius* Physician of Amida, Roman city in Mesopotamia, towards the end of the fifth century and the beginning of the sixth. His *Tetrabiblos,* a compilation of earlier physicians, was widely copied and known through the middle ages and, in part, printed in the sixteenth century.

946] *Oribasius* Famous Greek physician of the fourth century, born at Pergamum. He had the friendship of the Emperor Julian the Apostate, who attempted to restore paganism. His works are in part compilations and in part original. About a third were known through the middle ages and were printed in the sixteenth century.

946] *Galen* The greatest physician of antiquity, after Hippocrates, lived in the second century. No author of antiquity was so productive, though more than half of his works are lost. He was known through the middle ages, and the printing of his works began in the fifteenth century.

947] *Serapion* A Syrian physician of the tenth century. Two of his works survive.

947] *Avicenna* The greatest of Arabian physicians, born in Persia in 980. He died in 1037. He was an alchemist and a metaphysician as well. His *Canons,* translated into Latin, were used through the middle ages and into the eighteenth century, dominating medical study. He was primarily a compiler of Greek and Roman medical treatists, and his works were among the first of those of the traditional physicians to be printed, beginning in the fifteenth century.

947] *Averröes* Arabian physician and philosopher, born at Cordova, Spain, in the twelfth century. He died in Morocco in 1198. He was primarily a theoretical physician, rather than a practical one, and particularly dependent on Aristotle and Galen.

955–961] *Zwuinglius . . . Zurich . . . Luther . . . Wittenberg . . . Carolostadius* Ulrich Zwingli, the principal Swiss reformer, was born at Wildhaus, in the Toggenburg valley in NE Switzerland, January 1, 1484, and was killed in battle in 1531. He studied at Basel, Berne, and Vienna. At the age of eighteen he began teaching at Basel. In 1506 he was given the benefice at Glaris, in the bishopric of Constance. He devoted his study to Greek and the New Testament, the fathers of the church, and such moderns as the heretics Wycliffe and Hus. In 1515 he was appointed to Einsiedeln. He began to reform this ancient place of pilgrimage, the birthplace of Paracelsus, by burying relics, and the like, and discouraging pilgrims. In 1516 he was called to Zürich, which he made one of the chief centers of the Reformation. In 1520 he renounced his pension from Rome and began to teach nothing but the Gospel. By 1525, a year in which he became involved in a quarrel with Luther, he had married and had established the Reformation in Zürich. Carolostadius (Andrew Bodenstein, called Carlstadt (c. 1480–1541) originally the Greek tutor of Luther at the University of Wittenberg, and later his colleague) continued Luther's reforms while Luther was in refuge and hiding in the Wartburg, when he had been placed under the Ban of the Empire and his books had been condemned as heretical (l. 344n). Luther returned to Wittenberg in 1522 in defiance of the Ban and continued the reform, though more conservatively. Carlstadt, who had come to the conclusion that the Lord's supper was a commemorative rite only, denied the Real Presence in the consecrated bread and wine, a radical position which Luther rejected. Luther forced Carlstadt to leave Wittenberg for Strassburg, but his doctrines caught the attention of Zwingli and Oecolampadius (l. 293n). By 1525 Erasmus (l.

480n) was impressed, and did not see how the new doctrine could be refuted, though he preferred that the Old Catholic doctrine be preserved for the sake of peace. The argument centered on the word "is" in such Gospel passages as that found in Matthew 26:26–28, "And as they were eating, Jesus took bread and blessed it, and brake it, and gave it to the disciples, and said, Take, eat; this *is* my body. And he took the cup, and gave thanks, and gave it to them, saying, Drink ye all of it; for this *is* my blood of the new testament, which is shed for many for the remission of sins." Luther's doctrine, sometimes called consubstantiation, asserted that the body and blood were present, though the bread and wine were not transmuted, just as, in the simile often used, fire is present in red-hot iron, though the iron remains iron. The Carlstadt-Zwingli-Oecolampadius interpretation was that "is" in such statements is properly interpreted as "is a sign of." A pamphlet war began between Zwingli and Luther in 1526, but an open break did not occur until the following year.

993] *gangs of peasants . . . Suabia . . . Münzer . . . the duke, the landgrave and the elector* These lines refer to the Peasant's War. This revolt, the last of a series of such revolts in Germany, was inspired by the revolutionary and democratic character of the Reformation ideas. It began in the SW part of the Black Forest in June, 1524, and spread rapidly through SW Germany, i.e., Suabia and Württemberg. By the end of the year it had spread N to Saxony and Thuringia, in central Germany, the area in which Luther had his headquarters, was most powerful, and was under the protection of the Electoral Dukes of Saxony, first Frederick the Wise and then his brother John the Constant, who became Duke in 1525. ("Electoral" indicates the right to participate in the election of the Holy Roman Emperor; there were also non-electoral Dukes of another area of Saxony.) Here Thomas Müntzer, the Anabaptist, had set up a theocratic state in Mühlhausen, in central Germany. Anabaptism, which had many forms, started in Switzerland and was suppressed there in 1525 by Zwingli, and its leaders either killed or driven out; thus its ideas spread to N Germany. The heart of the position was an absolutely free church, one unconnected with any state or ecclesiastical system. In its extreme forms it was apocalyptic and communistic, anticipating the Last Judgement. This was the form it took when it combined with Müntzer's belief in ecstatic visions and freedom even from the Bible. He was attacked by Duke Henry of Brunswick (who was not sympathetic with the reforms and remained Catholic, but whose territories were not far from Mühlhausen); by Philip, the Landgrave of Hesse, sympathetic with the Reformation; and by Duke John, the Elector of Saxony. Müntzer was defeated and beheaded at Mühlhausen in May, 1525. The revolt did not last much longer; it was repressed with great brutality and slaughter. Luther's opposition to the Peasants cost him popular support and was in part responsible for the establishment of Lutheranism as a state religion.

Part IV

Scene] *Colmar* A town in E France forty mi. SSE of Strassburg. In 1528 it was an Imperial City, free from all feudal lords except the Holy Roman Emperor.

1] *Oporinus* John Herbst (in Latin, Oporinus) was born in Basel Jan. 25, 1507. Educated in Strassburg, he returned to Basel and went to work for Frobenius on the latter's edition of the Greek fathers of the church (III:l. 295n). He decided to study medicine and attached himself to Paracelsus, who promised to prepare him to receive the doctorate in a year. He followed him when he left Basel for Colmar, hoping to learn from him to prepare laudanum (Note: l. 209n), the composition of which was a secret. Wearied of losing his time with such a master, he solicited employment as a teacher, and the scholar Grunaeus obtained for him at the University of Basel the chair of Greek, which he filled with distinction. In 1539, being required to have the degree at least of Master of Arts, he left the University and founded a printing establishment. Despite poverty, he subsequently published excellent editions of the classics which he himself prepared for the press and also the work of Vesalius, the first modern anatomist. He died July 6, 1568, and was buried next to Erasmus. (See also B's Note, and his note 8).

1–7] *Von Visenburg . . . Torinus . . . Pütter* These names are apparently B's invention.

5] *Liechtenfels* See B's Note and his note 9.

82] *Saul* The first king of Israel. After Samuel had anointed him, "a company of prophets met him; and the Spirit of God came upon him, and he prophesied among them. And it came to pass, when all that knew him beforetime saw that, behold, he prophesied among the prophets, then the people said one to another, What is this that is come unto the son of Kish? Is Saul also among the prophets? And one of the same place answered and said, But who is their father? Therefore it became a proverb, Is Saul also among the prophets?" I Samuel 10:10–12.

112] *St. John* The fourth Gospel.

114] *stone* Bladder, kidney, or gall-bladder stones.

115] *Quid multa?* "Why many words?"

190] *sandal* The fruit of the Indo-Malayan sandal tree is cultivated for preserves and pickles.

190] *stripes* Strips.

192] *nard* An ointment made partly from nard, or spikenard.

199] *Egyptian's fine worm-eaten shroud* Mummy wrappings were much valued in the middle ages and later for medicinal purposes, principally for reasons given in l. 198.

213] *Luther's psalms* Luther (III:l. 344) wished to make congregational singing an important and dignified part of church service, thus signifying the believer's direct relation to God and God's Grace. To this end he composed a number of hymns, some original, some adapted from earlier Catholic hymns, and some based on the Psalms of the Bible. Of the last, the best known is "A mighty fortress is our God," derived from Psalm 46.

310] *Fiat . . . vili.* Let the experiment be performed on a body of no value.

588] *serviceable spirits . . . lamp's rubbing* In the *Arabian Nights* Aladdin procures a lamp by rubbing which he summons spirits, or genii, who do his bidding.

PART V

Scene] *Salzburg* A town in Austria, just over the border of Bavaria, seventy-five mi. E and a little S of Munich. At this time the Archbishop of Salzburg was a virtually independent prince within the Holy Roman Empire, and ruled a considerable territory, mostly to the S of the city.

St. Sebastian Paracelsus requested burial in the almshouse of St. Sebastian, but there is no evidence that he died there.

96] *Erasmus* See III:l. 480n.

97] *schools* The medical schools of Paris and Padua were among the most famous of the Medieval and Renaissance periods, particularly that of Padua.

123] *Jove strikes the Titans down* In Greek mythology the Titans were the children of Heaven and Earth, and Zeus (Jove) was himself a child of Titans. When he rebelled against his father, the other Titans came to his father's aid, but were defeated by Zeus. Subsequently Earth brought forth another race, the Giants, who attacked Zeus, piling the mountains Pelion and Ossa on one another in order to reach Olympus, or at least threatening to do so. The Titans and the Giants are often, indeed ordinarily, confused.

126] *Phaeton* Phaëthon, the son of Helios (Apollo) persuaded his father, against the latter's judgment, to let him drive the horses of the sun. He lost control, the chariot of the sun was swept close to the earth, which was in danger of being consumed by its fire, and on the appeal of Gaea (Earth) Zeus (Jove) killed Phaëthon with a thunderbolt; Helios resumed control of the horses.

161] *Latin, Arab, Jew, Greek* See III:ll. 946–947n.

181] *Galen of Pergamos and hell* Paracelsus "gloried in passing as a magician; he even boasts of having received from Hell letters from Galen, and of having had, in the vestibule of Hades, lively disputes with Avicenna about potable gold, the tincture of the philosophers, the quintessence, the mithridate, the philosopher's stone, etc." From the article in the *Biographie Universelle* part of which B translates in his Note. (Note: l. 92n)

187] *Zoroaster* The Greek form of Zarathustra, or Zarathushtra, the Persian religious prophet, founder of the Parsee or Magian religion, who lived perhaps around 600 B.C., perhaps as early as 1000 B.C. The heart of his teaching was that the world was divided between two principles of light and darkness, or good and evil. Various forms of this belief have penetrated to Europe and have been responsible for numerous Christian heresies. For B the best account of Zoroaster was probably in Chapter VIII of Gibbon's *Decline and Fall of the Roman Empire* (1776–1788).

320] *Cain* The son of Adam, who killed his brother Abel and was the first murderer. God put a mark upon him to protect him from all enemies. Genesis 4.

554] *Azoth* See B's Note: note 8, and annotations.

The Note

[B uses three kinds of notes to his Note: * and † for notes at the foot of the page; numbered notes printed after the Note; and * and † footnotes for his note 5. He re-arranged them slightly in 1849. Because of the complexities involved in presenting variants on the same page, in this edition the first two have been re-arranged in a single series. The following table shows B's changes and the changes made here.

Line	This edition Note number	1835 Note number	1849–1889 Note number
11	1	* (p. 203)	1
16	2	* (p. 204)	* (1888, p. 179)
23	3	1	2
36	4	2	3
47	5	3	4
56	6	* (p. 206)	* (1888, p. 180)
59	7	† (pp. 206–7)	† (1888, p. 181)
72	8	4	5
74	9	5	6
78	10	* (p. 208)	* (1888, p. 181)
209	*	* (p. 214)	* (1888, p. 185)
216	†	† (p. 214)	† (1888, p. 185)]

4] B does not translate the entire *Biographie Universelle* article. The more important omitted passages are translated below.

10] *Paracelsus* probably means "surpassing Celsus" (the Roman writer on medicine, first century A.D., or the opponent of Christianity, second century A.D.); the name was not used in print until 1536. It seems probable that the name was not self-invented but was given to him by his drinking companions at Colmar (1528). The name Theophrastus is not documented before 1526, and Philipp first appears on his tombstone.

11] *Hohenheim* famous alchemist and enthusiast of the sixteenth century, *was born in 1493*" He was probably born May 1, 1494.

14] *nearly related* Actually George Bombast, the Grand Prior, was Paracelsus' grandfather.
16] *Thomas Erastus* Thomas Liebler, called Erastus (1528–1583), Swiss physician and theologian, principally remembered for his doctrine that the church must be subordinate to the state. He attacked Paracelsean theories and teachings in his *Disputations on the New Medicine of Paracelsus,* in four parts, 1572–1573. He was professor at the University of Basel from 1580 until his death.
17] *"pretends.* The latter also relates (*Disput. de medic. nova Paracelsi,* Part I, p. 237) that Paracelsus suffered castration at the age of three years. Others say that he lost his virility as a consequence of the bite of a pig. What is certain is that he had no beard and that he detested women. *It appears"*
24] *Tritheim* See I:l. 241n.
24] *many German bishops* should be "several German bishops."
33] *Sigismond Fugger* Sigmund Fueger. Schwaz in Austria E of Innsbruck was the site of Frueger's mines. Paracelsus was also at the mining school of the Fuggers at Hutenberg near Villach, in Carinthia, south central Austria, where his father had been a physician.
34] *Magnum Opus* See I:ll. 351–358.
35] "Following the custom of alchemists, *Paracelsus travelled"*
43] *Khan of the Tartars* The Tartars, or Tatars, were remnants of the Empire of the Golden Horde of Chingis-khan or Genghis Khan 1167–1227). The Tartar Khanate of the Crimea, in Southern Russia, was a rich and powerful independent nation in the sixteenth century.
45] *Trismegistus* Certain sacred books of the last centuries before Christ, dealing with such divers matters as geology, astrology, medicine, temple ritual, and hymns in honor of the Gods, were believed to have been written by an ancient Egyptian priest, Hermes Trismegistus. Hermeticism was revived in the early Renaissance and mingled with alchemical tradition, which supposed itself derived from the writings of Hermes Trismegistus. The *tincture* was probably the oxide obtained from employing quicksilver in the process of separating gold and silver from the native matrix.
50] *Oecolampadius* See III:l. 293n.
51] *Basil* Basel. See III: *Scene* n.
53] *Avicenna* and *Galen* See III:ll. 946–947n. The sources indicate that only Avicenna was burned.
58] *Rhasis* See III:l. 211n. *Montagnana* Bartolommeo Montagnana, died 1470, one of the earliest collectors of *consilia,* descriptions of medical cases in a form meaningful to modern medicine. *Mesues* Arabian physician of the ninth century. By origin a Nestorian Christian, he supervised translations from Greek, Syrian, and Persian for Haroun-al-Raschid, the great Caliph of Bagdad. His medical writings were translated into Hebrew and Latin, and his works were printed in Venice and elsewhere before 1500.
59] *Paris, Montepellier,* etc. Seats of schools of medicine.

63] *"be mine*. The novelty of his doctrines, the emphasis with which he spoke of his success, the power he claimed to prolong life and to cure even incurable diseases, his practice of lecturing the vulgar, all these circumstances combined attracted to Basel a crew of the credulous, idlers and enthusiasts. We still possess the lectures that he gave on practical medicine: their language is a mixture of German and barbarous Latin; and they offer nothing but empirical remedies, recommended with the greatest pretentions possible. So much impudence, far from diminishing his fame, only made it grow, according to the witness of Ramus [Petrus Ramus or Pierre de la Rameé (1515–1572) French humanist and anti-Scholastic and anti-Aristotelian] to the point that Erasmus (III:l. 480n) himself, who had suffered a long time from the gravel, invoked the aid of Paracelsus; and this led to a correspondence between these two men, so differently famed, which has come to us. *But at Basil"*

69] *Oporinus* See IV:l. 1n.

80] *Alsatia* The present Alsace on the French side of the Rhine. Paracelsus fled to Colmar (IV:*Scene* n).

84] *St. Gall* St. Gallen, a city in NE Switzerland. *Pfeffers* Pfäfers near Bad Ragaz, a city twenty-five mi. S of St. Gallen, site of a monastery and an ancient spa. *Augsburg* City in S Germany.

85] *Moravia* Province in what is now central Czechoslovakia, in the sixteenth century a Margravate of the Holy Roman Empire which in 1526 became part of the Archduchy of Austria.

91] *Mindelheim* Town in S Germany, SW of Augsburg.

92] *"St. Stephen* (Sebastian *is meant*), (V:*Scene* n.) *September 24, 1541*. Thus ended his life, when he was only forty-eight, and well-nigh poverty-stricken, he who pretended to possess the double secret of transmuting metals and of prolonging life for several centuries.

His philosophical and medical system is interesting by its very absurdity. A summary follows. He takes as his first support religion and the sacred writings. He asserts that the contemplations of the perfections of Divinity is enough to procure all intelligence and wisdom; that the Holy Scripture leads to all truths; that the Bible is the key to the theory of sickness; that it is necessary to consult the Apocalypse to know what magical medicine is. The man who blindly obeys the will of God and succeeds in identifying himself with the celestial intelligences possesses the philosophic stone; he can cure all ills, and prolong life at his will, because he possesses the tincture which Adam and the patriarchs used before the flood to live for eight or nine centuries. Paracelsus professed the grossest pantheism; he owned the existence of pure spirits without soul. According to him, all beings, even minerals and fluids, partook of food and drink and expelled excrement. His physiologic theory, a confused heap of the most incoherent ideas, is built on the application of the laws of the Cabala to the demonstration of the functions of the human body. Thus the vital force is an emanation of the stars. The sun is *en rapport* with the heart, *etc*. . . . Paracelsus is not less absurd in his theory of pathology. Turning back always to magic, he asserts that it is the art of arts, that here one must find medical wisdom. He gloried in passing as a magician; he even boasts of having received from Hell letters from Galen, and of having had, in the vestibule of Hades, lively disputes with Avicenna about potable gold, the tincture of the philosophers, the quintessence, the mithridate, the philosopher's stone, *etc.* . . . In particular he explains every ill with the aid of his three principles out of chemical entities, which he substitutes for the four elements of the ancients (salt, sulphur, and mercury), *etc.* . . . One cannot dispute, however, the value of the effort he made to introduce into medicine the use of preparations of antimony, mercury, salt, and iron-bearing substances, which have so efficacious an effect on our organs. One cannot deny that alchemy, which has ruined so many adepts, was advantageous for the medical sciences, because of important discoveries of which it was the source. Paracelsus published very few works in his lifetime. Since those which are attributed to him offer numerous contradictions, one is led to the conclusion that several were composed by his students. If we wished to cite the titles of all of his writings, they would require several pages; we limit ourselves therefore to listing several complete collections. I. German editions: Basel, 1574, octavo; ibid. 1589–1590, ten volumes in quarto, edited by J. Huser: Strasburg, 1608–1618, four volumes in folio, also by J. Huser, who died after having published the first two volumes. The fourth is confined to apocryphal writings. II. Latin editions. *Opera omnia medico-chymico chirurgica,* Frankfurt, 1630, ten volumes in quarto; Geneva, 1658, three volumes in folio. III. French editions: *La Grande Chirurgie de Paracelse,* translated from the Latin edition of J. Dalhem, by Cl. Dariot, Lyon, 1593, quarto, 1603, quarto; Montbéliard, 1608, octavo.—*La petite chirurgie,* the same, Paris, 1623, octavo. These are almost the only works which have appeared in our tongue. For information about Paracelsus, and for his life, one can consult the following books. Michael Toxitis, *Onomasticum medicum et explicatio verborum* Paracelsi; P. Severini, *Ideae medicinae philosophicae;* D. Leclerc, *Histoire de la Médicine; Histoire Littéraire de Paracelse,* with a facsimile of his writings (in Volume 2, pp. 177–285, of the *Nouveau Journal des Arts et de la Littérature,* by The. de Murr); Adelung, *Histoire de la Folie Humaine,* Vol. 7; Sprengel, *Histoire Pragmatique de la Médicine,* Vol. III.

R——D——N"

In 1835 B purchased Oswald Croll, *Philosophy Reformed in Four Profound Tractates. The I. Discovering the great and deep mysteries of nature: by that learned chymist and physician Osw. Crollius. The other III. Discovering the wonderful mysteries of the creation, by Paracelsus: being his Philosophy to the Athenians.* Both made English by H. Pinnell. London, Lloyd, 1657. Croll (1580–1609) was one of the early Paracelseans. In these works Paracelsus discusses his theory that all matter (which he thought of as living) and all living things emanated in four stages from the Great Mystery, and did not come into existence by the special creation of God. These ideas may have been B's justification for Paracelsus' evolutionary vision in Part V, just before his death.

91] *Paracelsus* See l. 10n.

97] In 1941 H. E. Sigerist published an article in the *Bulletin of the History of Medicine* proving that the pejorative use of the term "Bombastic" does not refer to Paracelsus but derives from the Greek bombyx, silkworm, and designates its product silk and later cotton and cotton wadding. The first recorded metaphorical use of the word is from 1589.

100] *Hic . . . fuisse.* "This man (Erastus) says that Paracelsus was castrated as a three year old by a certain soldier, some others that it was done by a boar; at any rate he was beardless and hated women."

104] *Melander's "Jocoseria"* A collection of jokes and anecdotes by Otto Melander, *1597*.

105] *Tintoretto* Bitiskius (l. 119n.) used an engraving of a portrait he said was by Tintoretto (1518–1594) as his frontispiece. He refers to it on p. [2] of his Preface. I have been unable to confirm the existence of such a portrait.

106] *Helvetium . . . ediderit* "I can scarcely believe that Paracelsus was Swiss, for I can hardly imagine that region producing such a monster." For *Erastus* see l. 16n.

112] *Cornelius Agrippa* Henry Cornelius Agrippa of Nettesheim, physician and philosopher (1486–1535). An associate of Paracelsus, he wrote on the occult philosophy, particularly that ascribed to the tradition of Hermes Trismegistus (l. 42n), and on *The Uncertainty and Vanity of the Sciences,* Cologne, 1527, and elsewhere. His *On Occult Philosophy* was published at Antwerp and Paris in 1531. This contains both the dedicatory epistle to Tritheim and the latter's answer. He is perhaps best known today for his panegyric in praise of women, *On the Nobility and Pre-excellence of the Feminine Sex,* Antwerp, 1529, a declamation made to please Margaret of Austria, Regent of Flanders.

115] *Quum . . . contulissemus* "When recently the Reverend Father was with you in your cloister in Würzburg, a great many things were said about chemistry, magic, the occult, and other things which up to now lurked in secret, as well as the arcane science and art in which we had a common interest."

119] *Inexplebilis . . . obtineret* "The insatiable desire to scrutinize the secrets of nature and to fill the mind with the material of arcane science was his; he could not persist in any one place for any length of time but yet he mastered mercury and scattered the sparks of his knowledge gained from wandering many lands, nations, and cities. When he was with men of an observant nature, especially chemists, he attracted them, and obtained in one way or another those who had discovered something in the process of assiduous work." Bitiskius, Preface, p. [4]. The full title of Bitiskius' edition of the works of Paracelsus is, Aur. Philip Theoph. Paracelsi Bombast ab Hohenheim, medici et philosophi celeberrimi, chemicorumque principis, *Opera omnia medico-chemico-chirurgica, tribus voluminibus comprehensa.* Editio novissma et emendatissima, ad Germanica & Latina exemplaria accuratissimè collata: Variis tractatibus & opusculis summâ hinc inde diligentiä conquisitis, ut in voluminis primi praefatione indicatur, locupletata: Indicibusque; exactissimis instructa. Genevae, Sumptibus Ioan. Antonii, & Samuelis De Tournes. M. DC. LIIX. On p. [11] of his Preface Bitiskius identifies himself as a Polish knight, a "mystes naturae," and one justly known as a citizen of the world.

124] *Patris . . . neminem* "First with the aid of his father and then by his own industry, he acquired a set of followers, the most learned men in Germany, Italy, France, Spain, and other regions of Europe; men who by a liberal doctrine and through appropriate searching managed to accomplish so much, that many were willing to say that no mortal had ever been able to master in general philosophic terms, problems so arduous, so arcane, and so hidden." The passage is to be found on p. 28 of one of B's sources, Melchior Adam, *Vitae Germanorum medicorum: qui secula superiori, et quod excurrit, claruerunt: congestae & ad annum usque M DC XX deductae a Melchiore Adama. Cum indice triplici: personarum gemino, tertio rerum.* Haedelbergae, impensis heredum Jonae Rosae, exaudit Johannes Georgius Geyder, Acad. Typogr. Anno M. DC. XX.

130] *Paracelsus . . . videtur* "Paracelsus entered so deeply into the vitals of nature; the strengths of plants and animals; explored and understood with such incredible talent the powers and faculties of metals and plants; healing completely all dread diseases which in ordinary opinion were either hopeless or considered incurable; that it would have seemed that with Theophrastus the science of medicine was not only discovered but perhaps even concluded." This excerpt from Peter Ramus' *Oration on Basel* is to be found in Bitiskius, Preface, p. [6] and in Melchior Adam, p. 29 (ll. 111n and 116n). For *Ramus,* see l. 63n.

135] *Ecce . . . pigebit?* "And yet it did not bother this youthful lover of difficult journeys that he should catch a glimpse of a pretty girl or woman. Should it shame him that the labor and tedium of the most noble of arts should be alleviated by love?" *Seven Defenses against the Calumnies of his enemies.* "Fourth defense: Concerning my far wanderings." This work is, of course, in Bitiskius.

145–149] See III:l. 956n.

157] *Life of Bishop Fisher,* by Thomas Bayly, written in the sixteenth century but not published until the seventeenth.

159] *Crasso* Lorenzo Crasso, Italian of the seventeenth century. His *Elogies of Men of Letters* was published in Venice and elsewhere in 1656. For each there is a portrait, several pieces in prose and verse, in his praise, and a list of his works, both printed and manuscript.

160] *Quenstedt* Jean André Quenstedt (1617–1688), a learned Protestant theologian of Germany. In 1644 he started teaching geography and history at the University of Wittenberg, and in 1647 succeeded to the chair of theology. In 1654 he published a kind of literary history, *Dialogus de patriis illustrium doctrine et scriptis virorum, omnium ordinam ac facultatum, qui ab initio mundi per universum terrarum orben usque ad annum 1600 claruerunt.*

162] *Delrio* Martin-Antoine del Rio, born in Antwerp, died in Louvain, 1608; he taught in Styria and Spain, as well as the Low Countries, and was a learned man, though credulous. His most famous book, to which B refers, was his *Disquisition on Magic,* published in Louvain in 1599 and often reprinted.

162] *partim . . . haereticos* "in part atheists, in part heretics"

163] *Omnino . . . Christiani* "Although there is a great deal of theology in his writings, they smell almost entirely atheistic, and sound rather harshly on truly Christian ears."

165] *Clauderi* Daniel Gabriel Clauder, 1633–1691, German physician and chemist. His *Dissertation on the Universal Tincture, Vulgarly Called the Philosopher's Stone,* etc. was published in Altenburg, 1678.

166] *Oporinus . . . haerere* "Oporinus (IV:l. 1n) says that Paracelsus said that he could by some means reconcile the Pope and Luther, just as he had Galen and Hippocrates, for none of them up to this point had written anything on the scriptures, either old or new, that had in any way destroyed its basis. They seemed only to be stuck fast upon the outer and superficial surface of things." *Erastus,* see l. 16n. This quotation is from the famous letter of Oporinus to Rainerus Solenander and Johann Weyer. B could have found it in Daniel Sennert's *De chymicorum cum Aristotelcis et Galenicis consensu ac dissensu liber,* etc. Wittenberg, 1629. Solenander (1524–1601) was a follower of Johannes Argenterius (1513–1572), whose attack on Galenic medicine was quite independent of Paracelsus'. Johannes Wier or Weyer, called Vigerus (1515–1588), was a physician of the Low Countries and for a time in France. He was most famous for his demonstration that it was wrong to believe in the powers of witches and sorcerers. The first edition of his most famous work on the subject was printed in Basel, 1563. Daniel Sennert (1572–1637) attempted to reconcile the new chemical medicine, which owed much to Paracelsus, with the theory of the humors of the Galenic tradition.

171] *Oporinus* See IV:l 1n.

172] *Zuingerus* Theodore Zwinger, the elder, the first of a family of distinguished physicians and scientists, was born at Basel in 1533. He was the nephew of Oporinus (IV:l 1n). After study in France and Italy, he returned to Basel in 1559. At the University he taught in succession Greek, moral philosophy, and theoretical medicine. He died from attending and studying the poor victims of the plague in 1588. He published his *Theatrum vitae humanae* in Basel in 1565; it continued for a number of years, even after his death, and is a vast compilation of historical anecdotes and facts.

172] *longum . . . lueret* "And so he said a final farewell to him lest he also should pay the penalty someday to God on high for these horrendous blasphemies of his mentor, otherwise a very good friend."

175] *Erastus* See l. 16n.

175] *mirum . . . adjunxit* "It is a wonder that he did not add Africans, Indians, and English."

178] *anglum . . . Bacchonem* "A certain Englishman, Roger Bacon." (1214–1292) One of the first great medieval scientists.

182] *Nam . . . podicem* "Indeed I know that I have armed myself more and more against you and your mentors, Avicenna, Galen, Aristotle, etc. The peak of my bald head knows far, far more than either your Avicenna or all the followers of your whole profession. Come now, give us a sign what kind of men you are, what strength you have. Just what are you? Learned men and teachers, combing lice and scratching your ass." The passage may be found in Paracelsus' *Fragmenta ad operum medicorum,* Bitiskius, I, p. 346. (l. 119n.)

189] *Gentis . . . junctum* "This is but a trifling vice of the race, not really of this man. From the age of Tacitus to our own this vice has continued in an uninterrupted thread. Perhaps it is inherent in a true German, possibly linked indelibly, although I cannot guess how, by consanguinity." Bitiskius, p. [4]. (l. 119n.)

192] *Domi . . . putant* "As Oporinus his secretary has frequently said, he never left his house to go to his lectures unless drunk; and standing in the midst of the hall, he leaned blearily against a column; grasping the hilt of his sword in his hands, the hospitality of the hollow of which he offered, so they say, to his familiar spirit; he put forth his ideas and concepts:—some think that the hollow of his sword contained either a superb medicine or the philosopher's stone, which he called Azoth. Melchior Adam, p. 35 (l. 116n).

202] *Volpone* Play by Ben Jonson, acted in 1605 and published in 1607. The passage comes from a song, Act II, Scene ii, ll. 131–132 (ed. Herford-Simpson, Vol. V, Oxford, 1937, 1954).

208] *Hudibras* By Samuel Butler (1612–1680), Part I, 1662; Part II, 1663; Part III, 1678. The passage comes from Part II, Canto III, ll. 627–630.

209] *Azoth . . . laudanum suum* "Azoth" is a word used in later alchemical literature; it combines the first and last letter of the alphabet with the last letters of the Greek and Hebrew alphabets; it indicates the world-soul, penetrating and enlivening the universe. Current opinion surmises that it was related to the "Laudanum" which Paracelsus carried in the hilt of his famous long sword; the usual pictures of the sword shows "Azoth" inscribed on the pommel. This laudanum was not, as in modern times, an opiate, but the gum Laudanum of the pharmacopea or a compound remedy that contained pearls among its ingredients.

212] *Franciscus . . . Neander.* This information comes from Bitiskius p. [5] (l. 119n). Michael Neander published his *Orbis terrae partium succincta explicatio* at Leipzig in 1536. In it may be found a letter by Neander about Paracelsus.

215] *Degebat . . . testimonium* "While Theophrastus was in Nürnberg he was challenged by the healers of that city and called a boaster and a liar. In order to correct this slander he went to the governing officials of the Republic [Nürnberg was then an Imperial City, subject only to the Holy Roman Emperor] to remove the stain upon his reputation and to acquaint them with his skill and art; he promised that he would produce a specimen of it with no stipend or fee. At their order, and on the choice of another doctor, certain individuals were selected with obviously diseased elephantine ears which separated them from the community of other men and had thrust them aside into invalidism. And Theophrastus through the singular skill of his remedies cleansed them of this foul leprosy of the Greeks and restored their earlier health. That city has preserved an illustrious testimony to these cures in its archives." Bitiskius, Preface p. [5] (l. 119n).

224] Note* *Objectionem . . . suffocatur* "The argument that Paracelsus died fairly young some attribute to physical reasons. Perhaps so short a life was due to frequent overdoses of Tincture of which the greatest and most lasting effect would arise from a strength and an amount that would be fatal." *Clauderi* See l. 165n.

224] *Oporinus* See IV:l. 1n.

225] *Sed . . . inflixerant* "Finally he reconsidered, and the man whom he had reviled while still alive and in association with his intimates, he respected after he died, and the disrespect he paid to his mentor turned into stings of conscience, a penitence too late to heal the wounds of the dead which he had inflicted upon him living." Bitiskius, Preface, p. [3] l. 119n.

228] *Disput. Erasti.* See l. 16n.

229] *Andreae Jocisci* Jociscus, *Life of Oporinus,* Strassburg, 1569.

229] *Toxita* Michael Schütz, or, in Latin, Toxites. One of the early Paracelseans, author of *Onomastica* [specialized lexicon] *medicum et explicatio verborum Paracelsi,* Strassburg, 1574; and compiler of the *Testamentum Paracelsi,* Strassburg, 1574, which includes various documents, such as Paracelsus' will and his epitaph, also a preface, in which Toxites refers to Oporinus' (IV:l. 1) regret at having written as he did to Vigerus (l. 166n) and at having given away the books and preparations of Paracelsus. The *Testamentum* is incorporated at the end of the Vol. III of Bitiskius (l. 119n), with separate pagination.

230] *Conringius* Hermann Conring (1606–1681), an East Frisian, who spent most of his productive years at Helmstaedt in N Central Germany. He was one of the most learned and illustrious men of the seventeenth century, publishing over two hundred books on a great variety of subjects, including medicine. In 1648 he attacked Borrichius (see following note) for his defense of Paracelsus in *De hermetica Aegyptiorum veter et Paracelsicorum nova medicina liber.* A second edition (1669) defended his position against Borrichius' attacks.

231] Note† *Borrichius* Olaus Borrichius, chemist and physician of Denmark (1626–1690). He followed the principles of Paracelsus and of revived alchemy, but made important discoveries. He continued the Hermetic tradition (l. 42n) and was an opponent of Conring (see the preceding note). His principal attacks were published in 1668 and 1674. The second was *Hermetis, Aegyptiorum et chimicorum sapientia.* However fancifully developed, Paracelsus' great achievement, according to modern scholarship, was replacing the four humors by chemical entities in speculating about disease. That is, he conceived that man should be studied in his relation to his organic and inorganic environment. *Laudanum* See l. 209n.

234] *Vossius* Gerard-Jean Vossius (1577–?). Born in Heidelberg of Dutch parents, he grew up in Holland, and lived principally at Leyden and Amsterdam. Admired by Laud, archbishop of Canterbury, he was made Canon of Canterbury and granted a pension by Charles I, although he continued to live in Holland. He was one of the most learned and sensible men of letters of the seventeenth century, writing on a multitude of subjects. His *De philosophia et philosophorum sectis,* edited by his son Isaac, was published at the Hague in 1658. It was concerned with both speculative and practical philosophy, including medicine.

235] *Nobilem . . . Paracelsus* "This noble part of medicine, so long buried in the age of our fathers, has been recalled, as if from Hell, by Theophrastus Paracelsus."

238] *De Phlebotamia* The reference to the discovery of the circulation of the blood comes from Bitiskius' Preface to his second volume, p. [4] (l. 119n).

240] *Realdo Colombo* Famous Italian anatomist of the sixteenth century. He may have died in 1577. He studied living animals and observed that the heart contracts when the arteries dilate, and vice versa.

240] *Andrea Cesalpino of Arezzo,* Italy (1519–1603). A physician, botanist, and professor of medicine, as well as philosopher, he discovered the circulation of the blood, and, according to Bayle (see following note) was the first to do so.

241] *Bayle* Pierre Bayle (1647–1706), author of the famous *Dictionnaire Critique et Historique,* 2 vols., 1696, 2nd ed., 1720, subsequent editions revised and issued by others. The work was one of the principal sources for the anti-ecclesiastical struggle of the Enlightenment, and Bayle is usually identified with scepticism.

241] *Bartoli* Daniel Bartoli, Italian scholar (1608–1685), a Jesuit. He wrote about the history of the Jesuits and various other subjects, including freezing and coagulation, and tension and pressure.
241] *Lavater* Johann Kasper Lavater (1741–1801), Swiss writer, pastor, theologian, etc. He was most famous for his theories of physiognomy, his science of the soul, which had a wide-spread influence throughout Europe, and led to the founding of the pseudo-science of phrenology. His principal works on physiognomy appeared 1775–1778. Thomas *Holcroft* (1745–1809), English miscellaneous writer and dramatist, published his translation, *Essays on Physiognomy,* in 1789(?).
247] *Valentius (in Praefat. in Paramyr.)* Paracelsus' *Opus Paramirum (Work beyond Wonder)* was completed in 1531, when he was at St. Gallen (see B's Note). It contained his basic medical doctrines, but was not published until after his death. Valentius' Preface is in Bitiskius (l. 119n).
248] *quod . . . ingenii* "As far as the corpus of Paracelsus' work is concerned, I understand that the Germans have collected nearly three hundred works attributed to him. What productivity! How fertile his talent!"
250] *Bitiskius . . . good edition* See l. 119n.
251] *rejectis . . . numerus* "Those which fundamentally took pride only in his name have been rejected. There are a great many in circulation." Bitiskius, Preface, p. [1] (l. 119n.).
252] "charissimum . . . obtentum" "That priceless and invaluable author's mark which has been gleaned internally rather than merely alleged." Bitiskius, Preface, p. [1] (l. 119n).
254] *Jam . . . sunt* "And now indeed even without his aid or help the writings came to light; those shut up in a wall, in his absence, at the direction of some servant, were secretly removed and carried off."
256] *Valentius* See l. 247n.
258] *Petri Severini* Peter Soerenssen (1542–1602), an early Paracelsean, author of *Idea medicinae philosophicae fundamenta,* Basel, 1571 (l. 92n).
258] *Toxetis* See l. 229n.
259] *Dornei* See III l. 128n.
260] *Suavio* Leo Suavius, pseudonym of Jacques Gohorry, French translator, poet, historian, and alchemist of the 16th century. He had little learning, and less in the way of critical powers. In 1568 he published in Paris his *Theophrasti Paracelsi philosophiae et medicinae utriusque universae compendium, ex optimis quibus cumque eus libris, cum scholiis in libros iv ejusdem de vita larga.* It was vehemently attacked by Dorn (see III:l. 128) and other German Paracelseans.
261] *Liechtenfels* Modern scholarship tends to accept B's interpretation of this affair, that it was a deliberate trap set by Paracelsus' enemies. He had to flee because he had publicly insulted a judge, and thus made himself liable to arrest and severe—perhaps capital—punishment.
267] *Quis . . . administratur* "Who, may I ask, could possibly gain honor

from a profession manipulated and controlled by such criminal rascals." The works of Paracelsus are studded with hundreds of insults to the medical profession. B probably noted this from Bitiskius (l. 119n) and was unable to find it again. After considerable search, the present editor has not been able to find it either.

269] *Bona . . . erogavit* "He simply asked that his worldly possessions be collected and distributed among the poor." The alternative readings for *erogavit* come from Adam (l. 124n). The *Testamentum* (l. 230n) has "honoravit."

271] Note *10* also comes from the *Biographie Universelle,* as the variant for the first edition indicates. (l. 92n.)